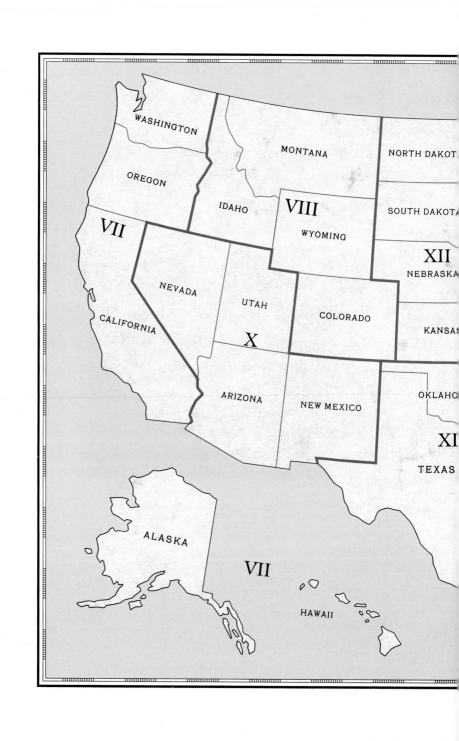

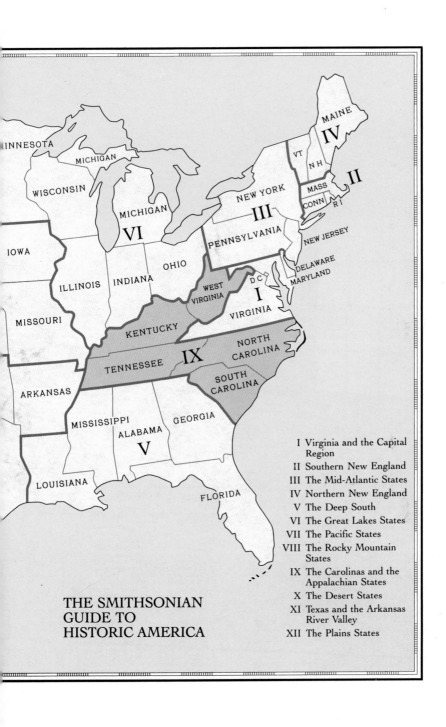

I Virginia and the Capital Region
II Southern New England
III The Mid-Atlantic States
IV Northern New England
V The Deep South
VI The Great Lakes States
VII The Pacific States
VIII The Rocky Mountain States
IX The Carolinas and the Appalachian States
X The Desert States
XI Texas and the Arkansas River Valley
XII The Plains States

THE SMITHSONIAN
GUIDE TO
HISTORIC AMERICA

THE
SMITHSONIAN
GUIDE TO
HISTORIC AMERICA

THE CAROLINAS AND THE APPALACHIAN STATES

TEXT BY
PATRICIA L. HUDSON
SANDRA L. BALLARD

SPECIAL PHOTOGRAPHY BY
JONATHAN WALLEN

EDITORIAL DIRECTOR
ROGER G. KENNEDY
DIRECTOR OF THE NATIONAL MUSEUM
OF AMERICAN HISTORY
OF THE SMITHSONIAN INSTITUTION

Stewart, Tabori & Chang
NEW YORK

Published in 1989 by Stewart, Tabori & Chang, Inc., 740 Broadway,
New York, NY 10003.

FRONT COVER: Pigeon Forge, TN
HALF-TITLE PAGE: Duke Homestead SHS, Durham, NC
FRONTISPIECE: Harpers Ferry, WVA
BACK COVER: Old Salem, NC

SERIES EDITOR: HENRY WIENCEK
EDITOR: MARY LUDERS
PHOTO EDITOR: MARY JENKINS
ART DIRECTOR: DIANA M. JONES
ASSOCIATE EDITOR: PAUL MURPHY
ASSISTANT PHOTO EDITORS: BARBARA J. SEYDA, FERRIS COOK
EDITORIAL ASSISTANT: MONINA MEDY
DESIGN ASSISTANT: KATHI R. PORTER
CARTOGRAPHIC DESIGN AND PRODUCTION: GUENTER VOLLATH
CARTOGRAPHIC COMPILATION: GEORGE COLBERT
DATA ENTRY: SUSAN KIRBY

LIBRARY OF CONGRESS CATALOGING-IN-PUBLICATION DATA
Hudson, Patricia L.
    The Carolinas and the Appalachian States / text by Patricia L. Hudson and Sandra L.
    Ballard; special photography by Jonathan Wallen; editorial director, Roger G. Kennedy. —
    1st ed.   p.   cm. — (The Smithsonian guide to historic America) Includes index.
    ISBN 1-55670-104-7 : $24.95. — ISBN 1-55670-108-X (pbk.) : $17.95
        1. Appalachian Region, Southern—Description and travel—Guide-books.
2. North Carolina—Description and travel—1981-   —Guide-books. 3. South Carolina—
Description and travel—1981-   —Guide-books. 4. Historic sites—Appalachian Region,
Southern—Guide-books. 5. Historic sites—North Carolina—Guide-books. 6. Historic sites—
South Carolina—Guide-books.
    I. Ballard, Sandra L. II. Wallen, Jonathan. III. Kennedy, Roger G. IV. Title. V. Series.
F217.A65H83   1989   89-4598
917.5—dc20   CIP

Distributed by Workman Publishing, 708 Broadway, New York, NY 10003

Printed in Japan

10 9 8 7 6 5 4 3 2 1
First Edition

CONTENTS

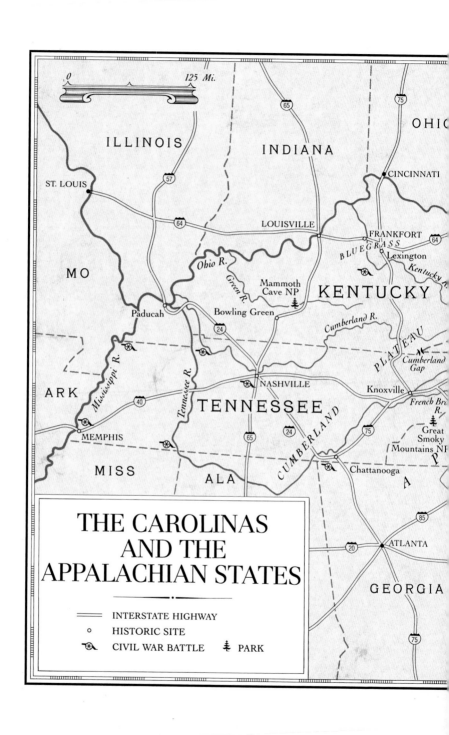

THE CAROLINAS AND THE APPALACHIAN STATES

——— INTERSTATE HIGHWAY

○ HISTORIC SITE

⚔ CIVIL WAR BATTLE 🌲 PARK

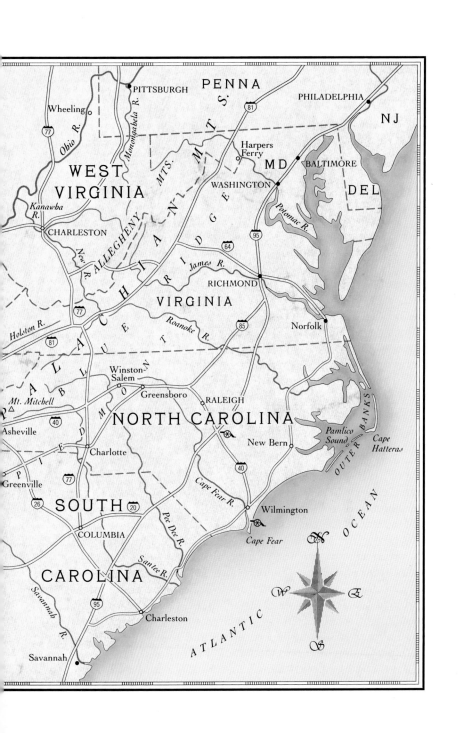

INTRODUCTION

The South has many voices: the blues of the Delta, migrating to Memphis and Nashville, becoming electronic rhythm and blues, country, and gospel, sung by blacks and whites in the hills and on the plains and in the cities; the hymns of the Shakers, still heard sometimes at Pleasant Hill; sentimental melodies spun around pianos throughout the South to the whirring of ceiling fans; work songs chanted by stoop labor in the fields; Moravian hymns in Winston-Salem; Robert Shaw's great orchestra and chorus in Atlanta. The South shares with the rest of America a special strength derived from the diversity of its origins. Compared to colonial Connecticut, for example, the Old South was as diverse as the Balkans; it is a false idea that it ever was a place of ethnic "purity." Austrian German was spoken among the "Salzburgers" at Ebenezer, Georgia, and Rhineland German among the Palatines nearby. Rhenish was also the patois of the "German Coast" of Louisiana, though by now it has merged with French-Canadian (Cajun) into a dialect that exists in close proximity to the slow African-English of the Louisiana parishes nearby. French-Swiss was spoken among the Huguenot traders of Georgia and South Carolina who had been sent to Geneva for schooling; names like Manigault and Huger are still pronounced in Charleston not as they are in Indianapolis, but in Geneva. Spanish was, and is, spoken in six dialects, including that of the Canary Islands. And thirty or more Indian dialects underwent their fusions (like Gullah) with African languages from Senegal to Angola.

The South remains now, even after many migrations to the North, the most African portion of the United States. In the Tidewater plain, any visitor from 1740 onward might have thought it an African colony, with a few Europeans keeping guard. Even before the Africans joined them there, whites had been a minority group in the Carolinas. As late as 1750, there were probably about 25,000 Europeans, 40,000 blacks and 60,000 Creek, Cherokee, Choctaw, and members of smaller tribes. Thereafter, while the Native American population was diminished by death and forced emigration, the black population increased more rapidly than the white.

The English applied their habit of using conquered people for slave labor as soon as they stepped ashore in the Old South. Coffles of conquered Indians dragged themselves eastward through the dust toward the Carolina coast, and met there blacks who, a few months

W. C. Handy playing trumpet in front of Noble Sissle's Band, around 1948.

earlier, had been marched westward toward the holding pens on the coast of Africa. The powerful but outnumbered whites assiduously fomented divisions among the Indians, and between the Indians and the blacks, to prevent a combination of these forces. The English in Charleston had great success in recruiting the Creek to join them in their slave-hunts among the Guale and Apalachee. In the first decade of the eighteenth century, ten to twelve thousand Indians were brought to market with the assistance of other Indians.

The English relied upon the colonial militia to protect the plantations from Indians and, of course, from slave revolts. But so skillful were the English in dividing potential opponents that, from 1708 to the middle of the century, the militia was composed of equal numbers of blacks and whites. Though the fear of slave rebellion led to a lowering of the recruitment targets to one third blacks, half the force by which the Governor of South Carolina barely succeeded in defeating the Yamasee in 1715 were blacks. African-Americans also joined in the campaigns against the Cherokee in the 1760s.

Blacks and Indians fought against each other and with each other against other blacks and Indians in wars that history has generally depicted as being between the European invaders of the continent. Blacks and Indians were actively deployed by the British in their wars against Spain in the early eighteenth century. The Spaniards invaded Georgia in 1742 with an army that included a regiment of blacks under black officers, "clothed in lace, [who] bore the same rank as the white officers."

The American Revolution brought a new set of racial complexities and tensions, for, in the presence of still-powerful confederacies of Cherokee and of a huge slave population, both sides attempted to recruit those leaning toward them and neutralize potential enemies. The British promised emancipation to the slaves in 1775. Thomas Jefferson estimated that 30,000 slaves responded and were "lost" in Virginia alone. Lost many of them were, for the British permitted thousands to die of starvation awaiting shipment to illusory freedom. Some, it is possible, actually went free, but the records are very unclear as to how many—it did not seem important at the time. Nor do we know much about the 25,000 from South Carolina and the 12,000 from Georgia who escaped to Florida or the West, or were "stolen" by the British. There were many free blacks in the French army aiding the Americans at Savannah in 1779 and many more in the Spanish expedition that took the great fortress at Pensacola from the British in 1781.

Blacks served in the American independence forces, more at sea than on land. In 1779, the Continental Congress offered freedom to 3,000 slaves in South Carolina and Georgia in return for service in the Continental army (a proposal strongly supported by George Washington). It is a further demonstration of the selective

OPPOSITE: *The distinctive knees of baldcypress emerge from still, swampy waters along the South Carolina coast.*

blindness of American historians that we have apparently lost track of what happened to those who accepted the offer. Because we possess records of the conversations and deliberations of slave-owners, but not of the behavior of slaves, we only know that John Laurens of South Carolina and Alexander Hamilton were unsuccessful in their effort to induce the Congress to make a fixed policy of enrolling blacks. We can only wonder how the history of the Old South might have proceeded had it been otherwise. (In 1865 Robert E. Lee favored recruiting blacks for the Confederate army in return for a promise of freedom. This policy, essentially that of Hamilton and Laurens eighty-five years earlier, was at the point of prevailing in the Confederacy when the Civil War came to an end.)

Slavery was not unique to the South; it was merely more successful there, and inextricably associated with race. Black slavery united the seacoast, the highlands, and the plains beyond, and distinguished the frontier experience of the South from that of the North. One may think of the Northerners as Europeans advancing—without Africans—in ever-expanding waves, waves lapping upon a smoothly graduated, sandy coast—too simple an image, but true enough. One cannot think this way at all about the pattern of advance across the South. There the frontier line was more like a marshy delta; Europeans, Africans, and Indians were mixed in paisley patterns of swirls and washes. In the southern Appalachians some Indian communities so stoutly resisted conquest or removal that the Europeans were forced to ooze about them and among them.

The consequences of slavery still hover above the rich agricultural lands on both sides of the Appalachians; less obvious, but real none the less, is the subtle persistence of African and Indian ways in the mountains between. Intermarriage among slaves who escaped from those plantations and the Native Americans yielded a mixed heritage that is manifest in the music of Appalachia, with African rhythms and African instruments like the banjo, and in "mountain clothing," including moccasins, beading, and neck-ornament. Storytelling in the epic tradition is Cherokee, Celtic, and African, and so is the peculiar eighteenth-century Highland speech still to be heard in the hill country (though less and less often in the age of electronic homogenization). The merger of African, Indian, and Celtic ballad patterns and inflections of both speech and song have made the southern mountains the laboratory for generations of ethnomusicologists and plain people who like old stories and music.

The polygenetic South has benefited from the presence of many
ethnic strains, but it is well to observe how richly the life of the
Appalachian highlands has been served by one set of immigrants
—people from the Celtic fringes of the British Isles. These Celts have
often been portrayed as if they were homogeneous. There were great
differences, however, in the ancestral memories brought to the
southern highlands by the Roman Catholic Highlanders of Scotland
and by the Presbyterian Scotch-Irish whose character had been
forged by life in Ireland under the heel of the English. Richard II
had set the tone for English policy in Ireland by denigrating the
inhabitants as "savages." After the English became Protestant they
were able to disparage the Irish as "Popish."

The Scotch-Irish were brought to Ireland by Anglican English
landlords to dispossess or intimidate the Roman Catholic natives,
whose place was to do the work of the fields. This Irish experience
left its mark upon the Scotch-Irish as well as the Irish themselves.
The Scotch-Irish Jacksons (Andrew and "Stonewall" among them),
Calhouns, and Hamptons came from a line that had endured the
discomfort of being interposed between the English, who disdained
and used them, and the Irish, who hated them. In Ireland theirs had
been a grim life, and the Scotch-Irish remained rather grim in
America, where, if they went to town, they might be reminded of
what they had left behind. The garrison-towns built by the English
from coastal Georgia to Fort Loudon, in Tennessee, had their prototypes in the fortified towns, such as Londonderry, which the English
built in Ireland and garrisoned with Scots. Savannah, for example,
was like the geometric *bastides* by which the Irish were to be over-
awed, and from which spread outward plantations of Scottish
Lowlanders who were to form agricultural garrisons throughout
Ulster and "the Pale."

Another Celtic strain entered the polygenetic South thanks to
the efforts of a Scottish laird, Sir Alexander Cuming, (who also
dreamed of settling 300,000 Jews from Europe among the Cherokee)
and other benign Scotsmen, who were successful in providing in
America some release from the sufferings of their own Highlanders.
Cuming sought to rescue the Highlanders threatened in their religion (Roman Catholic) and deprived of their lands—and of other
consolations like bagpipes and kilts—after their Jacobite revolt
against the English was suppressed in 1746. William, Duke of
Cumberland, had brought the revolt to a bloody end at the Battle of

Culloden, at which the Highlanders gallantly assaulted modern fire-power with claymores (broadswords) and pikes. Their leader, Prince Charles Stuart, escaped to exile and into sentimental tales as "Bonnie Prince Charlie." After Culloden, an increasing amount of Gaelic could be heard around Darien, Georgia, and in the Carolinas. And it expressed some sentiments uncomfortable to the English. Catholic Highlanders held out longer than others against the introduction of black slavery, and were very articulate in public papers against the imposition of forced labor upon any people, black or white. One learns such things in the Highlands, where the lairds could be as oppressive to their own people as the English were in Ireland.

Unimpressed by the aristocratic pretensions of the Tidewater planters, Highlanders in North Carolina provided the backbone of the upcountry "Regulator" revolt against those planters in the 1760s and 1770s. Their revolt against the King's governor and the Tidewater planters was put down in 1771, after the Battle of Alamance, with a ferocity equal to that of Cumberland after Culloden. The Regulator War anticipated the Revolution, though not in any direct or simple way. The rebels of 1770–1771 were rebels against the Tidewater *and* the Crown. In 1775–1783 many of the same men were rebels against the Tidewater and *for* the Crown.

Many Jacobite Catholics of Scotland, including the most famous of Highland heroines, Flora Macdonald, had emigrated to America. Flora had hidden Bonnie Prince Charlie from his enemies, and allowed him to slip away to France; now she had taken the oath of loyalty to the British King, and, having a long tradition of oath-taking to clan leaders, she, her husband, and their kin were serious about such things. Furthermore, Catholic Highlanders loathed Presbyterian Lowlanders, so it was natural for them to choose any side but that of Ulstermen and Lowlanders—who were heavily com-mitted to independence. Flora's husband fought and was imprisoned for his King; she fought too, and was wounded in her last battle, on the decks of a ship attacked by an American privateer.

A veteran of Culloden, the 80-year-old Donald McDonald, raised the King's standard in 1776 to gather the Loyalist Highlander force that went into battle at Moores Creek, North Carolina. McLeods and Stewarts, Campbells and McLeans rallied, with pipes skirling, tartans bright in the sunlight, pikes and claymores in their hands. Once again, as at Culloden in 1746, Scots charged into the face of modern military technology and died for it. Across the bridge at Moores Creek they went at dawn, crying "King George and Broadswords!"

A detail of Ann Rice O'Hanlon's mural depicting life in frontier Kentucky shows a one-room school and a pioneer woman dipping for water.

With a heavy fog hanging over the bridge they could not see that the cross-planks had been removed, and that the unchivalric foe had greased the stringers. Two cannons and a thousand marksmen were waiting on the other side.

Four years later, in the fall of 1780, the Scotch-Irish and the Highlanders demonstrated how quickly they could adapt to Indian ways, in dress and in warfare. They learned to give a close and terrifying approximation of the Cherokee war scream, and give it they did as they assaulted the Tories ranged on the crest of Kings Mountain under Major Patrick Ferguson of His Majesty's 71st Highland Regiment. (This was the same sound that became the "Rebel Yell" in 1861.) The scream of William Campbell's attack force came suddenly and frightfully over the battlefield; steadier was the wheeze and bleating of his pipers, answering those of Ferguson's Highlanders. A man of fixed prejudices, Ferguson had previously used the term "mongrel" to derogate his antagonists. In this his final battle, he was wrong in his tactics, wrong in his strategy, and wrong in his implication. It seems that he meant that the buckskinned men working their way up hill from tree to tree were more racially mixed and therefore less formidable than the brightly-uniformed Tories he commanded to defend it. Perhaps he felt that gentlemen do not hide behind trees, and that a polyglot people using Cherokee tactics could not be composed of gentlemen. In any case he ordered his men to respond with fixed volleys and feckless bayonet charges—and lost.

In fact nearly all the men on both sides at Kings Mountain were emigrants from Britain's Celtic fringe. (Ferguson's error has been compounded by subsequent historians who describe the battle as being fought between "the British" and "the Americans." The only person on the field who might have described himself as British was Ferguson himself.) If one heard the sound of battle and saw Colonel Campbell riding about wearing his claymore, indeed, it might have seemed that Kings Mountain was merely another scrap between the clans, transferred to North Carolina. Echoes of the pipes of Kings Mountain and the skirling that sounded at Moores Creek resound in the tales told by Appalachian Celts to this day.

After the Revolution the Piedmont of North and South Carolina remained lightly settled, and the mountains more sparsely still. In the hills the descendants of fierce Celts became fiercer, and watched their cousins growing rich in the Nashville basin with the same animosity that had turned them into Regulators and enemies of the Tidewater gentry. When the Confederacy was proclaimed under the leadership of the planter class, the mountaineers went into rebellion from rebellion. A convention in Winston County, Alabama, voted to take it out of the Confederacy; Rabun County, Georgia, never went *in*. The Ozarks of Arkansas sent 8,000 men to join the Union forces, and many more joined them from East Tennessee and the Cumberland region of Kentucky. West Virginia became a separate state, and East Tennessee tried to do likewise but it did not have the endorsement of a Union army in residence.

The Confederacy, like the Union, recruited forcibly. In the North there were draft riots. In the Celtic upcountry of the South, desertion was one remedy for conscription, and 100,000 Confederates deserted. The Confederates did not make nice distinctions between deserters and Union sympathizers. The historian Carl H. Moneyhon wrote that "They were driven from their homes . . . persecuted like wild beasts . . . hunted down in the mountains . . . . Perhaps no people on the face of the earth were ever more persecuted than were the loyal people of East Tennessee." The echoes of Ireland and of the Highlands after Culloden could still be heard.

East Tennessee, western North Carolina, and the mountain corners of South Carolina, Alabama, and Georgia remained Unionist throughout the war. General William Tecumseh Sherman was protected during his Georgia and Carolina campaign by a bodyguard of cavalry from Alabama. After the war the governors of North Carolina and Tennessee were able to call upon militia units from the highlands to put down the Ku Klux Klan in the plantation country. Reconstruction was less traumatic for the highland areas than for the Piedmont and Tidewater because there was less in the hills to reconstruct. The few slaves that were there to be freed became so in legal theory, and enjoyed a brief burst of hope that the poverty they shared with their white neighbors might somehow become less grinding. However, an economy of exploitation of natural resources replaced that of exploitation of human labor; coal and iron went to create prosperity elsewhere, with only a few pockets of affluence here and there in the mountains among the managers of mines and smelters. The mountaineers of the East shared with the mountaineers of the West their role as economic dependents of absentee owners. Very little of the profits derived from mining and lumbering in Appalachia went to the replacement of its own economic resources. Those profits were sucked away to distant cities. Absentee ownership has been as much a characteristic of West Virginia as of Colorado.

Blacks and whites together found work in the mines and on lumbering crews. But by the end of the nineteenth century, discriminatory wage rates began once again to undo the work of Reconstruction. Reconstruction gave way to Jim Crow, and it was no longer so easy to distinguish the old Unionists of the hills from the Dixiecrats of the flatland. It was only in the brief period of southern biracial Populism in the 1880s and 1890s that there were enough common aspirations among the poor country people of both races to bring them, briefly, together. After the Populist coalition came apart about 1895, Jim Crow prevailed everywhere, regardless of altitude.

Yet the politics of the Appalachians have roots more ancient than the era of Reconstruction, older than the Civil War. Long before they invaded America, the highlanders differed from the great landowners and merchants of the shore. That difference had been heard in the pipes at Moores Creek, as it had been heard not long before at Culloden. Now it is no longer the pipe but the whining of a mountain fiddle that speaks the contrariness, the separateness, the ancient, intractable, courageous cussedness of the highlander. And the descendants of Africans, Europeans, and Native Americans are still working things out.

NORTH CAROLINA

OPPOSITE: *The detached kitchen at Raleigh's Mordecai House, built in the 1840s, has herbs hanging to dry above the massive brick fireplace and an array of nineteenth-century household implements on the hearth.*

I n 1728 William Byrd, surveyor of the dividing line between his
native Virginia and this state, made himself notorious to future
North Carolinians when he declared that "tis a thorough
Aversion to Labor that makes People file off to N Carolina, where
Plenty and a Warm sun confirm them in their Disposition . . . here
People may live plentifully at a triffleing expense. . . . Surely there is
no place in the World where the Inhabitants live with less Labour
than in North Carolina." Like Byrd, who observed "the great felicity
of the Climate" and "the easiness of raising Provisions," North
Carolinians have long recognized the richness of their state, which is
probably why it continues to have one of the highest percentages of
native-born residents in the country—people who are born in North
Carolina like to live in North Carolina.

North Carolina was favorably described as a site for settlement
as early as 1584, when two British explorers returned to England
with the report that the land was "the most plentiful, fruitfull, and
wholesome of all the world." Such inviting reports heightened
interest in Sir Walter Raleigh's plans to establish a colony here. In
1585 North Carolina became the site of the first English settlement
in America, on Roanoke Island, which lasted only into the next year.
Raleigh's next colony added to American history one of its greatest
mysteries: the "Lost Colony." Led by Governor John White in 1587,
this group also landed on Roanoke Island. In 1591 a supply ship
arrived and found that the settlement had disappeared.

In the 1660s eight lords proprietors, friends of Charles II, were
granted the right to govern the territory between Virginia and
Spanish Florida, from the Atlantic to the "South Seas." North
Carolinians were never satisfied by proprietary rule: They deposed
six royal governors between 1663 and 1729. The region grew slowly
with only a few early towns, the oldest of which is Bath, incorporated
in 1705. Wilmington, founded in 1730, became the colony's main
port. Carolina became the royal colony of George II in 1729, when
the lords proprietors sold the territory to the crown. In 1730
Carolina was divided into its north and south provinces. The first
permanent settlers were primarily the English, who had gradually
migrated south from Virginia to the Albemarle Sound area. North
Carolina's population increased dramatically early in the eighteenth
century as German and Scotch-Irish settlers from Pennsylvania and

OPPOSITE: *A view of the Indian settlement of Secoton, drawn by John White, gover-*
nor of the "Lost Colony," in 1585, shows several aspects of life there, including agri-
cultural practice, eating habits, and religious observance (detail).

Their rype corne

Their greene corne

Corne newly sprong

Their sitting at meate

The place of solemne prayer

howse wherin the Tombe of their Herounds standeth.

SECOTON

A Ceremony in their prayers strange iestures an songes dansing abowt posts carued on the tops lyke mens faces.

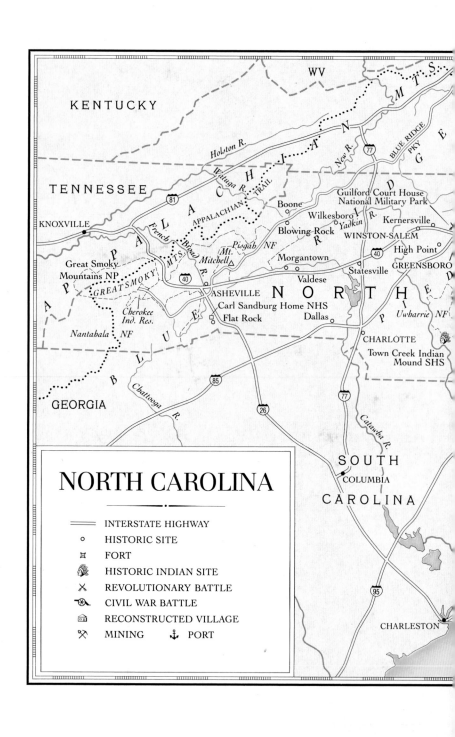

NORTH CAROLINA

═══	INTERSTATE HIGHWAY
○	HISTORIC SITE
⌻	FORT
⛊	HISTORIC INDIAN SITE
✕	REVOLUTIONARY BATTLE
⚔	CIVIL WAR BATTLE
⌂	RECONSTRUCTED VILLAGE
⚒	MINING ⚓ PORT

Map labels

KENTUCKY

WV

TENNESSEE

KNOXVILLE

Holston R.

Watauga R.

APPALACHIAN

TRAIL

Boone

Wilkesboro

Yadkin R.

Kernersville

Blowing Rock

WINSTON-SALEM

High Point

GREENSBORO

Guilford Court House National Military Park

French B.

APPALACHIAN MTS

Broad R.

Mt. Mitchell

Pisgah NF

Morgantown

Statesville

Great Smoky Mountains NP

GREAT SMOKY MTS

ASHEVILLE

Valdese

NORTH

Cherokee Ind. Res.

Carl Sandburg Home NHS

Flat Rock

Dallas

CHARLOTTE

Town Creek Indian Mound SHS

Uwharrie NF

Nantahala NF

BLUE RIDGE

Chattooga R.

GEORGIA

SOUTH

Catawba R.

COLUMBIA

CAROLINA

CHARLESTON

New R.

BLUE RIDGE PKY

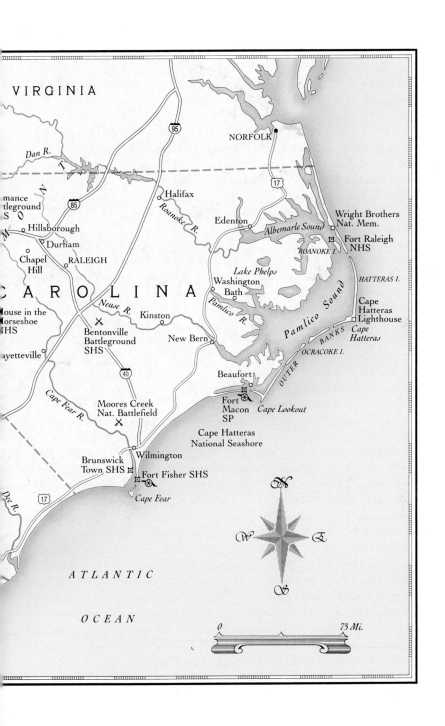

VIRGINIA

NORFOLK

Dan R.

95

17

mance
tleground
S O

85

Halifax

Hillsborough

Roanoke R.

Edenton

Wright Brothers
Nat. Mem.

Durham

Chapel
Hill

RALEIGH

Albemarle Sound

Fort Raleigh
NHS

ROANOKE I.

C A R O L I N A

Lake Phelps

Washington

HATTERAS I.

Neuse R.

Bath

Pamlico R.

Cape
Hatteras
Lighthouse

ouse in the
orseshoe
HS

Kinston

New Bern

Pamlico Sound

*Cape
Hatteras*

OUTER BANKS

ayetteville

Bentonville
Battleground
SHS

40

OCRACOKE I.

Beaufort

Cape Fear R.

Moores Creek
Nat. Battlefield

Fort
Macon
SP

Cape Lookout

Cape Hatteras
National Seashore

Brunswick
Town SHS

Wilmington

Fort Fisher SHS

ee R.

17

Cape Fear

N

W   E

S

A T L A N T I C

O C E A N

0   75 Mi.

Maryland began to settle the Piedmont, or as it was then called, the backcountry. More English settlers from South Carolina, as well as Highland Scots, arrived in the Cape Fear region later in the eighteenth century.

The British lost control of North Carolina early in the Revolutionary War, when a column of Loyalist Scots, on its way to join the royal governor, was halted by Patriots at the Battle of Moores Creek Bridge in February 1776. The fighting did not return to North Carolina until 1781, when Lord Cornwallis invaded from South Carolina, supposing that large numbers of secret Loyalists would rally to him. Instead, he found himself "in a damned rebellious country." After pursuing General Nathanael Greene's army through the wintry woods without resolution, Cornwallis finally got the major battle he wanted, at Guilford Courthouse in March 1781. Although the Americans were driven from the field, Lord Cornwallis paid a bloody price. "Another such victory would destroy the British Army," said one official in England. His army seriously weakened, Cornwallis abandoned North Carolina for, he hoped, easier pickings in Virginia.

North Carolina was the twelfth of the original thirteen colonies to join the Union in 1789. Legends about the nickname of the "Tar Heel State" go back to these days. Some say the name comes from the North Carolinians' tenacity, "sticking" to what they start; others claim that tar, dumped into rivers to prevent its capture by the British, left Cornwallis's soldiers who waded in North Carolina with "tar heels." North Carolina was the next-to-last state to secede from the Union in 1861. Some of its citizens, especially in the mountains, remained Union sympathizers and openly opposed slavery. The Confederacy had already been split by Sherman's march through Georgia and South Carolina when Wilmington, the last port open to the Confederacy, was captured by the Union navy in early 1865. After Robert E. Lee's surrender to Grant at Appomattox, the Confederate troops led by General Joseph E. Johnston surrendered to Sherman in North Carolina outside of Durham. North Carolina was readmitted to the Union in 1868, when the present state constitution was adopted.

Since the time William Byrd leveled his remarks at North Carolina, the state has distinguished itself with a number of contributions to America's heritage. The Cherokee, the strongest tribe in the area, controlled a section of the state until the 1830s, and still preserve their ancient crafts and culture in Oconaluftee Village, a

Confederate defenders repel one part of the Union attack on Fort Fisher, near Wilmington, in January 1865. Federal units penetrated the fort's defenses in another sector, and captured it. The fall of Fort Fisher closed the port of Wilmington, the last one open to the Confederacy.

part of the Cherokee Indian Reservation in the western mountains. The Blue Ridge Mountains have also been home to important writers such as the novelist Thomas Wolfe and the poet Carl Sandburg. In the Piedmont Moravians who settled the communities of Bethabara and Old Salem still practice their faith and customs and preserve the architecture of an entire mid-eighteenth century village in Winston-Salem. At Chapel Hill is the nation's oldest state university, the University of North Carolina, founded in 1795. And the North Carolina coast is known not only for its infamous pirate Blackbeard, the historic lighthouses along the Outer Banks, and mystery of the Lost Colony, but also for the flight experiments of the fathers of modern aviation, the Wright Brothers. This large and diverse state preserves a wealth of American history from its mountains to its coast.

This chapter is divided into three main sections. It begins in the coastal plain and the Outer Banks and moves from the Piedmont to the western mountains.

THE   COASTAL   PLAIN

North Carolina's history began on its coast. Sir Walter Raleigh's attempts to establish colonies in 1585 and 1587 resulted in one of the greatest mysteries in American history—the disappearance of the 150 colonists who have become known as the "Lost Colony." Among those missing was Virginia Dare, the first English child born in America and the granddaughter of the colony's governor, John White, who had returned to England for supplies.

The hazardous 150-mile stretch of water and islands beyond the mainland coast has long inspired fear. These islands, the Outer Banks, have been called the "Graveyard of the Atlantic," where over 650 ships have been lost. The Banks were made more treacherous during the reign of terror of such pirates as Edward Teach, known as "Blackbeard," whose favorite headquarters was around Ocracoke. The Outer Banks comprise one of the most beautiful coastal stretches of protected national seashore in the country, the largest on the Atlantic. Wild ponies still roam through this pristine setting. The flat beaches and favorable winds led Wilbur and Orville Wright to choose Kill Devil Hills and Kitty Hawk for their experiments with flight. The state's history of commerce and politics also begins in this region. Bath, the oldest town in the state, was founded in 1705 but has developed less than the other river port towns of its day. The towns of New Bern, Beaufort, and Edenton, all of which preserve important architecture, served as the cradle of growth and development in the colony.

This tour begins along the northwestern edge of the Coastal Plain, defined by the fall line beyond which river navigation cannot penetrate. The region extends southward from the Virginia border to South Carolina along the western boundaries of Northampton, Halifax, Nash, Johnston, Harnett, Hoke, and Scotland counties, and stretches eastward to the Outer Banks.

Hertford was incorporated in 1758 and named for the earl of Hertford. County records in the **Perquimans County Courthouse** (Church Street), one of two Federal-style courthouse buildings in North Carolina, extend uninterrupted from 1685 and include one

OPPOSITE: *Edenton's wooden Cupola House, with its second story overhang and massive chimneys, is the best surviving example of Jacobean building in the South. Like Mount Vernon, it presents an asymmetrical facade to the world.*

of the oldest deeds on record in the state, George Durant's purchase from the Yeopim Indians. South of town is the late-seventeenth-century **Newbold-White House** (Route 1336, 919–426–7567), one of the oldest buildings in the state, constructed of brick with glazed headers, interior end chimneys, and a steep gabled roof. North Carolina's oldest seat of local government, it was the meeting place of the proprietary general assembly, the governor and his council, and a number of courts between 1689 and 1704.

EDENTON

One of North Carolina's oldest and loveliest coastal communities, Edenton is an architectural and historical treasure, rich in important early Georgian structures and in pre-Revolutionary history. Though twentieth-century prosperity is more evident here than in its contemporaries, the towns of Bath and Beaufort, some outstanding structures survive. An early German traveller, Johann David Schöph, described Edenton as "consisting of not more than 100 framed houses, all standing apart and surrounded with galleries or piazzas." An architectural innovation from the West Indies, these full-length, often two-story, porches designed to catch breezes from the sound are typical in this region.

A London merchant, Robert Hunter, who visited Edenton around 1786, described what is visible today: "The town is laid out in the form of a square, built on the Albemarle Sound. . . . They have a tolerable good brick statehouse, a brick church, and a marketplace from whence they are supplied every day." Along streets lined with dogwood and crepe myrtle, Edenton preserves a number of charming private and public buildings from the early eighteenth and nineteenth centuries, including the 1767 **Chowan County Courthouse** (East King and Court streets), the "good brick statehouse" mentioned by the London visitor, as well as the brick Saint Paul's Episcopal Church, completed in 1766. The architectural variety includes Federal, Greek Revival, Gothic Revival, and Queen Anne styles.

Settled in the early 1700s on a bay between Queen Anne's Creek and Pembroke Creek, Edenton was adopted by the assembly in 1715 as the site where a courthouse and meeting place for future assemblies should be built. Known as "Ye Town on Queen Anne's Creek" until 1722, when it was incorporated and named for

Proprietary Governor Charles Eden, Edenton served as the capital
of the colony until 1743. It was also the home of such Revolutionary
leaders as Samuel Johnston, who served as both governor and U.S.
senator; James Iredell, a Supreme Court justice appointed by
George Washington; and Joseph Hewes, a signer of the Declaration
of Independence. Edenton prospered as a port city until about
1830, when the opening of the Dismal Swamp Canal diverted
shipping to Elizabeth City and Norfolk.

Barker House (southern end of Broad Street, 919–482–3663),
the former home of Thomas and Penelope Barker, is a frame
clapboard house built in 1782 with two-and-a-half stories, twin
exterior chimneys, a double gallery porch, and an entrance with
transom and sidelights. It was relocated to Edenton's waterfront in
1952 from its original site at 213 Broad Street. Thomas Barker, who
had served as a pre-Revolutionary colonial agent in London, was a
prominent planter and lawyer. Penelope Barker participated in the
Edenton Tea Party in 1774. The episode is a focal point of exhibits
in the house, which now serves as the visitor center for **Historic**

*Facing Edenton Bay along East Water Street are three cannons, the remnants of
more than forty that were purchased in France by Benjamin Franklin in 1777, and
several late-eighteenth- and early-nineteenth century houses.*

Edenton, whose tours include the two-and-a-half-story **Cupola House** (408 South Broad Street). Built in 1725 for Richard Sanderson and remodeled for Francis Corbin, Lord Granville's land agent, between 1756 and 1758, it is named for its central octagonal cupola. Unusual features include a second-story overhang (it claims to be the only extant house in the South with that feature); a Chinese Chippendale staircase leading up to the circular stairs that rise to the cupola; and wavy glass windows into which signatures were scratched in the panes in the 1830s. Although much of the downstairs woodwork was taken away in 1918 to the Brookland Museum of Fine Arts, some has been reproduced; the second-floor woodwork is original. The house, which is now open as a museum of the period 1725 to 1775, served as the county library for nearly fifty years.

Also on the Historic Edenton tour is the **James Iredell House State Historic Site** (107 East Church Street). This was the home of

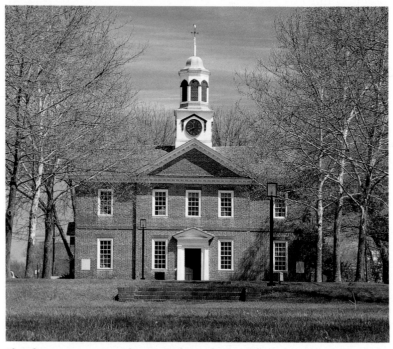

The Chowan County Courthouse in Edenton has an elaborate cupola, where a look-out was stationed at night to watch for fires.

James Iredell, who came to Edenton in 1768 as a collector of customs at Port Roanoke. He studied law under Samuel Johnston, was the state's first attorney general (from 1779 to 1782), and was appointed associate justice of the first U.S. Supreme Court by George Washington in 1790. His son and namesake became governor of North Carolina and a U.S. senator. In 1778 Iredell bought the house, a Georgian-style structure built in 1773. A Federal-style wing was added in 1815. Supreme Court Justice James Wilson, a friend of the Iredells, died in the house in 1798.

The second oldest of three surviving colonial churches in North Carolina, **Saint Paul's Episcopal Church** (West Church and Broad streets) was built between 1736 and 1766. Organized in 1701, it was the first chartered religious body in the state. The brick one-and-a-half-story building has a three-story tower topped by a shingled octagonal spire. The panelled double-door entrance features a fanlight and tripartite keystone. Inside the church are nineteenth-century box pews and reconstructed side balconies, and the communion silver from 1725 is still in use. The cemetery holds the graves of three colonial governors, Henderson Walker, Thomas Pollock, and Charles Eden. Possibly a design by Gilbert Leigh of Williamsburg, Virginia, the **Chowan County Courthouse** (East King Street), built in 1767, may be the oldest courthouse in continuous use in North Carolina. The two-story brick structure has a modified T shape, hipped roof, octagonal cupola, and single-story semicircular rear apse. It served as a meeting place for Patriots during the Revolutionary War, and on the green in front of the courthouse, a monument to Joseph Hewes recounts his contributions to the American Revolution, including his work as a delegate to the Continental Congress and one of North Carolina's three signers of the Declaration of Independence. President James Monroe was entertained at the courthouse when he visited Edenton in 1819.

Around 1815, outside Edenton, James Cathcart Johnston built **Hayes Plantation** (East Water Street, Extended, private) to the designs of William Nichols, one of the architects of the state capitol. Its exterior presages the Greek Revival. Two outlying wings are connected to the main structure, which has a hipped roof, a cupola, a two-story colonnade, and a fanlight above the doorway with flanking sidelights. The house remains a fine example of a Federal plantation house with early Greek Revival elements.

HOPE PLANTATION

The plantation home of David Stone, congressman, senator, and twice North Carolina governor, was built around 1803. The two-story frame house features a pedimented portico in the Neoclassical manner. Also on the property is the 1763 gambrel-roofed **King-Bazemore House,** built by William King, a Bertie County planter. Both houses are furnished with period pieces from the region, dating roughly from 1725 to 1830 and matching descriptions on estate inventories.

> LOCATION: Route 308, 4 miles west of Route 13 Bypass at Windsor. HOURS: March through December: 10–4 Monday–Saturday, 2–5 Sunday. FEE: Yes. TELEPHONE: 919-794-3140.

SOMERSET PLACE STATE HISTORIC SITE

Built around the 1830s, this plantation house was one of the finest in the state—a good early example of a transition to the Greek Revival architecture, with full-width verandahs on both stories on the front and rear wings. The house, built for Josiah Collins III, was constructed of hand-hewn cypress. In recent years the historical focus of the site has shifted from the house itself to the story of the slaves who worked on the Somerset Place rice plantation, one of the most successful in North Carolina.

In 1784 three Edenton residents, one of whom was Josiah Collins I, purchased 100,000 acres of swampy woodlands here. They brought eighty slaves directly from Africa to dig a six-mile canal, which, after two years of construction, joined Lake Phelps with the Scuppernong River to drain the swamps and make farming on the land possible. Because of the canal and its machinery, Somerset Plantation became the largest plantation along Lake Phelps.

An entry in an overseer's journal describes the unhappiness of the slaves and their profound homesickness: "At night they would begin to sing their native songs, and in a short while would become so wrought up that . . . they would grasp their bundles of personal effects, swing them on their shoulder, and setting their faces towards Africa, would march down into the water singing as they marched

OPPOSITE: *The hall at Hope Plantation, which was used as a summer living area, has been furnished according to the estate inventories of its builder, David Stone.*

till recalled to their senses only by the drowning of some of the party." The overseer also recorded the casual cruelty of plantation life. Slaves who were seriously injured digging the canal "would be left by the bank of the canal, and the next morning the returning gang would find them dead." During the Civil War, when Federal troops occupied the Albemarle Sound area, the Collins family left Somerset accompanied by their slaves. After Josiah Collins III died in Hillsborough, his widow and sons sold the plantation.

Recent archaeological digs have uncovered remnants of African culture as it existed on the plantation. An 1821 map shows the location and size of the slave quarters, including three two-story buildings, forty by twenty feet, where nearly 200 slaves were housed. Genealogical and social research on the blacks who lived here has been aided by the survival of extensive plantation records. As research continues, Somerset Place may become one of the country's most important sites for the interpretation of the slaves' experience.

LOCATION: Off Route 64, 7 miles south of Creswell, in Pettigrew State Park. HOURS: April through October: 9–5 Monday–Saturday, 1–5 Sunday; November through March: 10–4 Tuesday–Saturday, 1–4 Sunday. FEE: None. TELEPHONE: 919–797–4560.

WASHINGTON

An important supply port during the American Revolution, Washington was a crucial commercial center for the Continental army when the British controlled the ports of Savannah, Charleston, and Wilmington. Much of Washington, the seat of Beaufort County, was destroyed by fires set by Union forces in 1864; few houses date before that time. Residents rebuilt the town, but an accidental fire on September 3, 1900, destroyed it again. Two historically significant buildings survived the fires: The **Bank of Washington** (216 West Main Street), built around 1852, is a Greek Revival brick structure with a brick-lined roof. The **Old Beaufort County Courthouse** (158 North Market Street), a two-story brick structure built ca. 1786, is the second-oldest courthouse building extant in the state.

BATH

Surveyed in 1704 by John Lawson and chartered in 1705, Bath is the oldest incorporated town in North Carolina. Originally called Town

The Palmer-Marsh House's massive brick double chimney has two small windows, which light small closets on two stories.

of Pamlicoe on Old Town Creek, it is named for one of the lords proprietors, the earl of Bath. The sound and river retain the Indian name of Pamlico. European settlers entered the territory and made their homes along the Bath Creek and the Pamlico River, though settlers suffered an attack by the Tuscarora Indians on September 22, 1711. According to local legend, Edward Teach, better known as the pirate Blackbeard, married the sixteen-year-old daughter of a local citizen (she was Blackbeard's thirteenth or fourteenth wife) and settled here for some time around 1717. Stories that Blackbeard met in Bath with the royal governor Charles Eden are plausible, as the pirate did receive a royal pardon, but his return to piracy led to his death in 1718 near Ocracoke. Another legend, about the lack of growth in the small town, holds that the Great Awakening revivalist preacher George Whitfield visited Bath four times between 1747 and 1762. On the first three visits, the Englishman so harshly decried the sins he observed in this port town that citizens barred him from preaching during his fourth visit. Whitfield then cursed

Bath and declared that the village would never prosper. For whatever reason, Bath has changed little over the years, and the present town lies almost entirely within the original boundaries surveyed by John Lawson.

Historic Bath State Historic Site

The town preserves several restored eighteenth- and nineteenth-century brick and frame buildings within the Bath Historic District, bounded by Bath Creek, Route 92, and King Street. Several buildings here are among the oldest in North Carolina. The Georgian-style **Saint Thomas Episcopal Church** (Craven Street), built in 1734, is the oldest extant church in the state, with simple brick walls two feet thick and an unusual corbeled arch. The two-story clapboard **Bonner House** (Front Street), furnished with period pieces, is a fine example of early-nineteenth-century North Carolina architecture. It stands on land once owned by the town's founder, John Lawson, surveyor and author of *A New Voyage to Carolina*, the earliest description of the North Carolina colony. Also of note is the restored frame gambrel-roofed **Van Der Veer House** (Harding Street), built around 1795, which houses exhibits covering nearly three centuries of Bath's history. The Georgian **Palmer-Marsh House** (Main Street, south of Route 92), a two-story frame building constructed around 1744, served as both office and residence of Colonel Robert Palmer, a surveyor and later customs officer in Bath. One of its most unusual features is the double brick chimney, seventeen feet wide at its base and four feet thick, with two windows in the brick wall between the flues. The house contains late-eighteenth-century furnishings.

LOCATION: Route 92. HOURS: April through October: 9–5 Monday–Saturday, 1–5 Sunday; November through March: 10–4 Tuesday–Saturday, 1–4 Sunday. FEE: Yes. TELEPHONE: 919–923–3971.

RICHARD CASWELL MEMORIAL AND THE RAM CSS *NEUSE* STATE HISTORIC SITE

This site commemorates the life of Lenoir County native Richard Caswell, an influential Patriot in the American Revolution, and also

OPPOSITE: *Bath's Saint Thomas Episcopal Church was the home of the first public library in North Carolina, founded under the patronage of the English Society for the Propagation of the Gospel in Foreign Parts.*

preserves the hull of a Confederate warship that never saw action in
the Civil War. Exhibits and an audio-visual presentation illustrate
Caswell's military and political career. An important leader at the
battles of Moores Creek Bridge and Camden, South Carolina, he
was the first governor of the independent state of North Carolina, in
office from 1776 until 1780, and was reelected in 1784. He is buried
in a cemetery on the site. The CSS *Neuse* was an ironclad ramming
ship, one of twenty-two built by the Confederacy, that the
Confederate commander Joseph Price ordered sunk in March 1865
because Union forces had pushed to within five miles of Kinston
and the low waters of the Neuse River prevented the ship's use in
the Confederate war effort. Because Price did not want Union forces
to capture it, he ordered the ship set afire with explosives placed in
the bow. It sank quickly and remained on the bottom of the Neuse
River for nearly a century. Raised in 1964, the *Neuse* is one of two
remaining Confederate naval vessels.

LOCATION: West Vernon Avenue, off Route 70, west of Kinston.
HOURS: April through October: 9–5 Monday–Saturday, 1–5 Sunday;
November through March: 10–4 Tuesday–Saturday, 1–4 Sunday.
FEE: None. TELEPHONE: 919–522–2091.

NEW BERN

Founded in 1710, New Bern is generally accepted as the second-
oldest town in North Carolina. Its location at the confluence of the
Neuse and Trent rivers, approximately thirty-five miles from the
ocean, has contributed to its growth. The handsome **historic district,**
bounded roughly by the two rivers and Queen Street, preserves the
original town center with commercial, governmental, religious, and
residential buildings dating from the eighteenth and nineteenth
centuries, including examples of Georgian and Federal architecture.
New Bern was settled by Swiss and German colonists led by Baron
Christopher de Graffenried, a Swiss who named the town for the
Swiss capital, Bern. An attack by the Tuscarora in 1711 nearly ended
the colony, but the town revived under the leadership of Colonel
Thomas Pollock. When the Reverend George Whitfield visited in
1739, he recorded his displeasure at finding that the town, which
began with colonists seeking religious and political freedom,
supported a dancing teacher; Whitfield was also "grieved" to find a

During General Ambrose E. Burnside's occupation of New Bern, a group of Federal soldiers and former slaves stand among barrels of potatoes and boxes of hardtack.

local minister who tolerated dancing. Serving sporadically as the colonial and state capital from 1746 until 1792, New Bern became an important center of trade and commerce. The state's first newspaper, the *North Carolina Gazette,* was issued here in 1749. The seat of royal governors from 1770 to 1774, New Bern was the site of the governor's "Palace," constructed from 1767 to 1770 for William Tryon. Tryon Palace burned in 1798 but has been reconstructed.

It was Tryon who proposed establishing the port city as the colonial capital and building the palace; he believed, along with others, in creating a permanent capital. Previously, the colonial government had met at alternating locations, and public records were transported from place to place. Tryon Palace, however, was not originally the object of pride for many Carolinians. During construction, the editor of the *South Carolina Gazette* wrote that "the people cannot be reconciled to being taxed as they are for building the Governor's sumptious Palace at Newbern which is thought to stand in so much danger of being destroyed, that an entrenchment or barricade has lately been thrown up . . . the better to defend it." Resentment over using taxes for the building of Tryon Palace was one of many grievances of the Regulators, who organized to protest unfair taxation but were defeated by Tryon and the colonial militia in the Battle of Alamance Creek on May 16, 1771.

During the Civil War, the town served as Union headquarters for General Ambrose E. Burnside, who defeated Confederate general L. O'Bryan Branch on March 14, 1862, and occupied the town for the rest of the war. Confederate troops made unsuccessful attempts to retake the town on March 14, 1863, February 1, 1864, and February 5, 1864.

Tryon Palace

Tryon Palace served as the state house for both the colony and the state of North Carolina, as well as the family residence of Royal Governor William Tryon and his successor, Josiah Martin. Designed by the English architect John Hawks and constructed between 1767 and 1770, the red-brick Georgian mansion was originally furnished with Tryon's personal pieces. The furnishings seen today are of the period, arranged according to Tryon's inventory of his possessions. Hawks's English design included the colonial architectural feature of separating the stable and kitchen wings from the main structure, primarily to provide protection in the event of fire. After the state capital moved to Raleigh in 1794, the palace was vandalized, then used as offices, a school, and a hotel. Ironically, it finally was destroyed by fire in 1798. The stable wing survived the fire intact.

Between 1952 and 1959, the palace was completely researched and reconstructed on the original foundations, along with the surrounding eighteenth-century formal gardens. A brick two-story structure with attached two-story wings, the Tryon Palace mansion is the centerpiece of the complex. King George III's coat of arms mounted in the front pediment appears as it did when William Atmore visited the palace in 1787 and commented, "Considering the independent spirit of the people averse to every vestige of royalty, [it] appears something strange." The Council Chamber best illustrates the dual purpose of the palace. It is a ballroom featuring draperies of eighteenth-century red silk damask, two cut-glass chandeliers, pier glasses made by John Gumley in about 1720, and eight George II side chairs with narrow seats, typical of ballroom furnishings. The room also contains portraits of George I, George III, and Queen Charlotte, as well as the governor's master chair, a Chippendale table-desk, and twelve Gothic Chippendale elbow chairs with square seats, for council meetings. The impressive library, restored to its original ocher color (copied from paint found amid the palace ruins), holds over 400 original editions of books listed in Tryon's inventory. The parlor reflects the English tastes of the Tryons. It has a suite of George II carved mahogany chairs; a card table made by William Vile, cabinetmaker for George III; and early-eighteenth-century silver pieces by George Hindmarsh and Paul de Lamerie. The family living rooms are upstairs, as was the English custom. The great stair hall has a

The first-floor library at Tryon Palace contains copies of many books owned by William Tryon and listed in an inventory of his residence in Fort George, (now Albany), New York, where he was appointed royal governor after his service in North Carolina.

staircase of Santo Domingo mahogany and pegged walnut with a central skylight overhead. In addition to the drawing room and supper room with period furnishings are Mrs. Tryon's dressing room and bedroom with appointments in pink, Wedgwood blue, and white. The largest suite, Governor Tryon's bedroom, with a portrait of his father, adjoins his wife's dressing room. A child's room designed for the Tryons' nine-year-old daughter, Margaret, has small-scale furnishings, including a rare little walnut wing chair.

The family left the palace shortly after the Battle of Alamance in 1771, when Tryon accepted the post of royal governor of New York. During the Revolution, Tryon led a series of highly destructive raids against towns in Connecticut. The palace complex features impressive gardens and other buildings on fourteen acres in New Bern, overlooking the Trent River. Costumed guides and artisans interpret eighteenth-century life here. The complex includes the **Dixon-Stevenson House,** built about 1828 for a former New Bern mayor and merchant, and the **John Wright Stanly House** (307 George Street), built about 1780 and probably designed by Hawks. The home of a Patriot merchant and shipowner, it was described by George Washington in his diary as a place that provided "exceeding good lodgings" when he stayed there in 1791. The house also served as the headquarters of Union general Ambrose E. Burnside.

LOCATION: George and Pollock streets, just off Route 17 (Broad Street). HOURS: 9:30–4 Monday–Saturday, 1:30–4 Sunday. FEE: Yes. TELEPHONE: 919–638–1560.

Built ca. 1790 by Samuel Chapman, a first lieutenant under General Washington, the **Attmore-Oliver House** (510 Pollock Street, 919–638–8558) has an unusual set of four exterior end chimneys. It is now a house museum operated by the New Bern Historical Society, featuring period furnishings and Civil War artifacts.

Two of the oldest fire departments in continuous operation in the United States are in New Bern: the Atlantic Company, formed in 1845, and the Button Company, dating from 1865 and named

OPPOSITE: *Tryon Palace's parlor, fitted out for a summer concert with slip-covered chairs and an eighteenth-century French violin.*

for the New York Button Steam Company, manufacturers of steam-driven fire engines. The **New Bern Firemen's Museum** (420 Broad Street, 919–637–3111) preserves the head of a former fire horse named Fred; after years of service to the community, Fred died in his traces, answering an alarm. Also on display are antique firefighting equipment, photographs, and artifacts of local history, including gifts from Bern, Switzerland, New Bern's sister city.

BEAUFORT

One of the oldest towns in North Carolina, surveyed in 1713, with settlers as early as 1709, was this village named for Henry Somerset, duke of Beaufort. Spanish pirates occupied Beaufort for several days in 1749, until the citizens banded together to drive them out. The seat of Carteret County, Beaufort (pronounced Bo' furt, unlike the South Carolina town of Bew' furt) remains a fishing village with a historic district of houses showing the influence of trade with the West Indies. Most feature porches designed to catch sea breezes.

Old Town Beaufort Historic Site

The buildings here, rows of mostly white frame dwellings and commercial structures with porches, were built between 1710 and the 1900s and represent a wide variety of architectural styles, including Federal and Greek Revival. Centrally located in Beaufort's historic district are a number of sites open to the public. Guided tours begin at the Welcome Center located in the **Josiah Bell House,** built around 1825 and painted yellow with brown trim. The **Joseph Bell House,** painted conch red with white shutters, features original pine floors and woodwork and holds original and reproduction furnishings and appointments; it was built around 1767 as a townhouse for Bell, a planter, judge, and colonel in the local militia. These two houses are the only two structures in the complex that remain on their original sites.

The other houses in the complex have been relocated from within a five-block area and have been restored. The **Old Carteret County Courthouse,** built in 1796 as an Anglican meeting place and used to house the militia in 1812, is the oldest public building

OPPOSITE: *The 1796 Carteret County Courthouse, used also as an Anglican meeting place and a Masonic lodge during its long history, now displays a American flag of the 1790s.*

in the county. The 1859 **Apothecary Shop and Doctor's Office**
exhibits items used by early local physicians and dentists. The
Samuel Leffers House, dating from 1778, was the residence of
Beaufort's first schoolmaster. The **Rustell House,** completed in
1830, is used as a seasonal art gallery and also is the site of weaving
demonstrations on four-harness looms. The ca.-1829 **Carteret
County Jail** has two-foot-thick walls, two cells, and jailer's quarters.
The **Old Burying Ground,** on Ann Street between the Baptist and
Methodist churches, was deeded to the town in 1731. Graves here
include that of Captain Otway Burns, commander of the *Snap
Dragon* and a successful privateer in the War of 1812 (his grave lies
beneath a cannon from his ship); Josiah Pender, the commander
who captured Fort Macon in 1861; a British soldier, buried standing
upright; and the mass grave of the crew that froze to death on the
Chrissie Wright on January 11, 1886.

LOCATION: 100 block of Turner Street, off Route 70. HOURS:
9:30–4:30 Monday–Saturday. FEE: Yes. TELEPHONE: 919-728-5225.

FORT MACON STATE PARK

Begun in 1826 and completed in 1834 to the design of General
Simon Bernard, a French military engineer who designed a chain
of forts along the eastern seaboard, the fort was named for
Senator Nathaniel Macon. It was captured by the Confederates in
1861 but recaptured by Union forces on April 25, 1862, in a land
and sea attack. Confederate commander Moses J. White
surrendered the fort after eleven hours of bombardment when
Federal artillery batteries fired rifled-cannon shells, penetrating
rooms near those where gunpowder was stored. The Confederates
never regained control of the fort, which was deactivated in 1877,
garrisoned again during the Spanish-American War, and
deactivated again in 1903.

LOCATION: Route 58, off Route I-70. HOURS: June through August:
8–9 Daily; September through October: 8–8 Daily; November
through February: 8–5:30 Daily; March: 8–7 Daily; April through
May: 8–8 Daily. FEE: None. TELEPHONE: 919-726-3775.

OPPOSITE: *Fort Macon, a sophisticated example of early nineteenth century military
architecture, contains some of the most intricate brickwork of the period.*

THE   OUTER   BANKS

The 100-mile stretch of narrow peninsulas and islands off the North Carolina mainland holds national seashore beaches and sand dunes north of Nags Head, with lighthouses, wild ponies, and other wildlife. **Jockey's Ridge State Park** (Route 158 at milepost 12, 919–441–7132), the highest natural sand dune on the East Coast, has a rich history; the 391-square-mile area includes the first English settlement, in 1585; the sites of countless shipwrecks; the headquarters of the infamous Blackbeard; and the first flight of a power-driven airplane in 1903.

CAPE HATTERAS NATIONAL SEASHORE

Covering roughly forty-five square miles of North Carolina's Outer Banks, Cape Hatteras National Seashore, the largest protected seashore on the Atlantic coast, includes the southern part of Bodie Island, as well as Hatteras and Ocracoke islands (excluding the town areas). A toll-free bridge and a free ferry connect the islands. Within the national park is **Bodie Island Lighthouse** (eight miles south of the intersection of Routes 158 and 64); though the striped 150-foot-tall lighthouse is not open to climb, visitor information is available at the Whalebone Information Station, located in the Old Lighthouse Keeper's House on Park Road eight miles north. Off Route 12, eight miles south of Route 158, the *Laura Barnes*, wrecked in 1921, may be seen at Coquina Beach. The **Cape Hatteras Lighthouse,** built in 1870 at a height of 208 feet, is the tallest such brick structure in the United States. Its beacon warns ships about Diamond Shoals, a treacherous area also called the "Graveyard of the Atlantic." Though the lighthouse is closed to the public, the former keeper's residence has a visitor center with local-history exhibits.

LOCATION: Off Route 12 at Buxton. HOURS: June through September: 9–6 Daily; November through March: 9–5 Daily. FEE: None. TELEPHONE: 919–995–4474.

OPPOSITE: *Cape Hatteras Lighthouse, painted with distincitive black and white spiral stripes.*

OCRACOKE ISLAND

This island, with Pamlico Sound on one side and the Atlantic on the other, is fourteen to sixteen miles long and between one-half mile and two miles wide. Most of the island is part of the Cape Hatteras National Seashore. The fishing village of Ocracoke, located near the southern end of the island, was settled in the seventeenth century and was frequented by the pirate Edward Teach, known as "Blackbeard." The battle in which Blackbeard was killed in 1718 by Lieutenant Robert M. Maynard took place in a nearby inlet. During the Revolution Royal Governor Josiah Martin complained about "the contemptible Port of Ocracock," which had developed as "a great channel of supply to Rebels while the more considerable Ports of the Continent have been watched by the King's ships."

The area is also the site of the conical **Ocracoke Lighthouse** (Route 1326), a seventy-five-foot-tall brick structure that has been in use since 1823.

ROANOKE ISLAND

Situated between the Albemarle and Pamlico sounds, the island is twelve miles long and an average of three miles wide. **Manteo,** named for the Indian who befriended the first settlers, is the seat of Dare County, named for Virginia Dare, the first English child born in America. Roanoke Island was the site of a naval battle during the Civil War. When Union general Ambrose Burnside attacked Fort Bartow on February 7 and 8, 1862, a Confederate fleet attempted unsuccessfully to defend the island. Their defeat allowed Union control of most of North Carolina's inland waters.

The **Elizabeth II State Historic Site** (919–473–1144) is a museum focusing on sixteenth-century life. The visitor center offers exhibits interpreting Sir Walter Raleigh's voyages, and costumed guides lead tours through the *Elizabeth II*, a reproduction of a sixteenth-century square-rigged sailing ship.

Fort Raleigh National Historical Site

On this site originated one of the most fascinating mysteries in American history, the result of Sir Walter Raleigh's unsuccessful attempts to establish a colony. In 1585 Raleigh organized a settlement party under Sir Richard Grenville, who constructed Fort

At Fort Raleigh, an earthen fort constructed by Ralph Lane, governor of Sir Walter Raleigh's 1585 expedition to the New World, has been reconstructed, but the site of the colonists' dwellings remains unknown.

Raleigh on the northern tip of Roanoke Island. When Grenville sailed for England later that year, he left over 100 men on the island under the leadership of Ralph Lane. Hardships resulting from low supplies caused these first settlers to return to England the next year with Sir Francis Drake, who visited the colony and offered assistance. Only a few weeks after they left, Grenville returned with the supplies. Finding no colonists, he unloaded his ships and left fifteen men to hold Fort Raleigh while he returned to England.

Raleigh organized a second group of colonists in 1587. The men, women, and children who set out in May with Governor John White intended to collect the fifteen men at Fort Raleigh and sail north to Chesapeake Bay. But one of the first mysteries connected with the Lost Colony, as it came to be known, is why, after finding Grenville's men had been killed by Indians, at least some of the settlers reoccupied Fort Raleigh. Why did they not sail north as they had planned? Some accounts say that the ship's pilot, Simon Fernandez, refused to sail farther. A leading authority on the Lost Colony, Dr. David B. Quinn, contends that many of these colonists did travel overland to the Chesapeake region, where they were killed by members of the Powhatan tribe. In any case, members of the second group of colonists resettled Fort Raleigh in July 1587. On August 18 of that year Eleanor Dare, the daughter of Governor White, gave birth to a daughter, Virginia, the first English child born in the New World. Though crops were planted and the colony was surviving, White realized that their supplies would soon be exhausted. Reluctantly, he sailed for England on August 27 to obtain the needed provisions. He arrived as the English were preparing to meet the Spanish Armada, and it was nearly two years after Sir Francis Drake's victory over the Spanish in 1588 before White was able to procure the ships and supplies for his colonists. He returned to Roanoke on August 18, 1590.

When he arrived, he discovered a deserted fort and mysterious clues that still have not answered conclusively what happened to the Lost Colony. The primary clue left behind was the single word CROATOAN, the Indian name for Hatteras, carved on a tree. Before White had left for England, the colonists had agreed that, if relocation became necessary, they would leave the name of their new location carved on a tree, with a cross carved above the name if they moved under attack. No cross was found inscribed with the word CROATOAN, and no bodies were found, but bad weather prevented more extensive searching. White returned to England in 1591 without discovering the fate of the colonists. Myriad legends and theories explain the disappearance of the Lost Colony, but perhaps the most plausible is that the colonists moved south to the modern-day site of Hatteras, where they lived with the friendly tribe of Croatan. An eastern North Carolina tribe called the Lumbee, many of whom have blue eyes, claims ancestry from the Lost Colony.

In addition to a reconstruction of **Fort Raleigh,** the site includes the **Elizabethan Gardens** (919–473–3234). Honoring Queen Elizabeth and the Lost Colony, they were designed to resemble a sixteenth-century pleasure garden. The gardens cover more than ten acres with antique statuary and native and imported plants.

LOCATION: Off Route 64, 3 miles north of Manteo. HOURS: 9–5 Daily. FEE: None. TELEPHONE: 919–473–5772.

OPPOSITE: *Near Fort Raleigh, the Garden Club of North Carolina created a sixteenth-century formal garden to illustrate the land the early colonists had left, and that to which they had come. The Elizabethan Garden includes a collection of garden ornaments dating to the sixteenth century.*

KILL DEVIL HILLS

Legends suggest that Kill Devil Hills was named for rum so strong it would kill. In William Byrd's *History of the Dividing Line between Virginia and North Carolina,* he wrote that "most of the rum they get in this country comes from New England, and it is so bad and unwholesome, that it is not improperly call'd 'Kill Devil.'"

Wright Brothers National Memorial

On December 17, 1903, Kill Devil Hills was the site of the first powered airplane flight. Orville and Wilbur Wright, who chose the site for flight experiments because of the constant wind, took turns at the controls for their four flights; Orville's twelve-second flight, covering a distance of 120 feet, was the first. The fourth flight, piloted by Wilbur, covered 852 feet in fifty-nine seconds before a gust caused such damage to the aircraft that no further flights could be attempted. A reconstruction of the Wright brothers' 1903 camp is at the site, along with a public airstrip, markers explaining the four flight distances, a visitor center featuring a full-scale reproduction of the original plane, and a granite memorial to the Wright brothers. The monument has a star-shaped base with a sixty-foot-tall granite shaft; the inscription commemorates "the conquest of the air by the brothers Wilbur and Orville Wright conceived by Genius, achieved by Dauntless Resolution and Unconquerable Faith."

LOCATION: Route 158. HOURS: 9–5 Daily. FEE: Yes. TELEPHONE: 919-441-7430.

MOORES CREEK NATIONAL BATTLEFIELD

The first Revolutionary War battle in North Carolina took place here on February 27, 1776. Scottish Highland settlers along the Cape Fear River, loyal to the British crown, were marching toward the coast to join newly arrived Highlanders who had been persuaded to take up arms for the king by the royal governor, Josiah Martin. Martin had taken refuge on a warship in the Cape Fear River. To prevent the Highlanders from gathering, Patriot forces assembled under colonels James Moore, Alexander Lillington, James Kenan, and John Ashe.

OPPOSITE: *Orville Wright gliding at Kitty Hawk on a test flight in 1911. Kitty Hawk was chosen for its high winds, evident in the onlookers, determinedly clutching their hats.*

The double porches on two sides of Wilmington's 1770 Burgwin-Wright House are the descendents of architectural forms developed in the hot climate of the West Indies.

The Scottish leader, 70-year-old Donald McDonald, wanted to avoid a fight because his men were poorly equipped. He managed to outwit and evade the Patriots for several days, until one misty morning the Scots found their way blocked at Moores Creek Bridge. His second-in-command, Donald McLeod, took charge and ordered a frontal assault on the Patriot position, a strong earthen fortification protected by artillery. The attack would be led, in traditional Highland fashion, by eighty men wielding broadswords. Amid bloodcurdling battle cries and the braying of bagpipes, the Scots rushed forward across a crude bridge. In the early dawn light neither McLeod nor Captain John Campbell and his broadswordsmen could see that the rebels had removed a number of boards from the bridge and placed a small cannon and a swivel gun at the end of the span—in addition to the hundreds of muskets they had aimed in that direction. The Patriots easily drove back the swordsmen. Casualties were not high because many of the Highlanders quickly realized how uneven were the odds and retreated. The decisive Patriot victory delayed for years British attempts to gain control in the South through an uprising of Loyalists.

The eighty-six-acre national park includes the site of the battle, the remains of fortifications, partially restored earthworks, field exhibits and markers, and a visitor center with interpretive audio-visual presentations.

LOCATION: Route 210, near Currie, roughly 25 miles northwest of Wilmington. HOURS: 8–5 Daily. FEE: None. TELEPHONE: 919–283–5591.

WILMINGTON

Settled in 1732, Wilmington soon became a prosperous port city and was the site of events leading to the American Revolution. On November 16, 1765, at the old courthouse that once stood on the northeast corner of Front and Market streets, a Stamp Act protest forced the royal stamp officer to resign. In February 1781 Major James H. Craig, with a force of about 400 British and Loyalists, occupied the town. Lord Cornwallis and his army rested in Wilmington in the spring of 1781, after their Pyrrhic victory in the Battle of Guilford Courthouse and before marching to Virginia. Local citizens still refer to the John Burgwin house as "the Cornwallis house," believing that Cornwallis used the house as his area headquarters. During the Civil War the inlets at the mouth of the Cape Fear River were guarded by Forts Fisher, Caswell, and Johnston. Wilmington became the main Confederate port for blockade runners and was the last Confederate port to fall.

Historic churches include the Gothic Revival **Saint James Episcopal Church** (25 South 3d Street), designed by Thomas U. Walter in 1839 near the site of an earlier church used by British officers as their principal stronghold during the Revolution. In the church cemetery are the graves of Patriot Cornelius Harnett and early American playwright Thomas Godfrey. The Gothic Revival **First Presbyterian Church** (125 South 3d Street), completed in 1928, was designed by Hobart Upjohn. The 1876 **Temple of Israel** (1 South 4th Street), with its Moorish design by Alex Strausz, was the first synagogue in North Carolina. The Gothic Revival **First Baptist Church** (5th and Market streets), built between 1859 and 1870, was designed by Samuel Sloan. **Saint Mary's Church** (220 South Fifth Avenue), the Spanish Baroque Revival design of Rafael Guastavino, was built between 1909 and 1912 under the direction of the architect's namesake and son, who used Guastavino's famous tiles for the self-supporting dome—no steel, wood, or nails.

Burgwin-Wright House and Garden

The oldest house extant in Wilmington was built in 1770 for John Burgwin, colonial treasurer under the Carolina royal governor, Arthur Dobbs. The front part of the present house is the townhouse Burgwin built in 1770 on the stone foundation of the original town jail. Joshua Grainger Wright, the stepson of Burgwin's business partner, Charles Jewkes, bought the house after Jewkes's death, and the Wright family resided there until Cornwallis established his headquarters in the house for eighteen days after the Battle of Guilford Courthouse. Cornwallis chose the place he described as "the most considerable house in town." From Wilmington, Cornwallis moved north toward the site of his defeat and surrender at Yorktown. The house is now a museum featuring a collection of eighteenth-century furnishings and decorative arts. Of particular note are the upstairs drawing room with elaborate panelling and the three-story kitchen, which dates from the time of the jail and is even older than the house. An eighteenth-century formal garden is also on the property.

LOCATION: 224 Market Street. HOURS: 10–4 Tuesday–Saturday. FEE: Yes. TELEPHONE: 919–762–0570.

USS North Carolina Battleship Memorial

Commissioned on April 9, 1941, the USS *North Carolina* saw action in all the major offensives in the Pacific in World War II, from Guadalcanal to Tokyo Bay, and earned fifteen battle stars. The ship has been open as a memorial to World War II veterans since 1961. Self-guided tours include nine decks and levels, including the crew's quarters, officers' staterooms, galley, sick bay, engine room, machine shop, pilothouse, nine sixteen-inch gun turrets, twenty five-inch guns, twelve fifty-caliber guns, a Kingfisher float plane, and a museum.

LOCATION: Accessible from Routes 17, 74, 76, and 421. HOURS: May through August: 8–8 Daily; September through April: 8–Dusk Daily. FEE: Yes. TELEPHONE: 919–762–1829.

Zebulon Latimer House

Latimer, a dry goods merchant and bank director, built this house in 1852, and it remained in the Latimer family until 1963. The Lower Cape Fear Historical Society now uses the building for its headquarters and maintains it as a house museum. The Italianate residence has quoins, a stuccoed exterior, heavy cast-metal frieze brackets, and round vents. Ornate cornices cap the windows (the Corinthian-columned portico was added after 1889). The three-tiered cast-iron fountain in the south yard is a good example of Wilmington's street furniture and probably dates from the 1880s, when it was originally placed in the center plaza of South 3d Street. Roughly 70 percent of the furnishings are original to the Latimer family. The house also contains the original crystal chandeliers, family portraits, family clothing, and nineteenth- and twentieth-century decorative arts.

LOCATION: 126 South 3d Street. HOURS: February through December: 10–5 Tuesday–Saturday. FEE: Yes. TELEPHONE: 919–762–0492.

Thalian Hall

Variously called the "Wilmington Theater," the "Opera House," and the "Academy of Music" during its history, Thalian Hall stands as the only surviving American theater of some forty designed by architect John Montague Trimble. Built by the city in 1858 as a combination opera house and municipal building, the hall housed city offices in the south wing and the police department in the basement. The entire second floor was a ballroom. In the theater wing, the first tier of the balcony is supported by decorative cast-iron columns. There is a variety of equipment for special effects, including the "thunder run," a long wooden trough in which small cannonballs are rolled to approximate the sound of thunder. During its long and varied history, the theater has been the scene for performances by John Philip Sousa, General Tom Thumb, Oscar Wilde, and Lillian Russell.

LOCATION: 3d and Princess streets. HOURS: 10–3 Tuesday–Saturday. FEE: Yes. TELEPHONE: 919–252–8881.

The defense of Fort Fisher during the January 1865 battle, painted by Frank Vizetelly, who noted "I was present in the fort during the entire engagement, three days in all, and never could I have credited such formidable means of attack were possessed by the federals."

Saint John's Museum of Art (114 Orange Street, 919–763–0281) primarily features nineteenth- and twentieth-century North Carolina art. The central art gallery for the permanent collection, which includes a group of thirteen color prints by the American painter Mary Cassatt, is in Saint John's Lodge, built ca. 1804, home of the oldest Masonic lodge in North Carolina.

Established in 1898, the **New Hanover County Museum** (814 Market Street, 919–341–4350) is the oldest local-history museum in North Carolina. Central to the holdings is a 600-item Civil War collection featuring a seventeen-by-twenty-foot diorama of Wilmington's waterfront in 1863.

BRUNSWICK TOWN
STATE HISTORIC SITE

First settled in 1725 and involved in the Stamp Act resistance of 1765, Brunswick Town remained a prosperous port town until the Revolutionary War, when it was burned by British troops led by Sir Henry Clinton on May 12, 1776. The community was so thoroughly destroyed and so vulnerable to repeated attacks that the town was eventually abandoned. An earth fort on the site, Fort Anderson, was a Confederate stronghold and was taken by Union troops by February 1865. The site has archaeological remains of the eighteenth-century port town and the nineteenth-century fort in addition to a visitor center with interpretive exhibits.

LOCATION: Route 133, between Wilmington and Southport. HOURS: April through October: 9–5 Monday–Saturday, 1–5 Sunday; November through March: 10–4 Tuesday–Saturday, 1–4 Sunday. FEE: None. TELEPHONE: 919–371–6613.

FORT FISHER STATE HISTORIC SITE

One of the largest Confederate earthwork forts, Fort Fisher was the site of a heavy land and sea battle on January 13–15, 1865. Confederate colonel William Lamb was assigned to command in Fort Fisher. Influenced by his knowledge of the Russian Crimean War fort called Malakoff Tower, he redesigned the fort until, by January 1865, Fort Fisher offered one-third of a mile of inland defenses and one mile of sea defenses. It was heavily armed, and its earth and sand mound construction readily absorbed bombardment by heavy artillery. In December 1864 the fort was only slightly damaged when the Union navy blew up a ship, packed with explosives, in front of it. Determined to close the port of Wilmington to Confederate blockade runners, General Grant ordered a second attack in January 1865. As Federal gunboats pounded the fortifications, sailors and marines stormed across the beach under intense fire, suffering heavy casualties. Meanwhile, army units atacked from another side, entered through a breach made by the gunboats, and captured the fort in bitter hand-to-hand fighting.

The site has the remains of the earthen fort with a restored palisade fence. The visitor center houses interpretive exhibits and items recovered from sunken blockade runners.

LOCATION: Route 421, south of Kure Beach. HOURS: April through October: 9–5 Monday–Saturday, 1–5 Sunday; November through March: 10–4 Tuesday–Saturday, 1–4 Sunday. FEE: None. TELEPHONE: 919–458–5538.

T H E   P I E D M O N T

The Piedmont, literally "the foot of the mountains," covers the central part of the state and has long been the center of the state's growth. Settlers from Pennsylvania, Moravians who settled Bethabara, Old Salem, and Bethania, arrived here during the first half of the eighteenth century. Significant events in both the American Revolution and the Civil War occurred in this region. At Moores Creek Bridge in 1776, North Carolina Patriots won a victory over the Tories. The British drove the Patriots from the field of Guilford County Courthouse, the largest Revolutionary battle to take place in North Carolina, but suffered many casualties. The last major action of the Civil War took place in Durham, where Confederate general Joseph E. Johnston surrendered to General William T. Sherman on April 26, 1865.

After the Civil War, North Carolina's major industries, based on tobacco and natural resources, developed in the Piedmont. The region contains the state's main cities: Charlotte, the largest in the state; the capital city of Raleigh; and the other two points of the "Research Triangle," Chapel Hill and Durham. The region has also developed as the center of the state's numerous universities and private colleges. Bounded on the north by Virginia and on the south by South Carolina, the North Carolina Piedmont stretches from the Blue Ridge foothills in the west to the fall line where the coastal plain begins in the east. This area of rolling hills is the state's most fertile farmland and the most heavily populated. This tour begins at the Piedmont's eastern edge.

FAYETTEVILLE

Located at the head of navigation on the Cape Fear River, Fayetteville is best known as the home of Fort Bragg, one of the nation's largest military bases. Parts of the city preserve some interesting architecture, mostly from the nineteenth and twentieth centuries, although the **Cool Spring Tavern** (119 Cool Spring Street, 919–323–4111) dates to 1789. The town's three main historic districts are **Market House Square,** an area of ten commercial buildings surrounding the Market House; **Heritage Square,** a small nineteenth-century neighborhood; and **Liberty Row,** a cohesive nineteenth-century row of commercial structures.

Fayetteville's strategic location as North Carolina's farthest inland port made it a site of some interest during the Revolution. After the Battle of Guilford Courthouse, Lord Cornwallis retreated to the port, expecting to be met with supplies. Bands of Patriots, however, had forced the British supply boats to return down the Cape Fear River to Wilmington, where Cornwallis had to go to resupply his troops in April 1781. The city saw some military action in the Civil War, when it was occupied by Confederates in 1861. The **U.S. Arsenal** (Arsenal and Bradford avenues), equipped with machinery from the Federal arsenal at Harpers Ferry, West Virginia, produced Fayetteville rifles, prized by Confederate soldiers for their accuracy. Sherman's men destroyed the arsenal in March 1865, though they spared the **Arsenal House** (822 Arsenal Avenue), directly across the street.

Fayetteville has four historic churches, all open by appointment. **Saint John's Episcopal Church** (302 Green Street), organized in 1817 for the city's first Episcopal congregation, was rebuilt using its original walls after the Great Fire of 1831. The Gothic Revival structure features two lancet entrances and corner towers, each with a lancet opening, trefoil, and five surmounting pinnacles. Eight of the stained-glass windows were made by the Mayer Company of Munich, Germany, and installed between 1898 and 1900. **Saint Joseph's Episcopal Church** (Ramsey and Moore streets), chartered in 1873, is of Queen Anne style. Its stained-glass Resurrection Windows by Tiffany and Company are unique in the city and among the last installed by the company. The **Evans Metropolitan AME Zion Church** (301 North Cool Spring Street) was founded by a free black preacher, Henry Evans, in 1795. The present church was constructed in 1893, and Evans is buried in the basement. The brick **First Presbyterian Church** (corner of Bow and Ann streets), organized in 1800, constructed in 1816, and rebuilt in 1832 after the Great Fire, features two front entrances with fanlights, notable wooden roof trusses designed by Ithiel Town and built by Alexander Jackson Davis, a full-height Tuscan portico, and a four-part steeple designed by Hobart Upjohn in the Christopher Wren style, added in 1922.

The impressive two-story Flemish bond **Market House** (intersection of Hay, Green, Person, and Gillespie streets, 919–483–2073) was built on Market Square in 1838. Atop its hipped roof is a square clock tower surmounted by an octagonal cupola. Originally the lower floor served as the town marketplace and the upper floor as the town hall. Currently it holds a museum of local artifacts and the offices of the Old Fayetteville Association. The North Carolina state house stood on this site until it was destroyed in the Great Fire of 1831. The U.S. Constitution was ratified by North Carolina there on November 21, 1789, and Lafayette spoke from its balcony in 1825. The Greek Revival **Kyle House** (234 Green Street, 919–433–1994) was built in 1838 for a successful Scottish merchant, James Kyle. The exterior walls of handmade brick are eighteen inches thick and filled with sand for insulation and fire prevention. Interior details include elaborate plaster cornices, ceiling medallions, and a "builder's button," a mother-of-pearl inlay in the newel post, signifying that the owner paid for the house before moving in. The building now houses the mayor's and city manager's offices.

    Heritage Square (225 Dick Street, 919–483–6009) is a group of three buildings belonging to the Fayetteville Women's Club. The

OPPOSITE *and* ABOVE: *The ca. 1850 Harper house near Newton Grove served as a field hospital during the Civil War. Bullet holes can be found in the surrounding trees.*

Sanford House was constructed around 1800 by Duncan McLeran. From 1820 until 1836, the two-story townhouse was used as the central office of the Bank of the United States in North Carolina. The artist Elliott Daingerfield lived here as a teenager after the Civil War. The elegant Adamesque Oval Ballroom was formerly a part of the Halliday-Williams House, probably designed by William Nichols. The clapboard **Nimocks House,** built around 1804, features good interior Federal details and an unusual partially enclosed rear staircase. **Liberty Row,** part of the city's oldest commercial district, includes brick structures of two or three stories with such architectural features as parapeted gabled roofs and pressed-tin or cast-iron storefronts. **Liberty Point Store** (Bow and Person streets), the oldest block structure in town, was built around 1846 on the site where the anti-British Liberty Point Resolves were signed by fifty-four men on June 20, 1775. The present buildings were rebuilt after the 1831 fire.

At **Averasboro,** southeast of Erwin, Confederate generals William J. Hardee and W. B. Taliaferro, under General Joseph E. Johnston, led about 6,000 men in an unsuccessful attack against the Union troops of General H. W. Slocum, under General William T. Sherman, on March 15 and 16, 1865. The Confederates only temporarily slowed the advance of Union troops toward Goldsboro. The battle site is privately owned and no visible sign of the battle remains. Highway **markers** on Route 82 describe Averasboro battle strategy, and monuments in Averasboro's **Chicora Cemetery** also offer descriptions of the battle.

BENTONVILLE BATTLEGROUND STATE HISTORIC SITE

After the burning of Columbia, South Carolina, on February 17, 1865, General William T. Sherman's men headed toward Goldsboro, North Carolina, where they would get fresh supplies and rest after nearly two months of hard campaigning. But the Confederate troops of General Joseph E. Johnston sought to isolate and conquer the wings of Sherman's army before they reached their destination. At Averasborough (about thirty miles south of Raleigh) on March 15 and 16, two of Johnston's divisions met four of Sherman's but were unsuccessful in stopping the march to Goldsboro. Then, on March

19, Johnston tried again, with 17,000 infantrymen, near Bentonville. Though the attack by Johnston's troops first achieved limited success on the nineteenth, the Yankees repulsed attacks in the afternoon and evening and held their own on the twentieth. An eyewitness to the Union advance on Confederate lines recorded, ". . . nearer and nearer they came. . . . When not over forty or fifty paces from us, the order so anxiously awaited was given, and a sheet of fire blazed out from the hidden battle line . . . that was demoralizing and fatal to the enemy. They battled, reeled, and staggered, while we poured volley after volley into them, and great gaps were made in their line, as brave Federals fell everywhere."

Sherman's reinforcements arrived by March 21, when he interrupted the Union attacks on the Confederate left and allowed Johnston's troops, who were significantly outnumbered after the battle, to withdraw toward Smithfield during the night. It was the largest battle fought in North Carolina and the last important effort made to defeat Sherman as he marched north from Savannah to join forces with Grant in Virginia. Over 4,000 men were reported wounded, killed, or missing. The Civil War ended in the Carolinas after this battle when General Johnston surrendered to General Sherman on April 26, 1865, at Bennett Place near Durham.

The home of Amy and John Harper was used as a field hospital, primarily for Union soldiers, though some Confederates were also treated there. A colonel from the Ninth Ohio Cavalry recorded his memory of the bloody battle and its aftermath: "A dozen surgeons and attendants in their shirtsleeves stood at rude benches cutting off arms and legs and throwing them out of the windows, where they lay scattered on the grass. The legs of infantrymen would be distinguished from those of the cavalry by the size of their calves, as the march of 1,000 miles had increased the size of one and diminished the size of the other." The frame two-story **Harper House,** built around 1850, remains at the site and is open as a museum, furnished as a field hospital. Outdoor exhibits, monuments, original earthworks, Union trenches, a Confederate cemetery, and a visitor center are also here.

LOCATION: Route 1008, north of Newton Grove. HOURS: April through October: 9–5 Monday–Saturday, 1–5 Sunday; November through March: 10–4 Tuesday–Saturday, 1–4 Sunday. FEE: None. TELEPHONE: 919–594–0789.

Charles B. Aycock, governor of North Carolina from 1901 to 1905, is remembered as the state's "education governor," who built a schoolhouse for every day that he was governor, including Sundays. The **Charles B. Aycock Birthplace State Historic Site** (off Route 117, between Fremont and Pikeville, 919–242–5581) is part of the property once owned by the Aycock family. On its sixteen acres are eight restored and relocated nineteenth-century buildings: a farmhouse, outbuildings, and a one-room school, moved here from the Quaker community of Nahunta. Recently discovered lumber sales records indicate that Aycock's relatives built the original school for about $400 in 1893.

During the nearby Civil War Battle of Bentonville, the Greek Revival **Hastings House** (200 Front Street, Smithfield, 919–934–9721), built by William Hastings in the 1850s, was used as the Confederate headquarters of Generals Joseph E. Johnston, Wade Hampton, and Braxton Bragg. General Sherman, commanding the Union forces, used the **Johnston County Courthouse** (Market Street, 919–934–5969) as his headquarters after the Battle of Bentonville; while there, he learned of General Robert E. Lee's surrender.

The **Country Doctor Museum** (Vance Street, Bailey, 914–235–4165), which focuses on family doctors and medicine before 1925, is housed in two nineteenth-century doctor's offices. The clinic of Dr. Howard Franklin Freeman, built ca. 1857, forms the museum's library and apothecary shop, and Dr. Cornelius Henry Brantley's office, built ca. 1887, is furnished as a doctor's office and examining room with instruments and equipment of the day. The museum contains, among other things, the instruments used by Matthew Moore Butler in the amputation of Stonewall Jackson's arm.

HALIFAX

A visitor to this port in the 1770s described it as "a pretty town on the south side of the Roanoke," where "sloops, schooners, and flats, or lighters, of great burden, come . . . against the stream, which is deep and gentle." He stated further that "there are many handsome buildings in Halifax and vicinity, but they are almost all constructed of timber and painted white."

Founded in 1760, Halifax was the scene of important pre-Revolutionary political events. The Fourth Provincial Congress met here and, on April 12, 1776, adopted the "Halifax Resolves," calling

The 1838 jail and 1833 clerk's office in Historic Halifax were both built to be fire-proof, the jail after two previous structures were burned by escaping prisoners, and the clerk's office to safeguard records after the complete destruction by fire of the North Carolina Statehouse in Raleigh in 1831.

for independence from England. When the Fifth Provincial Congress met in the fall of 1776, North Carolina's first constitution was drafted and approved, and Richard Caswell was appointed the first governor. During the Revolution Halifax was important as a recruitment center, military depot, and public weapons factory. In May 1781, before marching into Virginia, General Cornwallis occupied a house here called "The Grove," of which only a large brick chimney remains today.

Historic Halifax

Covering several blocks near the head of the Roanoke River, this site preserves an eighteenth-century trading district of frame-and-brick buildings with eighteenth- and nineteenth-century stylistic elements. Among the original structures is the late-eighteenth-century **Eagle Tavern** (Saint Davids and King streets), likely to have been the building where the first North Carolina constitution was written in 1776. Its exterior has been restored. The **Constitution-Burgess House** (end of Market Street), owned by Thomas Burgess in the early nineteenth century, is now furnished as his townhouse and law office. The **Owens House** (Saint David's Street), a restored townhouse with a gambrel roof, was built around 1760 for the merchant George Owens. The **Sally-Billy Plantation House** (Saint Andrews Street), built around 1808, is typical of Federal-style architecture in the area. The brick **clerk's office,** completed in 1833, was constructed to be a fireproof court record depository. The brick **jail,** built in 1838 and restored on the exterior only, was also fireproof because the two previous jails on the site had been burned by escaping prisoners.

> LOCATION: Saint David's and Dobbs streets. HOURS: April through October: 9–5 Monday–Saturday, 1–5 Sunday; November through March: 10–4 Tuesday–Saturday, 1–4 Sunday. FEE: None. TELEPHONE: 919–583–7191.

DURHAM

In the 1850s a settlement called Prattsburg, for its main landholder, William Pratt, fought the advance of the North Carolina Railroad. When Pratt would not allow a right-of-way on his property, the railway detoured around it. Dr. Bartlett Durham, who granted the needed right-of-way about two miles west of Prattsburg, gave his name to the new station. Durham was incorporated in 1867 and named the seat of Durham County. The **Downtown Historic District,** along the Bull Durham traffic loop, features many early-twentieth-century commercial buildings, among them the **Central Carolina Bank Building** (Shreve, Lamb, and Harmon, architects for the Empire State Building in New York, contributed to the design), as well as the **Bull Durham Tobacco Factory** (201 West Pettigrew Street), built in 1875.

Duke Homestead State Historic Site

America's tobacco industry owes much to Washington Duke and his sons, who were born in this clapboard two-story farmhouse and who worked in the post–Civil War tobacco factory they established here. The Duke homestead complex, covering forty-three acres, preserves the main house, built in 1852, with a kitchen addition, the Dukes' third factory, built about 1870, a reconstruction of the first factory, outbuildings, a tobacco packing house, and a curing barn. The

OPPOSITE: *Washington Duke's third tobacco factory, where Bright Leaf tobacco was rubbed through a sieve, producing smoking tobacco. Duke's first factory, a former corn crib, is visible through the window.*

Dukes' American Tobacco Company had modest beginnings. To support his family after the Civil War, Washington Duke, who had once farmed cotton, used crude hand presses to process smoked tobacco. The family factory that the Dukes began in 1865 was soon successful enough to expand. In 1869 Washington Duke's son, Brodie, had set up a small factory, and in 1874 the elder Duke moved his business from the farm to Durham, hoping to share his son's success. By 1881 they were manufacturing a new product that gained popularity quickly—cigarettes. The company began the first mechanical mass production of cigarettes in 1884. Perhaps the best-known company to grow out of the original American Tobacco Company is R. J. Reynolds. The Dukes became wealthy contributors to charity and the endowment of colleges, in particular Trinity College, which became Duke University.

Adjacent to the farm is a modern visitor center housing a tobacco museum, with exhibits tracing the history of tobacco from its use by Native Americans to the present.

LOCATION: Duke Homestead Road, off Route I-85. HOURS: April through October: 9–5 Monday–Saturday, 1–5 Sunday; November through March: 10–4 Tuesday–Saturday, 1–4 Sunday. FEE: None. TELEPHONE: 919–477–5498.

Duke University was created in 1924 when James Buchanan Duke endowed Trinity College, a liberal arts college founded in 1838, as a memorial to his father, Washington Duke. Some of the original Georgian Revival Trinity College buildings survive on the East Campus (West Main Street). The **Duke Museum of Art** (919–684–5135), with collections of classical and medieval art and European and American paintings and sculpture, is also on this campus. The newer West Campus (Campus Drive), built to the designs of Horace Trumbauer, has notable Gothic Revival buildings, especially the **Duke University Chapel,** with its seventy-seven stained-glass windows, Flentrop organ, and 210-foot bell tower derived from that of England's Canterbury Cathedral.

The two-story clapboard **Saint John's Episcopal Church** (Route 1329, off Route 29) was built in 1772 with a gabled roof, side modillion cornices, and a central double door. The interior, with box pews and gallery, has undergone little alteration. Restored in

1956, the structure has some of the oldest and finest colonial church woodwork in the state.

RALEIGH

The centrally located capital city of North Carolina was first the seat of Wake County, and it continues to serve as the center of government for both the county and the state. The state capital was moved here from New Bern in 1788. Laid out in 1792, Raleigh was surveyed by William Christmas, who planned the central location of the capitol building and named the streets for the most prominent cities and people in the state. The first state house, completed in 1794, burned in 1831, and its replacement, the present capitol, was completed in 1840. Despite strong Union sentiment in the capital, on May 20, 1861, the state convention voted to secede. Raleigh became a headquarters for Confederate troops and supplies until the Union army led by General Sherman arrived on April 13, 1865, after the Battle of Bentonville, and occupied the city without resistance. North Carolina constitutional conventions were held in the capitol in 1865, 1868, and 1875.

North Carolina State Capitol

In the center of Capitol Square (also called Union Square) is the Greek Revival capitol building. Designed by William Nichols with further work by Ithiel Town, Alexander Jackson Davis, and David Paton, the capitol was begun in 1833 to replace an earlier building that burned in 1831. It was occupied by General Sherman's troops in 1865, and on May 31, 1893, Jefferson Davis lay in state in the rotunda. The exterior walls of the capitol are of gneiss quarried southeast of Raleigh and transported by the horse-drawn Experimental Railroad, the first railway in the state. The building is in the shape of a Greek cross, with a copper-domed rotunda at the point where the wings intersect. In the center of the rotunda is a reconstruction of Antonio Canova's marble statue of George Washington in a Roman tunic and armor, which was destroyed in the 1831 fire. Also in the rotunda are busts of Governors Samuel Johnston, John M. Morehead, and William A. Graham and Senator Matt Ransom, all completed between 1909 and 1912 by F. Wellington Ruckstuhl. The first floor houses the offices of the governor and lieutenant governor. On the second floor are additional offices and the chambers of the state senate and house of representatives. The mahogany desks and chairs in both chambers were handmade by Raleigh cabinetmaker William Thompson. Two rooms on the third floor, the State Library Room and the State Geologist's Office and Cabinet of Minerals, have been restored to their 1850s appearance. Both rooms were finished in the Gothic style, and both have domed, top-lit vestibules.

The thirteen monuments and statues on the capitol lawn honor important people and events in the history of the state. On July 4, 1857, the placement of the statuary began on the south lawn with a bronze statue of George Washington, one of six cast by William J. Hubard from a mold of a statue by Jean Houdon in the rotunda of the Virginia capitol. On the west lawn is a seventy-foot monument to Confederate soldiers of North Carolina by the Muldoon Monument Company. The bronze *Three Presidents Statue*, by Charles Keck, honors Presidents Andrew Jackson, James K. Polk, and Andrew Johnson, all of whom, though Tennessee residents when elected, were born in North Carolina. Johnson was born about 150 yards south of this statue, in a house now moved to Mordecai Historical Park.

LOCATION: Capitol Square, Wilmington Street. HOURS: 8–5 Monday–Friday, 9–5 Saturday, 1–5 Sunday. FEE: None. TELEPHONE: 919–733–4994.

On each corner of Capitol Square stands a historic church. The Gothic Revival **Christ Episcopal Church** (120 East Edenton Street) was built between 1848 and 1854 to designs by Richard Upjohn. The single-story granite structure is in the shape of a Latin cross with a freestanding tower, cross-gabled roof with outstanding hammer beams, corner buttresses, and lancet windows. The architect's grandson, Hobart Upjohn, designed the church's chapel and parish house in 1921. The **First Baptist Church** (Salisbury and Edenton streets), completed in 1859, is the Greek Revival design of William Percival. In 1868 the black members of this church formed their own congregation, and in 1904 they built the Gothic Revival **Wilmington Street Church** (Wilmington and Morgan streets), also known as the First Baptist Church. The **First Presbyterian Church,** designed by George Waring, is a Romanesque Revival structure built in 1900.

OPPOSITE: *In Raleigh, the North Carolina Executive Mansion, designed by Samuel Sloan, shows the influence of Charles Eastlake in its elaborately carved wooden trim.*

Constructed between 1883 and 1891, the forty-room **North Carolina Executive Mansion** (200 North Blount Street, 919–733–3456) was one of the last buildings designed by Samuel Sloan. Many of the red bricks, handmade of native clay by state prisoners, display the names of those who made them. First occupied by Daniel G. Fowle in 1891, the three-story residence has a patterned high-hipped roof with many steep, intersecting gables; a small rectangular cupola; and verandahs and balconies with ornate brackets and trim. The interior features woodwork of North Carolina heart of pine, crystal chandeliers, eighteenth- and nineteenth-century furnishings, and hand-loomed rugs. The **Capitol Area Visitor Center** (301 North Blount, 919–733–3456) is housed in the 1916 Andrews-London House, once the home of a Raleigh mayor.

The **Oakwood Inn** (411 North Bloodworth Street) is located in the Raynor-Stronach House, built in 1871 by Thomas H. Briggs. **Oakwood Cemetery** (Oakwood Avenue and Watauga Street), established in 1866 as a Confederate burial place, holds many examples of ornate statuary. At the western end of West Hargett Street stands **Wakefield** (728 West Hargett Street), or the Joel Lane House. The oldest dwelling in Raleigh, it was built before 1771 and named for Margaret Wake, the wife of Royal Governor William Tryon. Colleges in Raleigh include **Saint Mary's College** (900 Hillsborough Street, 919–828–2521), a women's Episcopal school opened in 1842. The Gothic Revival chapel is a board-and-batten structure built in 1856, another design by Richard Upjohn. **Saint Augustine's College** (1315 Oakwood Avenue, 919–828–4451), also Episcopal, was founded in 1867 in connection with the Freedmen's Bureau. **Peace College** (Peace and North Wilmington streets) is a Presbyterian women's college. The Greek Revival main building, built in 1857, was used during the Civil War as a Confederate hospital and after the war as headquarters for the Freedmen's Bureau. **Shaw University** (East South Street) was established as a freedmen's school in 1865 by Henry M. Tupper. The campus includes the Victorian Estey Hall, built in 1873, one of the first college structures for black women in America. **North Carolina State University** (2000 Hillsborough Street, 919–737–2850) was established as a land-grant college in 1887. Holladay Hall, completed in 1889 and built with brick made by inmates at the state prison in Raleigh, was the university's first building and housed the entire college—dormitories, classrooms, offices, dining room, and gym. The 115-foot Memorial Tower, completed in 1937, honors the thirty-three North Carolina State students killed in World War I; it is made of granite from Mount Airy.

The **North Carolina Museum of History** (109 East Jones Street, in the east wing of the Archives and History Building, 919–733–3894) has a permanent collection of more than 200,000 items, chiefly artifacts of everyday life in the state from prehistoric times to the present. The collection includes gold minted in North Carolina, Confederate uniforms and battle flags, Civil War handguns, tobacco items, inaugural gowns of governors' wives, and a significant collection of folk art and crafts. The museum plans to move to a larger building in 1992.

Mordecai Historic Park

In this small historic village are eight structures, three of them arranged to duplicate an early Raleigh street. Beside the Badger-Iredell Law Office, built around 1810, is a Neoclassical nineteenth-century office building, moved here in 1972, that probably was once used as the post office. Adjacent to these is Saint Mark's Chapel, dating from 1847 and moved here from Chatham County in 1979. The centerpiece of the village is the 1785 Mordecai House, the plantation home of Henry Lane, whose father, Joel Lane, sold the land on which Raleigh was founded in 1792. In the library is a locally made Chippendale secretary that may be where Joel Lane signed the deeds for the land. Other furnishings original to the family include a ca.-1815 American Sheraton clock and an early-nineteenth-century bedroom suite.

The house was named for its second owners: When Henry Lane's daughter Margaret married attorney Moses Mordecai, they occupied the one-and-a-half stories that make up the back (north) part of the present house. Five generations of the Mordecai family subsequently occupied the house, which was remodeled in 1826 by William Nichols, one of the architects who designed the state capitol. Its combination of eighteenth- and nineteenth-century architecture and its collection of books, portraits, and furnishings reflect the changing styles and tastes of the family members.

Three small structures surround the house, including an 1842 kitchen from Anson County, relocated and restored on the approximate site of the Mordecai kitchen. Also on the grounds is the tiny gambrel-roofed frame house, built ca. 1795, in which President Andrew Johnson was born in 1808. His parents lived in the small combination kitchen-dwelling in the yard of Casso's Inn, once located on the corner of Fayetteville and Morgan streets. The house, furnished with period pieces, was moved to Mordecai Park in 1975.

LOCATION: 1 Mimosa Street. HOURS: 10–2 Tuesday–Friday, 1–4 Saturday–Sunday. FEE: None. TELEPHONE: 919–834–4844.

The **North Carolina Museum of Art** (2110 Blue Ridge Boulevard, 919–833–1935), the first art museum to be sponsored by a state, features international, national, and regional exhibits of art from ancient Egypt to the present but is strongest in European paintings from the thirteenth to the nineteenth century and in American art.

CHAPEL HILL

Chapel Hill is the site of the first state university in America, the University of North Carolina, where the cornerstone for the first campus building, Old East, was laid on October 12, 1793. The central campus adjoins the eighteenth- and nineteenth-century homes along East Franklin and Rosemary streets, an excellent example of a well-planned university campus that is an attractive part of the surrounding community. The oldest private residence near the university is the **Hooper House** (504 East Franklin Street), built ca. 1814 by William Hooper, whose grandfather and namesake was a North Carolinian signer of the Declaration of Independence.

University of North Carolina

With a faculty of two, the school opened its doors on January 15, 1795, though the first student, Hinton James, did not arrive from his home in Wilmington until nearly four weeks later. He was the only student for about two weeks until others arrived to bring the university's first-term enrollment up to forty-one. The campus landmarks include the first state university building in the country, **Old East,** completed in 1794. Additions were made to Old East by the architects William Nichols and Alexander Jackson Davis. The ivy-covered **Davie Poplar,** named for William Davie, still grows where the first planners of the school may have met when choosing the building site. The **Old Well** (Cameron Avenue), a small temple-form structure that originally served as the students' central water source, now serves as the symbol of the university. The **Playmakers Theatre** (Cameron Avenue), a Greek Revival temple built in 1850, was the design of Alexander Jackson Davis. Also notable is the Gothic Revival **Chapel of the Cross** (304 East Franklin Street).

LOCATION: Off Route 85 or 40. TELEPHONE: 919–962–0045.

HILLSBOROUGH

This was the most important Piedmont town in western North Carolina until after the American Revolution, serving as a significant center of political activity and trade. Hillsborough preserves a number of late-eighteenth- and nineteenth-century buildings, most of them examples of Federal and Greek Revival architecture, though some have Victorian elements. Notable buildings include the brick **Orange County Courthouse** (106 East King Street), designed by John Berry and built in 1845. The early-nineteenth-century **Burwell School** (319 North Churton Street, 919–723–8648) is open by appointment with the Hillsborough Historical Society. The **Town Hall** (Churton and Orange streets), built in 1820, was the home of Thomas Ruffin, a former North Carolina chief justice, and it now holds the offices of the Hillsborough Historical Society.

Laid out in 1754 by William Churton, the earl of Granville's surveyor, Hillsborough was located near the Eno River and the important Occoneechee Indian Trading Path. **Markers** point out the site of **Edmund Fanning's home** (Churton Street, Route 70A), which the Regulators destroyed. East of town, a **sign** marks the spot where Royal Governor William Tryon hanged six Regulators after their defeat at Alamance Creek in 1771. During the Revolution Hillsborough served as headquarters for the Continental army under Baron Johann de Kalb and General Horatio Gates in 1780. Lord Cornwallis occupied the town for six days in February 1781 after General Morgan's triumph at Cowpens, South Carolina. Thomas Burke, a Hillsborough native, became governor in June of that year. Despite Burke's efforts to suppress Tory raiders around Hillsborough, the town was taken over on September 11 and 12 by Tories led by David Fanning, and Burke was taken prisoner.

ALAMANCE BATTLEGROUND
STATE HISTORIC SITE

In September 1770 North Carolina Regulators, armed backcountry farmers, rose up against the provincial government and Royal Governor William Tryon. The rebels congregated in Hillsborough and interrupted Judge Richard Henderson's court, then burned his home and attacked other local officials. (Among the latter, ironically, was William Hooper, who later signed the Declaration of Independence.) Tryon led the Tidewater militia against the up-country rebels by marching from New Bern to Hillsborough. Hugh Waddell led a smaller militia troop, which attempted to join Tryon but was prevented by Regulators from advancing to Hillsborough. Tryon took his 1,100 men to support Waddell in Salisbury, where he was met by 2,000 Regulators at Alamance Creek. Hermon Husband, the Regulators' original leader, had become a Quaker and objected to violence, but they dismissed his advice to avoid fighting the colonial governor. Another rebel leader, James Hunter, declined to command them, reportedly declaring, "We are all freemen, and everyone must command himself."

Though Tryon was outnumbered nearly two to one, his militia was well trained and well equipped, unlike the Regulators, many of whom were poorly armed and unskilled in battle. Though accounts vary as to the number of dead and wounded in the confrontation at Alamance Creek on May 16, 1771, no one disputes Tryon's victory. After executing one man on the spot (six others were hanged later), Tryon took the main agitators as his prisoners and issued pardons to all Regulators who would take an oath of allegiance. Many did, though many others moved westward to the mountains or the wilds of Tennessee and Kentucky, out of the British government's reach.

The forty-acre battlefield park includes a number of commemorative markers and monuments, a visitor center, and the relocated eighteenth-century dwelling of John Allen, whose sister married Hermon Husband.

LOCATION: Off Route 62, roughly 6 miles southwest of Burlington.
HOURS: April through October: 9–5 Monday–Saturday, 1–5 Sunday; November through March: 10–4 Tuesday–Saturday, 1–4 Sunday.
FEE: None. TELEPHONE: 919–227–4785.

On the grounds of eight-acre **Tannenbaum Park** is the **Hoskins-Wyrick House** (New Garden Road, at the gateway to Guilford Courthouse National Military Park, 919–288–8259), once the home of Joseph and Hannah Hoskins. The restored two-story cabin, built ca. 1778 of chestnut, poplar, and oak logs, was used as Cornwallis's British headquarters before the Battle of Guilford Courthouse and afterward as a hospital for British and American wounded. Some believe the property to hold the undiscovered mass grave of sixty British soldiers.

CHINQUA-PENN PLANTATION

Built between 1923 and 1925 by Thomas Jefferson Penn, whose father's business became the American Tobacco Company, and his wife Betsy Schoellkopf, whose family developed Niagara Falls as a power source, the twenty-seven-room stone-and-log residence resembles an English country home. The estate's name combines the Penn family name with *chinquapin,* a type of dwarf chestnut tree once abundant on the property. The thirty-acre estate includes five greenhouses, a formal garden, a rose garden, and an ornate Chinese pagoda. The Penns were avid art collectors; the house holds an amazing variety of treasures acquired from at least thirty countries, including a Shang libation bowl from 1100 B.C., rare Chinese sand paintings from the fifteenth century, and a sixteenth-century Spanish powderhorn of etched bone.

LOCATION: Off Route 29, 3 miles northwest of Reidsville. HOURS: March through mid-December: 10–4 Wednesday–Saturday; 1:30–4:30 Sunday. FEE: Yes. TELEPHONE: 919–349–4576.

Guilford Courthouse National Military Park

The 220-acre park preserves the site of the battle between Nathanael Greene's Continental army of about 4,400 men and Lord Cornwallis's veteran force of about 2,000 on March 15, 1781. After Daniel Morgan's victory over Tarleton at Cowpens in January, Cornwallis became determined to destroy the American army. For

OVERLEAF: *Near the American Third Line Monument at Guilford Courthouse National Military Park are cannon representing those lost by Nathanael Greene to Cornwallis during the battle on March 15, 1781.*

his part, Greene was reluctant to pit his ragged army against the British. He realized that his prime strategic goal should be to keep his army intact—its mere existence in the Carolinas would keep that territory out of British control. Thus, for several weeks in the winter of 1781, Greene fought what he called a "fugitive war," running from Cornwallis while waiting for the best opportunity to fight.

In early February Greene's troops, their bare feet leaving bloody tracks in the snow, fled across the Dan River into Virginia. Cornwallis set up headquarters in Hillsborough and issued a call to Carolina loyalists to join him. Few did, but false rumors reached Greene that the countryside was shifting its allegiance to the king. Alarmed, Greene recrossed the Dan, this time with additional troops dispatched from Virginia, and headed for a spot near Guilford Courthouse, which he had earlier chosen as favorable ground for a battle. Here the terrain rose from a valley, across a clearing, and into woods—troops holding the high wooded ground could fire down on attackers. Greene adopted the tactics Morgan had used successfully at Cowpens, arranging his troops in three lines: 1,000 North Carolina militia formed the first line, with cavalry units on their flanks led by William Washington and the famed Light-Horse Harry Lee (father of Robert E. Lee). About 300 yards behind them was a second line of infantry composed of Virginia militia. A third line, 500 yards farther back, was made up of crack Maryland, Virginia, and Delaware units, as well as some inexperienced troops.

When Cornwallis began his attack, the North Carolina militia fired two volleys, inflicting heavy casualties—a British officer wrote that "one half of the Highlanders dropped on that spot." Royal Welch Fusiliers bravely charged the line although they could see the Americans just forty yards away "taking aim with the nicest precision." The Carolinians had been told to withdraw in an orderly fashion after firing, but they panicked and ran. Lee's legion, isolated, held its own against repeated attacks but was not the important factor it could have been. The British broke through into the woods and pushed the second American line back, despite the fact that the British ranks were thrown into some confusion in the dense growth. The worst of the battle took place when the British reached the third line. "I never saw such fighting since God made me," Cornwallis wrote later. "The Americans fought like demons." Here the Continentals poured down a devastating fire, followed by a bayonet charge. Some British fell back, others surged forward, and the fighting was hand-to-hand—a situation that favored the Americans. At this moment, over the objections of his officers, Cornwallis ordered his gunners to fire grapeshot into the mob to drive the armies apart. Both British and American soldiers were killed, but the blasts did force both sides to fall back. The highly disciplined British quickly reformed their ranks and charged. Greene saw that his advantage had been lost and called for a retreat.

Although Greene had lost the field, the British victory cost Cornwallis one fourth of his troops. So many British soldiers were dead or wounded that Cornwallis was unable to pursue the retreating enemy to Greene's base at Troublesome Iron Works (about seven miles southwest of Reidsville). Cornwallis, after camping on the battlefield, led his crippled force toward Wilmington. In May, thoroughly sick of Greene and the Carolina backcountry, Cornwallis left for Virginia, where he was forced to surrender at Yorktown in October. The heavy British casualties suffered at Guilford Courthouse may have been a factor in Cornwallis's final defeat.

In 1917 the park became the first Revolutionary battle site to be part of the national park system, due to the efforts of Greensboro's Judge David Schenck, who formed the Guilford Battle Ground Company in 1886, sold stock, and bought the land to preserve and develop the battlefield. Though the exact location of the original Guilford Courthouse is undetermined, the park holds twenty-eight memorial markers and the graves of several Revolutionary War heroes, including two North Carolinians who signed the Declaration of Independence, William Hooper and John Penn.

LOCATION: New Garden Road, off Route 220, 6 miles northwest of downtown Greensboro. HOURS: 8:30–5 Daily. FEE: None. TELEPHONE: 919–288–1776.

GREENSBORO

Greensboro was named to honor General Nathanael Greene, a Patriot leader in the Revolutionary War. The short-story writer William Sydney Porter (O. Henry) was born here in 1862. During the Civil War, Greensboro was a Confederate supply headquarters and railway center. After Lee's surrender at Appomattox, Jefferson Davis came here on April 11, 1865, to meet General Joseph E.

Johnston to discuss the latter's surrender to General Sherman. The city preserves a late-nineteenth-century commercial district along Elm Street.

Greensboro Historical Museum

This museum comprises the First Presbyterian Church, built in 1892, and the Smith Memorial Building, completed in 1903. A reconstruction of Greensborough Village shows the town as it appeared in the 1880s, with a doctor's office, general store, drugstore, and one-room schoolhouse. The museum also has exhibits on two prominent Greensboro natives, First Lady Dolley Madison and short-story writer William Sydney Porter (O. Henry); collections of decorative arts and American historical glassware; and a display of North Carolina–made Civil War weapons, including the Tarpley carbine rifle, which was manufactured in Greensboro under a Confederate patent.

LOCATION: 130 Summit Avenue. HOURS: 10–5 Tuesday–Saturday, 2–5 Sunday. FEE: None. TELEPHONE: 919-373-2043.

Blandwood

Originally constructed as a two-story, four-room farmhouse around 1790 and expanded around 1820, Blandwood was the home of Governor John Motley Morehead, whose achievements as governor included the development of the North Carolina Railroad. The house was redesigned as an Italian villa by Alexander Jackson Davis in 1844, one of his early essays in the Italianate Villa style. The stuccoed building features a three-story entrance tower flanked with arcades leading to dependencies on either side. An arched entrance leads to a grand entrance hall and large twin parlors with elaborate friezework and moldings. Sliding pocket doors in front of each parlor's bay window and mirrors on the backs of the parlor doors allow for the control of sunlight and heat. A low-pitched tin hip roof covers the original farmhouse and the later addition. Blandwood remained in the Morehead family until 1907.; it is now a museum.

LOCATION: 447 West Washington Street. HOURS: 11–2 Monday–Friday, 2–5 Sunday, and by appointment. FEE: Yes. TELEPHONE: 919-272-5003.

HIGH POINT

Incorporated in 1859 and named because it was the "high point" on the rail line between Charlotte and Goldsboro, the city became a central trading place along the main highway in the state, the plank road between Fayetteville and Salem. Long a textile and furniture trade center, High Point is the state's leading furniture manufacturer and marketplace. The **High Point Museum and Industrial Park** (1805 East Lexington Avenue, 919–885–6859) features the 1786 home of John Haley, a brick structure built on the Quaker plan and reputedly the oldest dwelling in the city; a weaving house and blacksmith shop, both representative of the 1700s; and a museum of local history, with exhibits of furniture and textile industry items, early telephone equipment, Native American artifacts, and military items from the Revolutionary War to the present.

WINSTON–SALEM

The original town of Salem, now called Old Salem, is a remarkable historical survivor. Founded in 1766 by Moravians, a Protestant sect of German-speaking tradespeople from Pennsylvania, Old Salem is an outstanding example of a well-preserved eighteenth-century community. Closed at first to non-Moravians, Salem gradually began to accept outsiders under the watchful eye of the church. Despite the growth and success of their city, the Moravians did not want to become the center of local government, so the town of Winston began as the county seat in 1849. Originally a mile apart, Winston and Salem soon grew together, and Old Salem is now in the heart of the city, less than a mile from downtown.

Winston-Salem is an industrial center for the R. J. Reynolds Tobacco Company and textile mills. The 1927 **R. J. Reynolds Office Building** (401 North Main Street), one of the state's finest examples of the Art Deco style, was designed by New York City's Shreve and Lamb, the architects of the Empire State Building. The **Brookstown Inn** (200 Brookstown Avenue) was originally a mill, built in 1837 for the Salem Cotton Manufacturing Company. It was remodeled and renamed Arista Mills in 1880.

Historic Bethabara Park

Bethabara, meaning "House of Passage," is the site of a temporary settlement, the first Moravian community in North Carolina. It was

The Bethabara Gemeinhaus, built in 1788, included living quarters for the minister and his family. In the churchyard is a recontructed stockade where the Moravian settlers took refuge during the French and Indian War.

founded on November 17, 1753, by fifteen Moravian men who left Bethlehem, Pennsylvania, to settle the 100,000-acre tract called *Der Wachau* (Wachovia) that had been acquired from Lord John Carteret, earl of Granville. Bethabara served as a base community from 1766 to 1772 while the permanent settlement was being built at Salem. Bethabara Park maintains the 1788 Gemeinhaus, the oldest Moravian church in the southern United States; the 1782 Schaub (or Potters') House and the 1803 Buttner (or Brewers') House, each furnished with exhibits; the reconstruction, on its original site, of a palisade fort from the days of the French and Indian War; stabilized archaeological excavations of original foundations for over forty early buildings; God's Acre (a cemetery); a visitor center with exhibits and a scale model of the early village; and eighty acres of land. The Bethabara gardens were replanted according to information from the extensive daily records kept by the Moravians and may be the best-documented colonial gardens in the nation. The nearby communities at Bethania, begun in 1759, and Salem, begun in 1766, were formed from the community at Bethabara.

LOCATION: 2147 Bethabara Road. HOURS: *Grounds:* Open Daily. *Exhibits:* April through mid-December: 9:30–4:30 Monday–Friday, 1:30–4:30 Saturday–Sunday. FEE: None. TELEPHONE: 919–924–8191.

Old Salem

The Moravians who settled Salem brought with them many German ways as well as a strong Christian faith, industriousness, widely respected skills as tradespeople, and a love of music. Their best-known custom is the "lovefeast," a simple shared meal of coffee and bread, usually accompanied by music. Their brass bands are also well known, especially as they herald Easter Sunday morning. Moravians believed that they demonstrated spiritual growth by working with their own hands to produce food, pottery, candles, herbal medicines, and other products for the commercial profit of the community and the individual. In the early years of the settlement, Moravians practiced a form of communal living, a "choir" system in which people of like age, sex, or marital status lived and worshiped together. The Single Brothers, Widows, and Single Sisters, among other groups, lived in their own "choir" houses. Later, individuals could choose to live in their own houses, though their choices were subject to a "lend-lease" arrangement with the Moravian church, which owned the land and determined the building style of the structure.

Under the direction of the Moravian church, Old Salem was established in 1766, six miles southeast of Bethabara. Ninety-one original buildings built between 1766 and 1860 survive, covering roughly twenty-four city blocks, including exceptional examples of residential and commercial buildings, mostly of brick, frame, or half-timber construction. The majority are private residences, though ten of the restored buildings and two reconstructed ones serve as museums of the 100 years ending around 1850. The oldest original building is the **Fourth House,** built in 1768. The half-timbered **Single Brothers House,** where unmarried males came after the age of 14 to live and learn a trade, has been reconstructed as built in 1769 with a 1786 brick addition. Also on Main Street is the weatherboard log **Miksch Tobacco Shop,** built in 1783, which is

perhaps the oldest tobacco shop in America. As did many families in Salem, the Miksch family used the ground floor for their business and lived on the upper floor.

At the intersection of Main and Bank streets is the very large Greek Revival **Belo House,** once the property of cabinetmaker Edward Belo, who constructed the building on two lots. The first floor served as his mercantile shop, the second as his family residence, and the third as housing for his store clerks. Belo owned a foundry and manufactured much of the ironwork surrounding the property. Down Main Street is the **Winkler Bakery,** built in 1800, where traditional baking practices are demonstrated using an enormous oven. Adjacent to the bakery is the **Wachovia Museum,** housed in the Boys' School, built in 1794. Facing Salem Square is the **Salem College** campus, originally a girls' school established by Moravians in 1772, with a building constructed in 1805 that still serves as a dormitory. The sanctuary of the **Home Moravian Church,** designed by Frederic William Marshall, was consecrated in 1800 and continues to serve the congregation, which was organized in 1771. Farther along Church Street is the brick **Vierling House,** home and apothecary shop of Dr. Samuel Benjamin Vierling, who followed the same pattern for the arched door and other architectural features as those of Moravian churches in North Carolina.

On the corner of West and Main streets is the **John Vogler House,** built in 1819, the home and shop of a silversmith and clockmaker about whom it was said, "If his mind could conceive it, his hands could make it." Two doors away is the shoemaker shop of Samuel Shultz; built in 1827, it was the first shop in the community to be operated in a building separate from the owner's residence. On Main Street, at a point farthest from the church, is the first brick structure in the settlement, **Salem Tavern,** built in 1784 and operated by the church for its non-Moravian visitors—often customers for goods and services provided by the community. George Washington, once welcomed to town by a Moravian band, was a guest at the tavern in 1791. **God's Acre,** the Moravian cemetery on Cedar Avenue, has been used for burials since 1771.

On the grounds of Old Salem is the **Museum of Early Southern Decorative Arts** (924 South Main Street, 919–721–7360), featuring a

OPPOSITE:*The Single Brothers Workshop in Salem, which housed a bakery, black-smith's shop, weaving room, and joinery.* OVERLEAF: *The kitchen in the Single Brothers House, where teen-aged boys and unmarried men lived while learning a craft.*

collection of authentic southern furnishings and decorative art produced between 1640 and 1820. The inspiration for this collection was a remark made at the Williamsburg Forum in 1949, where it was said that "little of artistic merit was made south of Baltimore." Disproving that statement, the museum's six galleries and nineteen period rooms hold original furniture and art, including a 1640 court cupboard made in Tidewater, Virginia; pastels dating from 1711 by Henrietta Johnston, America's first professional female artist; needlework and other textiles; a collection of southern cast iron dating from 1769; and collections of silver, dating to 1711, and ceramics made and used in Maryland, Virginia, the Carolinas, Georgia, Tennessee, and Kentucky. Rooms from architecturally significant houses from these states have been transferred to the museum, with exhibits revealing a wide variety of influences on the surroundings of eighteenth-century Southerners.

LOCATION: Old Salem Road, off Route I-40. HOURS: 9:30–4:30 Monday–Saturday, 1:30–4:30 Sunday. FEE: Yes. TELEPHONE: 919–721–7300.

Reynolda House Museum of American Art

Built between 1914 and 1917 by Richard Joshua Reynolds, the founder of R. J. Reynolds Tobacco Company, and his wife, Katharine Smith, Reynolda House is furnished to reflect their tastes and features a permanent collection of 150 paintings and sculptures representing American art from 1755 to the present, including works by Jeremiah Theus, John Singleton Copley, Frederick Church, William Merritt Chase, Mary Cassatt, Thomas Eakins, Georgia O'Keeffe, and Andrew Wyeth. There is also a collection of women's clothing dating from 1905 to 1960. The 100-room house was designed by the Philadelphia architect Charles Barton Keen. The two-story living room has a cantilevered balcony, a wrought-iron balustrade and sconces by the Philadelphia ironmaster Samuel Yellin, and an aeolian organ with 2,500 pipes, built in 1915. The floor tiles on the porches adjacent to the living room were designed by Henry Chapman Mercer of Doylestown, Pennsylvania.

LOCATION: Reynolda Road, off Route I-40. HOURS: 9:30–4:30 Tuesday–Saturday, 1:30–4:30 Sunday. FEE: Yes. TELEPHONE: 919–725–5325.

STATESVILLE

Statesville, founded in 1789, suffered a fire in 1852 that destroyed most of the town. One of the best examples of Richardsonian Romanesque architecture in the state is the **Statesville City Hall** (227 South Center Street), formerly the U.S. Post Office, built in 1892 and designed by Willoughby J. Edbrook of Washington, DC. The **Zebulon Vance House,** built in 1832 and relocated to the corner of Woodward and West Sharpe from 219 West Broad Street, became the temporary executive mansion and state capitol when Union troops occupied Raleigh near the end of the Civil War, during Governor Vance's term.

Fort Dobbs State Historic Site (Route 1930, off Route 21, 704–873–5866) preserves the site of a fort built in 1756 by Commander Hugh Waddell and his rangers. Waddell's men defended the fort from attacking Cherokee on February 27, 1760, and it was apparently dismantled when pioneers moved westward after the conclusion of the French and Indian War in 1763. Archaeological investigation has revealed the exact location of the fort; the moat, cellar, magazine area, and well have been excavated. Exhibits explain the military and civilian life on the site.

SPENCER SHOPS STATE HISTORIC SITE

Located midway between Washington, DC, and Atlanta, the Southern Railroad's Spencer Shops opened in 1896 as the primary repair facility in the South. It serviced up to 100 steam locomotives daily until the development of diesel locomotives in the 1940s. The 1904 machine shop measures 600 by 150 feet and still houses the cranes used to lift a steam locomotive off its wheels. A thirty-seven-stall roundhouse built in 1924 holds the 100-foot-wide turntable. The centerpiece of the fifty-seven-acre complex is a sixty-six-year-old restored steam locomotive. The engine, repaired by retired Southern Railway workers, was once used to haul coal in the mountains of West Virginia and is now used seasonally as the locomotive for the site's excursion train.

LOCATION: On Salisbury Avenue, off Route 85, Spencer. HOURS: April through October: 9–5 Tuesday–Saturday, 1–5 Sunday; November through March: 10–4 Tuesday–Saturday, 1–4 Sunday. FEE: For excursion train. TELEPHONE: 704–636–2889.

CHARLOTTE

Organized in 1768 and named for Queen Charlotte of Mecklenburg, the wife of George III, Charlotte preserves a number of nineteenth- and twentieth-century structures. **The Fourth Ward,** near downtown, is a residential area of excellent Victorian restoration; one home of note is the **Victoria** (1600 The Plaza, 704–333–9395), built ca. 1895. Southeast of downtown are two streetcar suburbs: **Dilworth,** dating to 1891, and **Myers Park,** dating to 1912, with willow-lined streets planned by John Nolen and Earl Draper of Cambridge, Massachusetts. Edward Dilworth Latta, who owned the streetcars, developed the neighborhoods.

Charlotte was the site of a gathering that created a document sometimes called "the first Declaration of Independence" (there are other claimants to this title in other regions). Finding taxation and British rule under Governor Josiah Martin to be oppressive, Colonel Thomas Polk organized the delegation that wrote and signed the Mecklenburg Declaration of Independence on May 20, 1775, a date that appears on the state flag and seal.

British general Lord Cornwallis occupied Charlotte for about sixteen days after September 26, 1780, unsuccessfully opposed by Patriots under Colonel William R. Davie and Major Joseph Graham. The troops engaged in several skirmishes in the area, including one called the Battle of the Bees on October 3, 1780, at the **McIntyre Farm** (Beatties Ford Road at McIntyre Avenue, 704–336–3854), where the British were attacked not only by Patriots but also by a swarm of bees. After learning of the defeat of Colonel Patrick Ferguson at Kings Mountain on October 7, 1780, Cornwallis withdrew to South Carolina; legend has it that he declared, "Let's get out of here; this place is a damned hornets' nest." Local organizations and the city's seal continue to use the epithet. President George Washington visited the city in 1791. Jefferson Davis, the president of the Confederacy, was in Charlotte on April 19, 1865, when he received the news of Lincoln's assassination.

Notable buildings in Charlotte include the Norman Gothic Revival **First Presbyterian Church** (on West Trade Street between North Church and Poplar), a stuccoed brick structure built in 1857.

OPPOSITE: *The golden eagle at Charlotte's Mint Museum, fourteen feet from wing to wing and five feet high, required more than 165 books of gold leaf and 10 books of silver leaf to cover it when it was restored in the 1890s.*

At the left of the entrance is the McAden memorial window designed by Sir Edward Burne-Jones. **Spirit Square** (318 North Tryon Street) is a cultural and performing arts center housed in the Romanesque Revival First Baptist Church building, completed in 1908 to designs by J. M. McMichael, of yellow brick with a large green dome. Another domed building designed by McMichael is the 1908 **Old Little Rock AME Zion Church** (403 North Myers).

Mint Museum

The building housing the art and history museum is the reconstructed first branch of the U.S. Mint, which operated from 1837 to 1861 and from 1867 to 1913 to accommodate the 100 gold mines surrounding Charlotte in the early nineteenth century. Designed by William Strickland of Philadelphia, the mint is a Greek Revival two-story T-shaped building with vaulted ceilings. Domestic gold coined at the mint came exclusively from North Carolina from 1804 until 1828. Throughout the Civil War Confederate troops used the building as a hospital and headquarters. Chartered as a museum in 1933, it holds collections of pre-Columbian art, American and European paintings, the work of regional craftspeople, and Carolina currencies and coins of the gold-mining period.

LOCATION: 2730 Randolph Road. HOURS: 10–10 Tuesday, 10–5 Wednesday–Saturday, 1–6 Sunday. FEE: Yes. TELEPHONE: 704–337–2006.

Completed in 1774, the **Hezekiah Alexander Homesite and History Museum** (3500 Shamrock Drive, 704–568–1774), also known as the "Rock House," was the home of a Revolutionary leader and a writer of the first constitution and bill of rights of North Carolina. It is the oldest surviving dwelling in Mecklenburg County. Operated by the city of Charlotte, the site also includes a two-story stone springhouse, a reconstructed log kitchen, gardens, exhibits, and a history museum.

The **James K. Polk Memorial State Historic Site** (Route 521, Pineville, 704–889–7145) is located on property once owned by Jane and Samuel Polk, the parents of President James K. Polk, who was born here in 1795. The log buildings and furnishings, although not original to the farm, are of the same period as their occupancy.

James K. Polk, the eleventh president of the United States, who was born at this site in 1795, and lived here until his family moved to Tennessee eleven years later. The farmhouse was moved here from another site.

DALLAS

This town's historic district of nineteenth-century commercial and residential buildings includes a **jail,** a **train depot,** and the **old courthouse,** a Greek Revival structure built in 1847 and rebuilt in 1875. The Hoffman House Hotel, built in 1852, houses the **Gaston County Museum of Art and History** (131 West Main Street, 704–922–7681), which features twentieth-century American art, textiles, exhibits of local history, and the state's largest public collection of horse-drawn vehicles.

Town Creek Indian Mound State Historic Site (between Routes 731 and 73, southeast of Mount Gilead, 919–439–6802) includes an elliptical mound, about 16 feet in height and 100 feet across. The site probably dates from the sixteenth century or earlier, when it was used by Creek Indians of the Pee Dee River as a ceremonial center. A hypothetical reconstruction includes a temple mound, priests' dwelling, and stockaded village. Exhibits at the visitor center interpret the site.

THE   MOUNTAINS

Western North Carolina is the land of mountains—the Blue Ridge
Mountains, succeeded by the Great Smoky Mountains, both part of
the ancient Appalachian chain. The highlands cover roughly 6,000
square miles, with several hundred peaks exceeding 4,000 feet, and
over forty that rise above 6,000 feet—more than in any other eastern
state. Mount Mitchell, with an elevation of 6,684 feet, is the highest
peak east of the Mississippi. Geologists estimate the Appalachian
chain to be 250 million years old, and the Blue Ridge and the
Smokies are among its oldest ranges. The western mountains are
the home of the state's largest Indian nation, the Cherokee,
mentioned in de Soto's accounts of his explorations in the area
around 1540. Some Cherokee still live on the 56,000-acre
reservation in North Carolina.

In the 1750s a Moravian bishop from Pennsylvania, August
Gottlieb Spangenberg, explored the region, and Daniel Boone lived
in the area from 1760 to 1769 and blazed trails for incoming settlers.
But perhaps the greatest migration of white settlers to the
mountains occurred after the Battle of Alamance Creek in 1771.
Defeated by Governor William Tryon and his militia, many of the
Regulators decided to move west, out of the reach of the Tidewater
elite and the governor. At the time, North Carolina's boundaries
stretched westward to the Mississippi River. In 1772 the settlers west
of the mountains formed the Watauga Association, and in 1784, led
by John Sevier, they seceded from North Carolina and formed the
separate state of Franklin, with what is now Jonesboro, Tennessee, as
its capital. By 1788 Franklin had disbanded and rejoined North
Carolina, but in 1796 the state of Tennessee was formed from the
land west of the mountains. Much of this region is accessible via the
Blue Ridge Parkway, a scenic highway that extends uninterrupted
for almost 500 miles through three states. Begun in the early 1900s,
with construction interrupted by World War I, it opened in 1935, a
public works project of the Franklin D. Roosevelt administration.
The parkway links the Shenandoah National Park, the Blue Ridge
Mountains, and the Great Smoky Mountains National Park.

On the Blue Ridge Parkway is the **Brinegar Cabin** (milepost
238.5, in Doughton Park), a one-story, rectangular log building with

OPPOSITE: *The Great Smoky Mountains along the North Carolina-Tennessee border.*

lapped siding, a gabled roof, and a stone exterior end chimney. Built around 1880, the well-preserved structure is a good example of early housing in the region. A shed has been added to the rear, and one outbuilding, thought to have served as a dairy, still stands.

WILKESBORO

Wilkesboro, settled on the south bank of the Yadkin River before the Revolutionary War, is the seat of Wilkes County. Both were named for John Wilkes, an eighteenth-century English radical. The **Wilkesboro Historic District** encompasses a number of nineteenth-century buildings, including **Saint Paul's Episcopal Church** (Cowles Street), completed in 1849; the **Carl Lowe House,** built in 1889; the 1891 **Smithey Hotel,** with its original iron front; and the **Wilkesboro Presbyterian Church,** completed in 1850. The **Wilkes County Courthouse** (Bridge Street) is a Classic Revival brick-and-stone structure, built in 1902, with an oblong cupola and a monumental pedimented portico. Also on the Courthouse Square is the **Tory Oak,** from which five Tories were hanged by Colonel Benjamin Cleveland during the Revolutionary War.

Old Wilkes County Jail/Museum

Completed in 1860, the brick two-story jail with interior end chimneys and a low hipped roof is one of North Carolina's few well-preserved examples of penal architecture. Tom Dula (Tom Dooley), made famous in ballads after he was hanged for the murder of a sweetheart, was once held here. The jailer's quarters houses period artifacts, jail furnishings, and kitchen tools, and the cells have their original hardware. Next door is the **Robert Cleveland Log House,** built in 1779 and restored with period furniture.

LOCATION: Courthouse Square. HOURS: 9–4 Monday–Friday. FEE: None. TELEPHONE: 919–667–3712.

Moses H. Cone Memorial Park (Milepost 294, Blue Ridge Parkway, 704–295–3782) preserves a twenty-room Victorian mansion, the summer home and estate of Moses H. Cone, a Greensboro textile manufacturer. The house serves as the Parkway Crafts Center for the

OPPOSITE: *Old Wilkes County Jail in Wilkesboro, where Tom Dula, who has passed into American folkfore as Tom Dooley, was imprisoned after killing his faithless sweetheart.*

A view from the mansion at Moses Cone State Park, a summer estate set admist 3,600 acres along the Blue Ridge Parkway. Cone, a Greensboro textile manufacturer, was known as the "Blue Denim King."

Southern Highland Handicraft Guild. **Grandfather Mountain** (Route 221, near Linville, 704–733–4337) was named by pioneers because the mountain ridge resembles the profile of a reclining old man. Estimated by the U.S. Geological Survey to be 1 billion years old, the mountain of quartz, granite, slate, and other stone is among the oldest rock formations in the world.

BOONE

The seat of Watauga County was named for Daniel Boone, who had a home in the area from 1760 to 1769. At the corner of Faculty and Newland streets in Boone, an eighteen-foot-tall stone marker stands on the **site of Boone's cabin.** Boone entered the region through Deep Gap around 1760 and explored the Watauga River valley as well as the valleys of the New River and the Holston. In July and August, the Southern Appalachian Historical Association (704–264–2120) presents an outdoor drama depicting the

Revolutionary War struggle between Patriots in western North Carolina and Loyalists serving under British major Patrick Ferguson. Seven miles south of Boone is the **Mast General Store** (Route 194), one of the best examples of a nineteenth-century general store in the state. The first rooms were built in 1882 by Henry Taylor. The clapboard building with a gabled roof still houses the community's post office as well as a potbellied stove, original fixtures, and turn-of-the-century advertising posters. Once claiming to sell everything "from cradles to caskets," the store still carries a wide variety of merchandise. Just east of the store are the **Mast family log cabin,** dating from ca. 1812, and the **Mast Farm Inn.** The restored two-story farmhouse, built in 1885, preserves its original outbuildings, including an octagonal gazebo, a blacksmith shop, smokehouse, and weaving house. It is a good example of a self-sufficient nineteenth-century farm complex.

Blowing Rock, south of Boone, is one of North Carolina's oldest mountain resort towns. Developed in the 1880s, it was named for a rock cliff over the Johns River Gorge, where a strong updraft returns objects dropped from the cliff. Legend has it that an Indian woman prayed to the God of the Winds to save the warrior she loved when he disappeared over the ledge. The god responded to her plea by returning her lover to her, and has continued to return items that fall over the Blowing Rock. Located between Boone and Blowing Rock on Route 321 is what remains of the narrow-gauge railroad, built in 1886, that once traveled the sixty-six miles between Boone and Johnson City, Tennessee. **Tweetsie Railroad** (704–264–9061), named by local residents for the sound of the whistle on the coal-fired steam locomotive, now makes a three-mile run.

Built between 1788 and 1792 by Thomas Fields for General William Lenoir, **Fort Defiance** (Route 268, Happy Valley) is a frame clapboard house named for the early frontier Indian fort that once stood on the site. The house contains original furnishings as well as Indian artifacts and Revolutionary War relics.

At 6,684 feet above sea level, **Mount Mitchell** (Route 128, off the Blue Ridge Parkway, 704–675–4611) is the highest point east of the Mississippi River. Preserved as a park, the peak is named for Dr. Elisha Mitchell, professor at the University of North Carolina who made the first measurement of the peak and fell to his death in 1857 while verifying his data. Mitchell's claim had been contested by Congressman Thomas Clingman, who measured Clingman's Dome on the North Carolina–Tennessee border and declared it higher.

The mountain guide "Big Tom" Wilson followed Mitchell's trail when the professor failed to return and discovered the body at the foot of a waterfall. Mitchell is buried in the park.

ZEBULON B. VANCE BIRTHPLACE STATE HISTORIC SITE

Between 1790 and 1795, David Vance established his homestead here. David Vance served in the Continental army, fought at Kings Mountain, and was a commissioner in the establishment of the 1799 boundary between North Carolina and Tennessee. He is buried in the nearby family cemetery, and his two-story, five-room yellow-pine log house with a huge chimney has been reconstructed. The site also includes six log outbuildings and a museum highlighting the life of Vance's grandson, Governor Zebulon B. Vance, the Civil War governor of North Carolina. David Vance II served during the War of 1812, and his brother, Dr. Robert B. Vance, died in 1827 in a duel with Samuel P. Carson, an opponent for a seat in Congress.

LOCATION: Reems Creek Road, off Route 1923, 6 miles east of Weaverville. HOURS: April through October: 9–5 Monday–Saturday, 1–5 Sunday; November through March: 10–4 Tuesday–Saturday, 1–4 Sunday. FEE: None. TELEPHONE: 704-645-6706.

ASHEVILLE

Around the turn of the century Asheville became the most important summer resort in western North Carolina, particularly for the wealthy. Summer residents included John D. Rockefeller, Thomas Edison, Henry Ford, Grover Cleveland, and Theodore Roosevelt. The city preserves one of the most interesting collections of early-twentieth-century architecture in North Carolina, perhaps in the South. The resort hotels and other buildings are excellent examples of Georgian Revival, Romanesque Revival, Art Deco, and other architectural styles, including several buildings erected by Edwin Wiley Grove, an important city developer. Between 1912 and 1913 Grove built the original part of the **Grove Park Inn** (290 Macon Avenue), a monumental lodge and resort complex constructed of native granite with a red tile roof, at the foot of Sunset Mountain. He also built the **Arcade Building** (37 Battery Park), covering a city block with intersecting arcades made of stone and terra-cotta tile. Designed by the Asheville architect Charles Parker, it has a three-story atrium and spiral staircases connecting the first and second floors. Grove is also responsible for the fourteen-story Georgian Revival **Battery Park Apartments** (Battle Square), completed in 1924. **Riverside Cemetery** (Birch Street) contains the graves of novelist Thomas Wolfe, short-story writer William Sydney Porter (better known as O. Henry), and Civil War–era governor Zebulon B. Vance.

During the Civil War, Asheville and the Buncombe County area rallied to the Confederate cause: Asheville was a mustering place where seven of the ten North Carolina companies were raised, and Enfield rifles, accurate firearms valued by Confederate soldiers, were manufactured here. During the final months of the war Union troops occupied Asheville after a skirmish north of the city on April 6, 1865. Earthworks for that engagement remain on the Asheville campus of the University of North Carolina.

Much of downtown Asheville dates from the 1890s. Typical city blocks include rows of two- and four-story brick buildings with decorative pressed sheet-metal cornices. Among the most impressive Romanesque structures in the region is the **Drhumor Building** (48 Patton Avenue), a four-story brick office building built in 1895 and featuring limestone friezework by the English sculptor Frederick Miles, who also did carvings for George Vanderbilt's Biltmore House. The **Downtown Asheville Historic District,** located between the French Broad River and Beaucatcher Mountain, includes a number of nineteenth- and twentieth-century buildings. The brick Greek Revival **Ravenscroft School** (29 Ravenscroft Drive), built ca. 1840, is probably the oldest building in the district. A downtown landmark, **Pack Square** (Broadway at Biltmore and Patton avenues), is the site of a seventy-five-foot-tall granite obelisk set in place in 1896 to honor Governor Zebulon B. Vance. The nine-story Art Deco **City Hall** (70 Court Plaza), designed by Douglas Ellington, was built between 1926 and 1928 of brick, pink Georgia marble, and terra-cotta, with a multicolored tile roof. The seventeen-story **Buncombe County Courthouse** (60 Court Plaza), designed with some classical details by Washington, DC, architects Milburn and Heister, was constructed between 1925 and 1927 of light-colored brick, Indiana limestone, and granite. Other buildings designed by Ellington include the fine Art Deco **S and W Cafeteria** (56 Patton Avenue) and the **First Baptist Church** (corner of Oak and Woodfin), completed in 1927, combining front brick columns and such Art Deco details as an octagonal dome of varicolored tile. The **Catholic Church of Saint Lawrence** (97 Haywood Street), built in 1909, is the masterful design of Rafael Guastavino in the Mexican-Spanish style. Guastavino came to Asheville as one of the engineers who worked on the design of the Biltmore House. The church's interior features a self-supporting elliptical dome, eighty-two by fifty-eight feet, constructed entirely of tile.

On the east side of the city, perched on the west side of Sunset Mountain, is the small **Manor and Cottages Historic District** (Charlotte Street), dating from 1898 and designed by Thomas W. Raoul as a village in the English style. Also to the east is the **Saint Matthias Episcopal Church** (Valley Street). Built in 1896, the Gothic Revival structure serves the oldest black Episcopal congregation in western North Carolina, dating from 1865.

The Thomas Wolfe House

The novelist Thomas Wolfe lived in this twenty-nine-room Queen Anne boardinghouse from the age of six until about sixteen, when he left for the University of North Carolina. Known as the "Old Kentucky Home," the rambling two-story white frame house with a gabled roof and a wraparound porch was built in 1883 and expanded through the years. Wolfe's first novel, *Look Homeward, Angel* (1929), reflects his experiences growing up in this house, in which he was never allowed to have his own bedroom because his mother constantly shifted the children around to accommodate her boarders. His mother, Julia, bought the furnished house in 1906 and, against the wishes of his father (who refused to move from their Woodfin Street residence two blocks away), operated it as a boardinghouse until she died in 1945. Wolfe wrote that his mother's 1916 renovations were "made after her own plans, and of the cheapest material. It never lost the smell of raw wood, cheap varnish, and flimsy rough plastering."

The house was opened as a museum in 1949 with the original furnishings and personal items of the family, including the medallion bed on which all eight of the Wolfe children were born.

OPPOSITE: *The author Thomas Wolfe with his mother at her Asheville boarding house, the Old Kentucky House, in 1937.*

The children's playhouse from Woodfin Street was moved to the yard of the boardinghouse when the earlier residence was destroyed, and one upstairs room is furnished with items from Wolfe's final New York apartment.

LOCATION: 48 Spruce Street. HOURS: April through October: 9–5 Monday–Saturday, 1–5 Sunday; November through March: 10–4 Tuesday–Saturday, 1–4 Sunday. FEE: Yes. TELEPHONE: 704–253–8304.

The Biltmore Estate

Between 1888 and 1890, George Washington Vanderbilt, grandson of the railroad promoter Cornelius Vanderbilt, purchased a total of 125,000 acres of land for the estate he planned to build. Richard Morris Hunt, designer of the base of the Statue of Liberty and New York's *Tribune* building as well as many buildings in Newport, Rhode Island, and New York, designed Vanderbilt's 250-room French Renaissance chateau with hand-tooled native limestone, steeply hipped roof sections, chimneys, dormers, decorative windows, and roof cresting. Construction, which lasted from 1890 to 1895, incorporated much modern technology, including central heating, plumbing, refrigeration, electrical systems, elevators, and Edison's first filament light bulbs.

The Biltmore House is the largest private residence in the United States. The main entrance leads into a hall with a Guastavino tile ceiling seventy-five feet in height. To the right of the hall is an indoor winter garden, a sunken area of marble featuring a Karl Bitter sculpture surmounting a fountain; to the left is a spiral stairway circling a wrought-iron chandelier. Hand-tooled Spanish leather covers the walls of the breakfast room, which features a fireplace framed by Wedgwood tiles. The ceiling in the immense banquet hall arches seventy feet high, and a huge triple fireplace fills one end of the room. The ninety-foot-long gallery with stenciled ceiling, linen-fold panelling, and Brussels tapestries leads to the library, which features a Pelligrini ceiling painting, a black marble fireplace, walnut panelling, and carvings by Karl Bitter, as well as over 20,000 volumes. The house also contains an impressive collection of fine and decorative art, including paintings by Renoir, Boldini, Sargent, and

OPPOSITE: *Biltmore House, designed by Richard Morris Hunt for George Vanderbilt, is based on Loire Valley chateaus of the sixteenth century.*

Whistler; Meissen porcelains; and Albrecht Dürer engravings.

Frederick Law Olmsted, designer of New York's Central Park, managed the 250 acres surrounding the Biltmore House and designed 17 acres of spectacular gardens and the beautiful three-mile winding entrance drive. Much of the original acreage became the Pisgah National Forest after Vanderbilt's death in 1914. Many of the original farm buildings—barns, stables, carriage house—have been restored and are open to the public. The restored dairy complex now houses the Biltmore Estate winery.

LOCATION: Route 25, 3 blocks north of Route 40. HOURS: 9–5 Daily. FEE: Yes. TELEPHONE: 704-255-1700.

At the entrance to the estate is the **Biltmore Village Historic District,** a "model village" in the English Tudor style, designed by Richard Morris Hunt and Richard Sharp Smith, landscaped by Olmsted, to ornament the estate. **All Souls Episcopal Church and Parish House** (2 Angle Street) is a Romanesque structure of Hunt's design.

CHEROKEE INDIAN RESERVATION

Home of the eastern band of Cherokee, the reservation covers over 50,000 acres in Swain and Jackson counties and some 13,000 acres in Graham and Cherokee counties. The largest Indian reservation east of Wisconsin, it has a population of approximately 8,000 Cherokee, descendants of those who eluded General Winfield Scott by escaping into the Smoky Mountains in 1838, when he moved the majority of the tribe west to what is now Oklahoma on the infamous Trail of Tears. Nearly one quarter died en route during the forced relocation. The Cherokee land was recovered as the result of an interesting chain of events. The story goes that a small band of Cherokee led by an old Indian named Tsali killed a soldier under the command of General Scott. Weary of his efforts to capture and deport all of the Cherokee in the area, Scott offered to leave behind all those who had escaped capture in return for the lives of Tsali and his warriors. Believing they were exchanging their lives for a guarantee that the Smoky Mountains would be forever home to their kinspeople, Tsali and his men surrendered and were executed. North Carolinians, however, were not ready to recognize the

OPPOSITE: *The ceiling in Biltmore's 20,000 volume library is from the Pisani Palace in Venice.*

A cabin at the Oconaluftee Indian Village on the Cherokee Indian Reservation.

Cherokee as landowners until William H. Thomas arranged for the purchase of land with treaty money for this permanent reservation. Nearby are two sites associated with the Trail of Tears. In Cherokee County, near the town of Murphy, is **Fort Butler,** where Cherokee were housed before Scott moved them west in 1838. Near Hayesville, in Clay County, is *f***Fort Hembree,** a stockade where Scott assembled the Cherokee before forcing them to begin their 1,000-mile trek on the Trail of Tears. In Macon County, a mound in the center of the town of **Franklin** is the location of a **Nikwasi,** an old Cherokee village.

The **Museum of the Cherokee Indian** (Route 441, 704–497–3481) features the most comprehensive collection in this part of the country, focusing on the 10,000 years of Cherokee presence in the area. The museum interprets Cherokee history from prehistoric times to the present through displays of ancient weapons, household tools, pottery, and other artifacts. Audio exhibits explain the Cherokee language and the Sequoyan syllabary, which has preserved the language in written form since

A guide makes a dugout canoe using fire and an axe at Oconaluftee Indian Village.

1821. The **Oconaluftee Indian Village** (Route 441 North, 704–497–2315) is an excellent outdoor museum that re-creates lifestyles of 225 years ago.

In Pisgah National Forest, the **Cradle of Forestry Visitor Center** (Route 276, four miles southeast of Blue Ridge Parkway Milepost 412, 704–877–3130) is located on the site of the Biltmore Forest School, where scientific forest management was first practiced and taught. From 1898 until it closed in 1914 the school was directed by Carl A. Schenck, whose background in forestry led George Vanderbilt to bring him over from Germany to manage over 100,000 acres of forest around Mount Pisgah. The Biltmore Forest School Campus Trail leads to eight original and reconstructed buildings, mostly single-story frame residences, once used by Schenck's students, who gave them such names as "Little Bohemia" and "Rest for the Wicked." The Forest Festival Trail leads to such forestry equipment as a steam-powered portable saw dating from ca. 1900 and a restored 1915 Climax logging machine.

Carl Sandburg Home National Historic Site

Winner of two Pulitzer Prizes—in 1940 for the four-volume *Abraham Lincoln: The War Years* and in 1951 for his *Complete Poems*—Carl Sandburg lived here from 1945 until his death in 1967. In this house he worked on his only novel, *Remembrance Rock* (1948); his autobiography, *Always the Young Stranger* (1953); Hollywood screenplays (including George Stevens's *The Greatest Story Ever Told*); and numerous volumes of poetry. Lilian "Paula" Steichen, Sandburg's wife, ran the farm and raised many herds of prize-winning goats.

The farm, known as Connemara, was originally the summer home of the first secretary of the Confederate treasury, Christopher Gustavus Memminger of Charleston, South Carolina, who built the main residence around 1838. According to local legend, Memminger urged Jefferson Davis to relocate Confederate governmental headquarters from Richmond to Flat Rock, which was, he argued, a more easily defendable site. The grounds include a number of the

Carl Sandburg at work in his office in 1946. He would frequently begin writing between 8 and 11 P.M., and continue until 5 A.M., when he would fall into bed in the room next door.

original farm buildings and trails, as well as a goat herd maintained by the park staff. The Sandburg house preserves a great deal of memorabilia. Sandburg's guitar stands propped against a chair, and stacks of magazines, books, and notes are casually placed inside and on top of orange crates used as tables and file boxes. Because of a wartime shortage of lumber, nearly every room has floor-to-ceiling bookshelves made from shelving boards the Sandburgs brought with them from their previous home in Michigan. The walls hold photographs by Paula's brother, Edward Steichen.

LOCATION: Little River Road, off Route 25, 3 miles south of Hendersonville. HOURS: 9–5 Daily. FEE: Yes. TELEPHONE: 704–693–4178.

FLAT ROCK

Twenty-six miles south of Asheville, near Hendersonville, is the community of Flat Rock. Among the oldest summer resorts in western North Carolina, it was begun by residents of Charleston and Savannah escaping the heat and humidity of the coast. The **Flat Rock Historic District** includes a number of nineteenth-century summer estates, most set back from the narrow, winding Route 25. The wide variety of architectural styles includes Greek Revival, Gothic Revival, Second Empire, and Classic Revival. Of special note are the privately owned **Argyle Estate** (1830–1831); the Romanesque Revival **Saint John-in-the-Wilderness,** a chapel built between 1834 and 1836 on the estate of Charles S. Baring; and the **Saluda Cottages** (Little River Road), occupied in the late 1830s by the French consul of Savannah, Count de Choiseul. The graves of his family as well as the grave of Christopher Gustavus Memminger, first secretary of the Confederate treasury, are in the chapel cemetery.

MORGANTON

Named for the Revolutionary War general Daniel Morgan, Morganton is the seat of Burke County, which was formed from Rowan County in 1777 and once extended to the Mississippi River. The Greek Revival **Burke County Courthouse** (102 East Union Street), built in 1835, was raided in February 1865 by Federal troops under General George Stoneman. Nearly all of the county records were burned. John Sevier, governor of the state of Franklin (later part of Tennessee), was brought to trial on charges of treason in 1788 in an earlier log courthouse that once stood nearby. His friend James Cosby helped him to escape from the courtroom by creating a disturbance. Morganton was also the site of the trial and hanging of Frankie Silver, reputed to be the first woman hanged in the state (the ballad "Frankie and Johnny" told her story).

Settled in 1893 by the Waldenses, a religious group from the Italian Cottian Alps, **Valdese** is a charming town with brick sidewalks and a bocci court on Main Street. The **Waldensian Presbyterian Church Museum** (Rodoret Street, adjacent to the church, 704–874–2531) commemorates the Waldenses' escape from religious persecution and the history of their settlement. In the town of **Old Fort** the **Mountain Gateway Museum** (Catawba Avenue and Water Street, 704–668–9259) sits on the site of Davidson's (Old) Fort, built in 1776 by Griffith Rutherford's troops to protect settlers and their Catawba allies from the Cherokee. The museum's collection includes the log building that housed the first Presbyterian church in McDowell County.

KERNERSVILLE

Local legend has it that the site for Kernersville was purchased by Caleb Story around 1756 for several gallons of rum; the town was founded by German settlers around 1770. Washington's diary reports that he stopped here in 1791 en route to Guilford. **Korner's Folly** (400 block of South Main Street, 919–996–8644) is a three-story brick house built on seven levels in 1880 by the artist J. Gilmer Korner. It features marble floors, elaborately carved woodwork, frescoes by German artist Caesar Milch, and narrow staircases. The top floor was used as a theater in 1897.

REED GOLD MINE STATE HISTORIC SITE

John Reed's farm was the site of the first gold find in the United States. In 1799 Reed's son, Conrad, came upon a seventeen-pound yellow rock, which the family used for a doorstop until a Fayetteville jeweler recognized it as gold in 1802. Between 1803 and 1824, Reed and his two partners panned gold worth an estimated $100,000, and the gold discoveries spread to neighboring counties, making North Carolina the leading gold producer in the nation until the 1848

California gold rush drew miners westward. Areas open to the public include mining trails, the nineteenth-century stamp mill used to crush ore, a restored section of the underground mine shaft, and a visitor center with exhibits.

LOCATION: Route 200, off Route 601, about 10 miles southeast of Concord. HOURS: April through October: 9–5 Monday–Saturday, 1–5 Sunday; November through March: 10–4 Tuesday–Saturday, 1–4 Sunday. FEE: None. TELEPHONE: 704–786–8337.

HOUSE IN THE HORSESHOE STATE HISTORIC SITE

Located on a hill in a horseshoe bend of the Deep River, the Alston House was built ca. 1770. The plantation house belonged to Philip Alston, one of the wealthiest slaveholders in the region, who also held offices as justice of the peace, legislator, and leader of the local militia. During the Revolution, Colonel Alston's house was the site of a skirmish between his troops and those of a Tory officer, David Fanning. Alston's men had seized Kenneth Black, a close friend of Fanning, and beaten Black to death in an attempt to extract information. In revenge Fanning ambushed Alston on August 5, 1781, at the House in the Horseshoe. After a fierce fight, Fanning received Alston's surrender and his vow not to engage in further violence against the king's men. Bullet holes from this skirmish can be seen around the front and rear entrances to the house. Alston's subsequent political career was stormy, and he was implicated in other murders. After being forced out of the general assembly and the state in 1790, he was murdered in his bed in 1791 in Georgia.

Benjamin Williams bought the property in 1798. Also a planter and legislator, Williams served as governor for four years. In 1803, describing his property here, he claimed, "I think it may be justly ranked among the most valuable Estates in North Carolina." The two-and-a-half-story clapboard plantation house has a large brick chimney on each end and full-length shed porches on the front and back. The front door with a fanlight leads into a house museum with fine interior woodwork.

LOCATION: Route 1644, off Route 42, near Glennon. HOURS: April through October: 9–5 Monday–Saturday; 1–5 Sunday; November through March: 10–4 Tuesday–Saturday, 1–4 Sunday. FEE: None. TELEPHONE: 919–947–2051.

SOUTH CAROLINA

OPPOSITE: *Hampton Plantation in McClellanville, now a State Park. On this portico, Harriott Horry and her mother Eliza Lucas Pinckney stood to greet George Washington in 1791, wearing sashes painted with the president's likeness.*

B efore the English succeeded in settling South Carolina, two
unsuccessful attempts were made, the first in 1526 by the
Spaniard Lucas Vásquez de Ayllón and the second in 1562 by
the Frenchman Jean Ribault. In 1670 the first permanent English settlement, established on the Ashley River, was named Charles Towne,
or Charleston, as it was officially renamed in 1783. It was named for
King Charles II, who granted the Carolina province, originally
including both the Carolinas, Georgia, and the northern part of
Florida, to the eight lords proprietors. The city had moved, by 1680,
to the present site of Charleston, and the lords proprietors referred
to the surrounding area as Berkeley County. In 1682 they agreed that
county boundaries should be surveyed, with Craven County to the
northeast and Colleton to the southwest. Settled primarily by the
English (directly and from the West Indies) and by French
Huguenots, South Carolina also attracted settlers from North
Carolina, Virginia, and Pennsylvania, as well as from Scotland,
Germany, and other countries.

The diverse population united in opposition to proprietary rule
in 1719, and in a much more orderly revolt than was staged in North
Carolina a decade later, the legislative assembly voted to ignore the
rulings of the proprietors. However, they retained the proprietary
governor, Robert Johnson, and in May 1721 accepted the king's
appointed provisional governor, Sir Francis Nicholson, though royal
government offered no great improvement over proprietary rule.
Coastal settlers often came under attack by pirates, and up-country
farmers were often contending with Indians. Slaves from Africa and
the West Indies soon outnumbered the white planters, and there was
constant fear of insurrection. South Carolina was not in every way
the Eden described by its promoters. But it did grow and prosper,
producing many successful planters and agricultural innovations,
such as finding a way to grow and market indigo in the early 1740s.
The person chiefly responsible for making indigo a commercial crop
was a young woman named Eliza Lucas.

In 1729 the decision was made to divide the Carolina province
into North Carolina and South Carolina, though the boundary was
not officially settled until 1815. Indian trails were followed by settlers
and traders who journeyed to the up-country, which remained a
frontier until after the American Revolution. Indian trails have provided the routes for many of South Carolina's major highways; Route
I-26 approximately follows the most famous one, the Cherokee Path,

A View of Charles-Town, the Capital of South Carolina, *engraved from a painting by the English artist Thomas Leitch. Leitch, who visited the city in 1773. intended to create "so exact a portrait of the Town, as it appears from the Water, that every House in View will be distinctly known. . . ."*

leading from the northwest corner of the state to the Saluda River valley to the Congaree valley east of Columbia and ending at Charleston.

Although Governor James Glen recognized in 1753 that the up-country needed courts outside of Charleston, the low-country planters resisted any dispersal of power until 1769, when the king approved circuit court legislation allowing courts to meet in Beaufort, Orangeburg, Ninety Six, Camden, Cheraw, and Georgetown, as well as Charleston. Up-country settlers long resented Charleston's reluctance to acknowledge the rights of backcountry residents, whose undeveloped land was taxed at the same rate as that of the wealthy low-country planters. This resentment resulted in the up-countrymen's lacking the Charlestonians' "patriotic" sentiment over the affronts of English rule. Settlers outside Charleston had already experienced taxation without representation at the hands of Charleston legislators.

Despite the sharp divisions in the state, in 1774 South Carolina sent delegates to the Continental Congress. The next year, South Carolinians ousted their royal governor, William Campbell. In 1776 four delegates from South Carolina—Edward Rutledge, Thomas

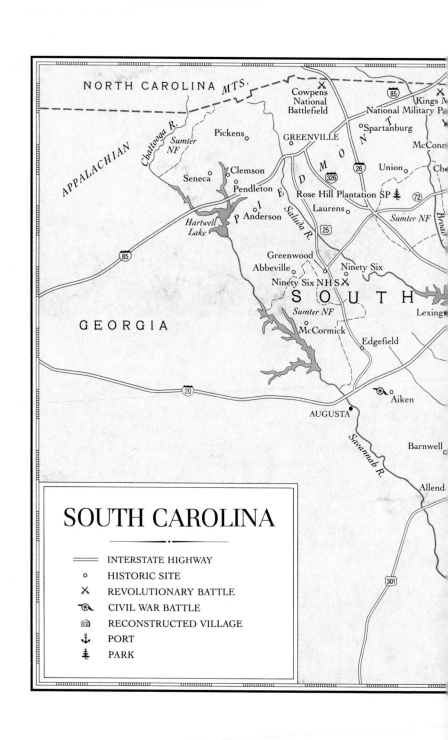

NORTH CAROLINA MTS.

APPALACHIAN

Chattooga R.

Sumter NF

Pickens ○

Cowpens National Battlefield ✕

85

Kings M
National Military Pa

○ Spartanburg

GREENVILLE ○

McConn

Seneca ○ ✕ Clemson ○

Pendleton ○

P
I
E
D
M
O
N
T

326

26

Union ○

Ch

72

Rose Hill Plantation SP ♣

Laurens ○

Saluda R.

Sumter NF

Broad

P ○ Anderson

Hartwell Lake

85

25

Greenwood ○

Abbeville ○

Ninety Six ○

Ninety Six NHS ✕

S O U T H

Lexing

Sumter NF

McCormick ○

Edgefield ○

G E O R G I A

20

Aiken ⚔

AUGUSTA ●

Savannah R.

Barnwell ○

Allend

301

SOUTH CAROLINA

—— • ——

═══	INTERSTATE HIGHWAY
○	HISTORIC SITE
✕	REVOLUTIONARY BATTLE
⚔	CIVIL WAR BATTLE
⌂	RECONSTRUCTED VILLAGE
⚓	PORT
♣	PARK

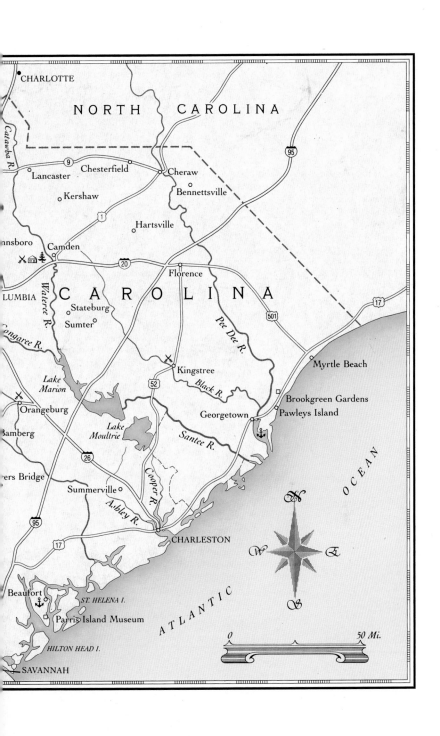

CHARLOTTE

NORTH CAROLINA

Catawba R.

⑨ Chesterfield
Lancaster
Kershaw
Cheraw
Bennettsville

①
Hartsville

nnsboro
Camden

LUMBIA
②⓪
Florence
⑤⓪①
⑰

C A R O L I N A
Waterree R.
Stateburg
Sumter
Pee Dee R.
Myrtle Beach

ongaree R.
Lake
Marion
Kingstree
⑤②
Black R.
Brookgreen Gardens
Pawleys Island

Orangeburg
Lake
Moultrie
Georgetown
Santee R.

Bamberg
②⑥

ers Bridge
Summerville
Cooper R.
Ashley R.

⑨⑤
⑰
CHARLESTON

OCEAN

Beaufort
ST. HELENA I.
Parris Island Museum

N
W ⚜ E
S

HILTON HEAD I.

SAVANNAH

ATLANTIC

0   50 Mi.

Lynch, Jr., Arthur Middleton, and Thomas Heyward—signed the Declaration of Independence, and the state drafted its own constitution. When the British attacked Charleston in 1776, troops under General William Moultrie successfully defended the city. In 1778 a second state constitution was adopted, asserting South Carolina's independence from England.

South Carolina saw a great deal of military action during the Revolutionary War. (Edward McCrady, in his two-volume *History of South Carolina in the Revolution,* described 137 military engagements, ranging from skirmishes to battles.) The British and their Loyalist allies suffered several important defeats in South Carolina during the Revolution, two of which were at the Battle of Kings Mountain on October 7, 1780, and the Battle of Cowpens on January 17, 1781. After Patriots under General Horatio Gates were defeated at Camden on August 16–17, 1780, George Washington sent General Nathanael Greene to replace Gates as the southern commander. As important as these major battles was the bitter and brutal guerrilla warfare waged by soldiers and civilians alike. One of the American commanders, Light-Horse Harry Lee, was horrified by the carnage of "this unnatural war" (although he himself was responsible for torture and other atrocities). He urged Greene to impose martial law on South Carolina, believing that the people were worse than "the Goths & Vandals in their schemes of plunder murder & iniquity. All this under pretence of supporting the virtuous cause of America." Three of the most celebrated American leaders of the Revolution were guerrilla fighters, Andrew Pickens, Francis Marion ("the Swamp Fox"), and Thomas Sumter ("the Carolina Gamecock"). They harassed the British forces under Lord Cornwallis and were pursued through the countryside by Sir Banastre Tarleton, a bold commander in his early twenties. After Cornwallis quit North Carolina in the spring of 1781, Greene marched into South Carolina to drive the British out. In one of the final actions of the Revolution, the British, who had occupied Charleston in 1780, were forced to withdraw from the city in 1782. A compromise between low-country planters and the steadily increasing population of up-country settlers was achieved in 1786, when the state capital was moved from Charleston to a central location, a new city planned for the purpose, Columbia. The legislature met there for the first time in 1790.

OPPOSITE: *The Bradley House, built ca. 1800, was moved in the 1970s from the Camden outskirts to the city's Revolutionary War Park for preservation. The stone chimney was rebuilt on the site.*

Federal troops under General Quincy Gillmore during the seige of Charleston in

The main concerns of most South Carolinians prior to the Civil War were agriculture and getting crops to market. Rivers provided the major routes to Charleston, but shoals and rapids above the fall line left the up-country settlers with the need for an easier way to transport their cotton and other crops. So systems of locks and canals were proposed, and some were constructed between the Santee and the Cooper rivers. The passage they afforded was never entirely efficient; interruptions often were caused by unreliable river levels and the need for expensive repairs. The canals were replaced by the coming of the railroad to South Carolina. By 1833 the first rail line was complete between Charleston and Hamburg, a site across the Savannah River from Augusta, chosen to attract shipments of cotton that had previously been routed through Georgia's ports. The 136-mile rail line was the longest in the world at the time.

A Charleston-born architect, Robert Mills, was instrumental in the construction of canals in the 1820s and of many county courthouses and other public buildings between 1820 and 1835, when Mills served as the civil and military engineer of South Carolina. One

1863. This photograph was taken by the South Carolina partnership Haas & Peale.

of the first native-born and -educated American architects, appointed as federal architect by President Andrew Jackson in 1836, Mills served under seven successive presidents, designing the Washington Monument, the Washington Post Office, the U.S. Treasury Building, the Patent Office, and other federal buildings. South Carolina structures designed by Mills include the Maxcy Monument at the University of South Carolina (1827), the State Hospital for the Insane (1828), the "Fireproof Building" in Charleston, and nine county courthouses (Chester, Walterboro, Bennettsville, Greenville, Newberry, Williamsburg, Camden, Lancaster, and York).

With civic improvements in transporting crops to market came the controversy over tariffs levied on these goods. Though he began as a Federalist, John C. Calhoun became one of South Carolina's main advocates of states' rights. After President Andrew Jackson sent federal warships to "show the flag" in South Carolina waters in 1833, Calhoun urged South Carolina to secede from the Union if troops were landed to force compliance with a high tariff, and he proposed that its legislature nullify the tariff. South Carolina neither seceded nor nullified; Jackson prevailed, but the economic tensions between the northern industrial states and the southern planters remained.

On December 17, 1860, a convention met in Columbia's First Baptist Church and moved its session to Charleston the next day (it was thought that a smallpox epidemic in Columbia made it an unsafe place to continue). The convention delegates voted unanimously on December 20 to accept the Ordinance of Secession, and less than two months later other states joined South Carolina in forming the Confederate States of America. Although secession was widely approved by South Carolinians, a few thought it was folly to embark on a political course that would surely lead to war. One Unionist wrote to a friend in 1860 that "South Carolina is too small for a republic, but too large for an insane asylum."

On April 12, 1861, the Confederate attack on Fort Sumter in Charleston harbor marked the beginning of the Civil War. Prominent South Carolinians who became Confederate leaders during the subsequent four years include generals Wade Hampton III, Joseph Kershaw, David D. Wallace, Richard H. Anderson, and Stephen D. Lee. Also from South Carolina came members of Jefferson Davis's cabinet and staff. Blockade runners into the ports of Charleston and Wilmington provided the Confederacy with some vital supplies, and the Confederates maintained control of Fort Sumter until they abandoned Charleston in February 1865. Though few Civil War battles were fought on South Carolina soil, a great number of South Carolinians served elsewhere and lost their lives: The death toll may have been as high as one-fourth of the 44,000 South Carolinians who entered the war as soldiers.

Most of the destruction in South Carolina was caused by General William Tecumseh Sherman's march north from Savannah, Georgia, to Columbia, where he arrived on February 16, 1865. One of Sherman's soldiers wrote that their object was to make South Carolina "suffer worse than she did at the time of the Revolutionary War. We will let her know that it isn't so sweet to secede as she thought it would be." The strategy was successful: One South Carolinian wrote on February 28, 1865, "Our army is demoralized and the people panic stricken. . . . The power to do has left us . . . to fight longer seems to be madness." A Union soldier, before setting out for a day's march, wrote, "There is not a rail upon any of the roads within twenty miles . . . but will be twisted into corkscrews before the sun sets."

With the end of the Civil War came the end of slavery. The loss of the slave labor force coupled with the destruction of many farms by Federal troops during the war left some areas of South Carolina on the verge of starvation. At the same time, blacks were insisting on their rights to work for fair wages and to own land. In 1867 a Republican state convention in Charleston called for an integrated public school system, state aid to the poor and elderly, the protection of small farms from foreclosure for debts, and a heavy tax on uncultivated land to force the breakup of large holdings and the distribution of the lands to the poor. Alarmed at the prospect of such reforms and at the determination of blacks that their rights be respected, many South Carolinians of all classes joined the Ku Klux Klan. Nowhere in the South was the Klan stronger than in the up-country region of South Carolina, where some of the worst outrages were perpetrated against blacks and white Republicans. In January 1871, 500 Klansmen attacked the Union County jail and lynched eight black prisoners. In response to this and other crimes, President Ulysses S. Grant declared nine South Carolina counties to be in "a condition of lawlessness"; he suspended the writ of habeas corpus and sent in federal troops to arrest Klansmen. Hundreds were arrested. Vigorous prosecution by the attorney general resulted in the imprisonment of a few dozen Klan leaders; perhaps as many as 2,000 Klansmen fled the state.

Economic recovery was slowed in the late 1860s by a collapse in cotton prices and by widespread corruption in state government. In particular, politicians were able to divert public funds earmarked for the construction of railroads. When the railroads were finally built and cotton prices began to rise in the 1870s, up-country cotton planters, mostly whites, began to feel some prosperity, but it was short-lived. Agriculture stagnated until about 1900. The manufacture of textiles became increasingly important to the state's economy. The boll weevil infestation of the 1920s dealt a hard blow to cotton, and the Depression set back manufacturing; but the economy revived during and after World War II. Reflecting the trials South Carolina has endured and overcome, the state's motto strikes the theme of perseverance: *Dum spiro spero*—"While I breathe, I hope."

This chapter is divided into three sections, covering the state's up-country, midlands, and coast. A subsequent chapter describes its greatest city, Charleston.

THE UP-COUNTRY

After 1725 or so, South Carolina's up-country was its frontier region. Poorly connected with the coast by narrow Indian trails and swampy rivers, some with treacherous rapids, the up-country at the edge of the Blue Ridge Mountains had little contact and little in common with the low-country around Charleston and the South Carolina coast. A region predominantly settled by small farmers, the up-country early developed its own independent personality.

This section on the up-country begins along the northern edge of the state with the military parks in York and Cherokee counties and extends west through the mountainous counties of Spartanburg, Greenville, Pickens, Oconee, and Anderson. The up-country region includes a seven-county northeastern section known as the Olde English District of York, Union, Fairfield, Chester, Lancaster, Kershaw, and Chesterfield counties, as well as the six-county northwestern district once called Ninety Six.

CHERAW

Established in the 1760s, Cheraw was named for a local Indian tribe. As the Great Pee Dee River became heavily traveled in the 1820s, the town grew as a commercial center. The thirteen-acre **Cheraw Historic District** contains more than fifty antebellum residential and public buildings, including frame or brick Greek Revival houses on tree-lined streets. Local residents explain the number of trees by referring to an old town law concerning public intoxication, which imposed the penalty of transplanting a tree from the woods to town. On the Town Green are the 1858 **Town Hall** and the 1836 **Market Hall** in which crops were sold on the first floor and court was held on the second. The 1825 **Lyceum,** which served many functions from Civil War telegraph office to town library, now houses a town museum (803–537–7692). Several blocks away is **Old Saint David's Episcopal Church** (100 Church Street); built in the early 1770s, it is one of South Carolina's few pre-Revolutionary-War churches.

In the town of **Lancaster,** the **Lancaster County Courthouse** (104 Main Street), constructed in 1828 and designed by Robert Mills, shows the typical influence of Jeffersonian Classicism: a four-columned portico with a fanlighted pediment on a high base with a lower arched entrance. Mills also designed the **Lancaster County Jail** (208 West Gay Street), built in 1823.

Between Lancaster and Rock Hill Route 21, in the **Landsford Canal State Park,** are the ruins of a canal built in the early 1820s on the Catawba–Wateree Rivers to allow barges safe passage to and from the South Carolina coast. Trails along a section of the canal parallel to the Catawba River pass three stone locks. An interpretive center is housed in the only remaining lockkeeper's house in the state.

CAMDEN

The oldest inland city in South Carolina, founded in 1733, Camden developed from a trading community at the head of navigation on the Wateree River. The store of Yorkshire native Joseph Kershaw was the nucleus of the village, which he named in honor of Lord Camden, a Parliamentary champion of colonial rights. Camden was the setting of two important Revolutionary War battles (highway markers designate the sites). The Battle of Camden (August 1780)

The 1777 Kershaw-Cornwallis House, originally the home of Camden's founder, Joseph Kershaw, was a casualty of the Union occupation of Camden in 1865. It has been reconstructed using archaeological and documentary evidence.

followed British occupation of the town in June. Lord Cornwallis, who had taken Joseph Kershaw's new mansion as British headquarters, dealt the American forces under General Horatio Gates a devastating defeat. Mortally wounded was Baron Johann de Kalb, a German nobleman who served as a major general of the Patriot forces. In the waning days of their occupation, the British were again victorious at the Battle of Hobkirk's Hill (April 1781). The American general Nathanael Greene had hoped to take the town (by then fortified by the British), but his forces were routed in a surprise attack by enemy forces under Lord Francis Rawdon-Hastings. George Washington visited Camden during his presidential tour in 1791. Another distinguished visitor was the marquis de Lafayette, who in 1825 officiated at the reinterment of Baron de Kalb's remains under a **monument** designed by the noted architect Robert Mills. Mills was also the architect of **Bethesda Presbyterian Church** (502 DeKalb Street), built in 1820, before which the de Kalb memorial stands.

During the Civil War Camden provided a rail terminal, a storehouse, and a hospital for the Confederate cause. Among the surgeons was Dr. George R. Todd, a brother of Mary Todd Lincoln. A staunch Confederate, he married a local woman and lies buried in Camden's **Quaker Cemetery** on Campbell Street. In addition, Kershaw County sent many men into the Confederate army, including six with the rank of general. Sherman's troops burned much of Camden in February 1865; lost at this time was the historic Joseph Kershaw mansion, by then known as the Cornwallis House.

The ninety-two-acre **Revolutionary War Park** (north of Route I-20, on South Broad Street/Route 521, 803–432–9841) is the site of the early town of Camden. Authentic restorations of the British fortifications are ongoing, including earthen breastworks and palisade walls. A reproduction of the Kershaw-Cornwallis house stands on its original foundations, and smaller houses of the eighteenth and nineteenth centuries have been moved to the site and serve as museums. The collection of the **Camden Archives and Museum** (1314 Broad Street, 803–432–3242) includes books, newspapers, original clockworks (ca. 1825), and exhibits relating to the town's history. The major portion, however, is the Genealogy section. The South Carolina Daughters of the American Revolution and the Colonial Dames seventeenth-century collections are also on exhibit.

WINNSBORO

The **Winnsboro Historic District,** roughly bounded by Gooding, Buchanan, Garden, and Fairfield streets, contains structures characteristic of an up-country town. The **Town Clock,** located in the Market House, has works that were shipped from France and hauled by ox cart from Charleston. It has kept time since 1833. Across the street, the **Fairfield County Courthouse** (Congress Street), built in 1823 from ballast brick, was designed by Robert Mills. In February 1865 Sherman's soldiers burned part of the village. The **Fairfield County Museum** (231 South Congress Street, 803–635–9811) is in the restored 1830 Cathcart-Ketchin house. Its exhibits include period furniture, a collection of textiles, kitchen implements, farm tools, and Indian and military artifacts.

CHESTER

Pennsylvania settlers founded Chester in the 1750s as a marketplace for the region. It was an important center of rail transport during the Civil War. The **Chester Historic District** is the downtown commercial area around the central public square, which includes nineteenth-century Greek Revival residences and Italianate commercial blocks. The **Chester City Hall** (West End and Columbia streets) is a notable focal point of the commercial district. Local citizens point to the rock at 103 Main Street as the one that Aaron Burr used in 1807 as a speaker's soapbox; while en route to Richmond, Virginia, to be tried for treason, Burr briefly escaped the grip of his captors and appealed to the citizens of Chester to rescue him. The **Chester County Historical Society Museum** (McAlily Street, 803–377–1991) displays local historical artifacts, including Indian relics and items from the Revolutionary and Civil wars. It occupies the 1914 jail building.

ROSE HILL PLANTATION STATE PARK

Owned by Governor William H. Gist in the early nineteenth century, this cotton plantation, named for its landscaped rose garden, is now a state park. Gist was the so-called Secession Governor, who presided over the state's break with the federal government. The centerpiece of the park, the Federal-style house of stuccoed brick, has fanlights, carved doors, a spiral staircase, and ca. 1860s furnishings. The sepa-

rate kitchen is occasionally the site of demonstrations of nineteenth-century cookery.

LOCATION: 8 miles south of Union on Sardis Road. HOURS: *Park:* 9–6 Thursday–Monday. *House:* 1–4 Saturday–Sunday. FEE: Yes. TELE-PHONE: 803-427-5966.

UNION

Union began as a twenty-block plat in 1787 called Unionville, after the Union Church east of the town, where Episcopal and Presbyterian congregations met together. Named the county seat in 1800, Union grew as a crossroads between the Broad and Tiger rivers. Of interest are the **Judge Thomas Dawkins House** (Dawkins Court, private), where state officials gathered to escape Federal forces as General William Tecumseh Sherman made his march from Savannah to Columbia. The **Union County Jail** (West Main Street) is the granite two-story design of Robert Mills, completed in 1823 during his tenure as the state engineer for public works. The front triple arches and twenty-one-inch-thick walls of locally quarried stone are distinguishing features of this building, reputed to be the state's oldest jail still in use. The **Episcopal Church of the Nativity** (Church and Pinckney streets), an excellent example of Gothic Revival ecclesiastical architecture, has stained-glass lancet windows and a marble baptismal font sculpted by Hiram Powers. The eclectic **Jeter-Sarratt House** (203 Thompson Boulevard, private), built around 1859, was the home of South Carolina statesman and governor Thomas B. Jeter. The **Union County Historical Museum** (American Federal Building, East Main and South Church streets, 803-427-9446) has regional artifacts dating to the 1730s.

BRATTONSVILLE

This land was first settled in the 1770s, by Colonel William Bratton, a local militia commander in the Revolutionary forces. On July 11, 1780, Captain Christian Huck's force of Tories and British soldiers looted Bratton's house and threatened his wife. The Loyalists camped about a mile from Bratton's house, at James Williamson's

OPPOSITE: *The parlor at Rose Hill, the nineteenth-century plantation of Governor William Henry Gist, contains period furnishings similar to those mentioned in family papers and estate inventories.*

plantation; they were awakened at daybreak by Patriot troops whose commanders included Colonel Bratton. Huck was killed in the battle, which bolstered Patriot morale as one of the first American militia victories over the British cavalry. Local patriots became more willing than ever to join in resisting the British at Kings Mountain on October 7, 1780, and at Cowpens in January 1781.

Historic Brattonsville District

This complex of restored eighteenth- and nineteenth-century structures occupies the site of three houses and a number of accompanying outbuildings developed by the Bratton family between 1776 and 1870. The buildings include Colonel Bratton's clapboard log house (ca. 1776), the Homestead (ca. 1830), and the Jeffersonian Classical "Bricks" (ca. 1845). First owned by Colonel William Bratton, then by his son, Dr. James Simpson Bratton, the village is on the site of a plantation where over 180 people once lived. The restored site illustrates lifestyles of the South Carolina Piedmont from 1750 to 1860.

LOCATION: Brattonsville Road, northeast of McConnells. HOURS: 10–4 Tuesday and Thursday, 2–5 Saturday–Sunday. FEE: Yes. TELEPHONE: 803–684–2327.

YORK

Settled by Scotch-Irish, Scots, English, and Germans from 1750 through the 1780s, York County was a community of small farmers. The town of York was established as the county seat in 1785. The **York Historic District,** one of the largest in the state, includes more than seventy structures. By the 1840s the town's 800 residents had one of the highest rates of per capita income in the nation. York was also a popular summer resort for planters from the coast.

After the Civil War, York County was one of the strongholds of the Ku Klux Klan. According to the historian Eric Foner, "Nearly the entire white male population [of the county] joined the Klan, and committed at least eleven murders and hundreds of whippings." Sixty black families fled the county to settle in Liberia, Africa. During the federal crackdown on the Klan in the 1870s, many members were confined in the county jail, now known as the **Wilson House** (3 South Congress Street, private).

KINGS MOUNTAIN NATIONAL
MILITARY PARK

Covering almost 4,000 acres, this park includes the site of one of the bitterest battles of the Revolution. On October 7, 1780, a Tory militia force of over 1,000 men commanded by Major Patrick Ferguson was surrounded here by about 900 Patriots. Despite common references to the "British" involved in this battle, the Scottish leader Patrick Ferguson was the only British soldier present. The Tory troops were all Americans.

Ferguson's Tories used the traditional British tactics of bayonet charges and firing volleys from formation. The Patriots fought in the backcountry manner, firing from behind trees and giving ground when the Tories charged. Ferguson's conventional tactics cost him the battle and his own life. About 225 Tories were killed, but only 28 of the Patriots lost their lives. The victory was not an entirely honorable one for the Patriots—on the spot they killed some of the prisoners and the wounded, left other wounded to die of thirst, and later hanged nine of their captured Loyalist countrymen.

Within the Kings Mountain State Park Living History Farm is a mule-drawn cotton gin from Lexington County, built in the 1840s. The building now houses a collection of historic farm implements.

The park's visitor center has a film, diorama, and other exhibits illustrating the battle strategies that marked this turning point of the Revolutionary War. The Battle of Kings Mountain was a significant American victory because it decreased the size of Cornwallis's army and convinced him to alter his plans for North Carolina. It was the first major defeat in a series of battles that led to the final American victory at Yorktown. Interpretive markers cover the battlefield.

LOCATION: Off Route 85, just south of the state line. HOURS: June through September: 9–6 Daily; October through May: 9–5 Daily. FEE: None. TELEPHONE: 803–936–7921.

KINGS MOUNTAIN STATE PARK

Adjacent to the Kings Mountain National Military Park, this 6,141-acre park has a living-history farm that demonstrates life during the mid-nineteenth century. The 1850s homestead features a two-story log house, barn, smokehouse, corn crib, cotton gin, and other structures that have been relocated here from sites in the South Carolina Piedmont or constructed by park staff using the materials and style of the region. Though the park was once the site of a farm, none of the buildings is original to the site.

LOCATION: Route 161, approximately 12 miles northwest of York. HOURS: June through September: 7 AM–9 PM Daily; October through May: 7–6 Saturday–Sunday. FEE: Yes. TELEPHONE: 803–222–3209.

COWPENS NATIONAL BATTLEFIELD

This National Revolutionary War park honors patriots who fought at the Battle of Cowpens under General Daniel Morgan, leader of the American victory here, and Loyalists in the ranks of their antagonists, who fought under Sir Banastre Tarleton on January 17, 1781, a date celebrated annually here. The area called Hannah's Cowpens was an elevated open pasture used for wintering cattle. The meadow gradually rises to seventy feet above the surrounding forest, and the landscape has been preserved and marked effectively so that a visitor can grasp General Morgan's strategic use of the terrain. Morgan's excellent group of officers included John Eager Howard, William Washington, and Andrew Pickens. They positioned several lines of riflemen at different elevations and instructed them to fire

This painting by William Ranney shows cavalry action between American Colonel William Washington and British commander Colonel Banastre Tarleton during the decisive American victory at the Battle of Cowpens on January 17, 1791. (detail)

only one or two shots but to make those shots count, and then to withdraw to the rear and stand in reserve. These tactics were extremely successful against Tarleton's troops, who charged head-long into the firing, one line after another, until finally the reserve cavalrymen refused to follow. British fatalities numbered about 100, and over 800 were captured. Estimates say that 12 Americans lost their lives and 60 were injured. The victory was particularly important to the Americans, who had suffered a sound defeat at the Battle of Camden on August 16, 1780.

The original one-and-one-quarter-acre Cowpens National Battlefield site has been enlarged to 845 acres. The park features exhibits and an audio·trail, as well as a restored 1830 cabin.

LOCATION: Approximately 20 miles west of Kings Mountain, 2 miles southeast of Chesnee at the intersection of Routes 11 and 110. HOURS: *Visitor Center:* 9–5 Daily; *Battlefield:* October through April: 9–5 Daily; May through September: 8:30–8:30 Daily. FEE: None. TELEPHONE: 803–461–2828.

SPARTANBURG

Settlements have been in the Spartanburg area since the 1760s, and the state's first ironworks opened within five miles of the town site in 1773. In 1785 the county and county seat were named for the South Carolina militia called the Spartan Regiment, formed here in 1776 and victorious in the Battle of Cowpens in 1781. Spartanburg was incorporated in 1831, and by 1859 the railroad reached it, providing vital shipping for the town's textile mills and other goods. The centennial celebration in 1881 of the Battle of Cowpens included the dedication of the **monument** to Cowpens commander General Daniel Morgan on the courthouse square, thereafter Morgan Square. Two college campuses in the area have been recognized as historic districts. **Wofford College** (North Church Street, 803–585–4821) was founded in 1854 with a $100,000 bequest from a local Methodist minister, the Reverend Benjamin Wofford. **Converse College** (580 East Main Street, 803–596–9000), founded in 1889 as an independent college for women, features nine brick buildings built between 1891 and 1915. Pell Hall, the oldest, built in 1891, combines Gothic Revival with Neoclassical Revival architectural styles. The area's history is the focus of the **Regional Museum of Spartanburg County** (501 Otis Boulevard, adjacent to the public library, 803–596–3501), whose exhibits include maps, dolls, and historic photographs.

Around 1795 Thomas Price, a slave-holding farmer who ran a general store, a post office, and a boardinghouse for stagecoach travelers, built a house on his 2,000-acre plantation. The **Price House** (1200 Oak View Farms Road, 803–476–2483) is of unusual design for this part of South Carolina, employing Flemish bond construction with bricks made on the site, with a steep Dutch gambrel roof and interior end chimneys.

The **Jammie Seay House** (106 Darby Road, 803–576–6546), built around 1790 for a Revolutionary War soldier, stands on its original site and is believed to be the oldest house in Spartanburg. The single-story, L-shaped log building is covered with vertical siding and clapboards on the ell. It has an exterior end chimney built of fieldstone, a type common in Virginia but rarely found in upstate South Carolina. The house, owned by family members until 1974, has original furnishings and period pieces predating 1820.

LAURENS

The seat of Laurens County was named for the Revolutionary War statesman Henry Laurens. The county was formed in 1783, one of six created from the Old Ninety Six District. The Greek Revival **Laurens County Courthouse,** a gray stone structure with a Corinthian portico, was constructed in 1838 and remodeled in 1911 and 1940. The seventeenth president, Andrew Johnson, once ran a tailor shop on the north side of the courthouse square. The **Octagon House** (619 East Main Street, private) was built in 1859 in an octagonal design with four porches, each with four octagonal columns; a two-story central hall with a curving stair is lighted by a central skylight, and the house has a pyramidal roof. It is undergoing restoration and will be opened as a museum. The **James Dunklin House** (544 West Main Street, 803–984–7219) is a typical example of up-country architecture, built in 1812 as a frame two-story house with Federal elements; it is furnished with southern antiques. Also on Main Street is the Greek Revival **William Dunlap Simpson House** (726 West Main Street, private), built in 1839, perhaps with the aid of a pattern book. Simpson served South Carolina as a state congressman, senator, governor, and state supreme court chief justice.

EDGEFIELD

Settled in the 1760s, this community saw much commercial growth by the 1780s and became the seat of Edgefield County in 1791. The county was the home of ten South Carolina governors, five lieutenant governors, and a number of U.S. representatives and senators. The **Edgefield Historic District,** on both sides of Route 25 through downtown, preserves the site of the original town, which was organized around the village green and courthouse square. The district contains forty nineteenth-century buildings, mostly residences. Confederate General Martin Witherspoon Gary lived at **Oakley Park** (300 Columbia Road, 803–637–6576) after the Civil War. The house, built in 1835 by Daniel Byrd, a descendant of the Byrds of Virginia, features carved mantels, chandeliers, ceiling medallions, portraits, decorative arts, and some family furnishings. **Magnolia Dale** (320 Norris Street, 803–637–5652), surrounded by magnolia trees over 100 years old, displays Edgefield County regional artifacts. The **Pottersville Museum** (just north of Edgefield on

Route 25, 803–637–3333), housed in a kitchen building built in 1810, displays a rare collection of locally made late-eighteenth- to mid-nineteenth-century stoneware pottery.

NINETY SIX NATIONAL HISTORIC SITE

The trading post established here in 1730 was named Ninety Six for the estimated ninety-six miles separating the site and the Cherokee trading post at Keowee, at the end of the Cherokee Path. The town, founded in 1769, became an important Loyalist stronghold. Located southeast of Ninety Six on Route 248 are the extensive ruins of the original settlement and fort at Ninety Six. The fort, the strongest inland fort in South Carolina, was the site in 1775 of the first Revolutionary War land battle fought in the South and the site of the Continental army's longest siege of the war. Major Patrick Ferguson mustered a force of 4,000 Loyalists here in the summer of 1780. Also that summer, the British and Loyalists built a stockade around Ninety Six, constructed the earthen Star Fort, and built a stockade fort at the west side of the village. Loyalist Colonel John Harris Cruger was the commanding officer at Ninety Six when General Nathanael Greene led nearly 1,000 Patriots in the twenty-eight-day siege of the Loyalist stronghold, beginning May 21, 1781. Though Greene's losses were twice those suffered by Cruger, Patriot forces cut off the Tory water supply, and fire arrows caused a great deal of damage. The assault resulted in the British abandonment of their last backcountry fort.

The site is well preserved because the village moved about two miles north when the railroad came through in 1855. A visitor center has exhibits and information about occurrences at the site.

LOCATION: Route 248. HOURS: 8–5 Daily. FEE: None. TELEPHONE: 803–543–4068.

ABBEVILLE

French Huguenot settlers founded this town in 1785. It became an early up-country center of commerce, agriculture, and culture. The **Abbeville Historic District** includes many nineteenth-century houses

OPPOSITE: *The stockade fort on the west side of Ninety Six was constructed to secure Spring Branch, the settlement's only reliable source of water.*

in architectural styles ranging from Greek Revival to Victorian, brick-paved streets, watering troughs, and the town fire bell. The three-story brick **Opera House** (Court Square), with an elaborate entrance and an auditorium with a three-tiered balcony, is one of the few opera houses remaining in the state.The **Episcopal Trinity Church** (Church Street), is a good example of Gothic Revival architecture with a tower, buttresses, and an arched entrance. Designed by George E. Walker and consecrated in 1860, it features fine hand-carved interior woodwork. The grounds contain two gardens laid out in the 1860s, including an intricate boxwood garden.

The **Burt-Stark House Museum** (306 North Main Street, 803–459–4297), built about 1840, was the home of Major Armistead Burt when Jefferson Davis came through Abbeville on his flight from Richmond at the end of the Civil War. It was the site of the final meeting of the Confederate Council of War on May 2, 1865. The **Abbeville County Museum** (215 Polar Street, 803–459–2740) displays a collection of local historical items in the three-story county jail building (ca. 1853). Prisoners' graffiti can still be seen on the third-floor walls. A log cabin is also on the property.

PENDLETON

Named for Judge Henry Pendleton, who strongly advocated up-country representation in state government, the town of Pendleton was established in 1790 as the seat of the Pendleton District, which once included the present counties of Anderson, Pickens, and Oconee. It was the first South Carolina town organized north of Camden. Located in the Blue Ridge Mountain foothills, at the inter-section of the Cherokee Path to the low-country and the Catawba Path to Virginia, Pendleton offered an active trade center as well as an attractive climate to low-country planters.

The **Pendleton Historical District** is a large area of more than fifty public and private eighteenth- and nineteenth-century build-ings, many bordering the village green. Architectural styles reflect building practices from Charleston and the mid-Atlantic region. Notable structures include the 1826 **Farmers' Society Hall,** the **Elam Sharpe House** (1802), and the **Old Stone Church** (1802). Centrally located in the business district is **Hunter's Store** (125 East Queen Street, 803–646–3782), built around 1850, which houses a local his-tory and genealogical library, exhibits, an arts-and-crafts center, and the visitor center for the district.

Pendleton's Old Stone Church, originally called the Stone Meeting House, was constructed in 1802 to replace a log Presbyterian church that had burned.

Lowther Hall (161 East Queen Street, private) is the oldest residence in Pendleton. It was built in the 1790s by a pioneer settler, Dr. William Hunter, who sold the property in 1815 to the trustees of William, Viscount Lowther, for $10,000. In 1838 one of Lowther's trustees sold the estate, where Lowther had never resided, for $100. It has since served as a Masonic hall and private residence. The **Elam Sharpe House** (229 East Queen Street, private), a typical up-country townhouse, has two stories with a center hallway and one room on either side on each level. It has hand-sawn exposed overbeams, original mantels and fireplaces, and a curved staircase in the central hall. Elam Sharpe was a prominent Pendleton citizen whose name appears frequently in early town documents.

The original meeting place for the Pendleton Farmers' Society was the **First Farmers Hall** (106 West Queen Street, private), built in 1819. On the same street is **Marshalsea** (112 West Queen Street, private), named in 1919 by Mrs. W. W. Simmons after a prison that Charles Dickens described in his novel *Little Dorritt*. The building, which was also once a female academy, was constructed as the district jail in the 1820s, after there was an outcry over the presence of the jail on the village green, where citizens could hear obscenities shouted by its inmates. The design of the structure is attributed to Robert Mills.

The **Pendleton Farmers' Society Hall** at the southern end of the village green is the oldest farmers' hall in continuous use in America. The society is the third one to have been established in the nation. Its former members include a vice president of the United States, John C. Calhoun, and Calhoun's son-in-law, the founder of Clemson University, Thomas Green Clemson. Begun in 1826 as the courthouse for the Pendleton District, the building was purchased that year by the Farmers' Society, formed in 1815. The hall was sufficiently complete for meetings by 1830; columns were added in front in 1848. It is built of brick covered with white plaster, a common up-country construction method.

Ashtabula (Route 88, 803–646–3847), built in the mid-1820s, is an excellent example of lowland plantation architecture brought to the up-country by settlers from Charleston. Named with an Indian word meaning "fish river," the plantation, built by Lewis Ladson Gibbes, is well restored and open as a museum. Its nine rooms and two great halls contain antique furnishings from several periods.

Woodburn

Several prominent members of South Carolinian's Pinckney family were named Charles Cotesworth Pinckney. One, born in 1789, was the builder of this early-nineteenth-century Greek Revival plantation house built ca. 1830. This Charles Cotesworth Pinckney, the son of the state's governor, Thomas Pinckney, who was also a Federalist vice presidential candidate in 1796, served as a South Carolina lieutenant governor and a member of the Nullification Convention of 1832. He was named for his uncle, who was an author of the U.S. Constitution and an unsuccessful presidential candidate against Thomas Jefferson and James Madison. The house has been restored, with eighteen rooms on four levels open as a museum.

LOCATION: Route 76 west of Pendleton. HOURS: April through October: 2–6 Sunday, and by appointment. FEE: Yes. TELEPHONE: 803–646–3655.

The **Pendleton District Agricultural Museum** (adjacent to Woodburn Plantation, 803–646–3782) displays antique (pre-1925) farm equipment, a cotton gin older than Eli Whitney's invention, a replica of a McCormick reaper, an 1876 thresher, a corn husker, and hand tools.

On Route 76 between Pendleton and Clemson is the **Old Stone Church,** begun in 1797 and completed in 1802. Buried in the cemetery are the first church elders, Generals Andrew Pickens and Robert Anderson, and Major Thomas Dickson, as well as English newspaperman Printer John Miller and other prominent citizens.

CLEMSON

The town of Clemson grew up around the land-grant campus of Clemson College, now **Clemson University** (803–656–4789). Founded in 1889 and named for Thomas Green Clemson, the agricultural college is located on the former plantation of the South Carolina statesman John C. Calhoun. On campus is **Fort Hill** (803–656–2475), built in 1803 by the pastor of the Old Stone Church, Dr. James McElhenny. From 1825 to 1850, it was the home of John C. Calhoun, vice president, secretary of war, senator, and a leading advocate of nullification in the 1828–1832 controversy. Calhoun's daughter, Anna Maria, married Thomas Green Clemson, who inherited the estate and bequeathed it for the establishment of Clemson Agricultural College. The frame two-story residence with three Doric-columned piazzas has fourteen rooms, many furnished with family heirlooms, including a mahogany sideboard made of panelling from the officers' quarters of the frigate *Constitution*, a separate kitchen, a restored springhouse, and an office and library on the south lawn. Also on the Clemson campus is **Hanover House** (803–656–2241), a museum house built before 1716 by a French Huguenot, Paul de St. Julien. The frame one-and-a-half-story residence has a gambrel roof, large exterior end chimneys, pedimented dormers, and fine interior panelling. It was dismantled, moved from Berkeley County near Moncks Corner in 1940, when the Santee-Cooper Dam was planned, and reassembled on campus.

SENECA

This town was founded in 1873 at the junction of the Blue Ridge Railroad and the Atlanta & Richmond Air Line Railway. The **Seneca Historic District** includes three churches and many residences featuring a wide variety of late-nineteenth- and early-twentieth-century architectural styles, reflecting the town's changing tastes. The large bungalow-style house built in 1909 by Dr. William J. Lunney and his wife, Lillian Mason Lunney, is now the **Lunney Museum** (211 West South First Street, 803–882–4811). It displays Victorian furniture, period costumes, and artifacts from Oconee County.

PICKENS

The county and county seat are named for Revolutionary War hero General Andrew Pickens, the great up-country leader. In the restored Gothic Revival **Pickens County Gaol** (Johnson and Pendleton streets, 803–878–7847) of 1903 is the **Pickens County Historical Museum,** with memorabilia from Pickens and exhibited artifacts depicting the history of the county. The second floor holds the **Pickens County Art Museum,** featuring exhibitions of the works of contemporary upstate South Carolina artists.

At 104 North Lewis Street is the **Irma Morris Museum of Fine Arts,** a collection of paintings and furniture housed in the **Hagood-**

The Walnut Grove Plantation house and its outbuildings are shaded by walnut trees planted nearly 200 years ago.

Mauldin House, one of the city's historic buildings. About three miles northwest of Pickens is the restored **Hagood Mill** (Route 178, 803–878–3207), a good example of up-country pioneer functional design. Built by James E. Hagood in 1825, the mill remained in his family until 1971 and is still in working order.

WALNUT GROVE PLANTATION

The Moore family plantation was built by Charles Moore around 1765 on a royal land grant. The house was also the home of Moore's daughter Margaret Katherine (Kate) Moore Barry, a Revolutionary War heroine who, the story is told, tied her young daughter Katie to a bedpost while she spread the word that Tarleton's Tory force was approaching. Around 1800 Kate Moore Barry planted the walnut trees that give the plantation its name. The two-story log house with clapboards is restored and authentically furnished. This early example of an up-country plantation complex also has a number of outbuildings, including a 1777 kitchen, barn, smokehouse, and well house, in addition to the Rocky Spring Academy (the first school in the area), and the office of Dr. Andrew Barry, the first physician in the county.

> LOCATION: 8 miles southeast of Spartanburg, near the intersection of Routes I-26 and 221. HOURS: April through October: 11–5 Tuesday–Saturday, 2–5 Sunday; November through March: 2–5 Sunday. FEE: Yes. TELEPHONE: 803–576–6546.

Poinsett Bridge (off Route 25 on Saluda Road), one of the oldest stone bridges in the state, is located north of Greenville. Built about 1820, it has a design attributed to Robert Mills. It was once part of the original state road connecting Greenville and Asheville, which was designed by South Carolina's director of public works, Joel Poinsett—hence, the name of the bridge. Poinsett introduced in the state a variety of flower he discovered while ambassador to Mexico: the poinsettia, which was named for him.

North of Greenville is **Gilreath's Mill** (four miles northwest of Greer on Route 101). Built around 1839 beside Shoal Creek, the frame mill structure retains its massive waterwheel and corn-grinding machinery, including two 250-pound millstones. South of Greenville is the

Fairview Presbyterian Church (Route 55, off Route I-385), whose congregation was organized in 1787. Built in 1857, the present church has family pews, a slave gallery, and unusual tombstones.

GREENVILLE

A 1777 treaty with the Cherokee gave whites access to the land in the Blue Ridge foothills. Prior to the treaty, the first white trader to settle here, about 1770, was Richard Pearis, who had a Cherokee wife in addition to a white family. Pearis accumulated land amounting to twelve square miles—the land on which the city was founded. After the Revolution, Pearis, a Loyalist, moved to the Bahamas on an English pension. Colonel Lemuel J. Alston acquired much of the Pearis plantation and laid out a village in 1797. When Alston sold his property in 1815 to Vardry McBee, McBee soon became known as the city's "father" because he actively began development of the area as a resort for low-country plantation owners: He opened a resort hotel, donated lands for four churches, built one of the first cotton mills alongside the Reedy River, and arranged for the railroad to come through the city. When the architect Robert Mills visited in 1825, he commented, "so much wealth, intelligence, and leisure are collected annually" here that he "anticipated a favorable result to the interior of the state." The country of "Greeneville," named in honor of Revolutionary hero Nathanael Greene, was established in 1786; the village was officially chartered as "Greenville" in 1831. In antebellum times Benjamin F. Perry led a strong contingent of Union sympathizers here. No Civil War battles were waged in this region, which lay outside of Sherman's path. Textile production flourished here after Reconstruction, and the area is still known for the beauty of its Blue Ridge foothills. The **Greenville County Museum of Art** (420 College Street, 803–271–7570) houses the world's largest collection of Andrew Wyeth's paintings outside of his own holdings. Featuring American artists from the colonial period to the present, and focusing on southern artists, the collection includes works by Washington Allston, George P. A. Healy, Georgia O'Keeffe, and Jasper Johns.

Located just outside the **Reedy River Falls Historic Park,** the site where the town was founded, is **Falls Cottage** (615 South Main Street), a nineteenth-century structure believed to have been the home of a working-class family. It was restored in 1977. The **John Wesley United Methodist Church** (101 East Court Street), organized by a former slave, the Reverend James R. Rosemond, was one of the state's first separate black congregations after the Civil War.

Andrew Wyeth's 1975 painting in tempera, The Quaker, *on display at the Greenville County Museum of Art.*

Built by a wealthy cotton planter, Josiah Kilgore, in about 1838, the **Kilgore-Lewis House** (560 North Academy at North Church Street, 803–232–3020) is one of the few remaining antebellum buildings in Greenville. A frame house with Greek Revival elements, it has hand-blown glass windows, wooden-peg construction, and copper roofing, and it serves as the headquarters for the Greenville Council of Garden Clubs. Nearby is **Christ Episcopal Church** (10 North Church Street), which began as the Saint James mission in 1820. The present church was constructed between 1852 and 1854. The red-brick building has Gothic Revival features: a square tower with buttresses and an octagonal belfry and tower with multiarched lancet windows over the main entrance. In the adjoining churchyard are buried former South Carolina governor Benjamin Franklin Perry, Confederate soldiers, and many local officials.

Whitehall (310 West Earle Street, private) is Greenville's oldest residence, built in 1813. It was constructed as the summer home of former South Carolina governor Henry Middleton, who served at another time as ambassador to Russia. His father, Arthur Middleton, was a signer of the Declaration of Independence. The **Bob Jones University Art Gallery and Museum** (1700 Wade Hampton Boulevard, 803–242–5100) has an important international collection of religious art, dating from the thirteenth to the nineteenth century, from Spain, Italy, France, Germany, and Holland, featuring works by Dolci, Rembrandt, Rubens, Titian, and Van Dyck.

In the town of **Conestee** is the **McBee Methodist Church Chapel** (Main Street), one of few octagonal churches remaining in America. The brick one-story structure with a pyramidal roof and an octagonal cupola was built around 1841.

T H E   M I D L A N D S

South Carolina was originally divided along the fall line stretching diagonally across the state from Aiken in the southwest to Cheraw in the northeast. The fall line thus divided the "civilized" low-country, including Charleston, from the "uncivilized" up-country north and west. Eventually the region that was not close enough to the mountains to be considered part of the up-country but too far north of Charleston to be claimed by the low-country began to be designated as the midlands. This tour begins in the capital city of Columbia and moves southwest toward Aiken and then southeast through the counties of Aiken, Barnwell, Allendale, and Bamberg. From there, it swings north to cover the midlands area south of Columbia and then turns northeast to the Pee Dee River country near Florence.

COLUMBIA

In 1786 the South Carolina legislature voted to establish a capital city near the geographic center of the state, where the Broad and Saluda rivers converge to become the Congaree River. The decision to move the seat of government from Charleston to the new site represented a compromise between up-country farmers and low-country planters.

OPPOSITE: *Columbia's First Presbyterian Church where Woodrow Wilson's father served as minister from 1870–1874, and where his parents are buried.*

The planned city was surveyed in 1787 on a two-mile-square plot. By laying out all streets 100 feet wide and main thoroughfares 150 feet wide, the planners created a spacious town where, they hoped, diseases would not spread rapidly from house to house. The city was named after Christopher Columbus.

James Hoban, later the architect of the White House, designed the first state house, where the South Carolina General Assembly met in 1790. When George Washington visited there in 1791, he described Columbia in his journal as "an uncleared wood with very few houses in it." Just west of the present State House, a granite **monument** marks the site of the first structure. The textile industry and other businesses were active in Columbia by the early 1800s. In 1801 the University of South Carolina (then South Carolina College) was chartered. The population grew and the economy thrived through the 1830s. A convention was held in Columbia at the First Baptist Church on December 17, 1860, to draw up the South Carolina Ordinance of Secession. The document was completed and signed in Charleston on December 20, after a smallpox epidemic caused the relocation of the convention. The First Baptist Church was the site of meetings of the South Carolina General Assembly during Reconstruction when the State House was under construction.

The **First Presbyterian Church** (1324 Marion Street) was organized in 1795. The present Gothic Revival building was built in 1853 and remodeled and enlarged in 1925. The **Ladson Presbyterian Church** (1720 Sumter Street) was organized in 1838 as a Sunday school for blacks by the First Presbyterian Church; the present building, the second on this site, was built in 1896. **Saint Peter's Catholic Church** (1529 Assembly Street) was first built in 1824 for Catholic immigrants who had moved to the area to construct the Columbia Canal; the present church was built in 1906. The High Victorian Gothic **Washington Street United Methodist Church** (1401 Washington Street) was rebuilt in 1866 and again in 1872 after it burned during Sherman's 1865 march through Columbia.

During the Civil War, hospitals, banks, a Confederate mint, and a weapons factory operated in the capital. As Sherman's army proceeded through the state, thousands of people took refuge here. Sherman and his Federal troops took the city on February 17, 1865, after shelling it from across the Congaree River on February 16. On the first night of Sherman's occupation of the city, most of Columbia was destroyed by fire. Eighty-four blocks were left in ashes. Some historians have pointed out that the fires that destroyed much of Columbia were in part the responsibility of evacuating Confederate troops who set fire to cotton bales, piled in the streets, to keep the cotton from Yankee hands. Others point to the fact that whiskey left behind by the Confederates fueled the passions of some Federal soldiers, who did indeed set fires in Columbia. Later, Sherman insisted that he never wanted to burn Columbia and pointed out that he led the effort to put out the fires.

In the area known as **Arsenal Hill,** which includes the Governor's Mansion Complex and the surrounding nineteenth-century residential district, is the **Columbia City Hall** (1737 Main at Laurel Street), built in 1874 to serve as a federal courthouse and post office. The **Columbia Historic District** is a residential area that includes the Robert Mills House and other mansions of various architectural styles built for the city's bankers, merchants, and lawmakers. A notable example is the **Seibels House** (1601 Richland Street, 803–252–7742). The oldest home in Columbia, built in the late 1700s and renovated in the 1920s, it is now headquarters for the Historic Columbia Foundation. Many of the homes burned during Sherman's occupation in 1865. The **Old Campus District** of the University of South Carolina includes the campus buildings designed by Robert Mills, the 1805 Rutledge College, and the 1827 Maxcy Monument. **Allen University** (1530 Harden Street), with a small campus built between 1881 and 1941, is named for the founder of the African Methodist Episcopal Church, Bishop Richard Allen. The brick Georgian Revival **Chapelle Administration Building** was built in 1922 to designs by John Anderson Lankford, a leading black architect of the day. The school emphasized training for the clergy and also offered industrial and agricultural courses and a law curriculum, a feature distinguishing it from other southern schools for blacks. The **Saluda Factory Historic District** (along the Saluda River in West Columbia, southeast of the intersection of Routes I-126 and I-26) was a Confederate prisoner-of-war camp. The granite foundations of the factory complex are all that remained standing after the burning of Columbia.

Fort Jackson, named for President Andrew Jackson, was built in 1917. On the post is the **Fort Jackson Museum** (Jackson Boulevard, 803–751–7419) with collections relating to the history of the fort.

South Carolina State Museum

Beside the Congaree River is the 1895 **Columbia Duck Mill** (formerly a manufacturer of heavy cotton duck fabric); it was among the
first cotton mills in America to be fully powered with electricity. The
renovated factory building now holds the state museum complex.
Each level of the massive, four-story brick mill highlights a different
aspect of life in the state. An art gallery features works by artists with
South Carolina connections. Natural history exhibits cover modern
and prehistoric animals and the geology of the region. Science and
technology exhibits include a section on the development of the
laser and maser by the 1964 Nobel Prize winner in physics, Charles
H. Townes, a South Carolinian. Cultural history exhibits display artifacts illustrating the region's history from about 12,000 B.C. to the
present. The complex is also the headquarters for the **Greater
Columbia Convention and Visitors Bureau** (803–254–0479).

> LOCATION: 301 Gervais Street. HOURS: 10–5 Monday–Saturday, 1–5
> Sunday. FEE: Yes. TELEPHONE: 803–737–4921.

Riverfront Park and Historic Columbia Canal (off Laurel Street,
803–733–8613) preserves a one-mile canal completed in 1824. It
allowed barges to bypass the rapids that presented the only navigational hazard where the Saluda and Broad rivers join to become the
Congaree. By 1895 the canal powered the Columbia Duck Mill, also
called the Mount Vernon Mill. The park surrounds the city's original hydroelectric plant and restored waterworks facility, which is
open to the public.

Governor's Mansion Complex

Two blocks north of the Canal Park is the nine-acre Governor's
Mansion Complex, which comprises the Governor's Mansion, Lace
House, and Boylston House. The **Governor's Mansion,** completed in
1855, is a two-story stucco structure with wrought-iron grillwork orna-
menting the flanking porches. Originally the officers' quarters of
the state arsenal's military academy, the building has been the governor's residence since 1868. Some rooms are open to the public.
Also enclosed in a block-long area surrounded by a wrought-iron
fence and gateway are the **Lace House** (803 Richland Street), built

OPPOSITE: *A palmetto, the South Carolina state tree, stands in front of the Governor's
Mansion in Columbia.*

in 1854 with Greek Revival elements, and the **Boylston House** (829 Richland Street), built in the 1820s.

LOCATION: 800 block of Richland Street. HOURS: By appointment only. FEE: None. TELEPHONE: 803–737–1710.

Mann-Simons Cottage

This cottage was built around 1850 by Celia Mann, a freed slave from Charleston, one of 200 free blacks in Columbia. Mann established the First Calvary Baptist Church here, one of the earliest post–Civil War black churches in South Carolina. The structure, restored to the period of the 1880s, was also home to Bill Simons, a black musician and music teacher. It houses a museum of African-American culture, including personal items that belonged to Mann and other black Columbia residents.

LOCATION: 1403 Richland Street. HOURS: 10–4 Tuesday–Friday, 11–2 Saturday. FEE: Yes. TELEPHONE: 803–254–1450.

Hampton-Preston Mansion

The mansion, built around 1818 and originally owned by the wealthy merchant Ainsley Hall, was the townhouse of the Hampton family from 1823 to 1873. This well-known South Carolina family included three Wade Hamptons: The first was a veteran of the American Revolution and a general in the War of 1812; his son inherited his plantations and became even richer; the third, a Civil War general, served later as a South Carolina governor and U.S. senator. The house passed to State Senator John S. Preston with his marriage to Caroline Hampton, and in the 1840s, they changed the red brick to stucco and added a suite of twenty-four rooms. The two-and-a-half-story structure, with Jeffersonian Classical elements, has a full-width Doric portico with a full entablature and a wrought-iron railing over a high arcaded basement.

During the Federal occupation of Columbia, the house was the headquarters of General John Logan, who intended to destroy it upon his departure. However, it was saved by an Ursuline nun, Sister Baptista, who had known General Sherman before the war. She asked Sherman to provide a shelter for the girls in her care after her convent had burned. The general instructed her to choose "any of the houses left in the city" for her use. According to the historian

Burke Davis, "Logan swore fearfully when he was handed Sherman's order" but yielded the house to the determined nun.

The house is furnished with family pieces from three plantations of the Hamptons and Prestons, including photographs, crystal, and china from the family's Millwood Plantation. The Rococo Revival furniture in the drawing room reflects Caroline Hampton Preston's tastes. A centerpiece of the Manning Room, which features fashions of the 1800s, is a gold silk brocade wedding dress. Other family pieces include General Wade Hampton II's gold-handled umbrella and his father's ivory and ebony dominoes.

LOCATION: 1615 Blanding Street. HOURS: 10:15–3:15 Tuesday–Saturday, 1–5 Sunday. FEE: Yes. TELEPHONE: 803–252–1770.

Robert Mills Historic House

One of the ten or so documented residences designed by Robert Mills, this house was built for Mills's friend Ainsley Hall, a prosperous merchant who had lived in the house across the street until he sold it in 1823 to Wade Hampton I. The story goes that Wade Hampton took his new bride on a buggy ride around Columbia and told her he would buy her any home she wanted. When Mrs. Hampton chose Ainsley Hall's house at 1615 Blanding Street, Hall sold quickly at a good price, but without consulting his wife, who refused to move until her husband agreed to build her a new house, bigger than the first, across the street and looking down on the old one.

The brick two-story house, with a two-story Ionic portico built over a high, aboveground arcaded basement, is one of the most ambitious of Mills's Greek Revival structures. The house, with three-part Venetian windows with movable interior shutters, has a symmetrical floor plan: four rooms to each floor, with curved ends in two rooms and the main hall. Mills is best known as the designer of the U.S. Treasury Building, Patent Office, and the Washington Monument in Washington, DC, although his plans for the monument were not followed. The Halls never occupied the house because Ainsley Hall died before it was completed. His widow sold it to the Presbyterian Synod for use as the Columbia Theological Seminary. The restored brick townhouse now houses a decorative-arts museum of early-nineteenth-century furnishings.

LOCATION: 1616 Blanding Street. HOURS: 10:15–3:15 Tuesday–Saturday, 1–5 Sunday. FEE: Yes. TELEPHONE: 803–252–1770.

The brick Greek Revival **First Baptist Church** (1306 Hampton Street), with four Tuscan columns of molded brick, was the site of the first meeting of the South Carolina Secession Convention held in 1860. Legend has it that the church escaped burning during the Federal occupation when a black sexton of the First Baptist gave soldiers directions to an old wooden structure instead of this one.

Woodrow Wilson Boyhood Home

Built in 1872 by the Reverend Joseph Ruggles Wilson and Jessie Woodrow Wilson, the Tuscan-villa-style house was the home of Thomas Woodrow Wilson from the age of 14 to 17. Known as "Tommy" to Columbians, Woodrow Wilson lived here while his father was a professor at the Columbia Theological Seminary and the minister of Columbia's First Presbyterian Church. The house, with gas lighting fixtures, Wilson family photographs, period pieces, and some original furnishings, is a good example of a Victorian middle-class Presbyterian home during the period of Reconstruction in South Carolina. Furnishings include the bed where the twenty-eighth president was born when the family lived in Virginia.

LOCATION: 1705 Hampton Street. HOURS: 10–4 Tuesday–Saturday, 1–5 Sunday. FEE: Yes. TELEPHONE: 803–252–1770.

Also on Hampton Street is the **Chesnut Cottage** (1718 Hampton Street, private), the Civil War home of Confederate general James Chesnut and his wife, writer Mary Boykin Miller Chesnut, author of *A Diary From Dixie,* written during the Civil War but published posthumously in 1905. The white frame one-and-a-half-story house is a good example of the "Columbia cottage": It has a central dormer with an arched window above the central entrance; the small porch has four octagonal columns and an ironwork balustrade. Mary Chesnut described a visit from Jefferson Davis to the house in 1864: When Davis was recognized on the porch by a passerby, a crowd gathered, and "the President's hand was nearly shaken off." The **Horry-Guignard House** (1527 Senate Street, private), a two-story frame residence with square front columns, is believed to have been built around 1813 by Revolutionary War colonel Peter Horry.

OPPOSITE: *The west parlor of the Robert Mills House, completed in 1825, contains an Aubusson rug and a pair of sofas from the period.*

South Carolina State House

The three-story Italian Renaissance Revival State House of iron, native granite, and brick was designed by John R. Niernsee. It is the only structure on Main Street that predates the burning of Columbia. When General Sherman first glimpsed the unfinished building as his army arrived outside the city on February 16, 1865, he allowed that it was a "handsome granite structure." But when he noticed the Confederate flag waving defiantly above the building he authorized his batteries to fire on it from a distance of more than one-half mile. Bronze stars on the south and west exterior walls mark the spots where the shells hit. Begun in 1851, the State House was not completed until 1907. After Niernsee's death in 1885, Frank Milburn designed the central dome with a square base, octagonal drum, and cupola. In 1907 Charles Coker Wilson added the north and south porticoes. Impressive granite stairs lead to these columns and the second-floor entrances.

LOCATION: Main and Gervais streets. HOURS: 9–12 and 1:30–4 Monday–Friday. FEE: None. TELEPHONE: 803–734–2430.

University of South Carolina–Horseshoe

Founded in 1801 and opened in 1805 as South Carolina College, the original part of the campus was laid out in the shape of a horseshoe and surrounded by a brick wall. Located in the center of the Horseshoe is the **Maxcy Monument,** designed by Robert Mills in 1827 to honor the first college president, Dr. Jonathan Maxcy. **Rutledge College,** also designed by Robert Mills and completed in 1805, was the first of five college buildings constructed here before the Civil War. It was used as a Confederate hospital, as quarters for Union troops, and as a General Assembly meeting place during Reconstruction. In 1865 the school was rechartered as the University of South Carolina. The **South Caroliniana Library,** located in a three-story brick Greek Revival building built in 1840, holds a large collection of South Carolina manuscripts, personal papers, maps, and prints. The **McKissick Museum** features collections of antique silver and cut gemstones, as well as exhibits on Southern folklife, history, modern art, and science. A popular gallery here continuously shows selections from the museum's extensive

The South Carolina State House is constructed of blue granite from local quarries. To transport the stone, a special three-mile railroad was built from Columbia to the quarries in 1857. OVERLEAF: *The ruins of Millwood, the house where the Confederate General Wade Hampton spent much of his boyhood.*

Movietone News film collection, newsreels shot worldwide from 1919 to 1963.

LOCATION: 900 Sumter Street. HOURS: 9–4 Monday–Friday, 10–5 Saturday, 1–5 Sunday. FEE: None. TELEPHONE: 803–777–7251.

Near the campus is the **South Carolina Confederate Relic Room and Museum** (920 Sumter Street, 803–734–9813), where exhibits focus on all periods of South Carolina history, with the primary collection devoted to the period of the Confederacy. Relics include firearms made in South Carolina, sabers, flags, currency, newspapers, photographs, and uniforms from the colonial period to the present.

Built in 1846 and designed by Edward Brickell White after the design of England's York Cathedral, **Trinity Cathedral** (1100 Sumter Street) is one of the South's finest examples of ecclesiastical Gothic Revival architecture. The structure survived the burning of the city in 1865. It has old-fashioned box pews, hand-carved choir stalls, a marble baptismal font designed by Hiram Powers, and a ceiling with

hammer-and-beam trusses. In the churchyard are buried the three Wade Hamptons; Henry Timrod, poet laureate of the Confederacy; and a number of South Carolina governors and military heroes from the Revolutionary War and other U.S. wars.

Millwood (Garner's Ferry Road, 803–252–7742), the home of Wade Hampton II and of his son, the Confederate general Wade Hampton III, was destroyed by fire during Sherman's occupation of Columbia. Five front columns on brick bases are all that remain of the Greek Revival plantation house. Many South Carolinians regard the ruins as a symbol of Sherman's destruction of the old slave-based plantation system in the state.

South of Columbia, on the Congaree River about two miles south of Cayce, is the site of the first frontier outpost in the South Carolina midlands. The **Congarees Historic District** here encompasses 160 acres of fields and forests, including the fort site and settlement area. Named for a lost tribe of Carolina, the Congaree Indians, the fort served as a base for military operations against the Indians. Route 378 from Columbia to Lexington follows an old Cherokee trail.

LEXINGTON COUNTY MUSEUM

Several eighteenth- and nineteenth-century structures are preserved in this museum complex. The oldest is a one-room log structure with a sleeping loft, built in 1772 by Revolutionary War soldier Lawrence Corley. The 1774 **Heinrich Senn House** is representative of colonial river houses built in the region; it is now used for exhibiting and demonstrating antique looms, spinning wheels, and quilt frames. The **Ernest L. Hazelius House,** built around 1830, was enlarged from four rooms to eight in 1834, when it became the site of the second-oldest Lutheran seminary in the United States; Hazelius, a renowned educator, was the headmaster. The 1832 **John Fox House,** originally used as a dormitory and classroom for the Lutheran seminary, was bought in 1855 by Fox, a county sheriff and clerk of court who became a state senator. The complex also includes a schoolhouse (ca. 1820), a cotton gin house and barn (ca. 1850), and other reconstructed outbuildings.

LOCATION: Route 378 and Fox Street, Lexington. HOURS: 10–4 Tuesday–Saturday, 1–4 Sunday. FEE: Yes. TELEPHONE: 803–359–8369.

The one-room China Springs Schoolhouse, ca. 1890, now part of the Aiken County Historical Museum.

AIKEN

Aiken was named for William Aiken, first president of the South Carolina Railroad and Canal Company, which built the railway between Charleston and Hamburg, South Carolina. On this line, *The Best Friend*, the first passenger train drawn by a steam engine and the first to carry U.S. mail, passed through Aiken. During Sherman's march through the state, a wild cavalry fight took place in the streets of this town when 2,000 mounted Confederates under General Joseph Wheeler ambushed General Hugh Kilpatrick's cavalry. Wheeler, who had been snapping at the flanks of Sherman's huge columns all the way from Georgia, drove the Federals from Aiken and nearly captured Kilpatrick.

An area known for its thoroughbred horses and polo matches, Aiken was a favorite wintering spot for the wealthy around the turn of the twentieth century, with vacation houses that seem too massive to be called "cottages." One of the largest is **Joye Cottage** (First Avenue SW, private), built in the middle of the nineteenth century. **Let's Pretend** (Horry Street and Colleton Avenue, private) is a large rambling colonial cottage, once the home of Governor Morris, a fiction writer, whose guests included Rudyard Kipling.

The **Aiken County Historical Museum** (433 Newberry Street, 803-642-2015) houses historical artifacts from the county, including an archaeological collection, textile exhibits, and a complete drugstore of the early 1900s. On the grounds are the 1808 **Frederick Ergle House,** a log cabin with period furnishings originally located near the Edisto River, and the 1890s one-room **China Springs Schoolhouse.** The **Aiken Thoroughbred Hall of Fame** (Whiskey Road and Dupree Place, 803-649-7700) displays paintings, photos, owners' silks, trophies, and other memorabilia related to champion thoroughbreds trained in Aiken County.

About seven miles southeast of North Augusta is **Redcliffe Plantation State Park** (Beach Island, off Route 278, 803-827-1473). This plantation house with Greek Revival elements was built in the 1850s as the home of U.S. senator and South Carolina governor James Henry Hammond and later John Shaw Billings, the managing editor of the first *Life* magazine. Located on the red clay hill for which it is named, the two-and-a-half-story house with a stucco basement is furnished entirely with family pieces.

BARNWELL

Established in 1785 from the Old Orangeburg District, Barnwell County initially included the area between the North Fork of the Edisto River and the Savannah River (later parts of Aiken, Allendale, and Bamberg counties). The county seat of this region of midland plantations was settled by Virginians who called it Red Hill. In February 1865 the town was looted and burned by the advance guard of Sherman's army. As the town burned General Hugh Kilpatrick and his officers held an impromptu ball at the hotel. When asked to restrain his troops from setting fires, an officer replied: "Madam, I have very little control over the boys, you must remember we are in South Carolina now; we entered this state with 'gloves off.'"

The present **Barnwell County Courthouse** (Wall and Main streets), completed in February 1879, has records dating to 1786. In front of the courthouse stands an unusual vertical sundial, given to the town in 1858. The 1857 **Church of the Holy Apostles** (1706 Hagood Avenue), though severely damaged during Kilpatrick's occupation, was repaired in 1883 and remains a fine example of Gothic Revival architecture, with an impressive stained-glass window that was the gift of Governor James Henry Hammond. It is one of the few antebellum structures remaining in town.

Local history is the focus at the **Barnwell County Museum** (Marboro and Hagood streets, 803–259–1916) and at the **A. Hammond Museum** (Old City Hall, Blackville, 803–284–2202), which contains artifacts relative to Blackville and Barnwell.

Rivers Bridge State Park (about seven miles southwest of Ehrhardt, 803–267–3675) preserves the site of a Confederate artillery emplacement that briefly impeded one wing of Sherman's army. The troops were more seriously delayed by having to slog through shoulder-deep swamps along the flooded Salkehatchie River. When told how Sherman's engineers had gotten the army through the seemingly impassable swamp over hastily built bridges and log roads, Confederate general Joseph E. Johnston said, "I made up my mind that there had been no such army since the days of Julius Caesar." The park contains extensive earthworks and a museum housing Civil War artifacts.

BAMBERG

Named for the man who owned the station on this stagecoach route between Charleston and Augusta, Bamberg was once the home of author William Gilmore Simms. About four miles east of town is Simms's home, **Woodlands Plantation** (Route 78, 803–245–4427). The house, burned during Sherman's raid through Columbia in 1865, has been reconstructed from one wing of the original building.

ORANGEBURG

Named for William, prince of Orange, and settled in the 1730s, Orangeburg began as a town at the crossing of two Indian paths. The **Orangeburg County Jail** (Saint John's Street), a masonry structure built in 1858, is one of the best examples of Tudor Gothic architecture in this part of the state. The jail was damaged in February 1865, when the Union Army under General Wiliam Tecumseh Sherman passed through the town. The **Orangeburg County Historical Society** (421 Middleton Street), has a collection that includes photographs and county records for genealogical and historical research.

STATEBURG

General Thomas Sumter founded this town with great hopes that it would become the capital of South Carolina. The site of Revolutionary War and Civil War activity, Stateburg suffered major damage during the latter. The **Stateburg Historic District** includes a number of eighteenth- and nineteenth-century residences in Greek Revival and Gothic Revival styles, unusual in that they were constructed from *pisé de terre*, air-dried bricks of earth shaped in wooden molds. Notable examples of the use of this material are the 1758 **Borough House Plantation** (Route 261, private) and the 1850 **Holy Cross Episcopal Church** (Route 261), a Gothic Revival church designed by Edward C. Jones. The staunch South Carolina Unionist statesman Joel Poinsett is buried here in the Holy Cross Cemetery.

Near Stateburg, signs from the intersection of Routes 76/378 and 261 lead to the **Tomb of Thomas Sumter,** the Revolutionary War general nicknamed "the Carolina Gamecock."

SUMTER

Named for Revolutionary War general Thomas Sumter, the settlement originally named Sumterville was chosen as the seat of Sumter County in 1798. A Citadel cadet from Sumter, George E. Haynsworth, is credited with firing the first shot of the War Between the States. The **Williams-Brice Museum/Archives** (122 North Washington Street, 803–775–0908) displays Sumter County historical artifacts in this Victorian Gothic house. The **South Carolina National Guard Museum** (National Guard Armory, North Pike West, 803–773–4151) holds a collection of cannons, other weapons, and military history exhibits.

In Sumter County, west of the town of Pinewood, is the finest Greek Revival residence in the state and one of the half-dozen finest in the nation. **Milford Plantation** (Route 261, private), with six front Corinthian columns, was constructed from 1839 to 1841 for Governor John L. Manning, who held office between 1852 and 1854. Nathaniel F. Potter oversaw the construction of the house, probably designed by Charles P. Reichardt and Russell Warren, with details taken from Minard Lafever's 1835 *Beauties of Modern Architecture* (Lafever had been associated with the architects in New York).

KINGSTREE

The town takes its name from the area's white pines, designated the king's trees because they were to be used only as masts for ships in the royal navy. The **Williamsburg County Courthouse,** designed by Robert Mills, was originally built in 1823. The courthouse grounds had served as the site for militia musters during the Revolutionary War. The Battle of Kingstree occurred northwest of the town on August 27, 1780, when the militia led by Major John James, who served as scout for General Francis Marion, attacked and captured a British company. About six miles south of Kingstree, General Marion and his men prevented Tory forces headed for Kingstree in March 1781 from crossing the Black River by burning Lower Bridge. Route 377 now crosses the Black River at the site where the battle occurred.

The elegant Milford, built for Governor John L. Manning, son-in-law of the first Wade Hampton, using granite imported from Rhode Island and bricks made on the plantation.

FLORENCE

Florence, founded in 1850, was named for the eldest daughter of General William Wallace Harllee, who brought the Wilmington & Manchester Railway to the town. During the Civil War, the railway made the city a major transportation center for supplies and troops. Wounded Confederate soldiers were treated here at Wayside Nursing Home; Union soldiers were held prisoner in Florence's prison, built for the purpose about three miles south of town. While the stockade was under construction, hundreds of Federal prisoners died in a typhoid fever epidemic as a result of being held in a makeshift compound with poor sanitary conditions in the center of the city. They were buried near Florence, on National Cemetery Road, in the six-acre **National Cemetery**.

HARTSVILLE MUSEUM

Housed in a restored passenger train station, built in 1908, this museum features exhibits on the history, arts, and crafts of the region. The permanent collection includes silverware and iron household implements, antique clothing and photographs, as well as a railroad caboose, open for viewing. The station, with stick-style elements, stands as a symbol of the railroad's key role in the growth and development of the town and Darlington County.

LOCATION: 114 South 4th Street, Hartsville. HOURS: 10–5 Monday–Friday, 3–5 Sunday. FEE: None. TELEPHONE: 803–383–3005.

BENNETTSVILLE

The seat of Marlboro County is located in the upper part of the old Welsh Neck settlement, established in 1737. The county, formed in 1785, was named for the duke of Marlborough, John Churchill, an ancestor of Winston Churchill. A popular local saying is that the farmland here was once so rich that it sold by the pound rather than by the acre.

Marlboro County Historical Museum

This museum traces county history back 300 years, through exhibits that include one of only a few known copies of the South Carolina Ordinance of Secession; antique farm implements; a county medical museum, which shows the history of medical practice for the past 150 years; and the Bennettsville Female Academy, which operated from 1834 to 1881. The centerpiece of the one-block museum complex is the **Jennings-Brown House,** furnished to illustrate life in Bennettsville in the 1850s. The saltbox-style house with fine interior woodwork, built in 1826, is one of the town's few remaining two-story houses constructed before 1850. General Frank P. Blair used the building as his Union headquarters in March 1865.

LOCATION: 119 South Marlboro Street. HOURS: 10–1 and 2–5 Monday–Tuesday and Thursday, 10–1 Wednesday and Friday. FEE: For Jennings-Brown House. TELEPHONE: 803–479–5624.

In the upper west corner of Marlboro County, near the North Carolina–South Carolina border, is **Pegues Place** (west of Route 1 on Route 266, private), the plantation home built around 1770 for Claudius Pegues. Though a rear wing was added in the nineteenth century, the house retains its original walnut-paneled dining room, carved woodwork, and many original furnishings. During the Revolution, in May 1781, this was the site of negotiations for the exchange of prisoners of war. The house has been owned by the same family since its construction.

T H E   C O A S T

South Carolina's Atlantic coast includes a stretch of commercially developed beaches popularly known as the Grand Strand or the Myrtle Beach area. The low-country begins around the seaport of Little River and extends southward to the Sea Islands just north of Savannah, Georgia.

BROOKGREEN GARDENS

In the 1930s Archer Huntington, a railroad heir, and his wife, Anna Hyatt Huntington, a sculptor, created a large outdoor collection of American sculpture on the grounds of a colonial rice and indigo plantation. Currently containing 450 works by 208 nineteenth- and twentieth-century artists, this large permanent outdoor collection of American figurative sculpture includes the work of Frederic

OVERLEAF: *South Carolina's Atlantic Coast encompasses sandy beaches and barrier islands.*

Remington, Augustus Saint-Gaudens, and Marshall Fredericks. Only the kitchen remains from the original Brookgreen Plantation, built in the mid-1700s.

LOCATION: On the west side of Route 17, 4 miles south of Murrells Inlet, 18 miles south of Myrtle Beach. HOURS: 9:30–4:45 Daily. FEE: Yes. TELEPHONE: 803–237–4218.

Pawleys Island contains one of South Carolina's oldest summer resort communities. Settled by rice plantation owners, the area was also the site of salt production during the American Revolution and the Civil War. Most of the old structures are one-and-a-half-story frame buildings with wide porches and high brick foundations.

GEORGETOWN

In 1526 the Spanish attempted, unsuccessfully, to settle this area. Some two hundred years later, in 1729, the town was established, surveyed, and named in honor of the prince of Wales, later King George II. It is the state's third-oldest city. The port is located at the head of Winyah Bay, where the Waccamaw, Great Pee Dee, Sampit, and Black rivers empty into the bay, making it one of South Carolina's three major harbors. Important as a Revolutionary War port of entry for supplies from Philadelphia, Georgetown was captured by the British in 1780. It was raided by Americans under Francis Marion on November 15, 1780, and again on January 24, 1781. Most of Georgetown was destroyed by the British on August 2, 1781, after General Thomas Sumter's raids on Loyalists.

Centrally located in the historic district is the **Prince George, Winyah, Episcopal Church** (Broad and Highmarket streets), constructed in 1750. It has a square tower surmounted by an octagonal clock tower, belfry, dome, and cross, all added in 1824. The **Winyah Masonic Lodge** (632 Prince Street), an inn built in 1740, was where George Washington addressed the Masons in 1790. The **Harold Kaminski House** (1003 Front Street, 803–546–7706), overlooking the Sampit River, is a rice planter's townhouse constructed ca. 1760. It displays eighteenth- and nineteenth-century antiques from Europe and America, including a fifteenth-century Spanish chest and a mahogany Chippendale banquet table. The 1842 **Old Market**

Building (Front and Screven streets), referred to locally as the Town Clock, has served as a market, jail, print shop, and police department. It now holds the **Rice Museum** (803–546–7423), with exhibits illustrating all phases of rice cultivation from 1700 to 1900 through dioramas, paintings, artifacts, and a scale model of a rice mill. In the mid-1800s Georgetown was the world's leading exporter of rice.

Twelve miles south of Georgetown is the **Hopsewee Plantation** (Route 17, 803–546–7891), built of black cypress around 1740. A frame clapboard house with a raised brick basement and a front double-tiered balustraded porch, it was the home of Thomas Lynch, a South Carolina delegate to the Continental Congress, and the birthplace of Thomas Lynch, Jr., a signer of the Declaration of Independence.

HAMPTON PLANTATION STATE PARK

Hampton, one of the most impressive of the South Carolina houses, stands beside the lower Santee River south of Georgetown on the

This classical portico was added to Hampton Plantation to honor George Washington on his visit in 1791. It may have been inspired by the work of the Adam Brothers, seen by Eliza Lucas Pinckney during a trip to England.

edge of the Francis Marion National Forest. The house may have been started as early as 1735 as a small frame residence for an early settler, Noah Serré. Some time between 1750 and 1785, the original six-room structure was greatly enlarged by Serré's son-in-law, Daniel Huger Horry, with a two-story ballroom on one end and large bedrooms and sitting rooms on the other end. The addition of the portico in 1791 was the idea of Eliza Lucas Pinckney, the mother of Horry's second wife, Harriott. (Pinckney had established the southern indigo industry while in her teens). The six column portico and pediment were completed in time for a visit by George Washington that year. The house has also been the home of Archibald Rutledge, a Horry descendant and poet laureate of South Carolina. Some walls and ceilings have been left unplastered to show how the house was constructed. The interior is undergoing restoration and will eventually be furnished with period pieces.

LOCATION: Off Routes 17 and 857, 8 miles north of McClellanville,.
HOURS: 1–4 Monday–Friday, 10–3 Saturday, 12–3 Sunday. FEE: Yes.
TELEPHONE: 803–546–9361.

BEAUFORT

Both the Spanish and the French planted short-lived settlements in this area in the sixteenth century. The first successful English traders arrived in the 1690s, and the town of Beaufort was chartered in 1710. Blessed with an excellent harbor, Beaufort was second only to Charleston in importance during the eighteenth century. The fledgling community was dealt a severe blow in 1715 when the Yemasee Indians, angered by white encroachment onto the mainland, killed a number of settlers and burned the town. Beaufort retains a wealth of antebellum and even pre-Revolutionary structures because early in the Civil War Federal forces occupied the town and held it for the war's duration. The 300-acre **Beaufort Historic District** includes more than 170 public and private buildings. Information is available at the chamber of commerce (1006 Bay Street, 803–524–3163).

The **Thomas Hepworth House** (214 New Street, private) was constructed around 1717, shortly after the Yamasee Indians had burned the town. It may be Beaufort's oldest surviving house. The **Joseph Johnson House** (411 Craven House, private), a Greek Revival

Beaufort's Henry Farmer House, built during a period of prosperity brought about by the introduction of long staple sea-island cotton and the cotton gin in the 1790s .

house built in 1859 with slave labor, is known as "the Castle" because of its large columns, massive paired octagonal chimneys, and double verandahs. The **Beaufort Museum** (713 Craven Street, 803–525–7471) is housed in an arsenal building first constructed in 1795 and rebuilt in 1852. The museum focuses on the history and culture of Beaufort County.

The **Milton Maxey House** (1113 Craven Street, private) is also known as the "Secession House" because tradition says that the first Ordinance of Secession to remove South Carolina from the Union was drafted here. During the Civil War period, the house was owned by Edmund Rhett, brother of Robert Barnwell Rhett, the "Father of Secession" and editor of the *Charleston Mercury*. **Marshlands** (501 Pinckney Street, private) was built by Dr. James Robert Verdier around 1814 after he completed his medical training at the University of Pennsylvania. Dr. Verdier was renowned for his successful treatment of yellow fever. The frame **Henry Farmer House** (412 East Street, private) was built in the early nineteenth century using wooden pegs and imported copper nails. **Tidalholm** (1 Laurens Street, private) was built around 1853 by Edgar Fripp, a wealthy planter of sea-island cotton. The second floor verandah was added after a storm in 1893 literally blew the roof off. The **Henry McKee–Robert Smalls House** (511 Prince Street, private) was constructed prior to 1830 by the planter Henry McKee. Robert Smalls, a slave, was raised in a cabin on the property. During the Civil War, Smalls and several fellow slaves seized the Confederate gunboat *Planter* and delivered it to the Federal forces blockading Charleston. Smalls bought the McKee house with the money he received for this prize. He was elected to the U.S. Congress in 1875.

Completed in 1790, the **John Mark Verdier House Museum** (801 Bay Street, 803–524–6334) is an outstanding example of the Federal style and contains particularly graceful interior details. Verdier was a well-to-do young merchant; the house has been restored to reflect his lifestyle from 1790 to 1825. Tradition says that Lafayette addressed the townsfolk from the portico of the home in 1825. From 1861–1865, the house was occupied by Federal officers.

The **George Parsons Elliott House Museum** (1001 Bay Street, 803–524–8450), a Greek Revival house overlooking the Beaufort

The restored Verdier House parlor contains the family's early-nineteenth-century Coleport tea service.

River, was built in 1844 for the planter and politician George Elliott. With its double verandahs and raised foundation, it is representative of the "Beaufort style." It served as a Federal hospital during the Civil War. Owned by the Historic Beaufort Foundation, it displays furnishings from the mid-nineteenth century to the twentieth century.

The congregation of **Saint Helena's Episcopal Church** (501 Church Street) was founded in 1712, and the present building, a brick-and-stucco structure, dates to 1724. The bricks used in its construction were made in England and arrived in South Carolina as ballast in the sailing ships that frequented the port. In 1734 Captain John Bull gave the church a set of communion silver in memory of his wife, who was taken prisoner by the Indians in a 1715 raid and never heard from again. The silver is still used on special occasions. During the Civil War, the church served as a hospital, and tradition says that some of the gravestones served as operating tables.

Approximately fifteen miles north of Beaufort are the ruins of **Old Sheldon Church** (Route 21). The first church on the site was built between 1745 and 1755 in the form of a Greek temple, the earliest use of this style in America. It was used to hide arms and ammunition from the British during the Revolution. In May 1779 the British burned the building. Rebuilt in 1826, this structure too was burned, this time by Sherman's Fifteenth Corps on January 14, 1865. The church's tall Tuscan columns and exterior walls remain. Also north of Beaufort, off Route 21 east of Yamasee, is one of the two South Carolina houses designed by Frank Lloyd Wright. **Old Brass,** or **Auldbrass Plantation** (private), was constructed between 1940 and 1951. The single-story main house with diagonal cypress siding has an irregular hexagonal shape; the house features abstract designs based on Spanish moss and arrowheads. Other buildings in the complex include a gatehouse, guest cottages, kennels, and stables.

PENN CENTER HISTORIC DISTRICT

Penn Center was founded in 1862 by Philadelphia Quakers led by Laura Towne and Ellen Murray, who came south to educate blacks in their transition from slavery to freedom. Over the years, programs have ranged from teaching basic literacy to promoting public health and demonstrating improved agricultural techniques. The **Brick**

Church, the oldest church on Saint Helena Island and built by slave labor, was one of the first buildings used for Penn School classes. The **York Bailey Museum** contains exhibits on the life of Sea Island African-Americans from slavery to the present. The museum also has a large collection of oral history recordings that preserve the language known as Gullah, a blend of English and African dialects.

LOCATION: Route 37, Lands End Road, Saint Helena Island. HOURS: 9–5 Monday–Friday. FEE: None. TELEPHONE: 803–838–2432.

East of Saint Helena Island, just off Route 21, is the **Hunting Island Lighthouse** (Hunting Island State Park, 803–838–2011). This 1875 structure replaced an antebellum lighthouse that was destroyed during the Civil War. Because of severe erosion along the beach, the lighthouse was built in cast-iron sections so that it could be moved; the first move was in 1889. Lighthouse service was discontinued in 1939, but the tower still offers a fine view of the ocean. A small exhibit on lighthouse technology is also on-site.

PARRIS ISLAND MUSEUM

Located at the Marine Corps Recruit Depot, the museum details the history of Parris Island and the Port Royal area, as well as the Marine Corps presence here. Exhibits on the Marines' history feature uniforms, weapons, and historic photographs. A portion of the collection tells the story of early European efforts to settle the island and of the Spanish village of Santa Elena, founded in 1566 and abandoned in 1587. Archaeologists have discovered Santa Elena's location, and items relating to the village are on display. A driving tour of the island, which includes the Santa Elena site, is available.

LOCATION: Route 281, Parris Island. HOURS: 10–4:30 Daily. FEE: None. TELEPHONE: 803–525–2951.

HILTON HEAD ISLAND

Named for the English sea captain William Hilton, the island was settled in the early 1770s by English planters who raised indigo as their staple crop. Its six Revolutionary War captains fought for independence, in contrast to the planters of nearby Daufuskie Island, known as "little Bermuda" for its Loyalist sympathies. Sea-island cotton, developed here about 1790 by William Elliott of Myrtle Bank Plantation, quickly enriched the planters of Hilton Head, who built townhouses in nearby Beaufort, Bluffton, and Savannah. On November 8, 1861, Union forces attacked and occupied the island, which they used as a fueling station for ships blockading the Confederate coastline and staging attacks on Charleston and Savannah. After a bridge to the mainland was opened in 1956, Hilton Head was developed as a resort and residential community. Places of historic interest include the **Fort Mitchell** earthwork fortifications, overlooking Skull Creek, and the **Bayard Ruins,** a 1796 tabby-built plantation house at Braddock's Point. The island also has several protected wildlife habitat areas: Sea Pines Forest Preserve, Newhall Audubon Preserve, and Pinckney Island Hilton Head Wildlife Preserve.

Federal soldiers of the 3rd New Hampshire Volunteers playing dominoes to pass the time during their occupation of Hilton Head Island, November 1861.

CHARLESTON
AND
ENVIRONS

OPPOSITE: *The celebrated "flying" staircase in Charleston's Nathaniel Russell House rises in three floors in a graceful spiral that never touches the walls. The portrait on the first landing, painted by George Romney in 1786, is of Mary Rutledge Smith, a prominent Charlestonian in the eighteenth century.*

The city of Charleston stands on a peninsula where, as the local saying goes, "the Ashley and Cooper rivers meet to form the Atlantic Ocean." Traveling southward down the peninsula, one sees twentieth-century buildings of steel and neon give way to structures of mellowed brick and weathered wood; as one crosses Broad Street, the past becomes present: Houses crowd in upon each other, shoulder to shoulder, piazzas facing the harbor awaiting an ocean breeze as they have for more than 200 years. The sheer number of eighteenth- and nineteenth-century structures standing on this tiny point of land is astounding.

Their collective survival can be traced to one cause: poverty. After the economic devastation of the Civil War, few Charlestonians possessed the capital to do more than patch existing structures. The city, which had once been very rich, took on a decidedly seedy look, leading to the oft-quoted observation that Charlestonians were "too poor to paint and too proud to whitewash."

As in many southern towns, the events surrounding the Civil War retain a sense of immediacy for many residents. Sometimes called the "War Between the States," sometimes the "War of Northern Aggression," sometimes the "Late Unpleasantness," the Civil War resulted in the loss of capital invested in slaves, and the devastation of some plantations reduced many once prosperous families to poverty. Those who were already poor became poorer still, and former slaves, though briefly exhilarated by nominal freedom, were soon restored to unrelenting toil. Struggling to adapt to such changed circumstances, the city turned inward, preferring to remember past glories.

The first English settlers arrived along this stretch of coast in 1670, sent by eight British gentlemen (known as the lord proprietors) to whom King Charles II had granted a domain that stretched from Florida to Virginia. Among the proprietors were some of the most influential men in Restoration England, men such as Lords Shaftesbury, Clarendon, and Albemarle. Pragmatists tempered by the intrigues of the English court, they expected a handsome return on their investment in the New World.

The colonists' original plan was to settle at a site near present-day Beaufort, but the Kiawah, searching for a powerful ally to protect them from neighboring tribes, openly courted the settlers and convinced them to consider more northerly sites. When Sir John Yeamans, governor of the colony, selected a site alongside a creek

An 1831 view of the East Battery, painted by S. Barnard, shows several varieties of the distinctive Charleston piazza, or porch, including one with three stories.

that flowed into the Ashley River, the colonists wearily agreed, "most of us being of a temper to follow though wee knew noe reason for it." One hundred and sixty settlers, among them several women, constructed a fort, dubbed Charles Towne, and lived "more like souldiers in a garrison than planters." In the spring of 1680, this site was abandoned in favor of the city's present location.

The new town was laid out following a formal plan sent from London, with a number of modifications to accommodate the marshy, creek-filled terrain. Surrounded by a wall to protect it from Indians, pirates, and the Spanish who sometimes sailed northward from Florida, the settlement was described by a visitor in 1682 as "regularly laid out into large and capacious streets. . . . In it they have reserved convenient places for a church, Town House and other public structures, an artillery ground for the exercise of their militia, and wharves for the convenience of trade and shipping."

From the beginning, trade was the lifeblood of the community. The riches of the backcountry (furs and timber) flowed into the city, and with the discovery that rice was an ideal cash crop for the coastal lowlands and the riverine marshes, plantations began to develop

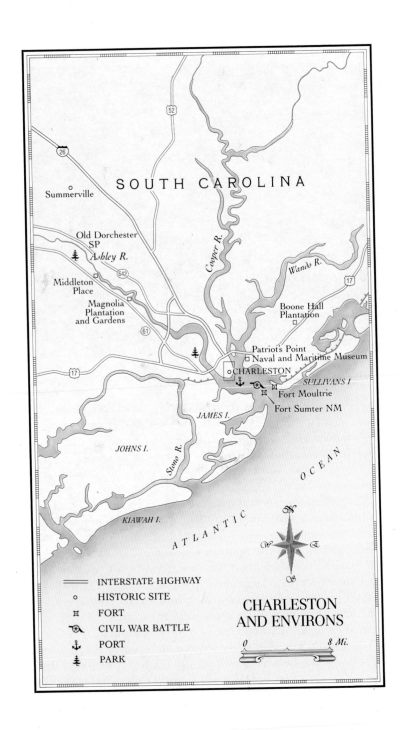

SOUTH CAROLINA

Summerville

Old Dorchester
SP
Ashley R.

Middleton
Place

Magnolia
Plantation
and Gardens

Cooper R.

Wando R.

Boone Hall
Plantation

Patriot's Point
Naval and Maritime Museum

CHARLESTON

SULLIVANS I

Fort Moultrie

Fort Sumter NM

JAMES I.

JOHNS I.

Stono R.

KIAWAH I.

ATLANTIC OCEAN

INTERSTATE HIGHWAY

HISTORIC SITE

FORT

CIVIL WAR BATTLE

PORT

PARK

CHARLESTON
AND ENVIRONS

0   8 Mi.

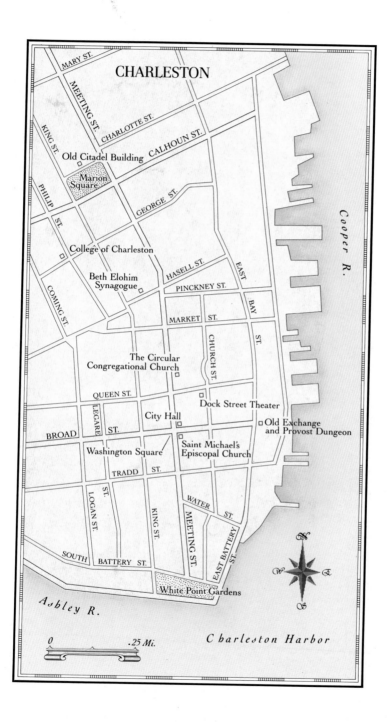

CHARLESTON

MARY ST.

MEETING ST.

KING ST.

CHARLOTTE ST.

CALHOUN ST.

PHILIP ST.

Old Citadel Building

Marion Square

GEORGE ST.

COMING ST.

College of Charleston

Beth Elohim Synagogue

HASELL ST.

PINCKNEY ST.

EAST

MARKET ST.

BAY

The Circular Congregational Church

CHURCH ST.

ST.

QUEEN ST.

LEGARE

ST.

City Hall

Dock Street Theater

Old Exchange and Provost Dungeon

BROAD

ST.

Washington Square

Saint Michael's Episcopal Church

TRADD ST.

LOGAN ST.

KING ST.

WATER ST.

MEETING ST.

EAST BATTERY ST.

SOUTH

BATTERY ST.

White Point Gardens

Cooper R.

Ashley R.

Charleston Harbor

0   .25 Mi.

N
W   E
S

along the major waterways. Soon the wealth of the entire region fun-
neled into this port city. By 1720 it was noted that "nearly 200 sail of
all sorts . . . [are] freighted behind Sullivan's Island for the export
trade." The presence of so many merchant ships attracted bands of
buccaneers from the West Indies to Carolina waters. A series of expe-
ditions were mounted against the marauders after the infamous
Blackbeard held hostage several prominent Charlestonians, finally
exchanging them for medical supplies. In 1718 alone, city officials
executed forty-nine buccaneers, including Stede Bonnet, the
"Gentleman Pirate."

As the cultivation of rice, and then cotton, spread throughout
the coastal area, the colony's leading merchants acquired plantations. Unlike their counterparts in Virginia, who remained on their
estates more or less year-round, these low-country planters sustained
their mercantile activity and spent much of the year in Charleston.
They had additional reason to do so because the marshy lowlands
surrounding the town were unhealthy. The old saying that "Carolina
is in the spring a paradise, in the summer a hell, and in the autumn a
hospital" was all too true. The well-to-do merchant-planters remained
in the city, with its cleansing ocean breezes, from May through late
autumn and as a result lavished a great deal of attention (and
money) on their city residences.

Rather early, Charleston developed its own architectural style
which was well suited to the sultry climate by incorporating certain
elements of design from the English colony of Barbados. A
Charleston "single" house was only one room wide and sat with a
gable end facing the street. Instead of opening into the house, the
door used by social visitors opened onto a porch, known locally as a
piazza, one floor above, while another door led directly from the
street to the merchant's quarters on the ground floor. Another for-
mat, two rooms wide, was referred to as a "double" house. The piazzas may not have existed before 1730 or so (the evidence is unclear),
but after that visitors complained that the city's houses, of whatever
style, were "generally encumbered with Balconies or Piazzas . . . con-
trived for coolness, a very necessary Consideration." Houses, though
generally close together, were often staggered along the street, each
jutting a bit farther out than its neighbor to catch the prevailing
winds. Good manners dictated that north-side windows stay shuttered
if they overlooked a neighbor's piazza.

OPPOSITE: *The front door of this single house leads directly into the piazza, the
Charlestonian porch that is really an outdoor room.*

Even though the planter and his family resided in town much of the year, life continued on the plantation year-round with a work force composed mainly of slaves brought from Africa or the West Indies. Some blacks had acquired some genetic resistance to malaria, a trait that accompanied their susceptibility to sickle-cell disease; others suffered from the same fevers that killed the white settlers. Many had learned the cultivation of rice in Africa and could instruct their owners. In 1755 a Charleston slave dealer wrote: "There was such pulling and hauling [as to] who should get the good slaves that some of them [the buyers] came . . . very nearly to blows. There was people enough in town that day to have taken off a thousand good slaves." Charleston rapidly became America's major slave port, and any of its fine dwellings, such as the Miles Brewton house, not built on profits realized from the trade were nevertheless the products of slavery.

On the eve of the American Revolution, Charleston was the busiest port in the colonies, a hustling, bustling city that wore with pride its nickname, "Little London." A New Englander visiting in 1773, Josiah Quincy, wrote in wonder: "I can only say, in general, that in grandeur, splendour of buildings, decorations, equipages, numbers, commerce, shipping, and indeed in almost every thing, it [Charleston] far surpasses all I ever saw, or ever expect to see, in America." A great deal of fine furniture was imported from England, but high shipping costs encouraged the development of home-grown artisans. (After the Revolution, heavy duties on imported furniture were further inducements to domestic crafts.) Hundreds of "cabinetmakers" plied their trade in Charleston, the most famous being Thomas Elfe, known for his distinctive fretwork. Mahogany, which was readily available from the West Indies, was the wood of choice.

Charlestonians were known for their pursuit of pleasure. Cock fighting, horse racing, theater, concerts, dancing, and cards were all favorite pastimes. The all-night "drinking bout" was an accepted form of entertainment. The botanist Alexander Gardner wrote, "The gentlemen planters . . . are absolutely above every occupation but eating, drinking, lolling, smoking and sleeping, which five modes of action constitute the essence of their life and existence." News of the Boston Tea Party elicited an equally effective, if less dramatic, response from Charlestonians: Their shipment of British-taxed tea was unloaded and allowed to rot in the cellars of the Old Exchange. On June 28, 1776, a British fleet attempted to enter Charleston harbor and was driven back by artillery fire from a fort hastily constructed of palmetto logs on Sullivans Island, the present-day site of Fort Moultrie. British cannonballs buried themselves in the spongy wood, causing little damage, and the fleet was forced to withdraw.

In 1779 the British tried and failed again. Finally, in 1780 the British lay siege to the town and forced its surrender after heavy shelling ignited fires in the heart of the city. Captured American officers were initially allowed to keep their swords, but their shouts of "Long Live Congress" so irritated the British that the swords were finally confiscated. The British occupied the city for two years, commandeering the finest homes and imprisoning Patriot leaders such as Thomas Heyward and Edward Rutledge. When they abandoned the city in 1782 they took with them many spoils of war, including silver, books, and even the bells from Saint Michael's steeple. The bells, at least, were eventually returned.

After the Revolution, Charleston's economy slowly, almost imperceptibly, began to decline. The city lacked its own merchant marine and eschewed, with few exceptions, banking, factoring, and insuring. It allowed Northern financial centers to become the middlemen in its commerce.After 1800 it was increasingly tied to a single cash crop, cotton. Wealth became concentrated in the hands of a very few, and the combination of enormous privilege and unquestioned control over the lives of other human beings inevitably led to a certain arrogance among the planter class and a growing disdain for those outside their circle. Moreover, that class tended to forget its mercantile origin and lose touch with the evolving capitalist economy of the nineteenth century. As slavery was abolished in most of the Western Hemisphere, Charleston's elite became increasingly furious in its defense. A young army officer from Ohio, stationed at Fort Moultrie in the 1840s, wrote derisively, "Carolinians boast . . . of this state, this aristocracy, this age, patriotism, chivalry and glory—all trash." The writer, William Tecumseh Sherman, was destined to return at the head of an invading army.

As the nineteenth century progressed, Charlestonians, zealously protective of their "peculiar institution," were at the forefront of the southern secession movement. At 4:30 AM on April 12, 1861, the first shots of the Civil War were directed at the federal stronghold of Fort Sumter. Residents of the city flocked to the tip of the peninsula to view the bombardment. "Every house, housetop and spire was crowded," wrote Emma Holmes in her diary. "Every body seems relieved that what has been so long dreaded has come at last and so confident of victory that they seem not to think of the danger of their friends." Defense of the city was in the hands of General Pierre G. T. Beauregard, a dashing Creole whose very presence inspired confidence. Following the Confederate capture of Fort Sumter, a popular bit of doggerel went:

> With cannon and musket, with shell and petard,
> We salute the North with our Beau - regard.

Strong Confederate batteries bristled from the city and though federal ships soon blockaded the harbor, some southern vessels were able to elude capture; blockade running became not only profitable but patriotic. Beauregard strengthened his defenses and waited for the inevitable Union assault. On April 7, 1863, the federal fleet began a bombardment that continued, with only occasional pauses, for the next two years.

Union troops acquired a land base from which to shell the city when they captured Battery Wagner on Morris Island in July 1863. The battle received enormous attention in the northern press because the assault was led by the Fifty-fourth Massachusetts, an all-black regiment led by Robert Gould Shaw, a white Bostonian. Shaw and half of his regiment were killed. By late August Union shells were landing in the heart of the city, and so many inhabitants had fled that the southern end of the peninsula was virtually a ghost town. As one resident observed: "The whole life and business of the place were crowded into the few squares above Calhoun Street . . . where the shells did not reach." The few who remained in their homes complained about the scream of Yankee shells and kept tubs of water handy in each room to fight fires. The long siege, which was virtually a stalemate for a year and a half, took its toll on the soldiers as well as the civilians. The Union admiral John Dahlgren confided in his journal: "The worst of this place is that one only stops getting weaker. One does not get stronger."

On February 18, 1865, the Confederate army quietly evacuated the city, falling back toward North Carolina in an attempt to halt the relentless advance of Sherman's troops. To many in the north, South Carolina in general—and Charleston in particular—bore much of the responsibility for the outbreak of the Civil War and the

OPPOSITE: *An extra edition of the Charleston* Mercury *announces South Carolina's Ordinance of Secession from the Union on December 20, 1860, in response to the election of Abraham Lincoln as the first Republican president.*

CHARLESTON

MERCURY

EXTRA:

Passed unanimously at 1.15 o'clock, P. M., December 20th, 1860.

AN ORDINANCE

To dissolve the Union between the State of South Carolina and other States united with her under the compact entitled " The Constitution of the United States of America."

We, the People of the State of South Carolina, *in* Convention *assembled, do declare and ordain,* and *it is hereby declared and ordained,*

That the Ordinance adopted by us in Convention, on the twenty-third day of May, in the year of our Lord one thousand seven hundred and eighty-eight, whereby the Constitution of the United States of America was ratified, and also, all Acts and parts of Acts of the General Assembly of this State, ratifying amendments of the said Constitution, are hereby repealed; and that the union now subsisting between South Carolina and other States, under the name of *The United States of America," is hereby dissolved.

THE

UNION

IS

DISSOLVED!

bloodshed that followed. General Henry Halleck wrote to Sherman, "Should you capture Charleston, I hope that by some accident the place may be destroyed, and if a little salt should be sown upon its site it may prevent the growth of future crops of nullification and secession." Charleston itself was spared Sherman's presence.With its inland communications cut, it was, in his words, "a dead cock in the pit." Though the main body of Sherman's army veered northward toward Columbia, a small detachment marched east, and only one of the elegant plantation homes that lined the Ashley River west of Charleston escaped their torches. The owner of Drayton Hall sent his slaves to greet the advancing Union troops with the news that the home was being used as a yellow fever hospital. Whether true or not, the soldiers skirted the property, and the house survived.

When the war ended in April 1865, Charleston lay desolate. After years of stagnation, the regeneration of the city's business and social fabric had only just begun when a massive earthquake struck in August 1886. Buildings were flattened and roads made impassable. Few structures escaped damage, but because of the city's economic woes, buildings were repaired rather than razed. Earthquake rods were run through houses and tightened with exterior bolts to pull weakened structures back together. These bolts, which are visible on many buildings throughout the city, have become a status symbol of sorts, as their presence indicates the structure was built prior to 1886.

Charleston slumbered until after the turn of the century when yet another war, this time a worldwide conflict, brought a naval shipyard to the area. With the influx of workers came a wave of development and the realization that many of the city's old buildings were threatened. In 1929 Charleston passed the country's first historic zoning laws, and the city continues to be at the forefront of American preservation efforts.

This chapter is divided into several sections. The first begins on East Bay Street in the downtown historic district and works its way south to the tip of the peninsula before turning north. In this manner the tour route weaves its way up and down the city's main thoroughfares. The second section covers sites north of Market Street. The next section deals with sites along the Ashley River, northwest of the city, and the final portion covers sites in the eastern environs.

OPPOSITE: *Federal ships blockading Charleston Harbor can be seen in the distance of Conrad Chapman's painting* The Flag of Sumter, October 20, 1863 *(detail).*

DOWNTOWN CHARLESTON

EAST BAY/EAST BATTERY

Construction of the imposing marble **U.S. Custom House** (200 East Bay Street, 803–724–4233) was begun in 1853. Progress was interrupted by the war, and the building was finally completed in 1879. It stands near the site of Craven's Bastion, the northeasternmost corner of the original walled city. The city's early wharves crowded along the Cooper River from Queen Street southward; the short streets that jut into the river along East Bay are lined with rows of old warehouses, which once housed the goods that flowed through the city port. Many have been renovated for commercial use.

Old Exchange and Provost Dungeon

This stuccoed brick Palladian structure, built by the British in 1771, was the political and economic heart of eighteenth-century Charleston. Its main floor served as an arcade for the trade of rice, indigo, and other Carolina products at a time when more than a hundred sailing ships sometimes lined the harbor wharves. During the Revolutionary War, three signers of the Declaration of Independence and other Americans were imprisoned in the cellar by the British when they occupied the city from mid-1780 through 1782. A portion of the wall that originally enclosed the city is still visible in the dungeon. The building's Great Hall witnessed the selection of South Carolina's delegates to the Continental Congress, South Carolina's ratification of the U.S. Constitution, and a gala ball given for President George Washington in 1791.

LOCATION: 122 East Bay Street. HOURS: 9:30–5 Monday–Saturday.
FEE: Yes. TELEPHONE: 803–792–5020.

The attached buildings known as **Rainbow Row** (79–107 East Bay Street, private) were built between 1740 and 1789 and are a good example of the West Indian style redeployed by early Charlestonians. The ground floors served as shops with residences for the merchants located above. Entrance to the second-floor quarters was originally by way of an outside staircase. At one time East Bay Street fronted directly on the wharves, making it a particularly convenient business address. After a fire in 1740, detached dwellings became increasingly popular, since the open spaces served as firebreaks. **Vanderhorst Row** (76–80 East Bay Street, private) was built in 1800 by General Arnoldus Vanderhorst, who served as mayor of Charleston, governor of South Carolina, and an officer in the War of 1812. Designed as a multifamily dwelling, it is a good example of a tenement, a term that was not originally pejorative.

The **Missroon House** (44 East Battery Street, private), an eighteenth-century structure, stands on the site of the Granville Bastion, which was at the southeastern corner of the original walled city. An unusual mansion at **25 East Battery Street** (private) combines Chinese and Tudor Gothic elements. It was built in 1885 by Charles H. Drayton, whose family plantation was Drayton Hall.

The Edmondston-Alston House

Charles Edmondston, a Scottish merchant who made his fortune in the import/export business, built this stately house with its fine view of the Charleston harbor in 1828. The financial panic of 1837 forced Edmondston to sell the mansion. Charles Alston, whose father purchased the house for him in 1838, immediately set about remodeling it; the result was this exceedingly handsome Greek Revival mansion with its three-story piazzas (probably added by Charles Reichardt in the 1838 remodeling).

The house has remained in the family since its purchase, and Alston descendants still reside on the mansion's third floor. The house retains a lived-in feel that is rare in a museum-house. Most of the furnishings are original to the family, including such diverse items as an original set of Audubon prints, family silver, and portraits. The most inviting room is the library, where nearly 1,000 leatherbound volumes line the walls and an Empire settee invites the reader. A slant-top desk, equipped with handles to facilitate moving, reflects the frequent pilgrimages Charleston families made from plantation to town and back again.

LOCATION: 21 East Battery Street. HOURS: 10–5 Monday–Saturday, 2–5 Sunday. FEE: Yes. TELEPHONE: 803–722–7171.

The three-story brick mansion at **9 East Battery Street** (private) is an early example of Greek Revival architecture, built in 1838 by Robert William Roper, a wealthy planter. The massive, unfluted columns on the two-tiered piazza dwarf those on other Charleston homes. The rope-shaped molding was conventional at the time and could be pur-

OVERLEAF: *Along Charleston's famous Battery, piazzas provide a unifying feature for a row of houses that are otherwise architecturally diverse.*

The second floor drawing room of the Edmonston–Alston House is furnished with many Alston family pieces. OPPOSITE: *The house's Corinthian-columned third story piazza was added by Charles Alston in 1838.*

chased "by the yard" from northern lumber suppliers. During the Civil War a fragment from an exploding cannon was hurled through the roof and landed in the attic, where it remains today. Earthquake rods, camouflaged by iron lion heads, are visible on the facade.

Built around 1849, **5 East Battery Street** (private) was the home of Dr. St. Julien Ravenel, a physician-scientist who helped design a semisubmersible vessel for use by the Confederacy. Ravenel's experiments with the area's phosphorus deposits for use in fertilizer helped establish a new industry that kept some plantation owners afloat after the economic devastation of the Civil War. Constructed about 1858, **1 East Battery Street** (private) overlooks the Charleston harbor. Its wide piazzas provided onlookers with a front-row seat during the Confederate bombardment of Fort Sumter on April 12, 1861. The *New York Herald* reported that "every available place has been thronged by ladies and gentlemen, viewing the solemn spectacle through their glasses."

White Point Gardens

These gardens, commonly referred to as the Battery, serve as a city park at the tip of the Charleston peninsula. The name White Point

A Confederate battery at Fort Johnson bombards Fort Sumter in a contemporary engraving of the first military engagement of the Civil War.

came from the mounds of white oyster shells found on the site by the early colonists. The settlers crushed the shells and used them to cover streets and walkways. During the Revolution a redoubt of palmetto logs was erected here and armed with sixteen heavy guns in anticipation of a British invasion by sea. The gardens were laid out in the 1830s, but when the Civil War erupted, the site was once again fortified. Confederate troops installed a thirty-eight-ton Blakely gun; when they evacuated the city in February 1865, they blew up the gun rather than have it fall into Union hands. Its fragments were thrown so high that they damaged the roofs of several mansions along East Battery Street. Today the park contains cannons and other war memorials, reminders of its martial past.

Fort Sumter National Monument

Fort Sumter stands on a man-made granite island at the entrance to Charleston harbor, and is accessible only by boat (call 803–722–1691 for times of departure). The opening shots of the Civil War were directed at this federal stronghold on April 12, 1861, by Confederate

Ruins of the officers' quarters and powder magazine, Fort Sumter. Most of the wooden portions of the building burned during the Confederate bombardment in 1861.

guns located at Fort Johnson on nearby James Island. The decision to fire, relayed to General Pierre G. T. Beauregard from the Confederate cabinet in Montgomery, Alabama, was the culmination of days of negotiation on the issue of resupplying the federal garrison at Sumter. The Confederate government declared any resupply effort would be viewed as a hostile act. When Lincoln announced his intention to send additional provisions to the island, the Confederates issued an ultimatum to the fort's commander, Major Robert Anderson, demanding surrender.

Mary Boykin Chesnut recorded in her diary the anticipation that gripped the city. "I do not pretend to sleep. How can I? If Anderson does not accept terms—at four A.M.—the orders are—he shall be fired upon. I count four—St. Michael chimes. I begin to hope. At half-past four, the heavy booming of a cannon. . . . There was a sound of stir all over the house—pattering of feet in the corridor—all seemed hurrying one way. I put on my double gown and shawl and went, too. It was to the housetop. The shells were bursting. . . . Prayers from the women and imprecations from the men, and then a shell would light up the scene."

After thirty-four hours of bombardment by Confederate batteries, Major Anderson surrendered. (Ironically, Anderson had been Beauregard's artillery instructor at West Point.) On April 14 the southern flag was raised over the fort and remained there until February 1865, when southern forces evacuated Charleston and its defenses. On April 14, 1865, Anderson, then a general, returned to the island, four years to the day after his surrender, and raised the Stars and Stripes over the fort's battered remains.

> LOCATION: Tour boats depart from two locations: the City Marina (17 Lockwood Boulevard) and Patriot's Point (off Route 17). Site interpretation and information can be found at the Fort Moultrie visitor center, 1214 Middle Street, Sullivan's Island. HOURS: Late May through early September: 9–6 Daily; mid-September through mid-May: 9–5 Daily. FEE: Yes. TELEPHONE: 803–883–3123.

SOUTH BATTERY

South Battery Street was originally called Fort Street; both names reflect Charleston's beginnings as a walled fortress-garrison. The houses along this street possessed an unrestricted view of the harbor until the mud flats that stretched from the west end of White Point Gardens to the west end of Tradd Street were reclaimed and Murray Boulevard was constructed between 1909 and 1911. The Italian Renaissance Revival mansion at **4 South Battery Street** (private) was constructed in 1894; shortly after 1905 it was converted into a popular hotel called the Villa Marguerita. Guests included Alexander Graham Bell, Theodore Roosevelt, and Henry Ford. The **William Washington House** (8 South Battery Street, private) was constructed around 1768 in the Georgian style and was purchased in 1785 by a Virginia kinsman of George Washington. William Washington arrived in South Carolina during the Revolutionary War as a cavalry officer. When he lamented his lack of a battle flag, a young lady named Jane Elliot cut up one of her mother's crimson curtains and set to work with her needle. After the war she became his bride.

The cupola on **32 South Battery Street** (private) is an architectural element worthy of note because it is only occasionally seen on Charleston homes. The house dates to the 1780s. The **Moreland House** (39 South Battery Street, private) was built in 1827 on a foundation of palmetto logs sunk into the marshy ground. This "floating" foundation helped the house survive the 1886 earthquake with little damage. The **William Gibbes House** (64 South Battery Street, private) is an impressive example of Georgian architecture, with the doorway's wide entablature and pediment. Built between 1772 and 1788 as the westernmost house along this street, the house overlooked Gibbes's own wharf, which once stood along the River.

CHURCH STREET

One of the original streets laid out in 1680, Church Street extended the length of the seventeenth-century town, from what is now Cumberland Street to Vanderhorst Creek, which ran along present-day Water Street. As marshy land was filled in, the street was extended, creating a jog in the road as it crosses Water Street.

During the Civil War, **15 Church Street** (private) was the residence of Dr. William Snowden and served as a hospital. The Snowden family buried their silver in the garden during the conflict, and it was not recovered until 1922. The **Young-Johnson House** (35 Church Street, private) was built around 1770 and was, for a time, the home of Dr. Joseph Johnson, a mayor of Charleston. The **George Mathews House** (37 Church Street, private) was constructed in 1750 in the Georgian style. The handwrought balcony is typical of early Charleston ironwork. Tradition says that one owner stored his gold in a water cask that stood on the porch in the belief that thieves would never suspect such an obvious hiding place.

The 1819 Regency-style house at **38 Church Street** was built by Dr. Vincent LeSeigneur, who fled to Charleston after the Santo Domingan slave rebellion in 1793. The crenellated north bay was added sometime after 1894. The picturesque **George Eveleigh House** (39 Church Street, private) dates to the 1740s. It has a two-story piazza and a front door placed asymmetrically, thereby flouting one of the basic rules of the Georgian architecture, a style that emphasizes balance. Eveleigh, who made a fortune trading furs with the Indians, returned to England with his hard-won wealth. In 1795 the noted botanist Dr. Jean Louis Polony purchased the home.

A relatively recent addition to the street is **41 Church Street** (private). It was built in 1909, supposedly on a wager that a building this large would not fit on such a narrow lot. The house is set at an angle, and the garage entrance is through the chimney. A Baptist church has stood on the site of the **First Baptist Church** (61 Church Street) since 1699. The members of the original congregation fled to South Carolina in 1683 to escape religious persecution in Maine. During the Revolution, the church's minister was Reverend Richard Furman, founder of Furman University. The present Greek Revival building, with its Doric portico, dates from 1822. It was designed by Robert Mills, who proudly declared this structure "the best specimen of correct taste in architecture in the city."

The stuccoed, brick **Colonel Robert Brewton House** (71 Church Street, private), which was constructed around 1730, is believed to be the city's oldest surviving example of a single house. The house's wrought-iron balcony and heavily molded cornice are notable features. Mary Brewton Foster was banished from the city in 1781 after offending the notoriously cranky British officer Banastre Tarleton. Tarleton had been soundly beaten by the Americans, including the Charlestonian William Washington, at the Battle of Cowpens. When he acidly remarked to Mrs. Foster that he would like to meet this Washington fellow, she supposedly replied, "What a pity you did not look behind you at Cowpens."

The small house at **76 Church Street** (private, now part of 78 Church) was the home of the writer DuBose Heyward. It was while living here in the 1920s that he wrote *Porgy,* the novel that inspired George Gershwin's opera *Porgy and Bess.*

The Charleston Museum's Heyward-Washington House

The severe brick facade of the Heyward-Washington house does not hint at the wealth of eighteenth-century woodwork and furnishings within. Built in 1772, it served as the townhouse for Thomas Heyward, a wealthy rice planter who studied law in London and became a Patriot leader. Heyward served in the Continental Congress and was a signer of the Declaration of Independence. When the British occupied the city in 1780, Heyward was arrested and imprisoned in Saint Augustine, Florida. His family remained in the house, and in 1781 when the British ordered residents to place lighted candles in their windows in celebration of the occupation, Heyward's wife, Elizabeth, refused, remaining adamant even when faced with an angry mob that gathered in the streets and threw debris at the house windows. In April 1791 George Washington stayed in the house for an entire week (thus, it seems probable,

OPPOSITE: *A pine dough box covered with a variety of cooking utensils in the Heyward–Washington House kitchen, located in an outbuilding behind the house.*

sleeping here) during his triumphal tour of the south. This brief encounter accounts for the latter part of the house's name.

The first-floor rooms, with their restrained Georgian woodwork, were where Heyward conducted the in-town duties obligatory for every successful planter. As with many Charleston houses, the second floor, more removed from the noise of the street and able to catch whatever breeze was available, was the heart of the home. The spacious drawing room displays marvelously detailed Georgian woodwork, such as the mahogany fretwork above the fireplace, thought to be the work of Thomas Elfe. The furnishings are outstanding representatives of the period. One example is a finely carved mahogany bed; the headboard is removable, as was the case with many Charleston-made beds, permitting increased ventilation in the steamy summer months. The Holmes library bookcase, a massive mahogany piece with delicate brass pulls and satinwood and ivory inlay, was created around 1775 by an unknown Charlestonian. It is one of the finest examples of colonial craftsmanship.

The outbuildings at the rear of the property, including a two-story kitchen building with a huge hearth and beehive oven, offer an interesting glimpse of eighteenth-century domestic life.

LOCATION: 87 Church Street. HOURS: 10–5 Monday–Saturday, 1–5 Sunday. FEE: Yes. TELEPHONE: 803–722–0354.

Cabbage Row (private) is the colorful name given to the tenement at 89–91 Church Street. Rowhouses such as these reflect the West Indian influence on the city's architecture. DuBose Heyward used the building as the prototype for Catfish Row in his novel *Porgy*. For dramatic purposes, Heyward placed the building along East Bay Street, two blocks east. The character of Porgy was based on a black Charlestonian, Sammy Smalls, a crippled beggar who drove through the streets in a cart pulled by a goat.

The **Thomas Bee House** (94 Church Street, private) a brick, single-style structure, was built between 1760 and 1765 by John Cooper, a merchant. Bee served in both the First and Second Continental Congresses. The house was later purchased by Governor Joseph Alston, whose wife was Theodosia Burr, the daughter of Aaron Burr. On her way to visit her father in 1812, Theodosia was lost at sea. In 1832 John C. Calhoun and others met in the second-floor drawing room to draft the Ordinance of Nullification, by which they intended to make federal tariff laws null and void in South Carolina. President Andrew Jackson, a South Carolina native, called the act treasonous and prepared to enforce the law with federal troops. A compromise on the tariffs defused the crisis, but the issue of a state's right to nullify a federal law remained alive.

Dock Street Theatre

A theater was built on this site in 1735—one of the earliest playhouses in America. At the beginning of the nineteenth century, the Planter's Hotel replaced the original structure and became a favorite gathering place for Charleston's wealthier citizens (it is said that the drink called planter's punch originated here). The present building incorporates the hotel as well as a reconstruction of an eighteenth-century playhouse, which is used for performances. The interior features fine Federal-style details on ceilings, mantels, and doorways, some of which were rescued from homes of the period that were slated for demolition.

LOCATION: 135 Church Street. HOURS: Noon–6 Monday–Friday. FEE: Yes. TELEPHONE: 803-723-5648.

The **French Protestant (Huguenot) Church** (136 Church Street), an elaborate structure erected in 1845 to designs by Edward B. White, was the first Charleston church to use the Gothic Revival style. The first church on this site was built by French Protestant immigrants in 1687. The original building survived until 1796, when fire swept the city and the church was deliberately blown up in an attempt to halt the flames' progress.

The congregation of **Saint Philip's Episcopal Church** (146 Church Street) was established in 1680, making it the first Anglican church organized south of Virginia. Tradition says that the first rector, "confusing spirits with spirituality," once christened a young bear. The present building was built in 1835 after fire destroyed an eighteenth-century edifice. The octagonal steeple, designed by Edward Brickell White, was added in 1848. For years the light burning there was a landmark for mariners. During the Civil War, the steeple was a favorite target of the Union batteries on nearby Morris Island, and the building sustained extensive damage. The church's bells were melted down for the Confederate cause and were not replaced until

In Charleston, colonial artisans used wrought iron—iron hammered when red hot into a desired shape—to create these decorative and utilitarian objects. In the mid-nineteenth century, cast iron—iron poured into molds and allowed to harden —became increasingly popular, particularly for designs that were composed of multiple units, such as fences. Cast iron was frequently used in conjunction with wrought iron to create the beautifully patterned fences, balconies, and gates that add distinction to the city's historic buildings. Among the abundant examples of elaborate architectural ironwork are the gate of 27 Meeting Street (opposite left); the spiky chevaux de frise, a method of fortification developed in the Netherlands, at the Miles Brewton House (above); and the gate of 37 Meeting Street (opposite right).

1976. The graveyard, which lies on both sides of Church Street, contains the graves of John C. Calhoun, DuBose Heyward, and Edward Rutledge, a signer of the Declaration of Independence.

MARKET STREET

The market hall and sheds that stand in the center of Market Street extend from Meeting Street to East Bay Street. Designed by Edward Brickell White in 1841, the buildings are on the site used as the city's marketplace since the early nineteenth century. The buzzards that helped keep the market clean were affectionately known as "Charleston Eagles." **Market Hall** (188 Meeting Street), which was patterned after a Greek temple, now houses the **Confederate Museum** (803–723–1541 or 803–588–2291). Founded in 1898 and still maintained by the Daughters of the Confederacy, the museum contains uniforms, weapons, and other Confederate memorabilia. The arcaded basement houses shops, and the one-story sheds that extend for several blocks to the rear of the hall are still lined with merchants' stalls.

MEETING STREET

Present-day Meeting Street, one of the city's main north–south thoroughfares, corresponds roughly to what was once the western boundary of the original walled city.

Established in 1681 by a combination of French Huguenots, Presbyterians, and Congregationalists, the **Circular Congregational Church** (150 Meeting Street), was the earliest dissenting congregation in South Carolina. This massive brick structure is the fourth to stand on the site. Built in 1892 in the Richardsonian Romanesque style, it incorporates bricks salvaged from an 1806 structure designed by Robert Mills. The first church at this location, known as the White Meeting House, gave Meeting Street its name. This structure was replaced in 1732, and the second church served as a British hospital during the Revolutionary War. The first circular building, constructed in 1806, was destroyed by fire in 1861; its ruins stood until 1886 when the Charleston earthquake leveled what remained. The graveyard, one of the city's oldest, contains numerous eighteenth-century stones. The church's interior has recently been restored.

Frances R. Edmunds Center for Historic Preservation

The center houses the Preservation Programs Division of the Historic Charleston Foundation, a nonprofit organization established in 1947 to help preserve Charleston's architectural heritage. The foundation's goal is to preserve specific endangered buildings and sites, as well as the architectural integrity of entire neighborhoods. This work is accomplished by a revolving fund; old structures are purchased, stabilized, and then sold with restrictions regarding future alterations and use. Each spring the foundation sponsors "A Festival of Houses," enabling visitors to tour a sampling of the city's historic private homes. The center also offers exhibits on Charleston's architecture and the preservation movement.

LOCATION: 108 Meeting Street. HOURS: 10–5 Monday–Saturday, 2–5 Sunday. FEE: None. TELEPHONE: 803–723–8485.

Hibernian Society Hall (105 Meeting Street), a two-story Greek Revival building constructed of brick which has been stuccoed and painted, was completed in 1841 as the headquarters of a society founded in 1799 by eight Irishmen. It was one of a number of ethnic organizations founded in eighteenth-century Charleston to provide charity to the needy in the days before governmental agencies provided such relief. Tradition demands that the society's presidency alternate between Catholic and Protestant members. The portico was rebuilt after its collapse during the 1886 earthquake. The white-stuccoed **Fireproof Building** (100 Meeting Street, 803–723–3225) is a freely adapted Palladian structure designed by Robert Mills, constructed from 1822 to 1827, the first fireproof building in the United States. Originally built to store governmental records, today it houses the South Carolina Historical Society. The society's library and collection, which includes documents dating to the seventeenth century, are open to the public for research purposes only. The **Charleston County Courthouse** (77 Meeting Street) dates to 1792 and incorporates the foundation and walls of the 1752 Provincial State House, which was gutted by fire. The intersection in front of the courthouse is known as the **Four Corners of Law,** because the building on each corner represents a different form of government: county (Courthouse), federal (U.S. Courthouse), municipal (City Hall), and religious (Saint Michael's Episcopal Church).

The **City Hall** (Meeting and Broad streets) was designed by
Charleston native Gabriel Manigault. Constructed in about 1802 as a
branch of the Bank of the United States, it was purchased by the city
in 1818. Jefferson Davis delivered "an eloquent and patriotic
address" here in the autumn of 1863 while the town was under siege
by Union forces. A portrait gallery in the council chamber contains
paintings acquired over the years as a result of the custom of commis-
sioning likenesses of famous visitors to the city. Most notable is John
Trumbull's 1791 portrait of George Washington. Adjacent to the hall
is **Washington Square,** also known as City Hall Park. The park contains a number of monuments.

Saint Michael's Episcopal Church

The oldest surviving church building in the city, Saint Michael's was
built between 1752 and 1761 in a style reminiscent of London's
Saint Martin-in-the-Fields, quite possibly from designs by the same
architect, James Gibbs. The church's soaring steeple, one of the
city's most enduring landmarks, has long served as a beacon for
mariners and for much of the nineteenth century doubled as the
city's fire tower. The church bells have had an eventful existence.
Originally imported from England in 1764, they were shipped back
to England as British booty during the Revolutionary period but
were later returned. During the Civil War, they were damaged by fire
and sent back to England yet again, this time for recasting, before
recrossing the Atlantic for the fifth time. The original pulpit, with its
massive sounding board, is intact, and pew forty-three was used for
worship by George Washington and Robert E. Lee during visits to
the city.

LOCATION: Meeting and Broad streets. HOURS: 9–5 Monday–Friday,
9–12 Saturday. TELEPHONE: 803–723–0603.

South Carolina Society Hall (72 Meeting Street, private) is a prime
example of Federal architecture. Designed by Gabriel Manigault,
the hall was constructed in 1804 to house the society, which was
founded in 1737 by several prominent Huguenots. The first floor

OPPOSITE: *The steeple of St. Michael's Church rises 182 feet from the ground. Its*
four-faced clock has been a Charleston landmark since 1764.

was used as a charity school, which operated until the advent of the public school system; the second floor served as the society's meeting hall. A two-story, Greek Revival portico was added in 1825. The **Branford-Horry House** (59 Meeting Street, private), a handsome double house, was built in about 1767 by William Branford. The two-story portico, which extends over the sidewalk, was added in the 1830s by Elias Horry, Branford's great-grandson.

The congregation of the **First (Scots) Presbyterian Church** (57 Meeting Street) was founded in 1731 by twelve Scottish families, and the present building, with its heavy, twin towers, was constructed in 1814. The seal of the Church of Scotland can be seen over the main entrance. The church bells were donated to the Confederacy in 1863 and have never been replaced.

Nathaniel Russell House

Though the name of the architect responsible for this three-story brick mansion is unknown, his disdain for convention is evidenced

Nathaniel Russell's initials adorn a second-story balcony of his elegant brick house. The Rhode Island merchant spent $80,000 for the house and its furnishings—a remarkable amount for 1808.

by the omission of a piazza, a standard architectural feature in Charleston houses of the period, as well as by the floor plan that results in a delightful variety of room shapes: oval, square, and rectangular. The builder's ultimate statement was the exquisite three-story staircase, which spirals upward without touching the walls, seemingly with no means of support. Nathaniel Russell, a native of Rhode Island, arrived in Charleston in 1765 and established a mercantile empire based on rice, indigo, cotton, and slaves. He built this mansion in 1808. The house is furnished with pieces produced prior to 1820, many of them made in Charleston, including a fine Hepplewhite table that graces the dining room. The woodwork throughout the house is one of the best examples of the Federal style in the city. The second-floor music room, with its fluted pilasters framing windowlike mirrors, renders the room both elegant and inviting. Adequate ventilation, despite the absence of a piazza, was ensured by the installation of tall windows, which extend to the floor and open onto iron balconies. The balcony above the

The Russell House's oval second-floor drawing room contains a harp made in Paris ca. 1803 and an Empire sofa made in New York in the same period. On the sofa is an English lyre from the 1760s, which belonged to Eliza Lucas Pinckney.

front door contains the initials "N.R." within the elaborate ironwork, a lasting reminder of the house's original owner.

LOCATION: 51 Meeting Street. HOURS: 10–5 Monday–Saturday, 2–5 Sunday. FEE: Yes. TELEPHONE: 803–723–1623.

Number **37 Meeting Street** (private), served as General Pierre G. T. Beauregard's headquarters until 1863, when Union shelling forced him to relocate farther north on the peninsula. Tradition says that the general, who had an ulcer, kept a cow in the backyard to keep him freshly supplied with milk.

The house at **35 Meeting Street** (private) was built around 1720 by William Bull, the lieutenant governor of the province, and is one of the oldest in the city. The porticoes were not part of the original design. The **Bull-Huger House** (34 Meeting Street, private) is typical of a Charleston double house and was built around 1760. It was the residence of Lord William Campbell, South Carolina's last royal governor. In September 1775 Campbell slipped out of the house after dark and fled to a British man-of-war anchored in the harbor. He died nine months later of wounds suffered in the British attack on Sullivans Island. In 1825 the marquis de Lafayette was entertained in the house by the Huger family.

The Georgian-style single house at **30 Meeting Street** (private) was built around 1770. Tradition says that deserting Hessian soldiers hid in the home's chimneys to avoid being evacuated with the British troops in 1782. One of the signers of the Declaration of Independence, Thomas Heyward, built the three-story brick house at **18 Meeting Street** (private) around 1803. Heyward had resided previously at the Heyward-Washington House on Church Street. Captured by the British in 1780, Heyward was imprisoned at Saint Augustine, Florida, for the duration of the war.

Calhoun Mansion

This thirty-five-room mansion was built by George W. Williams in 1876. It is often said locally that it is an anomaly, but though few homes of its size were built in the city so soon after the Civil War, Charleston did have a modest resurgence in the 1870s. Williams, a banker, spared no expense. His son-in-law, Patrick Calhoun (a grandson of John C. Calhoun), inherited the house, but when it passed out of the family in the 1930s, most of the original furnishings and many of the chandeliers were sold. In 1977, when restoration began, the mansion was on the verge of being condemned. Still a private residence, only the first and second floors are open to the public. The quality of materials used in the mansion's construction is typified by its solid walnut front doors, each of which weigh 300 pounds. The woodwork in each of the rooms features a different type of wood, such as walnut, cherry, or bird's-eye maple. The focal point of the spacious ballroom is a coved glass skylight arching forty-five feet overhead. The house contains many fine nineteenth-century furnishings, though only a few are original to the home; these include a mahogany dining table, various gilt mirrors, and a set of early-nineteenth-century Senate records (discovered in the attic) with marginal notes made by John C. Calhoun.

LOCATION: 16 Meeting Street. HOURS: 10–4 Daily. FEE: Yes. TELEPHONE: 803–722–8205.

Josiah Smith, the builder of **7 Meeting Street** (private), was responsible for reclaiming much of the marshland between Meeting and King streets, enabling the city to grow in that direction. The house was constructed during the 1780s. The Queen Anne mansion now known as **2 Meeting Street Inn** (803–723–7322) was built in 1892 and features a number of "Tiffany" windows, some of which, though unsigned, may be the work of Tiffany and Company. The house has offered bed-and-breakfast accommodations since 1931.

KING STREET

One of the city's main thoroughfares, King Street was laid out along a low ridge of ground that rose above creeks and marshes that once pockmarked the peninsula. It has long been a center of commerce for the city. The **Patrick O'Donnell House** (21 King Street, private) was built in the Italianate style during the 1850s. O'Donnell was an Irish immigrant and master builder who built this house for his fiancé; the construction took so long she married someone else.

The handsome brick **Miles Brewton House** (27 King Street, private), with its two-tiered portico, has been called "the most elegant expression of South Carolina Palladianism." The house was the work of a Londoner, Ezra Waite, who completed the building in 1769 for Brewton, a colonial merchant and leading slave trader. When

The Miles Brewton House is thought to be the supreme example of the Charleston double house. The two-story piazza takes the form of a Palladian portico with Portland stone pillars painted white.

Brewton entertained the Bostonian merchant Josiah Quincy here, Quincy wrote glowingly of "the grandest hall I ever beheld, azure blue satin window curtains, rich blue paper with gilt . . . excessive grand and costly looking glasses." Brewton and his family were lost at sea in 1775. The house served as headquarters for Sir Henry Clinton and Lord Cornwallis during the American Revolution as well as Union generals George Meade and Edward Hatch during the Civil War. During its occupation by the British, the lady of the house, Rebecca Motte, supposedly hid her three daughters in the attic and thought her deception had been successful until the British commander, upon taking his leave, stared up at the ceiling and lamented having been unable to meet the rest of her family. The ominous-looking spikes that top the house's wrought-iron fence are called "chevaux-de-frise," after the military defensive use of brush and uprooted trees. The local story goes that they were put in place after a major slave revolt in 1822. The houses at **50 and 52 King Street** are examples of early Georgian architecture; both date from around 1730.

The **Preservation Society** (147 King Street, 803–723–4381) was founded in 1920. Largely through the efforts of its members, Charleston adopted the nation's first historic district zoning ordinance in 1931. The society's headquarters maintains a large library on Charleston and the Carolina low country. Each autumn the society offers its annual "House and Garden Candlelight Tours" when a variety of Charleston's private homes and gardens are opened.

ARCHDALE STREET

This short street was named for John Archdale, a Quaker who served as provincial governor from 1695 to 1696. The first church on the site of **Saint John's Lutheran Church** (10 Archdale Street) was constructed between 1759 and 1764. A wood-frame structure, it stood along Clifford Street, to the rear of the property. During the British occupation of Charleston in 1780–1782, the church's pastor, John Nicholas Martin, refused to pray for the king; he was banished from the city and all his property was confiscated. In 1816–1818 the present building was constructed under the leadership of Dr. John Bachman. Of particular note are the tall iron gates crafted in 1822. Bachman was interested in natural science as well as theology, and he collaborated with John James Audubon on the book *The Viviparous Quadrupeds of North America*. Two of Bachman's daughters married two of Audubon's sons.

The congregation of the **Unitarian Church** (6 Archdale Street), the oldest Unitarian church in the south, was chartered in 1817, but the building is even older. Originally built as a Congregational church, it was constructed between 1772 and 1787. In 1852 extensive remodeling was undertaken by Francis D. Lee, a prominent Charleston architect. The Gothic Revival style was extremely popular at that time, though seldom used with Lee's virtuosity. He retained the eighteenth-century walls, adding the Gothic arched window, buttresses, and a fan-tracery vaulted ceiling based upon that of Gloucester Cathedral.

LEGARE STREET

Sword Gates House (32 Legare Street, private) gets its name from the ornate iron gates mounted in the tall brick wall that surrounds the property. Crafted by Christopher Werner in the 1830s, they were

installed here in 1849 by George Hopley, then British consul. The handsome ca. 1789 frame house at **31 Legare Street** (private) is said to be haunted by the ghost of young James Heyward, the nephew of Thomas Heyward, a signer of the Declaration of Independence. After serving in the Revolutionary War and escaping unscathed, Heyward was killed in a hunting accident. His sister claimed that, on the morning of his death, she walked into the house's library and saw the misty figure of her brother seated in a chair, head in hand.

British officers on the staffs of Lord Cornwallis and Sir Henry Clinton occupied the frame single house at **15 Legare Street** (private) from 1780 to 1782. Of special note are the house's ornamental window casings. The single Federal-style house at **14 Legare Street** (private) was built around 1800 by Francis Simmons, a wealthy planter. The next owner, George Edwards, enlarged the house sometime after 1818 and added the "pineapple" gates as well as the lovely ironwork.

TRADD STREET

This street was named for Robert Tradd, who was born in about 1679 and was probably the first male white child born in the city. The house at **143 Tradd Street** (private) was constructed between 1797 and 1801. It is unusual for that period because it is set well back from the road. The three-story **Colonel John Stuart House** (106 Tradd Street, private) was built prior to 1772 of black cypress, which is sometimes called the "everlasting" wood. Stuart was a Tory who served as superintendent for Indian affairs. He fled Charleston in 1775 amid accusations of inciting several tribes to side with the British. Portions of the house's original interiors, including its Siena marble mantels, were sold and are now on display at the Minneapolis Institute of Art.

The double house at **72 Tradd Street** (private) was constructed around 1765 to serve as the residence of two physicians. One of them, Dr. Archibald MacNeill, had a grandniece who won immortality as "Whistler's Mother." It is said that Jacob Motte, a prominent Huguenot, built **61 Tradd Street** (private) in 1731. Motte

OPPOSITE: *The iron fence at 14 Legare Street was added by its second owner, George Edwards, who incorporated his initial in the design.*

served as royal treasurer of the province. The Motte house and the early Georgian house at **60 Tradd Street** (private), which dates to 1732, were two of only a handful to escape the frequent fires that raged inside the original walled city during the eighteenth century. The unimposing structure at **54 Tradd Street** (private) was built around 1740 and is thought to have served as Charleston's first post office.

The **Studio-Museum of Elizabeth O'Neill Verner** (38 Tradd Street, 803–722–4246) was the studio of this native Charlestonian (1883–1979) whose subject matter was frequently the city's houses, churches, and natural beauty. The building was built by a Huguenot cooper in around 1694 and is the earliest surviving house in the city. Number **7 Tradd Street** (private) is a classic example of the earliest form of dwelling that once lined Charleston harbor. The arched passage leads off the street to a private garden and family entrance.

BROAD STREET

This street was originally called Cooper Street, after Lord Anthony Ashley-Cooper, earl of Shaftesbury, one of the province's lord proprietors. Within a generation or so, the street was known as Broad because it was the widest roadway in the original city. The area "south of Broad" is largely residential, and those Charlestonians who inhabit this prime real estate are playfully referred to as SOBs.

For more than 250 years, the owner of **68 Broad Street** (private) has been named Daniel Ravenel, the only exception being a solitary Henry. The brick three-story single house was constructed shortly after a 1796 fire destroyed a previous dwelling on the site. The glazed brick window lintels were probably imported from Holland.

The Georgian frame house at **92 Broad Street** (private) was built around 1740; during the Revolutionary period it was the residence of Dr. David Ramsey, a member of the Continental Congress and a surgeon for the Continental Army who had trained under Dr. Benjamin Rush. Imprisoned by the British, Ramsey conceived the idea of writing a history of the Revolution, a work he completed after his release.

The house at **110 Broad Street** (private) was constructed prior to 1728 and may have served for a time as the home of one of the provincial governors, James Glen. A later resident, Joel Roberts Poinsett, was the first U.S. ambassador to Mexico; he is credited with introducing the poinsettia into this country.

The **Colonel Thomas Pinckney, Jr., House** (114 Broad Street, private) served as one of General Beauregard's headquarters during the Civil War siege of Charleston. The general was forced to move his place of residence from time to time to avoid Union shelling. The mansion at **116 Broad Street** (private) was the home of John Rutledge, a prominent colonial leader and friend of George Washington. Rutledge helped draft the U.S. Constitution and held numerous other public positions, including chief justice of the Supreme Court and governor of South Carolina. The iron balconies, fence, and stair rails were added in 1835 and are the work of Christopher Werner, one of the city's foremost iron craftsmen. The house is now an inn. John's brother, Edward Rutledge, who lived across the street at **117 Broad Street** (private), was a signer of the Declaration of Independence. Both houses were built prior to the Revolution.

CHALMERS STREET

Chalmers Street is still paved with cobblestones, a type of surface once found on many Charleston streets. The stones arrived in the city as ballast in ships from European ports. Their extra weight was not needed for the return trip, as cargoes shipped from Charleston were frequently composed of bulky materials such as timber or barrels of rice. The diminutive **Pink House** (17 Chalmers Street), constructed of Bermuda stone, was built early in the eighteenth century and served as a tavern and bordello frequented by sailors. In 1800 this particular red-light district was cleaned up by order of the city council; the businesses soon relocated to an area west of King Street.

The **Old Slave Mart** (6 Chalmers Street) was originally called Ryan's Auction Mart. Constructed in 1853 by Thomas Ryan, it was one of a number of auction houses located within the city. Everything from livestock to furniture was sold here. For generations, slaves were sold near the wharves just north of the exchange on East Bay Street, but in 1856 a city ordinance forbade such street sales because of traffic problems. From that point Ryan's became increasingly known for its slave auctions.

QUEEN STREET

The **Thomas Elfe Workshop** (54 Queen Street, 803–722–2130) was the residence of one of Charleston's eighteenth-century master craftsmen. The house, a scaled-down single house, was built by Elfe around 1760, and his craftsmanship is evident in the home's woodwork. A collection of eighteenth-and nineteenth-century woodworking tools are on display. Elfe's exquisite furniture graced Charleston's finest homes, and a number of his pieces can be seen at the Heyward-Washington House.

One block north is the **Powder Magazine** (79 Cumberland Street, 803–722–3767), the city's oldest surviving public building. Constructed in 1713, the walls of the square, one-story building are composed of brick and tabby, a cementlike mixture made from lime, sand, and ground oyster shells. The magazine served the Carteret Bastion at the northwestern corner of the original walled city and now houses a small museum operated by the Colonial Dames of America.

GREATER CHARLESTON

Although the heaviest concentration of restored historic structures is in the area from Market Street southward, revitalization of historic neighborhoods elsewhere on the peninsula is occurring at an increasingly rapid rate. By the middle of the eighteenth century, a number of "suburbs" began to develop north of the original city. The first was **Ansonborough,** named for Baron George Anson, an admiral in the Royal Navy. This area (which stretches from Market to Calhoun Street) contains more than 100 antebellum houses and a number of notable churches. **Wraggborough** (roughly bounded by Calhoun, Meeting, and Mary streets) is another such suburb that contains many noteworthy structures. The following sites are a sampling of the many interesting buildings found in such "outlying" areas. There are several historic structures on Hasell Street. **Saint Johannes Evangelical Lutheran Church of Charleston** (48 Hasell Street) was constructed in 1841–1842 and is the work of Edward Brickell White. The **Colonel William Rhett House** (54 Hasell Street, private) was once the main house for Rhettsbury plantation. Built around 1714, it is one of the city's oldest surviving structures. Colonel Rhett won the gratitude of early Charlestonians by capturing the pirate Stede Bonnet in 1718. Rhett returned Bonnet and his men to the city, and they were hanged near present-day White Point Gardens. The Confederate general Wade Hampton III was born here in 1818. One of the wealthiest planters in the South, Hampton personally financed and commanded his own Confederate "legion," a combination of artillery, infantry, and cavalry.

A large number of Jews seeking religious freedom settled in Charleston in the early part of the eighteenth century. There has been a synagogue on the site of the **Beth Elohim Synagogue** (90 Hasell Street) since 1792. The original structure was destroyed by fire and replaced by this impressive Greek Revival building, designed by the German architect Charles Reichardt, in 1840–1841. The synagogue is the second-oldest in the country (the oldest is the Touro Synagogue in Newport, Rhode Island). A small museum of Jewish artifacts is housed here.

Established in 1789, **Saint Mary's Roman Catholic Church** (95 Hasell Street) is the mother church of Catholicism in the Carolinas and Georgia. Worship was originally conducted in a frame building, which was replaced in 1801 by a brick structure, which was later destroyed by fire. The present church was constructed in 1838–1839. A portion of the early congregation were French-speaking refugees who fled Santo Domingo after a bloody slave rebellion in the 1790s. Many of the tombstones lining the churchyard are inscribed in French.

The **College of Charleston** (George and Saint Philip streets), which has occupied the present campus since 1790, contains a complex of three nineteenth-century stuccoed brick buildings. The main building, which dates to 1829, was constructed in the Greek Revival style from a design by William Strickland, a student of Benjamin Latrobe. Also noteworthy is the 1854 **library** and the 1852 Renaissance Revival **Gate Lodge.**

A public park on Calhoun Street, between King and Meeting streets, **Marion Square** is dominated by the **Old Citadel Building.** This structure, which originally served as an arsenal and barracks, was built in 1822 after an aborted slave rebellion led by Denmark Vesey, a carpenter and former slave. The building later housed the South Carolina Military Academy, known today as the Citadel. A

portion of the tabby wall that once marked the town's northern fortifications can still be seen. In 1780 these land defenses were besieged by British troops under the command of Sir Henry Clinton. Though the fortifications held, the colonists were forced to surrender when British shelling sparked fires within the city.

Construction of the **Second Presbyterian Church** (342 Meeting Street) was begun in 1809 for a growing congregation whose earliest members had begun worshipping together in Charleston in 1731. Property for the church was obtained from the Wragg family, for whom the Wraggsborough area of Charleston is named, and the church was completed in 1811 at a cost of $100,000. The brick-and-stucco building is in the Classic Revival style and features a square tower with an octagonal belfry. The simple yet elegant facade displays a projecting pediment supported by four columns.

CHARLESTON MUSEUM

The museum, founded in 1773, is the oldest such institution in the United States. In 1826 Charlestonians, for twenty-five cents, could view such novelties as "the head of a New Zealand chief and shoes of the Chinese ladies, four inches long." Today exhibits focus on the city and the South Carolina low country, covering such subjects as plantation life, natural history, slavery, rice culture, and the Civil War; featured is an illuminating explanation of the city's many architectural styles. Fine examples of Charleston-made furniture can be seen, including a design indigenous to the region known as a "rice" bed, so called because the carved motif reflected this source of wealth in early Carolina. An extensive collection of silver, which was either made in Charleston or imported for use by early Charleston households, is also on display. Many of the museum's most notable pieces of furniture grace three historic houses (Heyward-Washington, Aiken-Rhett, and Joseph Manigault), which are museum-owned and operated. The museum offers a clear, concise introduction to the region, making it an excellent place to begin one's exploration of coastal South Carolina.

LOCATION: 360 Meeting Street. HOURS: 9–5 Monday–Saturday, 1–5 Sunday. FEE: Yes. TELEPHONE: 803-722-2996.

OPPOSITE: *This 1865 photograph shows ruins seen from the Circular Congregational Church on Meeting Street. Fire and bombardment leveled many structures in downtown Charleston.*

Joseph Manigault House

This magnificent Federal-style mansion—a three-story, brick hip-roofed house—was built in 1803 as the townhouse for Joseph Manigault, a wealthy planter. Joseph's brother, Gabriel, a European-trained lawyer and amateur architect, designed the house, a grand departure from the traditional Charleston single or double house. Gabriel adapted the Franco-English villa style to the city's semitropical climate; the result is a spacious residence bisected by a wide stair hall with doors on either end to form an elegant breezeway. Seen from the front door, an archway in the hall forms the perfect frame for the graceful curve of the staircase.

None of the home's period furnishings actually belonged to the Manigaults, but many pieces on display are the work of Charleston craftsmen, such as a three-part dining room table and a mahogany-and-satinwood desk. In the garden stands the house's original "folly," a circular gatehouse representing a small Roman temple.

The Manigault family, like many other Huguenots, arrived in South Carolina in 1685 as refugees from religious persecution in France. Pierre Manigault was a weaver turned distiller, and his wife, Judith, supplemented the family income by taking in boarders. In a letter home, Judith wrote, "We have seen ourselves since our departure from France, in every sort of affliction; sickness, pestilence, famine, poverty, very hard work. I was in this country a full six months, without tasting bread, and whilst I worked the ground, like a slave." Just three generations later, despite such desperate beginnings, the family had risen to the gracious lifestyle exemplified by this elegant Meeting Street mansion.

LOCATION: 350 Meeting Street. HOURS: 10–5 Monday–Saturday, 1–5 Sunday. FEE: Yes. TELEPHONE: 803-723-2926.

Aiken-Rhett Mansion

This massive house, built in 1817 in the late Federal style, was the home of Governor William Aiken from 1833 to 1887. When Aiken inherited the house from his father in 1833, he remodeled it with Greek Revival features. To furnish his new residence, he spent three years in Europe collecting household items, including chan-

Charles Manigault, son of the architect Gabriel, with his family on a European grand tour in 1831 (detail).

deliers and furniture, some of which are still in the house today. An 1858 addition to the house created a remodeled Victorian doorway and a Rococo Revival art gallery.

Aiken entertained Jefferson Davis here as a house guest during his week-long visit to Charleston in November 1863. Another notable visitor was General Pierre G. T. Beauregard, who used the house as his headquarters when Union shelling forced his removal from the heart of the city in 1864. One of the wealthiest men in the state, Aiken lost most of his fortune during the war, and his house was ransacked by Federal troops.

The mansion remained in the family until 1975, when it was given to the Charleston Museum. Portions of the house had been closed off in 1873 and 1918, and when they were reopened in the 1970s, furniture and paintings stood undisturbed, a time capsule of nineteenth-century life. The mansion offers visitors the oppor-

tunity to see a historic house in the early stages of restoration. A remarkable number of the house's original outbuildings have survived, including the carriage house, stables, kitchen, servants' quarters, and Gothic Revival privies.

LOCATION: 48 Elizabeth Street. HOURS: 10–5 Daily. FEE: Yes. TELEPHONE: 803–723–1159.

The Military College of South Carolina was founded in 1842 and was originally housed in the arsenal building at Marion Square. In 1922 the school moved to its present campus alongside the Ashley River. The **Citadel Museum** (25 Elmwood Avenue, 803–792–6846) depicts the history of the college and contains uniforms and weaponry that date to the school's earliest days.

A S H L E Y   R I V E R   R E G I O N

CHARLES TOWNE LANDING–1670

This living-history park is located on the site of the original seventeenth-century Charles Towne settlement. The English colonists chose this location along the Ashley River, known as Albemarle Point, because it was secluded and less likely to attract the attention of either Spaniards or pirates. The site was eventually abandoned in favor of the city's present location. Remains of the seventeenth-century fortifications have been preserved, a replica of a typical trading vessel of the period can be boarded, and costumed interpreters depict everyday life. An underground **Interpretive Center** contains artifacts and exhibits that detail the colony's first hundred years.

LOCATION: Off Route 171 at 1500 Old Towne Road. HOURS: June through August: 9–6 Daily; September through May: 9–5 Daily. FEE: Yes. TELEPHONE: 803–556–4450.

The **River Road** (Route 61) follows the Ashley River in a northwesterly direction. Portions of the highway are lined with large, moss-draped oaks that have shaded the road for centuries. It was along

OPPOSITE: *The circular gatehouse of Joseph Manigault's Charleston house, which was designed by his brother Gabriel, takes the form of a small Roman temple.*

Although the designer of Drayton Hall is unknown, some of its details can be found in eighteenth-century architectural books, such as William Kent's Designs of Inigo Jones.

the Ashley that many of South Carolina's most prominent families had their plantations. When Union troops marched through the area in the early months of 1865, they systematically destroyed everything in their path. A single plantation house, Drayton Hall, was spared and only remnants of others remain.

DRAYTON HALL

This red-brick Georgian-Palladian villa was built between 1738 and 1742 by John Drayton, a son of the owner of nearby Magnolia Plantation. The house remained in the Drayton family for seven generations until purchased by the National Trust for Historic Preservation in 1974. Remarkably, the family never added plumbing, electric lighting, or central heating and the house remains much as it was in the eighteenth century. This is the only planta-

The interior of Drayton Hall, built in the mid-eighteenth century, has been painted only twice, allowing the intricate details of its carving to remain distinct.

tion house along the Ashley River to survive the Civil War, it is said because Charles Drayton, a doctor, had his slaves tell Union soldiers that the house was being used as a smallpox hospital. Whether they believed the tale or not, the house was spared.

The National Trust has left the house unfurnished, enabling visitors to focus on architectural details, such as the impressive two-story portico, a cleverly concealed servants' staircase, and an eighteenth century hand-molded plaster ceiling. Unlike the later cast-plaster method, to make this ceiling the craftsman worked the wet plaster by hand on the spot. The ceiling is unique in America.

LOCATION: On Route 61, 9 miles from downtown Charleston, at 3380 Ashley River Road. HOURS: March through December: 10–4 Daily; November through February: 10–3 Daily. FEE: Yes. TELE-PHONE: 803–766–0188.

MAGNOLIA PLANTATION AND GARDENS

Magnolia Plantation has belonged to the Drayton family for 300 years. There have been three plantation houses on the site; the first was accidentally destroyed by fire, and the second was deliberately torched by Union soldiers in 1865. The gardens and the original family tomb survived, though the cherubs adorning the monument were used for target practice.

After the war the family disassembled a pre–Revolutionary War summer cottage in Summerville, floated it down the Ashley River, and set it on the foundation of the previous structure. In the 1880s Victorian elements, including a tower, were added. The house was occupied by the family until 1976. The plantation gardens fared better than the residence. The earliest portion, known as Flowerdale, dates to the 1680s. In the years prior to the Civil War, Reverend John Drayton married and greatly expanded this original garden, hoping, he wrote, "to create an earthly paradise in which my dear Julia may forever forget Philadelphia and her desire to return there." By the 1870s tourists journeyed up the Ashley by steamboat to view the lush plantings. Today the fifty-acre gardens, planted for year-round color, are at the heart of a 500-acre estate, which includes a waterfowl refuge, cypress swamp, and canoe and foot trails.

LOCATION: 10 miles northwest of downtown Charleston on Route 61. HOURS: 8–5 Daily. FEE: Yes. TELEPHONE: 803–571–1266.

MIDDLETON PLACE

Henry Middleton and his bride moved to Middleton Place in 1741 and immediately began the creation of a formally landscaped garden. It took 100 slaves ten years to complete Middleton's grand design, which incorporated a canal, terraces, and twin lakes. Henry Middleton served in the First Continental Congress, and his son, Arthur, was a signer of the Declaration of Independence.

Prior to the Civil War, the Middleton residence consisted of a brick main house built sometime before 1741 and two flanking buildings constructed in 1755. A detachment of Sherman's army ransacked and burned the mansion on February 22, 1865. The family salvaged what they could of the south flank, which had been

Middleton Place includes what may be the oldest landscaped garden in the United States, created by an English landscape architect brought to South Carolina by Henry Middleton. OVERLEAF: *Exotic flowering plants flourished in gardens such as Middleton Place after their introduction to the lush South Carolina climate in the late eighteenth century.*

a gentlemen's guest wing, and rebuilt it in a Tudor-Gothic Revival style. Although many of the Middletons' possessions were lost in the fire, the house contains items that the family managed to hide or that were carried off by Union soldiers and later recovered. The house's main living area displays family portraits, including a massive 1771 painting by Benjamin West. An elegant mahogany breakfast table with Chinese Chippendale fretwork dates to 1770 and is attributed to Charleston craftsman Thomas Elfe. In an upstairs bedroom at the foot of a four-poster "rice" bed stands a large leather trunk that had been secreted in a barn and was not discovered until the 1930s. Inside, in excellent condition, were eighteenth-century men's clothes. The once neglected gardens have been restored to their eighteenth-century splendor, and the stable-

yard features craftsmen practicing traditional plantation trades
such as blacksmithing, woodworking, and weaving.

LOCATION: Route 61, 14 miles northwest of Charleston. HOURS:
Garden: 9–5 Daily. *House:* 10–4:30 Tuesday–Sunday, 1:30–4:30
Monday. FEE: Yes. TELEPHONE: 803–556–6020.

OLD DORCHESTER STATE PARK

Located at the head of navigation of the Ashley River, the town of
Dorchester was laid out in 1697 by a group of Congregationalists
from Dorchester, Massachusetts. Their reason for venturing into
the South Carolina wilderness was to "settell the gospell their."
The village quickly became a center of trade and during the eighteenth century was South Carolina's third-largest town, behind
Charleston and Beaufort. In 1757, during the French and Indian
War, a powder magazine enclosed by an eight-foot tabby wall was
constructed. In 1780 the fort was occupied by the British, who
were driven out the following year by troops under the command
of Colonel Wade Hampton. Before evacuating, the British left the
town in ruins. In 1788 the well-known Methodist circuit rider
Francis Asbury wrote: "Passed Dorchester where there are remains
of what appears to have been once a considerable town. There are
ruins of an elegant church and the vestiges of several well-built
houses." Today the brick church tower and tabby-walled fort are all
that remain.

LOCATION: Route 642, 6 miles south of Summerville. HOURS: 9–6
Thursday–Monday. FEE: None. TELEPHONE: 803–873–1740.

E A S T E R N   E N V I R O N S

PATRIOTS POINT NAVAL
& MARITIME MUSEUM

The centerpiece of this maritime park is the USS *Yorktown,* a
decommissioned aircraft carrier that served in the Okinawa invasion in World War II and in the Korean and Vietnam wars. The
ship housed a crew of over 3,000 men, and visitors may tour the living quarters, as well as the bridge, engine room, and flight deck.
The hanger deck houses a museum of carrier aviation and a the-

ater where a 1944 documentary on the Yorktown is shown. Other vessels that may be toured include a nuclear-powered merchant ship, destroyer, and submarine. (Tour boats may also be boarded at this point for excursions to Fort Sumter.)

LOCATION: 2 miles east of Charleston on Route 17. HOURS: April through October: 9–6 Daily; November through March: 9–5 Daily. FEE: Yes. TELEPHONE: 803–844–2727 or 800–327–5723.

FORT MOULTRIE

The first fort on Sullivans Island was built in 1776 to protect Charleston harbor from the British. Constructed of palmetto logs, the spongy wood absorbed the cannonballs fired by British ships. (The palmetto is honored to this day on the South Carolina flag.) A second eighteenth-century fort made of earth and timber was destroyed by a hurricane in 1804.

When South Carolina seceded from the Union in December 1860, Federal troops spiked the guns and abandoned the site for the more secure position at Fort Sumter in Charleston harbor. Moultrie, which had become a Confederate stronghold, was one of several Confederate batteries to shell Fort Sumter on April 12, 1861. Though pounded intermittently by Union gunboats for a year and a half beginning in 1863, it remained in Confederate hands until 1865 when all southern forces evacuated the city.

The present structure is the third to stand on the site and was used, with continual modifications, from 1809 through World War II. The visitor center features exhibits and a film on the history of the fort. A young recruit named Edgar Allan Poe was stationed here briefly and used the island as the setting for his story "The Gold Bug." From 1842 to 1846 a young West Point graduate, William Tecumseh Sherman, was stationed here. Since the island was a summer resort, the young men spent much of their time at one ball after another. Sherman wrote to his brother, "A life of this kind does well enough for a while, but soon surfeits with its flippancy— mingling with people in whom you feel no permanent interest."

LOCATION: 1214 Middle Street, Sullivans Island, off Route 17. HOURS: Late May through early September: 9–6 Daily; mid-September through mid-May: 9–5 Daily. FEE: None. TELEPHONE: 803–883–3123.

Nine original cabins that were once inhabited by house slaves survive at Boone Hall Plantation. They are constructed of bricks made on the plantation.

BOONE HALL PLANTATION

A three-quarter-mile avenue of moss-draped live oaks leads to Boone Hall. They were planted in 1743 by Captain Thomas Boone, a cotton planter whose estate covered more than 17,000 acres. A brick- and tile-making yard was in operation here during the eighteenth century, and these products were used in the construction of many fine Charleston homes. The original plantation house fell into ruin; the present structure was built in 1935 in a Georgian style similar to its predecessor. Nine original slave cabins border the approach to the house. They date to 1743 and constitute one of the few surviving "slave streets" in the south. Other original buildings include the gin house, circular smokehouse, and commissary. The plantation has been a working estate since 1681. Once a major producer of indigo and cotton, today's products include cattle, sheep, and pecans.

LOCATION: 6 miles northeast of Charleston, just off Route 17.
HOURS: April through Labor Day: 8:30–6:30 Monday–Saturday, 1–5
Sunday; Labor Day through March: 9–5 Monday–Saturday, 1–4
Sunday. FEE: Yes. TELEPHONE: 803–884–4371.

On Route 17 at the turnoff for Boone Hall stands **Christ Episcopal
Church.** Founded in 1706, the church was burned by the British in
1782. The gutted church was rebuilt in 1787. Set aflame once again,
this time by Union soldiers in 1865, the structure was rebuilt in 1874
using the eighteenth-century walls. A number of graves in the
churchyard belong to members of the prominent Pinckney family,
whose plantation, Snee Farm, was nearby.

The simple farmhouse built in 1754 at **Snee Farm** was the plantation home of the Pinckneys, a powerful South Carolina family
whose most illustrious member, Charles Pinckney, was a delegate to
the Constitutional Convention in 1787, three-time governor of the
state, a U.S. senator, and minister to Spain. Recently acquired by the
National Park Service, the house is being restored.

*A watercolor painting from about 1800 shows black slaves on a plantation near
Charleston singing and dancing accompanied by African instruments including a
molo, the prototype for a banjo.*

TENNESSEE

OPPOSITE: *The library of the Tennessee State Capitol contains intricate cast-iron railings and spiral staircase.*

Tennessee is divided into three distinct regions: East, Middle, and West Tennessee. The sections have long acknowledged a sense of separateness, which is even symbolized by three stars on the Tennessee state flag. The East is largely mountainous, beautiful but rugged; Middle Tennessee is bluegrass country, rich and rolling; while much of West Tennessee is more akin to the Mississippi delta than to its sister sections. Before the arrival of white settlers, East Tennessee was the land of the Cherokee, while the western portion of the state was claimed by the Chickasaw, who lived on the bluffs overlooking the Mississippi River. Middle Tennessee was a hunting ground shared by several tribes. The Indians called the long, looping river that cut the state into sections the Tanasi (Tennessee), a musical word whose exact meaning has been lost.

The first whites to venture across the Appalachians were Indian traders and "long hunters," so called because of the lengthy journeys they made into the backcountry. One such explorer recorded his presence in the Tennessee wilderness by carving on a beech tree: "D. Boone killed a bar on tree in the year 1760." Settlers, intent on putting down roots, began to trickle into upper East Tennessee around 1770 despite a proclamation from the king designating all the lands west of the Appalachians as Indian territory. These hardy souls, who defied both the royal government and the Cherokee, came to be known as Overmountain men. Removed from the protective arm of government, they banded together, formulating and administering their own laws. The earliest such frontier government was the Watauga Association, formed in 1772 at Sycamore Shoals, but the most dramatic such experiment was the state of Franklin, an attempt in 1784 to found the nation's fourteenth state in territory in East Tennessee. After the American Revolution, land speculators and war veterans, who had been paid with backcountry land grants, scrambled to stake their claims. Many treaties were signed with the Cherokee, only to be broken, and Cherokee resistance to white invasions grew. Chief Dragging Canoe, who had watched his people's land melt away "like balls of snow in the sun," vowed to fight, and his warriors, known as the Chickamauga, terrorized settlers throughout the territory until the Indian's village, near present-day Chattanooga, was annihilated.

The early frontiersman possessed a hardy constitution and an independent spirit. John Sevier, an Indian fighter, became the state's

Painting by William Jorgerson showing federal mortar scows attempting to batter Island No. 10 into submission in April 1862; General John Pope's army was able to cross the Mississippi under their cover fire and capture the Confederate post.

first governor in 1796. Earlier, during the American Revolution, he had led a band of Overmountain men into North Carolina, where they defeated the British at King's Mountain, and then he warred against the Indians for twenty years, never losing a battle. Noted one historian, "He could outride and outshoot—and, it is said, outswear—the best and the worst of the men who followed him." Perhaps the most famous Tennessee frontiersman was Davy Crockett. Born in East Tennessee in 1786, he settled first in Middle, then West Tennessee. He served three terms in the U.S. Congress, becoming famous for his homespun humor and backwoods naïve wisdom, but when he lost his bid for a fourth term, he headed for Texas, where he died in 1836 defending the Alamo.

A circuit-riding lawyer who traveled the Tennessee wilderness, Andrew Jackson became the soldier-hero of the Battle of New Orleans. Elected the nation's seventh president, he forced the Cherokee to relinquish the remainder of their native land. The route the tribe followed in its removal to Oklahoma, in which a quarter of

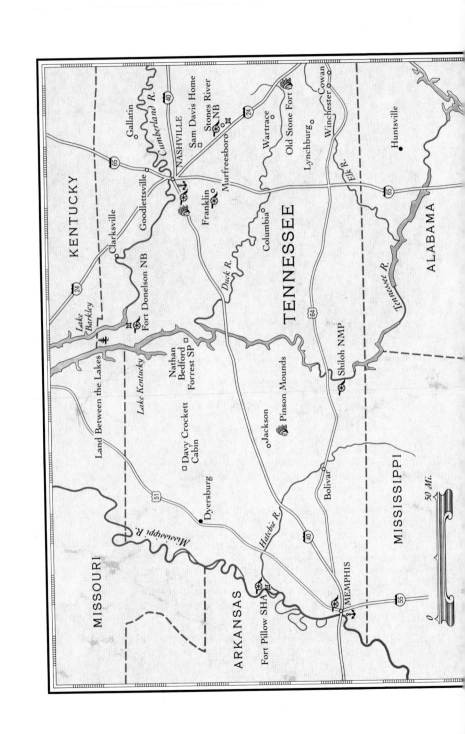

KENTUCKY

TENNESSEE

ALABAMA

MISSOURI

ARKANSAS

MISSISSIPPI

Gallatin

Cumberland R.

NASHVILLE

Sam Davis Home

Stones River NB

Murfreesboro

Clarksville

Goodlettsville

Franklin

Wartrace

Old Stone Fort

Lynchburg

Winchester

Cowan

Huntsville

Elk R.

Duck R.

Columbia

Fort Donelson NB

Lake Barkley

Lake Kentucky

Land Between the Lakes

Nathan Bedford Forrest SP

Tennessee R.

Shiloh NMP

Pinson Mounds

Davy Crockett Cabin

Jackson

Dyersburg

Mississippi R.

Hatchie R.

Bolivar

MEMPHIS

Fort Pillow SHA

50 Mi.

0

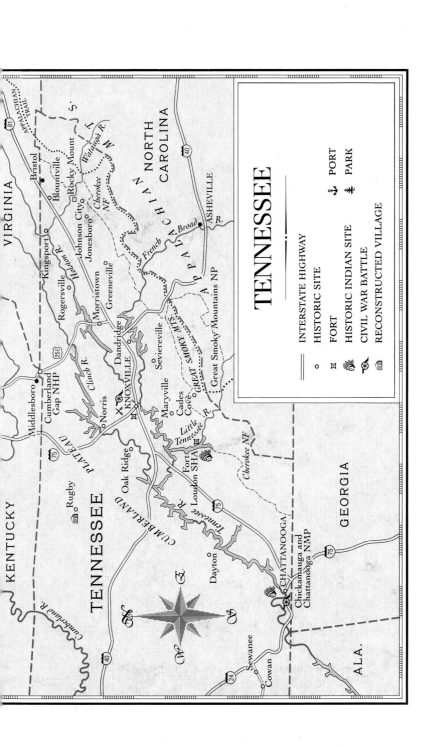

TENNESSEE

	INTERSTATE HIGHWAY
○	HISTORIC SITE
⌗	FORT
🌿	HISTORIC INDIAN SITE
⚔	CIVIL WAR BATTLE
🏠	RECONSTRUCTED VILLAGE
⚓	PORT
🌲	PARK

KENTUCKY

VIRGINIA

NORTH CAROLINA

GEORGIA

ALA.

TENNESSEE

Cumberland R.

Middlesboro

Cumberland Gap NHP

Rugby

Oak Ridge

Norris

KNOXVILLE

Clinch R.

CUMBERLAND PLATEAU

Dayton

CHATTANOOGA

Chickamauga and Chattanooga NMP

Sewanee

Cowan

Kingsport

Bristol

Blountville

Rocky Mount

Rogersville

Johnson City

Jonesboro

Morristown

Greeneville

Dandridge

Sevierville

Maryville

Cades Cove

Fort Loudon SHA

Holston R.

Watauga R.

Cherokee NF

French Broad

ASHEVILLE

French Broad R.

APPALACHIAN MTS

GREAT SMOKY MTS.

Great Smoky Mountains NP

Little Tennessee R.

Tennessee R.

Cherokee NF

Appalachian Trail

their number died, is known as the Trail of Tears. By the 1840s Tennesseans were no longer preoccupied with simple survival, and they turned their attention to national affairs. When the state asked for 2,800 soldiers to fight the war with Mexico, 30,000 tried to enlist, earning Tennessee its nickname, the Volunteer State.

By the time of Jackson's death in 1845, a plantation economy based on slave labor was dominant in Middle and West Tennessee, while the mountainous East remained a region of small subsistence farms. This divergence became critical with the outbreak of the Civil War; though officially part of a Confederate state, East Tennessee remained a Unionist stronghold and a thorn in the side of southern authorities. One Knoxville Unionist who refused to be silenced was William G. Brownlow, a newspaper editor. When it was rumored that he might support the Confederates, Brownlow thundered, "When I shall have made up my mind to go to hell, I will cut my throat and go direct, and not travel round by way of the Southern Confederacy."

Some of the Civil War's bloodiest battles were fought on Tennessee soil: Shiloh, Stones River, Franklin. From 1862 on, most of Tennessee was occupied by Federal forces, though General Nathan Bedford Forrest and his cavalry continued to stage successful raids. Guerrilla activity made life dangerous for soldiers and civilians alike, and basic necessities—food, medicine, clothing—were scarce. Unable to acquire coffee or tea, Tennesseans improvised with drinks made from dried sweet potatoes, okra, or peanuts.

Thrust into the presidency by Lincoln's assassination in 1865, Andrew Johnson, a Tennessean, faced the task of rebuilding the shattered nation following the war. Johnson's southern origins and mild Reconstruction policies made many northerners suspect him of duplicity. In 1868 he was impeached by the House but acquitted by the Senate by the margin of a single vote.

The federal government's Reconstruction policies met great resistance from some Southern whites. The most violent opposition came from the Ku Klux Klan, which had been founded with benign intentions as a Confederate verterans organization in Pulaski, Tennessee in 1865. In 1867 Nathan Bedford Forrest, a famous Confederate cavalry leader, became the first Grand Wizard. When some Klansmen were persecuting blacks, Forrest dissolved the organization in 1869, but cells had already been formed throughout the

South. Through a campaign of terror Klansmen sought to reestablish white supremacy, regain control of the black labor force, and
thwart the progressive efforts of the Republican party. Wearing
ghost-like white robes with hoods shielding their faces, Klansmen
raided the homes of white Republicans and raped, tortured, and
lynched blacks. Any black who ran for public office was particularly
at risk. When Andrew Flowers of Chattanooga was elected justice of
the peace in 1870, defeating a white candidate, he was whipped by
Klansmen. He said, "they didn't dispute I was a very good fellow. . .
but they did not intend any nigger to hold office in the United
States." In February 1869 Governor William G. Brownlow suppressed the Klan by declaring martial law in nine Middle Tennessee
counties and sending in militia units from the part of the state that
had been Unioninst during the war—East Tennessee. Several other
Southern governors took similar measures, and Klan violence subsided. The organization emerged again in 1915 and reached its
peak membership in the 1920s with broader hatreds, targeting
Jews, Catholics, and various immigrant goups as well as blacks.

    In the 1930s Roosevelt's New Deal policies brought tremendous
changes to the state. The Tennessee Valley Authority was created to
harness the unruly Tennessee River, providing flood control, much-
needed jobs, and a source of cheap energy. Norris Dam, completed
in 1936, was the first of a chain of TVA dams that have transformed
the Tennessee and its tributaries. Several new styles of music that
emerged during the twentieth century became associated with the
state. Nashville became the center of country music, which sprang
from traditional ballad making, while Memphis witnessed the birth
of the blues, a style that attracted worldwide attention thanks to the
work of a black composer, W. C. Handy.

    This tour begins in upper East Tennessee along the Virginia border
and travels southwest through the Tennessee Valley until it reaches
Knoxville. From there the chapter turns north to sites near the
Kentucky border before returning to Knoxville and heading south
to Chattanooga. The route then traverses the rolling countryside of
the bluegrass region south of Nashville. After exploring the state
capital, it continues north and then west to the Tennessee River.
Finally, the chapter winds its way to Memphis and from there heads
north along the Mississippi River.

E A S T   T E N N E S S E E

This mountainous region, with its forested peaks and rushing streams, was the first area of the state to be settled. Pioneers, primarily of Scotch-Irish extraction, filtered into the isolated coves and ridges during the late eighteenth century, built log structures, and lived relatively undisturbed until the first half of the twentieth century. With the arrival of the Tennessee Valley Authority in the 1930s, the region began to stir, attracting industry, research facilities, and tourists seeking outdoor adventure on the area's lakes and in the Great Smoky Mountains National Park and a variety of state parks.

KINGSPORT

In the eighteenth and early nineteenth centuries, Kingsport was known by a variety of names: Island Flats, Fort Patrick Henry, Christianville, and the Boat Yard. Located on the Holston River, the

The Netherland Inn, on the Holston River in Kingsport. Long, narrow, and tall, the inn is typical of Tennessee's domestic architecture of the ante-bellum decades.

town was a center of Indian activity; Long Island, in the middle of the river, was sacred to the Cherokee. It was also the starting point for the Wilderness Road cut into Kentucky by Daniel Boone in 1775. Around 1802 William King built a wharf along the Holston that was called first the Boat Yard and later King's Port. From this point flatboats loaded with salt and other goods could navigate all the way to New Orleans.

In 1818 Richard Netherland opened a stage stop called the **Netherland Inn** (2144 Netherland Inn Road, 615–247–3211). The three-story stone-and-frame structure served as an inn for over 100 years and hosted such notables as presidents Andrew Jackson, Andrew Johnson, and James K. Polk. Restored to its original condition, it is furnished with numerous Netherland family pieces and contains antebellum graffiti as well as the original taproom and bar. In front of the inn is the site of King's boatyard. Long Island is located just upriver; a **Cherokee Memorial** may be reached by a swinging bridge from Riverfront Park.

Exchange Place (4812 Orebank Road, 615–288–6071), an antebellum homestead, was also a stop on the Great Stage Road, which ran from Washington, DC, to points west. The main house was constructed in 1820 in the saddlebag style, in which two separate cabins were connected by a central chimney and every room had to be entered through an outside door. The site acquired its name from the exchange of stage horses and Virginia and Tennessee currencies that occurred here. Eight antebellum structures remain, including a store, granary, smokehouse, and slaves' cabin and a springhouse whose upper floor served as a schoolhouse.

The nearby town of **Blountville** was laid out in 1795, and its Main Street (Route 126) is lined with log, frame, and brick houses that date to the frontier period. A portion of the **Old Deery Inn** (private) was built in 1794. Plaques bearing the dates of the houses and historical markers with additional information provide a self-guided tour.

ELIZABETHTON

At the edge of Elizabethton's business district stands the **Doe River Covered Bridge.** Built in 1882 at a cost of $3,000, the 134-foot white clapboard structure is still open to traffic.

Sycamore Shoals State Historic Area

The first permanent white settlement at Sycamore Shoals was established in 1772. Sixteen families from North Carolina made the strenuous journey over the mountains and settled along the banks of the Watauga River in defiance of the king's proclamation of 1763 that designated the area west of the Appalachians as Indian territory. Recognizing that they were now living beyond the protection of colonial authority, the settlers organized their own government, the Watauga Association, creating the first written constitution by white settlers of American birth.

In 1775 the leaders of the Cherokee nation gathered at the Shoals to negotiate with the land speculator Richard Henderson. The result was the Transylvania Purchase, the largest private real estate transaction in American history; over 20 million acres of Indian land changed hands and was made available for white settlement. Not all of the Indian chiefs agreed to the sale, and in July 1776 a force of 300 Indians led by Dragging Canoe attacked 200 men, women, and children in tiny Fort Watauga. During the siege John Sevier, destined to be Tennessee's first governor, met his bride-to-be when he pulled her to safety over the palisade walls. During the Revolutionary War, Sycamore Shoals was the muster point for the group of Overmountain men who crossed the Appalachians and played a decisive role in the American victory at the Battle of King's Mountain in South Carolina.

The park's visitor center features a film and a small museum. A reconstruction of the frontier fort (which originally stood a mile south) overlooks the Watauga River, and a walking trail leads to the shoals where the Cherokee met with Richard Henderson.

LOCATION: Route 321. HOURS: 8–4:30 Monday–Saturday, 1–4:30 Sunday. FEE: None. TELEPHONE: 615–543–5808.

John and Landon Carter Mansion

Administered as part of the Sycamore Shoals State Historic Area, this two-and-a-half-story frame house was begun in 1780 by John Carter and completed in 1781 by his son Landon, after John Carter's death. John Carter was one of the founders of the Watauga Association, and his son, a soldier in the Revolutionary War, also gained fame in the Tennessee territory as an Indian fighter. This amazing house is one of the most arresting artifacts of the Western migration. Inside are two rare overmantel paintings and remarkably opulent baroque pine panelling. Although it is unfurnished, ninety percent of the house is original, and three of the rooms retain their original wall finishes.

LOCATION: North of the Sycamore Shoals State Historic Area, on the Broad Street Extension. HOURS: May through September: 9–6 Wednesday–Saturday, 1–5:30 Sunday. FEE: None. TELEPHONE: 615–543–6140.

ROCKY MOUNT

Built in 1770 by William Cobb, Rocky Mount served as the first capital for the Territory of the United States South of the River Ohio, as this frontier region was known from 1790 to 1792, before it was divided into states. The two-and-a-half-story log home sits high on a hill overlooking the forks of the Holston and Watauga rivers. The site is strewn with large limestone outcroppings, which gave the house its name.

Rocky Mount, one of the oldest surviving houses in Tennessee, has been restored as a living-history museum, re-creating daily life in 1791.

During his stay at Rocky Mount the territorial governor, William Blount, wrote: "I am very well accommodated with a Room with Glass Windows, Fireplace, etc." Mrs. Cobb's first cousin, Andrew Jackson, was a frequent visitor. The house remained in the Cobb family until 1959, when it was purchased by the state and restored to its eighteenth-century appearance. It is now operated as a living-history site, re-creating the year 1791—the year for which there exist the most detailed records of who was at Rocky Mount and what happened there. Costumed interpreters portray people known to have been at Rocky Mount in 1791 and perform such household tasks and farming chores as putting up preserves, making soap and candles, weaving, and planting crops. The site also includes the **Massengill Museum of Overmountain History,** with numerous displays depicting the region's early history.

LOCATION: 4 miles northeast of Johnson City on Route 11E. HOURS: January through February: 10–5 Monday–Friday; March through mid-December: 10–5 Monday–Saturday, 2–6 Sunday. FEE: Yes. TELEPHONE: 615–538–7396.

TIPTON-HAYNES HISTORIC SITE

In 1673 two Indian traders, James Needham and Gabriel Arthur, followed a buffalo trail to this site and camped in the cave at the foot of the hill. Colonel John Tipton, a Virginian who had fought in the Revolutionary War, purchased the site in 1784 and built a two-story log home with one unusual feature: Stone was used between the logs in addition to traditional mud chinking. A number of log farm buildings that remain on the property date to this period.

Purchased in 1838 by the Carter Haynes family, the log house disappeared under clapboard and was substantially enlarged. Haynes, who served in 1849 as Speaker of the Tennessee House of Representatives and later as a Confederate senator, built a law office on the property and altered the clapboard house to match the Neoclassical style of the office. The house and grounds have been restored to reflect the style of the 1850s and 1860s.

LOCATION: 2620 South Roan Street (Exit 31 off Route I-181), Johnson City. HOURS: April through October: 10–4 Monday–Friday, 2–5 Saturday–Sunday. FEE: Yes. TELEPHONE: 615–926–3631.

JONESBORO

One of the oldest towns in the Tennessee territory, Jonesboro was chartered by North Carolina in 1779. It became the first capital of the state of Franklin when settlers held preliminary conventions here in August and December of 1784 in an attempt to found the nation's fourteenth state. The founders of Franklin adopted a constitution, created an assembly, elected a governor, and organized a court and a militia. However, Franklin was never recognized by the U.S. government, and after four turbulent years, the experiment failed. Many of Franklin's leaders went on to govern the state of Tennessee after 1796. Jonesboro was a planned community from its inception. Each property owner was required to build "one brick, stone, or well-framed house, 20 feet long and 16 feet wide" or forfeit his title. In the center of town, the **Jonesboro Historic District** contains over 150 structures in styles ranging from Federal to Italianate. A significant feature of the town's architecture is the frequent use of stepped gables.

The **Christopher Taylor House** (Main Street), a two-story cabin constructed of chestnut logs, was built in 1778 on a site two miles west of town; it has been restored and moved to the heart of Jonesboro. Andrew Jackson boarded with the Taylors while practicing law here for about two years. Nearby is the site where Jacob Howard's print shop once stood. It was here in 1819 that Elihu Embree established the country's first abolitionist periodical, the *Manumission Intelligencer,* which later became *The Emancipator.* The town's oldest frame structure is the **Chester Inn** (106 West Main Street), built in 1797, which is undergoing reconstruction.

The **Davy Crockett Birthplace State Park** (615–257–2167) is located just off Route 11E, near the tiny community of **Limestone.** Davy Crockett was born in a log cabin beside Limestone Creek in 1786. Though the site had long been noted, all that remained was a large limestone slab, said to be the cabin's doorstep. In 1986, as part of the celebration of the 200th anniversary of Crockett's birth, a replica of the cabin was built on the site. Furnishings typical of the period of Crockett's birth can be viewed inside the cabin. The visitor center houses a museum with exhibits that detail aspects of Crockett's life as a hunter, businessman, farmer, and politician.

GREENEVILLE

The cool waters of Big Spring, located in the heart of Greeneville, first attracted settlers to this site in 1783. From 1785 to 1788 Greeneville served as capital of the short-lived state of Franklin. In 1861 pro-Unionists held a convention here to plot the region's secession from the rest of the state, a plan that proved unsuccessful. The **Greeneville Cumberland Presbyterian Church** (Church and Main streets) was shelled during the Civil War, and a cannonball remains lodged in one wall. On the same day that the church was shelled, September 4, 1864, Confederate General John H. Morgan was killed in an ambush in the Williams garden across the street from the church. The **Dickson-Williams Mansion** (Church and Irish streets), constructed in 1815, hosted such notables as Davy Crockett, the marquis de Lafayette, presidents Andrew Jackson and James K. Polk, Henry Clay, author Frances Hodgson Burnett, and General Wade Hampton.

Andrew Johnson National Historic Site

Greeneville's most famous resident was Andrew Johnson, the seventeenth president of the United States. A tailor by trade, Johnson had little formal schooling; his wife taught him to write after their marriage. A powerful debater, Johnson became mayor of Greeneville, state representative, U.S. congressman, governor of Tennessee, and U.S. senator. A devoted Unionist, Johnson remained in the Senate despite Tennessee's secession in 1861. Chosen as Lincoln's running mate in 1864, he became president after Lincoln's assassination in 1865, soon after the Civil War ended. Viewed as a traitor by many southerners and distrusted by many northerners, Johnson faced the task of leading the divided nation. Intent on offering generous terms to the defeated states, as Lincoln had intended to do, the new president disagreed with the punitive measures demanded by Congress. In 1868 the House impeached him, but he was acquitted by trial in the Senate by a single vote.

The **visitor center** complex (Depot and College streets) includes Johnson's tailor shop, where his wife read aloud to him while he worked, a museum, and Johnson's 1830 residence. The **Homestead** (South Main Street, 615–638–7131) was Johnson's home from 1851 until his death in 1875 and is furnished with many family pieces. The **Andrew Johnson National Cemetery** (Monument

Avenue), where the president and his family are buried, stands at
the edge of town.

LOCATION: Downtown Greeneville. HOURS: 9–5 Daily. FEE: For
Homestead. TELEPHONE: 615–638–3551.

Just east of Greeneville is the **Tusculum College Historic District.**
Tusculum is the consolidation of Greeneville College (1794) and
Tusculum Academy (1818) and is the oldest coeducational college
in the United States associated with the Presbyterian Church. **Doak
House,** the residence of the college's founder, Reverend Samuel
Doak, was erected in 1818 and was occupied by Doak descendants
until 1965. Also of interest is **Old College,** constructed in 1841.

Alongside Route 321, just east of Parrottsville, is the **Swaggerty
Blockhouse** (private), a small eighteenth-century log structure built
for protection against the Indians. The square two-story building
was constructed over a spring to ensure an adequate supply of water
for those taking refuge inside. Such structures were once a common
sight on the Tennessee frontier.

ROGERSVILLE

Crockett's Creek, which flows through Rogersville, was the site of an
Indian massacre in 1777 that took the lives of Davy Crockett's grandparents. In the early 1780s Joseph Rogers, an Irishman, settled on
the site and developed several businesses including a store and a tavern. Situated along a major stage road, the town prospered, and by
1834 it had 300 residents. One of the most prominent citizens was
John McKinney, an Irish-born lawyer who is responsible for the
design of a number of the town's finest buildings. **Three Oaks** (306
Colonial Road, private) was constructed in 1815 as McKinney's residence. The brickwork of the house's twelve chimneys is particularly
notable. Nearby stand the **Spring House** (306 Colonial Road, private), an 1816 structure that served as McKinney's law office, and
Rosemont (500 East Main Street, private), which was built in 1842. It
was the home of McKinney's daughter Susan and her husband, John
Netherland. In 1824 McKinney constructed the **Hale Springs Inn**
(110 West Main Street, 615–272–5171). Recently restored, it is the
oldest continuously operating inn in the state. During the Civil War
it served as Federal headquarters, the McKinneys being staunch

Unionists; the **Kyle House** (111 West Main Street, private) across the street was used by the Confederates when they held the town. Control of the town changed hands several times, and for years after the war, residents, according to their sympathies, would cross the street to avoid walking in front of "enemy" headquarters.

The **Hawkins County Courthouse,** on the town square, was constructed in 1836 and is the oldest still in use in the state. The **Rogers Graveyard,** just off East Main Street, contains the grave of the town's founder as well as those of Crockett's grandparents. A complete walking tour of the town is available at the **Rogersville Depot** (415 South Depot Street, 615–272–2186), which was constructed in 1890.

MORRISTOWN

In the 1790s John Crockett and his wife, Rebecca, moved from Davy Crockett's birthplace near Limestone, Tennessee, and built a six-

Front porch of the Homestead House, or Great House, built ca. 1840, at the Museum of Appalachia.

room tavern alongside the main road between Abingdon and Knoxville. The **Crockett Tavern Museum** (2002 Morningside Drive, 615–586–6382) is a reconstruction of their tavern and home. Davy moved out in 1799 at the age of 13 after refusing to attend school, in defiance of his father's wishes. The tavern contains a variety of period furnishings. Also of interest is **Rose Center** (442 West Second North Street, 615–581–4330), built in 1892 as Morristown's first public high school. It operated as a school until the 1970s and now serves as a community center.

DANDRIDGE

Dandridge, named in honor of Martha Dandridge Custis Washington, is a small community with many antebellum buildings. Founded in 1783, the town grew up along the banks of the French Broad River and soon became a regular stop for the boats plying the river and for the stagecoaches that journeyed between White's Fort (Knoxville) and Abingdon, Virginia. Several of the taverns that accommodated travelers during the early nineteenth century have survived. **Shepard's Inn** (Main Street, private) was built in 1820, and the original logs are intact beneath a Victorian frame exterior. Guests at the inn included Presidents Andrew Jackson, James K. Polk, and Andrew Johnson. Across Main Street, **Hickman's Tavern** (1845) now serves as the city hall. When the Tennessee Valley Authority dammed the French Broad River in the early 1940s, the town was threatened with inundation. President Franklin Roosevelt intervened, and a massive dike now serves as a backdrop along the southeast side of Main Street. The **Jefferson County Courthouse** in the center of town provides information about walking tours. The two-story brick structure was built in 1845 and contains a number of exhibits on the county's history.

SEVIERVILLE

Situated between the east and west prongs of the Little Pigeon River, Sevierville was established in 1795 and named in honor of Revolutionary War hero John Sevier, soon to be Tennessee's first governor. As a result of several devastating fires, few buildings survive from before the latter part of the nineteenth century. The town is dominated by the **Sevier County Courthouse** (Court

The Old Mill at Pigeon Forge, along the Little Pigeon River.

Avenue), which was completed in 1896 in an eclectic style that features an elaborate central clock tower and a number of small domes.

Off Route 441, in the heart of **Pigeon Forge,** stands the **Old Mill** (202 Middle Creek Road, 615–453–4628). Built in 1830 along the Little Pigeon River, the structure was once the focus of a tiny farming community named for the river and an iron forge that stood nearby. The mill is still in operation, producing a variety of stone-ground flours.

CADES COVE HISTORIC DISTRICT

In the heart of the Great Smoky Mountains National Park near Townsend stands a collection of pioneer structures that reflect the lifestyle of the people who lost their land in the 1930s when the park was formed. The first settler in the cove, John Oliver, arrived in 1818.

Isolated by poor mountain roads, cove residents (who numbered around 700 by 1900) preserved their folk traditions well into the twentieth century. A number of cabins and churches and a gristmill have been preserved. An eleven-mile road circles the cove. A small visitor center with exhibits on cove life is adjacent to the cable mill.

LOCATION: 7 miles south of Townsend off Route 73. HOURS: Dawn–Dusk Daily. FEE: None. TELEPHONE: 615–448–2472.

KNOXVILLE

In 1786 James White, a Revolutionary War veteran, settled on a hill overlooking the Tennessee River, northeast of the Cherokee towns that dotted the lower Tennessee Valley. White erected a stockade and several cabins, and the settlement became known as White's Fort. When William Blount was appointed governor of the Territory South of the River Ohio in 1790, he chose the fledgling community as the site of his territorial capital. At his urging lots were surveyed and the outpost was renamed Knoxville, in honor of General Henry Knox, President Washington's secretary of war. When Tennessee was admitted to the Union in 1796, Knoxville became the first state capital. During these early years, the town was frequented by such notables as Andrew Jackson and John Sevier; bitter political enemies, the two men narrowly avoided a duel after an angry encounter on a Knoxville street corner in which Sevier made disparaging remarks about Jackson's marriage. (In 1812 the state capital was moved to Middle Tennessee; it was located alternately at Murfreesboro and Nashville until an 1843 decision placed it permanently in Nashville.)

The Civil War created particular hardships for the citizens of East Tennessee. A substantial portion of the population supported the Union cause even though the state was officially part of the Confederacy. Knoxville, the center of Union sympathies, was placed under martial law and over 1,000 residents were imprisoned. When William G. Brownlow, the editor of a Unionist newspaper, defiantly continued to fly the Stars and Stripes atop his home, a group of Confederate soldiers decided to pull it down while he was away. As they approached the house, one of Brownlow's daughters stepped onto the front porch armed with a pistol. The flag remained in place. Late in the summer of 1863, Union forces moved into the city after the Confederates withdrew toward Chattanooga. Federal

troops, commanded by General Ambrose Burnside, proceeded to build a series of earthwork forts around the city. When General James Longstreet's Confederates moved to regain the town, Fort Sanders, surrounded by a water-filled ditch and strands of telegraph wire, stood in their path. An unsuccessful twenty-minute assault cost Longstreet over 800 men, and Knoxville remained in Union hands for the duration of the war.

The **James White Fort** (205 East Hill Avenue, 615–525–6514) stands in downtown Knoxville, not far from its original location. The 1786 log home of the city's founder was moved to this location in 1968, and the fort was reconstructed around it. Other reconstructed log houses in the fort include a guest house, a smokehouse, a loom house, and a blacksmith shop, each with furnishings and artifacts of the period. There is also a museum. The Graveyard of the **First Presbyterian Church** (620 State Street) contains the graves of many early settlers, including James White and William Blount. One of the settlement's first cleared plots, the site was originally the White family's turnip patch. The **Lamar House–Bijou Theater** (803 Gay Street, private) was constructed in 1816 to serve as a hotel. It was here that Union General William P. Sanders was brought after he was fatally wounded by a Confederate sharpshooter in November 1863. The theater was added to the structure in 1909. The **Knox County Courthouse** (330 West Main Street, 615–521–2000), designed by the New York firm Palliser, Palliser, and Company, was built in 1885 in an eclectic style that combines Colonial and Gothic elements. On the grounds are the graves of John Sevier, Tennessee's first governor, and his two wives. It was on this site that a federal blockhouse was built in 1793 to protect settlers from Indian attack.

Blount Mansion

When the territorial governor, William Blount, built this white frame house on the banks of the Tennessee River in 1792, it was a mansion compared to the rude log structures that surrounded it. A wealthy North Carolinian, Blount had served at the Constitutional Convention alongside George Washington, and he brought an aura of sophistication to the frontier setting. His house became the center of political and social activities, and the mansion hosted such

OPPOSITE: *The skyscrapers of modern Knoxville surround the log home of the city's founder, James White. He built the house in 1786.*

diverse guests as French botanist André Michaux, Andrew Jackson, and possibly Louis-Philippe, a future king of France. Restored to its eighteenth-century appearance, the house contains period furnishings. On the grounds is the **Governor's Office,** where territorial business was conducted and portions of the Tennessee state constitution were drafted. A visitor center, located in the **Craighead Jackson House,** built in 1818, features a small museum.

LOCATION: 200 West Hill Avenue. HOURS: April through October: 9:30–5 Tuesday–Saturday, 2–5 Sunday; November through December and March: 9:30–4:30 Tuesday–Saturday; January and February: 9:30–4:30 Tuesday–Friday. FEE: Yes. TELEPHONE: 615–525–2375.

The **James Park House** (422 West Cumberland Avenue, private) is said to have been designed by the English architect Thomas Hope as a city residence for Governor John Sevier. He never resided here, however, and in 1812 the unfinished house was sold to James Park, a wealthy merchant. **Old City Hall** (Western Avenue, private) is a Greek Revival structure built in 1848 as a school for the deaf. During the Civil War it was used as a hospital by both armies. For much of the twentieth century it served as Knoxville's city hall. The massive **Louisville and Nashville Station** (700 Western Avenue) was completed in 1904. It was restored for the 1982 World's Fair and now houses a variety of businesses. The **Old Gray Cemetery** (543 North Broadway, 615–522–1424) was established in 1850. Many prominent Tennesseans, including William G. Brownlow, are buried here.

The **Armstrong-Lockett House** (2728 Kingston Pike, 615–637–4163), also known as "Crescent Bend," was built in 1834 beside the Tennessee River. Once part of a large plantation owned by Drury P. Armstrong, the structure now houses the Toms Collection of eighteenth-century American and English furniture and decorative arts, as well as a collection of English silver from 1640 to 1820. The **W. P. Toms Memorial Gardens,** extensive terraced gardens and fountains, descend from the house to the river. **Confederate Memorial Hall** (3148 Kingston Pike SW, 615–522–2371) is a fifteen-room antebellum mansion that served as Confederate General James Longstreet's headquarters during the siege of Knoxville in 1863. A southern sharpshooter stationed in the tower of the home fatally wounded Union General William P. Sanders during that engagement, and Civil War graffiti are still visible on the tower walls.

Knoxville's Old City Hall, built in 1848 as a school for the deaf.

Ramsey House

This house, the first stone residence in the Knoxville area, was built about 1797 by Colonel Francis Alexander Ramsey, a Pennsylvanian who arrived in East Tennessee as a young surveyor and quickly established himself as a man of consequence. He hired Thomas Hope, an English architect who had previously worked in Charleston, South Carolina, to design the house. Hope produced a simple yet elegant structure made of rough marble and limestone. Colonel Ramsey was one of the original trustees of Blount College, the institution that became the University of Tennessee. One son, James, was a prominent physician and historian, while another, William, served as Tennessee's first secretary of state. The house was the largest and most expensive in the area at the time it was built and boasted the first attached kitchen in the state. It has been furnished in accordance with an 1821 Ramsey inventory.

LOCATION: 2614 Thorngrove Pike. HOURS: April through October: 10–5 Tuesday–Saturday, 1–5 Sunday. FEE: Yes. TELEPHONE: 615–546–0745.

Governor John Sevier Farm Home–Marble Springs

This simple log structure was the farm home of John "Chucky Jack" Sevier, Tennessee's first governor. Sevier had a distinguished public career and was known as a fierce Indian fighter. In 1771 he helped organize the Watauga Association, the earliest governing body that settlers attempted to establish in the Tennessee wilderness. Prior to Tennessee statehood, he served as governor of the state of Franklin, a short-lived (1784–1788) attempt to create a fourteenth state in the Tennessee territory. Sevier served as governor from 1796 to 1801 and 1803 to 1809 and as a member of the House of Representatives from 1811 to 1815.

Sevier was married twice, first to Sarah Hawkins and later to Katherine Sherrill, and fathered eighteen children. The Sevier family lived at Marble Springs from about 1790 until 1815. In addition to the original three-room log house, there are a number of other restored buildings on the forty-acre farm, named by Sevier for its numerous springs and marble deposits. The house is furnished with family and period pieces.

LOCATION: 1220 Governor John Sevier Highway. HOURS: April through October: 10–12 and 2–5 Monday–Saturday, 2–5 Sunday. FEE: Yes. TELEPHONE: 615–573–5508.

Six miles north of Maryville stands the **Sam Houston Schoolhouse** (Sam Houston Schoolhouse Road, off Route 33, 615–983–1550). Constructed in 1794, it is believed to be the oldest original school building in Tennessee. Sam Houston, who served as governor successively of Tennessee and Texas, taught in the one-room log building in 1812. A small museum is on the grounds.

OAK RIDGE

Oak Ridge came into existence because of the federal government's decision to develop the atomic bomb during World War II. In September 1942 War Department officials chose a rural area twenty-five miles northwest of Knoxville as the site for a top-secret facility. Approximately 1,100 farm families were given only a few months to vacate their homes. Armed guards were stationed at checkpoints, and the name Oak Ridge was chosen because officials thought its rural connotation would help disguise the sophisticated nature of the project. The first atomic bomb was made from enriched uranium created here. Today a wide range of energy-related research is conducted at several facilities here under the direction of the Department of Energy.

The **American Museum of Science and Energy** (300 South Tulane Avenue, 615–576–3200) has one of the world's largest collections of energy-related exhibits. The **Graphite Reactor** (Bethel Valley Road, 615–574–4160), the world's first full-scale nuclear reactor, is open to the public. The **Oak Ridge Gaseous Diffusion Plant,** the largest original facility at Oak Ridge, may be viewed from an overlook, complete with an audio-visual display, on Route 58.

NORRIS

Norris was established during the New Deal years of the 1930s as a model town to be administered by the Tennessee Valley Authority. Mandated by Congress in 1933, TVA was to harness the region's river power and provide economic opportunities to area residents. **Norris Dam** (615–494–7111), the first of a number of such facilities that the TVA would build throughout the valley, was constructed from 1933 to 1936. The **Lenoir Museum** (Route 441, 615–494–9688), in the Norris Dam State Park, contains pioneer artifacts.

Museum of Appalachia

This seventy-five-acre outdoor museum features more than thirty-five pioneer structures as well as more than 200,000 artifacts, ranging from homemade musical instruments to fanciful pieces of folk art. John Rice Irwin began the museum in the 1960s. The collection is unique not only in its scope but also in the way it is displayed. Cabins are furnished with the odds and ends of mountain life, such as a sunbonnet hanging on a ladderback chair or a square of handmade soap sitting next to a wooden bucket of spring water. The museum buildings, which include numerous cabins, a log church, and a schoolhouse, all look as if their original owners have just stepped out for a few moments. Irwin has taken great pains to preserve the stories of the people behind the artifacts, so that exhibits bring to life such diverse figures as Henny Copeland, a mountain midwife, or Jacob Vowell, a coal miner who scribbled a poignant farewell note to his wife while waiting for rescuers who

Pioneer tools and furniture fill a porch at the Museum of Appalachia in Norris. More than thirty-five buildings are on site, each furnished according to the period.

arrived too late. Oxen and other animals dot the pastures, and pioneer activities such as sorghum making, plowing, and rail splitting are often in progress.

LOCATION: Route 61. HOURS: April through October: 8–Dusk Daily; November through March: 9–5 Daily. FEE: Yes. TELEPHONE: 615–494–7680.

Northeast, along the Kentucky border near the town of **Harrogate,** is **Lincoln Memorial University** (Cumberland Gap Parkway, 615–869–6237). The eastern portion of Tennessee, though officially part of the Confederacy, remained staunchly Unionist during the Civil War. The university was founded in 1897 by General Oliver O. Howard (who also founded Howard University), a friend of Lincoln who recalled the president's desire to "do something for these people." Located on the university campus, the **Abraham Lincoln Museum** contains over 25,000 items related to Lincoln and his times, including the cane Lincoln was carrying in Ford's Theater on

The log church at the Museum of Appalachia was built ca. 1840 and moved to the museum from Madison County, North Carolina.

the night he was assassinated, a tea set used by the Lincoln family when they lived in Springfield, Illinois, and Civil War weapons, uniforms, and medical instruments.

Just a few miles north at Cumberland Gap is an entrance to the **Cumberland Gap National Historical Park.** The main **visitor center** (606–248–2817) is in Middlesboro, Kentucky.

HISTORIC RUGBY

Founded in 1880 by English author Thomas Hughes as a cooperative community, Rugby was designed to give the younger sons of the English gentry a place to learn farming and other practical skills away from the social strictures of their own country. The British custom of primogeniture, in which the eldest son inherited everything, left additional siblings with few options. Only a few crowded professions (ministry, medicine, law) were considered socially acceptable; Hughes wrote scornfully that the British gentry "would rather see their sons starve like gentlemen than thrive in a trade or profession that is beneath them." For a time the colony flourished as a summer resort, but it suffered from a series of disasters, including destructive fires and a typhoid epidemic. By the turn of the century, most of the original colonists had departed.

Rugby drowsed through the next fifty years but was never entirely deserted. Under the direction of Historic Rugby, twenty of Rugby's seventy original structures have been restored, with a number of buildings reconstructed. The **Schoolhouse Visitors Center** contains photographs and exhibits detailing the colony's history. The **Thomas Hughes Free Public Library** has changed very little since it opened in 1882 and still contains its original 7,000 volumes, constituting one of the finest collections of Victorian literature in the country. **Christ Church, Episcopal,** built in 1887 in the Carpenter Gothic style, is also still in use. German stained glass,

Christ Church, one of the surviving buildings from a Utopian community established at Rugby in 1880 by Thomas Hughes with the income from his highly popular novel Tom Brown's School Days. *The English aristocrats who settled at Rugby were a great source of amusement to the farming folk of East Tennessee.*

hand-carved walnut altar furniture, and English hanging lamps are all original. The rosewood organ, built in London in 1849, is believed to be the oldest of its type still in use in the United States. **Kingstone Lisle** was the home of Thomas Hughes during his regular visits to the community. Many items belonging to the colonists, including Hughes's writing table, furnish the home. **Newbury House,** the colony's first boardinghouse, has been restored and offers overnight accommodations.

LOCATION: Route 52, 17 miles southeast of Jamestown. HOURS: February through December: 10–4:30 Monday–Saturday, 12–4:30 Sunday. FEE: Yes. TELEPHONE: 615–628–2441.

ALVIN C. YORK STATE HISTORIC SITE

Sergeant Alvin C. York, one of the most decorated soldiers of World War I, almost declared himself a conscientious objector because of his religious convictions, but after spending several solitary days meditating in the Tennessee mountains, he joined the army. On October 8, 1918, he singlehandedly knocked out three German machine-gun emplacements in the Argonne Forest in France and took 132 prisoners—an exploit that won him the Congressional Medal of Honor.

The historic area includes the family gristmill along the Wolf River, which York operated after the war; his simple frame home across the river from the mill; the Wolf River Methodist Church, where he was converted; and his grave in the church graveyard.

LOCATION: Route 127, about 10 miles north of Jamestown. HOURS: April through October: 8–6 Daily. FEE: None. TELEPHONE: 615–879–4026.

Cordell Hull served as Franklin Delano Roosevelt's secretary of state. Often referred to as the father of the United Nations, he was award-ed the Nobel Peace Prize in 1945 for his work in improving interna-tional relations. The simple log cabin where he was born has been restored as the **Cordell Hull Birthplace** (Route 325, 2 miles west of Byrdstown off Route 42), and an adjacent museum contains his desk, personal library, political cartoons, photographs, and numerous items collected during his world travels.

FORT LOUDOUN STATE HISTORIC AREA

The original log fort was built by the British from 1756 to 1757 in the heart of Cherokee territory along the Little Tennessee River. The diamond-shaped structure was protected by twelve cannon, which had been transported across the mountains by pack horse. The tiny outpost served as a trading center with the Cherokee until 1760, when hostilities flared after the execution of twenty-three Cherokee hostages held in South Carolina. By March of that year the fort was under siege, and by June rations were reduced to one quart of corn per three persons per day. In August the garrison surrendered, and the Cherokee agreed to their safe passage to Charleston. Instead, the party was attacked a day's march from the fort; more than twenty were killed and the remainder were taken prisoner. Most were eventually ransomed.

Reconstruction of the fort on its original site began in the 1930s. In the 1970s the site underwent extensive archaeological studies and was protected when the Tellico Lake inundated much of the surrounding area. The William C. Watson Visitors Center offers a slide orientation and displays numerous artifacts, including one of the fort's original cannon.

LOCATION: Route 360, off Route 411 near Vonore. HOURS: 8–Dusk Daily. FEE: None. TELEPHONE: 615–884–6217.

Nearby, just off Route 411, are the remains of the **Tellico Blockhouse.** Built in 1794, the blockhouse served as the center of trade between the U.S. government and the Cherokee.

SEQUOYAH BIRTHPLACE MUSEUM

Sequoyah, one of the most respected members of the Cherokee tribe, was born near this site along the Little Tennessee River in 1776. Fascinated by the white settlers' ability to communicate in writing, Sequoyah spent twelve years developing a written language for his people. After his wife, disgusted by his constant scribbling, burned all his work, Sequoyah doggedly began again; in 1821 he perfected his Cherokee syllabary. The museum, which is owned by the tribe, offers audio-visual programs, including one that relates Cherokee myths and legends and another on how to pronounce the Cherokee syllabary. Exhibits on Sequoyah and on Cherokee history

Sequoyah displaying the Cherokee syllabary he developed, in an 1836 color lithograph by I. T. Bowen.

and culture include artifacts excavated in the Little Tennessee River valley, such as 700- to 800-year-old Cherokee pottery and grinding stones and projectile points dating back 1,000 years.

LOCATION: Just off Route 411 on Route 360, adjacent to Fort Loudoun State Historic Area. HOURS: March through December: 10–6 Monday–Saturday, 12–6 Sunday. FEE: Yes. TELEPHONE: 615–884–6246.

DAYTON

For eight days during the summer of 1925, the tiny town of Dayton was the focus of worldwide attention. It was here in a crowded courtroom at the **Rhea County Courthouse** (Courthouse Square, 615–775–0187) that two of the country's most celebrated lawyers, Clarence Darrow and William Jennings Bryan, confronted each other in the Scopes trial. Earlier that year the American Civil

Clarence Darrow, the attorney defending John T. Scopes at the famed "monkey trial," addressing the court of July 10, 1925. Scopes is the young man in shirtsleeves seated with his arms folded, behind Darrow.

Liberties Union had offered to pay expenses to any schoolteacher willing to test Tennessee's new anti-evolution law, which banned the teaching of any theory that disputed the biblical story of the divine creation of man. Dayton businessmen seized on the idea as a way to energize the local economy and enlisted the help of a young teacher, John T. Scopes. Scopes was accused of violating the law; Darrow defended him, and Bryan, an eloquent orator, prosecuted. The jury was convinced by Bryan's arguments, convicting Scopes and fining him $100. (The Tennessee Supreme Court reversed the conviction on a technicality.) Bryan died five days after the trial. From a business perspective the "monkey trial" was a tremendous success, drawing 10,000 spectators daily, including some 200 reporters. The third-floor courtroom has been restored to its 1925 appearance, and a museum contains memorabilia relating to the trial.

RED CLAY STATE HISTORIC PARK

Red Clay served as the council ground of the Cherokee nation from 1832 to 1838, when they were "removed" from their traditional homelands and forced to travel to Oklahoma for resettlement, a journey known as the Trail of Tears. One-quarter of the 14,000 Cherokee who began the journey died en route of disease and exposure. Prior to 1832 the Cherokee capital was at New Echota, Georgia, but after the Georgia legislature passed punitive laws making it illegal for Indians to gather except to sign away their lands, the Cherokee council ground was moved to Red Clay, just north of the Georgia-Tennessee line. It was at Red Clay that the Cherokee leaders tried desperately to negotiate a way to retain a remnant of their eastern lands. Eleven general councils were held here, attracting up to 5,000 people.

An interpretive center features an audio-visual program and exhibits depicting Cherokee life prior to the removal. Replicas of a council house, sleeping huts, and a typical Cherokee homestead of the nineteenth century are on the grounds. The Sacred Council Spring, or Blue Hole, provided water during council gatherings; the large, tree-shaded natural spring produces over 280 gallons a minute.

LOCATION: Route 6, off Route I-75. HOURS: *Visitor center:* 8–4:30 Daily. *Park grounds:* March through September: 8–Dusk Daily; December through February: 8–4:30 Daily. FEE: None. TELEPHONE: 615–478–0339.

CHATTANOOGA

Nestled in a valley and surrounded by steep ridges, Chattanooga has served as a crossroads since prehistoric days. A number of Indian trails converged at this site along the Tennessee River, and white trade routes followed these ancient paths. After the influx of settlers into East Tennessee, Chief Dragging Canoe and his followers declared war on the whites. They broke away from the Cherokee tribe and established themselves near Chattanooga. Known as the Chickamauga, they waged war throughout the frontier region until 1794, when they were crushed and their village destroyed. A ferry established along the Tennessee River in the opening years of the nineteenth century came to be known as Ross's Landing, for the Cherokee-Scottish family who operated it; when the federal government ordered the removal of the Cherokee in 1838, the landing became an embarkation point for the Indians on their way west. In that same year the town's name was changed to Chattanooga, possibly a corruption of a Creek word

The vista from Lookout Mountain in Chattanooga National Military Park. Because the slope was so steep, the Confederate guns on the top of the mountain could not be aimed down on the attacking Federals.

that means "rock that comes to a point," believed to be a reference to Lookout Mountain, which dominates the skyline.

During the Civil War, Chattanooga was important because four major rail lines converged here, and it was considered the gateway to the Deep South. The town changed hands several times. Union victories in the Chattanooga area during the autumn of 1863 caught the country's imagination when the struggle for the fog-laden heights of Lookout Mountain was dubbed the "Battle Above the Clouds" by journalists. Observed Ulysses S. Grant, "The battle of Lookout Mountain is one of the romances of the war . . . it is all poetry." Grant's success at Chattanooga led to his promotion to lieutenant general and commander in chief of the U.S. armies.

At the close of the war, the town was extremely anxious to rebuild its shattered economy. In December 1868 the following message appeared on the front page of the *Daily Republican:* WANTED IMMEDIATELY ANY NUMBER OF CARBET-BAGGERS TO COME TO CHATTANOOGA AND SETTLE. The ad went on to extol the city's virtues and inform interested parties that "those who wish to come can be assured they will not be required to renounce their political and religious tenets, as the jurisdiction of the Ku Klux and other vermin does not extend over these parts."

A number of industries, including iron and coal, contributed to the town's postwar recovery. In 1899 a new business, destined for international success, was born in the city when two enterprising lawyers along with Benjamin Franklin, Tomas and Joseph Whitehead hit upon the idea of bottling Coca-Cola, a drink that had previously been available only at soda fountains. Downtown, along the Tennessee River, is the site of **Ross's Landing** (Riverfront Parkway), now a city park. The **Chattanooga Regional History Museum** (400 Chestnut Street, 615–265–3247), housed in a 1910 school building, features exhibits on the city and the surrounding region from prehistoric times to the present. The **Tivoli Theater** (709 Broad Street, 615–757–5048), constructed in 1921, has undergone an extensive renovation and is now a cultural center.

The **Dome Building** (Georgia and East 8th streets, private) was built in 1891 as the headquarters of the *Chattanooga Times,* a newspaper owned by Adolph S. Ochs, who later purchased the struggling *New York Times,* which he built into one of the country's most respected papers. Chattanooga's Southern Railway terminal was built in the Beaux-Arts style between 1906 and 1909 and is now a hotel known as the **Chattanooga Choo-Choo** (1400 Market Street).

The Dome Building, built in 1891 by newspaperman Adolph S. Ochs.

The domed waiting room serves as the hotel lobby. At the foot of Lookout Mountain is the **Incline Railway** (827 East Brow Road, 615–821–4224), a cable-car system constructed in 1895 to connect the city with the mountain's summit. The mile-long track has a grade of 72.7 degrees, among the steepest in the world.

TENNESSEE VALLEY RAILROAD

Dedicated to the preservation of steam railroading, this museum offers a six-mile round-trip excursion along a rail line that dates to 1852. The two depots are reproductions of turn-of-the-century train stations, one of which utilized parts of a demolished station from Athens, Tennessee. The track crosses four bridges, including one over Chickamauga Creek, and penetrates Missionary Ridge through a 986-foot, horseshoe-shaped, antebellum tunnel. An 80-foot turntable in East Chattanooga is used to turn the locomotive after each trip. The East Chattanooga repair shop and equipment display is open for tours. The museum's locomotive collection numbers six, including the celebrated Engine No. 4501, the first steam locomotive of its type, purchased by the Southern Railway in 1911.

LOCATION: East Chattanooga Depot, 2200 North Chamberlain Avenue, or Grand Junction Depot, 4119 Cromwell Road. HOURS: April through May and September through November: 10–5 Saturday, 12–5 Sunday; June through August: 10–5 Monday–Saturday, 12–5 Sunday. FEE: Yes. TELEPHONE: 615-894-8028.

Chickamauga and Chattanooga National Military Park

A series of battles occurred in the Chattanooga area from September to November 1863. On September 19 and 20, 1863, the Confederate forces under General Braxton Bragg met General William Rosecrans's army at Chickamauga Creek in Georgia. The battle took place largely in woodlands, and before the fighting was over the casualties numbered 16,000 Federal soldiers and 20,000 of the Confederate forces. Rosecrans retreated into Chattanooga and prepared to defend the city. Generals James Longstreet and Nathan Bedford Forrest urged Bragg, their superior officer, to destroy the Union army before it could be reinforced, but Bragg chose to encircle Chattanooga and besiege it by fortifying the surrounding heights. For a time it appeared the Union forces would be starved into submission. One Hoosier private wrote that the men were allowed but two meals a day, "one cracker for each meal. We generally eat them up in three days and starve the other two. I was nearer starved here than ever." Unable to break the stalemate, Rosecrans was relieved of his command by General George Thomas in mid-October by order of Rosecrans's newly appointed superior, General Ulysses S. Grant.

With the arrival of Grant, the weeks of inactivity ended abruptly. A supply line was opened by a daring river raid west into Confederate-held territory, and in late November Grant launched a series of attacks against the Confederate positions on Orchard Knob, Lookout Mountain, and Missionary Ridge. Orchard Knob was taken on November 23, Lookout Mountain the following day. Fog concealed the progress of the Union troops scaling the mountain, but when the sun broke through the next morning, both armies were greeted by the sight of the Stars and Stripes flying from Lookout's point.

The final day of fighting, November 25, was along Missionary Ridge where Bragg's Confederate troops defended three lines of rifle pits: one near the base of the mountain, a second halfway up, and a third along the crest. When Grant ordered George H. Thomas's Army of the Cumberland to attack the center in an effort to divert attention from action on the flanks, both generals were stunned to see the men overrun the first line of defense and then, contrary to orders, continue up the steep slopes. With cries of "Remember Chickamauga" the Union forces surged forward, sending the Confederates fleeing up and over the top of the ridge. Wrote a blue-coat from Kansas, "Our men pursued the fugitives with an eagerness only equaled by their own to escape . . . all that remained of the defiant rebel army that had so long besieged Chattanooga was captured guns, disarmed prisoners, moaning wounded, ghastly dead." The debacle cost General Bragg his command and left the Federal troops in undisputed control of Chattanooga.

The military park covers over 8,000 acres in both Georgia and Tennessee and is the nation's oldest military park. The park's main **visitor center** is in Georgia on the Chickamauga battlefield, but a smaller center is located on Lookout Mountain at **Point Park,** which offers a breathtaking view of the city. Exhibits offered at both centers tell the story of the battles that took place here. On the slopes of the mountain stands **Cravens House** (off Route 148, 615–821–7786), which was caught in the midst of the fighting. Prior to the battle, the house was Confederate General E. C. Walthall's headquarters, but as the Confederates were pushed up and over the mountain's crest, the house served as a hospital and the headquarters of Joe Hooker. Heavily damaged by cannon and small arms fire, the house was rebuilt by the Craven family after the war. In addition to sites on Lookout Mountain, the park preserves a number of other areas. **Orchard Knob** was the site of Grant's headquarters, and a number of monuments line the crest of **Missionary Ridge.** Maps of the park are available at both the Georgia and the Tennessee visitor centers.

LOCATION: Point Park, off Route 148, at 1101 Brow Road on Lookout Mountain. HOURS: *Point Park:* 9–5 Daily. *Chickamauga battlefield:* 8–4:45 Daily; June through August: 8–Dusk Daily. *Cravens House:* March through November: 8–5 Monday–Saturday, 1–5 Sunday. FEE: For Cravens House. TELEPHONE: 404–866–9241.

OPPOSITE: *A portion of the Chickamauga battlefield, on the Tennessee–Georgia border. The Confederates were victorious at Chickamauga, but allowed the Union army to escape into Chattanooga.*

The **Chattanooga National Cemetery** (1200 Bailey Avenue, 615–855–6590) was established by General George H. Thomas. Union dead from battles throughout the area were buried here; by 1865 more than 12,000 interments had been made, 5,000 of them of unknown soldiers. When the chaplain charged with laying out the cemetery asked Thomas if the dead from each state should be buried together, Thomas replied, "No, no; mix 'em up, mix 'em up. I'm tired of states' rights." A **Confederate Cemetery,** founded in 1865, is located between East 3d and East 5th streets. The cemetery is open for tours only by request to the city park department (615–757–5054).

MIDDLE TENNESSEE

A region of gently rolling hills and fertile fields, Middle Tennessee is bounded by the Cumberland Plateau on the east and the Tennessee River on the west. The plantation system prospered here during the first half of the nineteenth century, nurturing a lifestyle similar to that of the Deep South. Hundreds of fine antebellum houses attest to the region's prosperity during the years prior to the Civil War.

SEWANEE

Home of the **University of the South** (Route 24E, 615–598–5931), the small town of Sewanee retains a feeling of unhurried southern charm. The university (commonly referred to as Sewanee) was formed in 1857 by the Episcopal church, and one of the school's founders was Leonidas Polk, Bishop of Louisiana, who went on to become a general in the Confederate army. The first cornerstone was destroyed by Union troops in July 1863, but the institution flourished after the war, with a number of former Confederate officers, including General Edmund Kirby-Smith, on the faculty. The focal point of the campus is **All Saints' Chapel,** which was constructed around 1907 and features English stained glass and a massive Casavant pipe organ. The chapel's **Shaphard Tower** contains the fifty-six-bell Leonidas Polk Memorial Carillon. **Convocation Hall,** an impressive example of Victorian Gothic architecture, and the attached **Breslin Tower,** which was modeled after Magdalene Tower at Oxford University, were constructed in 1886. In the tower are the Douglas Chimes, the result of a gift in 1900, and a Seth Thomas clock installed in 1935.

West of Sewanee on Route 64 is the small railroad town of **Cowan,** once the site of an active depot for pusher engines used to negoti- ate the steep inclines in the Cumberland Mountains. In the heart of town, a restored train station, dating to 1904, houses the **Cowan Railroad Museum** (Route 64/41A). The museum collection includes railroad lanterns, watches, caps, and schedules; a fifty- inch model engine built in 1910; the original benches from the 1904 depot; a link-and-pin train coupler dating to before 1887; a library of railroading books, and other railroad relics. Also on the museum grounds are a 1920 Porter steam locomotive, a flatcar, a caboose, and the one-story log structure that served as Franklin County's first courthouse from 1807 to 1814. On the rail line out- side of town is the **Cumberland Mountain Tunnel.** From 1849 until 1851, slaves owned by the North Carolina and Saint Louis rail- roads, Irish immigrants, and other laborers bored through lime- stone with hand drills, sledges, picks, and shovels to open the tun- nel, which is still in use today.

WINCHESTER

On February 24, 1861, a mass meeting was held in Winchester in which citizens of Franklin County voted to secede from the state of Tennessee and request annexation to the nearby Confederate state of Alabama. Twelve hundred volunteers led by a Winchester attor- ney, Peter Turney, formed the First Tennessee Regiment—the first Confederate regiment organized in the state. They journeyed to Virginia where they served under General Lee until his surrender at Appomattox. The subsequent secession of Tennessee from the Union on June 24, 1861, ended the county's brief mini-secession. The **Old Jail Museum** (400 First Avenue NE, 615–967–0524) is housed in a jail that dates to 1897 and contains artifacts and pho- tographs depicting the history of Franklin County.

   Hundred Oaks Castle (off Route 64, west of the town square, 615–967–0100) is a massive brick house with a four-story crenelat- ed tower. It was built in 1889 for Arthur Handy Marks, the son of Albert S. Marks, Tennessee's twenty-first governor. The younger Marks served in the consular service in England and became a great admirer of English and Scottish architecture; except for a few minor deviations, the house's study is a replica of Sir Walter Scott's study at Abbotsford, Scotland.

Twelve miles west of Winchester off Route 64 is **Falls Mill** (615–469–7161). Built in 1873, the gristmill is powered by a thirty-two-foot overshot wheel and still produces stone-ground flour and meal. Davy Crockett lived in this vicinity from 1812 to 1817 on a farm he called Kentuck. His first wife, Polly Finlay, died in 1815 and was buried in a small cemetery near Maxwell. Crockett subsequently moved farther west to Lawrence County.

LYNCHBURG

The tiny town of Lynchburg has changed very little since the turn of the century. The **Moore County Courthouse** in the town square dates to 1884 and is one of the oldest buildings in town—a fire in December 1883 destroyed many earlier structures. **Jack Daniel's Distillery** (Route 55, 615–759–4221), the nation's oldest registered distillery, was founded here in 1866. Daniel chose the location because of a large nearby spring that produces hundreds of gallons of mineral-free water each minute, a key ingredient in the produc-

The nineteenth-century office of the Jack Daniel's Distillery, the nation's oldest registered distillery founded in 1866.

tion of high-quality whiskey. The nineteenth-century distillery office has been preserved and contains its original furnishings, including the safe said to be responsible for the founder's death—one day, so the story goes, the safe would not open, and Daniel kicked it in disgust, injuring his leg. The resulting infection proved fatal. Tour guides explain the process of making charcoal-mellowed sour-mash whiskey.

East of Lynchburg stands the **Ledford Mill and Museum** (off Route 41A, north of the junction with Route 55, 615-455-2546). Built in 1884, it is the second mill on the site and contains a collection of eighteenth- and nineteenth-century hand tools.

OLD STONE FORT
STATE ARCHAEOLOGICAL AREA

For generations the origins of these stone and earth walls, which enclose forty acres on a peninsula formed by the Duck River, have been shrouded in mystery. Archaeological evidence indicates that the walls were in place by A.D. 430 and that their purpose was ceremonial rather than defensive. The enclosure walls average four- and-a-half feet, and in the entrance complex the wall reaches six feet. Few pottery shards or other indications of human habitation have been uncovered. Archaeologists believe that the builders were Indians of the Middle Woodland era, who viewed the site as sacred and probably used it only for religious observances and other ceremonies. The walls have been the subject of much speculation: One early theory had attributed them to the Spanish explorer Hernando de Soto, who passed through Tennessee on his sixteenth-century expedition. Others theorized they were of Viking, Welsh, or Phoenician construction—remnants of contact between Europe and the New World long before the voyage of Columbus. No evidence of influence by any non-native group in the construction of the walls has been found, however.

The park's visitor center features displays on the legends surrounding the site as well as the archaeological findings. A number of audio-visual programs illuminate the Indian culture believed responsible for the fort's construction, and an interpretive path provides a view of the walls and the forks of the Duck River below.

LOCATION: Off Route 41, just north of Manchester. HOURS: *Park:* 8–Dusk Daily. *Visitor center:* 8–4:30 Daily. FEE: None. TELEPHONE: 615–728–0751.

WARTRACE

Known as the Cradle of the Tennessee Walking Horse, Wartrace was founded in 1851 along the Nashville & Chattanooga Railroad. It was in the rolling countryside surrounding Wartrace that a new breed of horse, known for its distinctive "running walk," was born. Generations of plantation owners and farmers in the region, who spent long hours on horseback surveying their crops, prized mounts with particularly smooth gaits and bred their animals accordingly. In 1950 the U.S. Department of Agriculture officially recognized the Tennessee walking horse as a distinctive breed.

A number of nineteenth-century structures remain in Wartrace. The **Walking Horse Hotel** (Route 64), a three-story brick building with inviting verandahs, was built in 1917 by Jessie Overall to serve railroad passengers. In 1938 a horse trainer, Floyd Carothers, purchased the hotel, and it was here he trained a chestnut sorrel colt named Strolling Jim, winner of the first Tennessee walking horse world championship in 1939. The hotel is still open for business and boasts a large collection of walking-horse memorabilia.

MURFREESBORO

Originally known as Cannonsburgh, the town was laid out in 1811 and served as the state capital from 1819 to 1826, after which the legislature moved to Nashville. For a number of years, the issue of a permanent capital was debated, with Murfreesboro and Nashville being viewed as equally desirable. In 1840 the state legislature voted to return to Murfreesboro if the city would bear the cost of moving the state records, which amounted to $100. The city fathers refused to foot the bill, and Nashville remained the seat of government.

Situated along the Nashville & Chattanooga rail line, Murfreesboro was strategically important to both sides during the Civil War. After Union victories at Forts Henry and Donelson, northern troops occupied the town from March 1862 until July of that year, when General Nathan Bedford Forrest drove them out in a surprise attack. In December 1862 the town changed hands again as General William Rosecrans's troops gained control of the region following the Battle of Stones River. To solidify his control, the general had a massive earthwork fort built at the edge of town, and it was from this major supply depot that provisions were later shipped southward for General Sherman as he made his march to the sea through Georgia.

The **Rutherford County Courthouse** dominates the public square. The third courthouse on this site, it dates from 1859 and features Corinthian columns and an octagonal cupola. In 1913 a tornado completely demolished two sides of the square, and many of the buildings that surround the courthouse date from the rebuilding period that followed. The **General Palmer House** (434 East Main Street, private) was constructed in 1870 by Joseph B. Palmer, who served in the Civil War. The French Second Empire **Collier-Crichlow-Smythe House** (511 East Main Street, 615–896–0765) dates to 1880. **Old Fort Park,** on Route 96 at the edge of town, is the site of Fort Rosecrans, the Civil War's largest earthwork fort. The original structure consisted of nine outer forts and four inner forts. Portions of the walls remain.

Cannonsburgh

A village composed of more than twenty historic buildings gathered from around the region, Cannonsburgh celebrates life in the rural south during the nineteenth and early twentieth centuries. The village is entered through a toll gate, a reminder of the turnpike system once prevalent throughout the region. An 1870s cotton warehouse, original to the site, houses exhibits tracing community life from 1796 to 1876. The gristmill is a scaled-down reproduction of a nineteenth-century mill that once stood on nearby Stones River. It contains 150-year-old machinery and the original grindstones. The Stones River Garage evokes the early days of the automobile, while the blacksmith shop speaks of even earlier means of transportation.

LOCATION: South Front Street. HOURS: May through October: 10–5 Tuesday–Saturday, 1–5 Sunday. FEE: None. TELEPHONE: 615–893–6565.

Oaklands Historic House Museum and Medical Museum

Oaklands is an antebellum house built in stages over a period of forty years. The original section was a one-and-a-half-story house constructed in 1818 by James Maney, a physician whose wife was a Murfree, the family for whom the town was named. In the 1820s the west section and a full second story were added, and a rear wing was built in the 1830s. The basic style of the house was Federal until 1858, when Major Lewis Maney and his bride, Rachel Adeline

Oaklands, a Federal house with Italianate additions made between 1858 and 1860, includes elaborate carved wooden "eyebrows" above the windows.

Cannon, the daughter of a Tennessee governor, began a final round of construction that added the front three rooms and Italianate facade. The Maneys owned 1,500 acres and 100 slaves, making Oaklands one of the area's largest cotton plantations. During the Civil War the estate was used by Union forces from March to July 1862. One of the Union officers headquartered at the home, Colonel William Duffield, became a family friend; when he was wounded during General Nathan Bedford Forrest's raid on the town, the family helped nurse him back to health. The formal surrender of Duffield's garrison to Forrest took place in the mansion's back parlor. With the Confederate reoccupation of Murfreesboro, Oaklands hosted President Jefferson Davis for several days in December 1862 while he reviewed General Braxton Bragg's troops.

The house has been restored to its appearance prior to 1862, and a number of the furnishings are original to the Maney family. A semicircular stairway and formal parlor with gasoliers attest to the Maneys' elegant lifestyle prior to the war. The brick plantation office

One of the two niches holding classical busts that decorate Oaklands' semi-circular stairway, which was installed during renovations in 1858.

on the grounds houses a collection of nineteenth-century medical instruments and artifacts, including Doctor Maney's medical books.

LOCATION: 900 North Maney Avenue. HOURS: April through October: 10–4 Tuesday–Saturday, 1–4 Sunday; November through March: 11–3 Tuesday–Saturday, 1–3 Sunday. FEE: Yes. TELEPHONE: 615–893–0022.

Stones River National Battlefield

On the evening of December 30, 1862, 45,000 Union soldiers under the command of General William Rosecrans camped within sight of 38,000 Confederates led by General Braxton Bragg. To hearten the troops, the military bands struck up, each trying to outdo the other, but when the strains of "Home Sweet Home" were heard, everyone, Union and Confederate alike, joined in and sang together. At dawn the next morning the Confederates attacked, and by 10 AM the Union troops had been forced back to the Nashville Pike. By late

Federals retreat before a Confederate charge at Murfreesboro on December 31, 1862. The Northerners recovered, however, and held their line against further attacks. This

afternoon, General Rosecrans rallied his men along the pike and formed a new line, which held until the end of the day's fighting. On New Year's Day 1863 the guns remained almost silent, but on January 2 Bragg ordered General John Breckinridge's brigades to resume the attack. They were stopped by massive artillery fire, but the battle ended with both sides claiming victory. The Confederates lost 10,000 men, killed or wounded, while the Union army suffered 13,000 casualties. Bragg's forces retreated southward, leaving Rosecrans in control of the rail line. The loss of the rich agricultural stores of Middle Tennessee was a severe blow to the Confederacy.

A museum in the **visitor center** details the battle. A self-guided driving tour covers major points of interest on the battlefield, such as the **Slaughter Pens,** an area of rock outcroppings that Union General Philip S. Sheridan's division held until running out of ammunition. As a Union officer recalled, "The fighting at this point

painting by William Travis is part of a 528-foot panorama chronicling the exploits of the Federal Army of the Cumberland (detail).

was terrific. All along the front the dead and wounded lay in heaps, and over their bodies came the assaulting host." Across the Old Nashville Highway (Nashville Pike) stands the **Hazen Monument.** Erected by survivors of Colonel William B. Hazen's Union brigade while they wintered in Murfreesboro, it is the oldest Civil War memorial in the nation. In the midst of the battle, when Hazen was informed that he would have to fall back, he replied, "I'd like to know where in hell I'll fall back to?" With bayonets fixed, Hazen's men held the line. The **Stones River National Cemetery** contains the Union dead from Stones River, Franklin, and several other engagements. The unknown Confederate dead are interred in a mass grave in Murfreesboro's **Evergreen Cemetery.**

LOCATION: At the edge of Murfreesboro, off Route 41/70S. HOURS: 8–5 Daily. FEE: None. TELEPHONE: 615–893–9501.

SAM DAVIS HOME

North of Murfreesboro stands the boyhood home of Sam Davis, a Confederate scout who was hanged as a spy at the age of 21 after refusing to betray his informant. The oldest of nine children, Davis was 18 when he enlisted in the Confederate army. He was wounded at the Battle of Shiloh and again at Perryville.

In 1862 and 1863 he was assigned to Coleman's Scouts, Cheatham's Division, and on November 20, 1863, he was captured by Federal troops near Pulaski, Tennessee, carrying papers addressed to General Braxton Bragg that accurately detailed Union plans. Offered his freedom if he would reveal his source, Davis refused, saying, "If I had a thousand lives to live, I would give them all gladly rather than betray a friend."

The front portion of the Davis home was built in 1810. The Davis family purchased the house in 1845 and moved into it in the late 1840s after having made additions to the back of the house. Their home exemplifies the lifestyle of the region's rural middle class just prior to the Civil War. The farm produced cotton, wheat, and tobacco as its main crops, and the family owned about fifty slaves. The house and 168 acres, which were purchased by the state from the Davis family in 1927, remain much as they were in the mid-nineteenth century. Original Davis family pieces are found throughout the house, including their 1840 gold-leaf china, a chest of drawers brought from Virginia in 1825, and the parlor's original Brussels carpet. The overseer's house, plantation kitchen, smokehouse, and three-seat privy are among the original outbuildings that have survived. On the grounds are the Davis family gardens and burial grounds. Sam Davis's grave is marked by a monument. A small museum features Middle Tennessee Civil War objects and Davis family artifacts.

LOCATION: Sam Davis Road, near Smyrna. HOURS: March through October: 9–5 Monday–Saturday, 1–5 Sunday; November through February: 10–4 Monday–Saturday, 1–4 Sunday. FEE: Yes. TELEPHONE: 615–459–2341.

FRANKLIN

Franklin, founded in 1799, prospered as an agricultural center as well as the seat of Williamson County. By the time of the Civil War,

Williamson County was one of the richest in the state. More than two dozen fine antebellum structures are visible along Route 31 between Brentwood and Spring Hill.

On November 30, 1864, the Battle of Franklin was fought on the southern edge of town. Confederate General John Bell Hood, in a desperate effort to revive southern fortunes, planned to march from Alabama through Tennessee into Kentucky, where he hoped to pick up recruits, defeat Union forces there, and move east to Virginia, to meet up with Robert E. Lee's army. Capturing Nashville was the first step in Hood's scheme. Federal troops, under the command of General John M. Schofield, were entrenched across the Columbia Pike (Route 31) in Franklin, south of Nashville, when Hood, angered at having been outmaneuvered by Schofield the previous day, ordered his infantry to make a frontal assault. In the face of vehement opposition from his fellow officers, Hood announced, "We will make the fight. . . . Drive the enemy from his position . . . at all hazards."

At around 4 PM, 22,000 Confederate soldiers marched forward across an open field, banners flying, to attack the enemy fortifications. Wrote one Union officer: "For the moment we were spellbound with admiration . . . we knew that in a few brief moments . . . thousands of those valorous men of the South, with their chivalric officers, would pour out their life's blood on the fair fields in front of us." Fighting was hand to hand along the entrenchments, and repeated assaults were launched until well after dark. George W. Gordon, a Confederate general who was taken prisoner, recalled: "For some time, we fought them across the breastworks, both sides lying low . . . firing rapidly and at random and not exposing any part of the body except the hand that fired the gun. . . . It was fatal to leave the ditch and endeavor to escape to the rear. Every man who attempted it . . . was shot down without exception." Another soldier declared, "I never saw the dead lay so thick. I saw them upon each other . . . ghastly in the powder-dimmed starlight." Some time after midnight the Federal troops withdrew toward Nashville, but Hood could hardly claim the battle as a victory. While the Union suffered 2,300 casualties, the Confederates lost more than 6,000 men, including twelve generals: Five had been killed outright, one had been captured, and six more were wounded, one fatally. Of approximately 100 regimental commanders, the Confederates had lost 54.

Carnton Mansion

This twenty-two-room mansion was built in 1826 by Randal McGavock, a former mayor of Nashville. The McGavock plantation was known for its formal gardens and fine thoroughbreds. Such notables as Andrew Jackson, James K. Polk, and Sam Houston were entertained by the family. After the Battle of Franklin, the house was filled with over 200 wounded Confederate soldiers, and the bodies of four southern generals were laid on the long back porch. The parlor and the nursery were turned into operating rooms, and bloodstains are still visible on the wood floors.The house, which passed out of the family in 1911, is in the process of restoration. Paint analysis indicates the rooms were originally painted in deep purples and greens and that the entry hall was trimmed in gold leaf. One-third of the present furnishings are McGavock pieces, and others are of the period. The family cemetery holds the graves of 1,481 Confederate soldiers.

LOCATION: Off Route 431, 1 mile southeast of Franklin. HOURS: January through March: 9–4 Monday–Friday; April through December: 9–4 Monday–Saturday, 1–4 Sunday. FEE: Yes. TELEPHONE: 615–794–0903.

ABOVE and OPPOSITE: An upstairs bedroom at Carnton Mansion, where General Quarles is said to have had his arm amputated. Bloodstains near the fireplace remain from the period. Over the mantle is a childhood portrait of Frank McGavock.

Carter House

Located just behind the Federal breastworks át the site of the Battle of Franklin's heaviest fighting, the outbuildings surrounding the Carter House are still pockmarked with bullet holes on their south side. The Carter family and servants huddled in the cellar of the small 1830s brick home as the battle raged around them. When they emerged word reached them that a son, Captain Tod Carter, lay wounded on the field. His father and sisters found him, just a few hundred yards from the house, and carried him home to die. The house has been restored and is furnished with family and other period pieces dating from 1828 to 1870.

LOCATION: 1140 Columbia Avenue (Route 31S). HOURS: April through October: 9–5 Monday–Saturday, 9–2 Sunday; November through March: 9–4 Monday–Saturday, 9–2 Sunday. FEE: Yes. TELE-PHONE: 615–791–1861.

As with many towns in Middle Tennessee, Franklin is laid out around a square. The **Confederate Monument,** in the center of the square, was erected in 1899 and dedicated by General George W. Gordon, who fought and was captured at the Battle of Franklin. The **Williamson County Courthouse** was built in 1859 to replace an 1809 structure. South of the square stands the **Moran House** (120 Third Avenue South, private), built in the 1820s by Charles Moran, a cabinetmaker whose clients included Andrew Jackson. On the next block is the **Marshall House** (224 Third Avenue South, private), constructed prior to 1805. In the 1840s Supreme Court Justice John Marshall purchased the house, which remains in the Marshall family. The 1823 Gothic Revival–style **Hiram Masonic Lodge** (Second Avenue South, private) is believed to be the oldest three-story building in the state. In 1830 a treaty with the Chickasaw was negotiated on the grounds by Andrew Jackson and John Henry Eaton.

The **Eaton House** (125 Third Avenue North, private) dates to 1818 and was the home of Elizabeth Eaton, the mother of John Henry Eaton, Andrew Jackson's secretary of war. Jackson was often a guest at the house. Eaton's marriage to Margaret (Peggy) O'Neale, the daughter of a Washington innkeeper, was used by John C. Calhoun and his wife as fuel for Calhoun's political ambitions. The Calhouns and their friends ostracized Mrs. Eaton, purportedly because of her low birth and alleged premarital intimacy with John Eaton, but in reality to drive Eaton from office and garner political power. The social and political pressure caused by the scandal forced Eaton to resign his cabinet post in 1831. The insult caused by the Washington socialites deeply offended President Andrew Jackson, the Eatons' close friend and supporter, contributing to his severance of relations with Calhoun and ultimately to Calhoun's resignation from the vice-presidency in 1832.

Saint Paul's Episcopal Church (Fifth Avenue North) was constructed in 1831 and suffered tremendous damage during the Civil War. The pews and pulpit were used for firewood and horse troughs, but the church silver and records escaped unscathed, having been buried across the street.

COLUMBIA

Settlement of the area south of the Duck River (traditional hunting grounds of the Cherokee, Chickasaw, and Creek) began after the Dearborne Treaty of 1806. A series of disasters struck Columbia during its infancy: In 1811 the Duck River flooded, and from December 1811 to March 1812 the town was shaken by a series of earthquakes. Despite fears that the site was cursed, most families chose to remain. For over 100 years Columbia has been a major trading center for mules, and in 1934 the town began a tradition of celebrating "Mule Day" in April.

The **Maury County Courthouse** dominates the public square and is the third to stand on the site. The second building suffered irreparable damage while occupied by Federal troops. The present stone structure was completed in 1906 and features an octagonal clock tower. Across Courthouse Square stands the **Courthouse Square Building,** which dates to 1859. The exterior has recently been restored to its original appearance. The parish of **Saint Peter's Episcopal Church** (311 West 7th Street) was founded in 1828, and the church was constructed in 1860. During the Civil War it was commandeered by Federal forces who established a provost marshall's office here. Saint Peter's witnessed the funerals of Confederate Generals Earl Van Dorn, Patrick Cleburne, Otho Strahl, and Hiram Granbury, the last three of whom fell at the Battle of Franklin in November 1864. The church was restored and reconsecrated in 1871. The **Athenaeum** (808 Athenaeum Street, 615–381–4822) was constructed in 1835 in the Gothic Revival style and served as the rectory for the Columbia Athenaeum, a finishing school for girls. Designed by Colonel Adolphus Heiman of Nashville, it was built by Nathan Vaught, Maury County's master builder, for Samuel Polk Walker, a nephew of President James K. Polk. Walker never lived in the house, however, and it was soon acquired by Reverend Frank Gillette Smith, rector of the Columbia Athenaeum. The house contains some original furnishings.

James K. Polk Home

The only surviving home in which President James K. Polk resided, the house was built in 1816 by Samuel Polk, the father of the president. James began his law career in Columbia and served seven terms in the U.S. House of Representatives. He became governor of Tennessee in 1839 and was elected president in 1844. An ardent expansionist, Polk added the Texas, Oregon, and California territories to the country during his administration. The house is furnished with Polk family items, including many pieces from the White House years, as well as Mrs. Polk's pianoforte and rosewood Victorian furniture. Next door is the **Sisters' House,** built in 1818 in the Federal style as a residence for two Polk sisters. It now houses a museum.

LOCATION: 301 West 7th Street. HOURS: April through October: 9–5 Monday–Saturday, 1–5 Sunday; November through March: 9–4 Monday–Saturday, 1–5 Sunday. FEE: Yes. TELEPHONE: 615–388–2354.

A large number of antebellum houses still stand in the vicinity of Columbia. In southwest Columbia, off Route 43, is **Blythewood,** built in 1858 in the Italianate style for Thomas Keesee, a coachmaker from Richmond. It is now a bank. Especially noteworthy is the original, highly detailed wallpaper by the Swiss firm Zuber ete Zie. Several miles farther south at Ashwood stands **Saint John's Episcopal Church,** constructed in 1841 by Bishop Leonidas Polk and his brothers at the junction of their four plantations. The church, which is

OPPOSITE: *The colonnade of Rattle and Snap has ten fluted columns topped with acanthus-leaf Corinthian capitals. According to family tradition, the mansion was named after a game of chance—probably a dice game—in which Polk's father won 5,600 acres of land from the governor of North Carolina.*

Entrance hall of Rattle and Snap. During the Civil War Northern and Southern soldiers skirmished on the road in front of the mansion, but it escaped damage.

rarely used for services, has not been altered since its construction—there is still no heat or electricity. The bricks were made by the Polk family slaves, and the building is a fine example.of a Gothic Revival plantation church. Leonidas Polk was an Episcopal bishop, founder of the University of the South in Sewanee, and a general in the Confederate army. After fighting at Shiloh, Perryville, Murfreesboro, Chickamauga, and Atlanta he was killed in action in June 1864 at Pine Mountain, Georgia. At the church are the graves of five Episcopal bishops of Tennessee and the Polk burial grounds.

South on Route 43 is **Rattle and Snap** (private), built in 1845 by George W. Polk, younger brother of Bishop Leonidas Polk. It is one of the finest examples of the Tennessee-style, Roman-proportioned "Greek Revival" architecture in the country, displaying a lofty two-story portico with ten Corinthian columns. Six miles west of

Columbia off Route 99 stands **Zion Presbyterian Church,** which was built in 1847 to replace a log structure erected on the site in 1808 by a group of Presbyterian settlers from South Carolina. The graveyard contains many pioneer graves, including a number of Revolutionary War veterans.

From 1817 to 1822 frontiersman Davy Crockett lived in the vicinity of **Lawrenceburg,** where he operated a gristmill, a powder mill, and a distillery along Shoal Creek until flood waters destroyed the businesses and left him bankrupt. **David Crockett State Park** (Route 64, west of Lawrenceburg, 615–762–9408) contains a gristmill reconstructed near the site of the original.

NATCHEZ TRACE PARKWAY

Once the most heavily traveled roads in the Old Southwest, the Natchez Trace began as a series of Indian paths. The trails wound their way for 400 miles from Natchez, Mississippi, into the heart of Middle Tennessee. Travel along the trace was dangerous, as lonely stretches of wilderness often harbored highwaymen. One of the most notorious was John A. Murrell, who wandered the trace in the first half of the nineteenth century posing as an itinerant preacher. Dapper and eloquent, Murrell ingratiated himself with his victims and then shot them, leaving no witnesses.

With the advent of the steamboat, traffic along the trace dwindled, and portions of it were all but forgotten. In the 1930s the National Park Service began the construction of a parkway that closely follows the original route. Roadside markers point out sites of historic significance. At milepost 385.9, east of **Howenwald,** is the **Meriwether Lewis Monument,** which marks the grave of the famous explorer. On October 11, 1809, Lewis died of a gunshot wound at Grinder's Inn, a hostelry beside the trace. Labeled suicide by some and murder by others, the incident is still a mystery. All that remains of the inn are a few foundation stones. Nearby is a pioneer cemetery with Lewis's grave marked by a monument put up in 1848.

NASHVILLE

In 1779 James Robertson led a party of men and livestock overland from East Tennessee to a site along the Cumberland River in Middle Tennessee known as the French Lick. A second group, which included women and children, journeyed by flatboat from Long Island (Kingsport, Tennessee) on a four-month river voyage. Attacked by Indians and beset by cold weather and smallpox, the settlers had to pole the boats upriver for the last 200 miles. Among the passengers was 13-year-old Rachel Donelson, the future wife of Andrew Jackson. Named Fort Nashborough, the settlement was so far removed from civilization that the leaders drew up a document, known as the Cumberland Compact, establishing a civil government. Indian war parties resisted the invasion and on one occasion ambushed a group of settlers near the fort. They were saved by the quick wit of Robertson's wife, Charlotte, who loosed the fort's hunting dogs, forcing the Indians to beat a hasty retreat.

Around 1818 the first steamboat reached the settlement, making Nashville an increasingly important river port. River trade remained strong, even after the completion of the Nashville, Chattanooga & St. Louis Railroad in 1854. Though Nashville had served as one of a number of temporary state capitals, not until

The city of Nashville had its origins in the settlement of Fort Nashborough, founded in 1779 and today commemorated with a reconstructed fort near the original site.

1843 was it chosen as the permanent seat of government. The ante-bellum years were prosperous ones, with large plantations scattered throughout the countryside surrounding the city. When the Civil War erupted, most of Nashville's sympathy lay with the Confederacy. After the Confederate forces lost Fort Donelson in 1862, many residents fled. The Union occupation brought much destruction: Trees lining the city streets were chopped down for firewood, and fortifications and barracks dotted the lawns of fashionable mansions. In December 1864 General John Bell Hood's Confederate troops approached Nashville in a desperate bid to regain the city. On December 15 and 16 the Battle of Nashville, pitting Hood's outnumbered army against General George Thomas's troops, was a rout that left the Confederates racing for the safety of the Alabama border. A portion of the Federal breastworks, which extended for seven miles, can be seen on the Vanderbilt University campus, and numerous historical markers throughout the city's south side pertain to the battle.

A one-quarter-scale reconstruction of **Fort Nashborough** (170 First Avenue North, 615–255–8192) stands in downtown Nashville near its original site along the Cumberland River. Pioneer artifacts are exhibited, and interpreters demonstrate frontier activities. The **Ryman Auditorium** (116 Fifth Avenue North, 615–254–1445) is a Victorian Gothic building constructed in the 1890s as an all-faith meeting hall for revival meetings. From 1943 to 1974 it was the home of the Grand Ole Opry, a showcase for country music performers. The **Downtown Presbyterian Church** (154 Fifth Avenue North), a rare example of Egyptian Revival architecture, is the work of architect William Strickland, who designed a number of Nashville's public buildings, including the State Capitol. The interior walls and half-columns were painted later with vivid Egyptian motifs. In the bell tower hangs a 4,000-pound bell given to the church in 1867 by Adelicia Acklen (owner of Belmont Mansion). Between the 1870s and 1890s, the bell served as Nashville's fire alarm. The **Arcade** (between Fourth and Fifth avenues) is a reminder of a vanishing style of commercial building once common in America's downtowns. Constructed in 1903, the Arcade houses over fifty shops under an iron-and-glass roof.

OVERLEAF: *Guns were placed on the steps of the Tennessee State Capitol when Union forces under General George H. Thomas fortified Nashville in 1864.*

Union Station (1001 Broadway, 615–726–1001) was built in 1900 in the Richardsonian Romanesque style by the Louisville & Nashville Railroad. The massive stone structure now serves as a hotel, and all of the original stained glass and detailed woodwork and plaster-work are still in place. The **Hermitage Hotel** (231 Sixth Avenue North, 615–244–3121), which opened in 1910, is Beaux-Arts in style and was designed by J. E. R. Carpenter, a native Tennessean. Carpenter was commissioned in 1908 to design the hotel, and it was built at a cost of $1 million. The new hotel advertised its rooms as "fireproof, noiseproof, and dustproof, $2.00 and up." Each room provided hot and cold running water (distilled to avoid typhoid), a private bath, a telephone, an electric fan, and a device to announce the arrival of mail. Each room of the hotel was magnificently fur-nished with velvet upholstered furniture, Persian carpets, palm trees, and mahogany panelling. The entrance to the hotel features Italian Siena marble and a combination of Tennessee and Grecian marble in the steps, floors, and walls of the lobby. The skylight in the lobby and its surrounding glass panels were crafted by the Italian artisan Hotojy. The main dining room is paneled in Russian walnut and has an ornate, hand-crafted plaster-and-wood ceiling.

Tennessee State Museum

The museum preserves the history and culture of Tennessee through extensive exhibits on Indian culture, the frontier, the Jackson era, antebellum Tennessee, the Civil War, and turn-of-the-century life. Artifacts and audio-visual programs combine to paint a vivid portrait of the state. Items of note include Davy Crockett's rifle, Daniel Boone's pocketknife, Andrew Jackson's felt inaugural hat, and General P. G. T. Beauregard's hand-drawn map of Shiloh. A branch of the museum is dedicated to America's overseas conflicts, from the Spanish-American War to Vietnam.

LOCATION: James K. Polk Building, 505 Deaderick Street. HOURS: 10–5 Monday–Saturday, 1–5 Sunday. FEE: None. TELEPHONE: 615-741-2692.

Tennessee State Capitol

This striking Greek Revival structure, built on the highest hill in the center city from 1845 to 1859, was designed by William Strickland, who had studied with noted American architect

Benjamin Henry Latrobe. Strickland declared the building to be his finest achievement. After his death in 1854, the legislature granted his request to be entombed in the building's northeast corner. The exterior of the building is limestone that was quarried nearby, while the interior features East Tennessee marble and a great deal of wrought-iron work. Strickland used all three Greek orders—Ionic, Doric, and Corinthian—in his design. A number of the rooms, including the Legislative Lounge and Supreme Court Chamber, have been restored to their original condition.

On the grounds is an equestrian statue of Andrew Jackson by Clark Mills. This statue, which was the original artist's proof, was made before 1850 but not exhibited until 1880. Two other castings of the work are located in Lafayette Park across from the White House and in Jackson Square in New Orleans. Nearby is the tomb of President James K. Polk and his wife, Sarah.

LOCATION: Charlotte and Seventh avenues. HOURS: 9–4 Daily. FEE: None. TELEPHONE: 615–741–1621.

The Tennessee State Capitol building, designed in the Greek Revival style by William Strickland and built between 1845 and 1859.

MIDDLE TENNESSEE

The Parthenon

A full-scale replica of the ancient Greek temple that crowns the Acropolis in Athens, this structure was the centerpiece of the Tennessee Centennial Exposition held in 1897. Rebuilt in 1931, the massive building was extensively renovated in 1988 and now serves as an art museum. Work by sculptor Alan LeQuire is in progress on a forty-two-foot-high statue of Athena which, when completed, will dominate the main floor of the building.

LOCATION: In Centennial Park, off West End Avenue, between 25th and 29th streets. HOURS: 9–4:30 Tuesday–Saturday, 9–8 Thursday, 1–4:30 Sunday. FEE: Yes. TELEPHONE: 615–259–6358.

Belmont Mansion

Adelicia Acklen was the driving force behind the opulent estate known as Belle Monte. A spirited woman, Adelicia managed to retain much of her wealth during the vicissitudes of the Civil War by charming Union and Confederate officers alike. The family holdings included cotton plantations in Louisiana, and when they were threatened with destruction in 1864, Acklen traveled to New Orleans and managed to save her cotton crop from both sides. Wrote a Union officer: "It is my opinion that Mrs. Acklin [sic] has been playing a very deep game. . . . She had all the time her cotton was being removed, a company of rebels under a captain guarding it, and had our [Federal] army wagons hauling it." Acklen had the cotton shipped to Liverpool, where it brought almost $1 million in gold at a time when many plantation owners were watching their crops go up in smoke.

The thirty-two-room mansion was constructed in 1850 in the Italianate style. The Grand Salon, with its Corinthian columns and massive double staircase, is now considered the most elaborate domestic interior built in Tennessee before the Civil War. Acklen filled her house with paintings and statuary purchased in Europe, and one visitor remarked that he felt as if he were touring "some great art gallery." The estate's grounds contained a bear house (a

OPPOSITE: *Belle Meade Mansion was built in the Greek Revival style by William Giles Harding in 1853.*

playhouse), a bowling alley, and an artificial lake stocked with alligators brought from Louisiana. Acklen sold the mansion in 1887, and the building became a women's college and later a coeducational facility, Belmont College. The mansion was opened to the public in 1976; a number of Acklen pieces remain in the house, and restoration is ongoing.

LOCATION: 1900 Belmont Avenue, on the campus of Belmont College. HOURS: June through August: 10–4 Monday–Saturday; September through May: 10–4 Tuesday–Saturday. FEE: Yes. TELEPHONE: 615–269–9537.

Belle Meade Mansion

Once the plantation home of the Harding family, Belle Meade was known throughout nineteenth-century America for its fine thoroughbred horses. John Harding settled on the property in 1807 in a cabin that still stands beside Richland Creek. The present Greek Revival mansion with its six limestone columns was completed in 1853 as a simplified version of Milford, a South Carolina mansion of the 1840s. At its zenith the plantation consisted of over 5,000 acres, including a deer park and racetrack. William Giles Harding, an ardent Confederate, was arrested soon after Federal troops marched into Nashville in 1862. He was imprisoned at Fort Mackinac, Michigan, and one Union sympathizer wrote that during Harding's absence "There was grand hunting after those deer and buffalo [in the park]. Hundreds of tons of his hay and thousands of bushels of his grain were hauled into our camps. Miles of his fencing were burned."

The plantation remained in the Harding family until 1904; the house and twenty-four acres were purchased by the state in 1953; the mansion contains family and period furnishings. A collection of horse-drawn vehicles is on display in the enormous carriage house adjacent to the mansion.

LOCATION: 110 Leake Avenue. HOURS: 9–5 Monday–Saturday, 1–5 Sunday. FEE: Yes. TELEPHONE: 615–356–0501.

OPPOSITE: *Entrance to the double parlor off the front hallway at the Belle Meade Mansion. In the nineteenth century, the Harding family was famous as breeders of thoroughbred horses.*

Travellers' Rest Historic House Museum

The home of John Overton, a prominent lawyer, Travellers' Rest represents the period from 1789 to 1833, when Middle Tennessee developed from frontier to a plantation economy. When Overton first arrived in the Cumberland settlements in 1789, he roomed with another young attorney, Andrew Jackson, and the two became lifelong friends. Judge Overton began construction of Travellers' Rest in 1799; originally a modest clapboard structure, it was enlarged several times throughout the years. The two-and-a-half-story house is a rambling L-shaped structure with a two-story porch on the inside of the ell. It was from here that Overton ran Jackson's political campaigns in Tennessee, though his role may never be fully appreciated since he ordered the destruction of his correspondence with Jackson, saying, "I have protected my friend in life, I will not betray him in death." The house has been restored to the period of Overton's residence, and the grounds contain a small museum.

LOCATION: 636 Farrell Parkway. HOURS: June through August: 9–5 Monday–Saturday, 1–5 Sunday; September through May: 9–4 Monday–Saturday, 1–4 Sunday. FEE: Yes. TELEPHONE: 615–832–2962.

Not far from Travellers' Rest is the **Oscar L. Farris Agricultural Museum** (Ellington Agricultural Center, between Routes 24 and 65, 615–360–0197), which contains an extensive collection of agricultural artifacts dating to 1800, including farming and household tools and blacksmithing, logging, and woodworking equipment.

The Hermitage

The Hermitage was the home of President Andrew Jackson from 1804 until his death in 1845. A lawyer, soldier, farmer, and politician, Jackson served as the nation's seventh president. The farm was aptly named, providing a refuge from the frequent attacks, both political and personal, that Jackson suffered during the election campaigns of 1824 and 1828.

The original Hermitage consisted of several log structures clustered near a spring at the rear of the present mansion. A young visitor, Jefferson Davis, described the Jacksons' early home as "a

OPPOSITE: *Portrait of Andrew Jackson painted by Ralph E. W. Earl about 1830. The original brick Hermitage, with its white portico, is in the background at right.*

roomy log house. In front was a grove of fine forest trees, and behind it were his cotton and grain fields." In 1819 Jackson began construction of a two-story Federal-style house on a site selected by his wife, Rachel. At this same time Jackson had an English gardener, William Frost, design the flower garden alongside the new house. Rachel Jackson's first marriage had ended in divorce, a rare occurrence in nineteenth-century America, and Jackson's enemies capitalized on the fact that Rachel's divorce may not have been legally completed before she married Andrew. Shortly after her husband's election to the presidency, Rachel died suddenly at the Hermitage and was buried in a corner of her flower garden. Jackson blamed his rumor-mongering enemies for her death.

During Jackson's first presidential term the house underwent a major remodeling and wings were added, but a fire in October 1834 gutted the house, sparing only the dining-room wing. The present structure dates from a period of rebuilding that began in 1835, during Jackson's second term in Washington. Though the basic structure remained the same, imposing two-story porticoes (front and back) were added and the front of the house was painted white to enhance the Greek Revival effect. Jackson retired to the Hermitage in 1837 for the final eight years of his life. Every evening at sundown he walked through the garden to Rachel's tomb; in 1845 he was buried alongside her. The state purchased the Hermitage in 1856, though members of the Jackson family were allowed to remain as life tenants. In 1889 the Ladies Hermitage Association was formed to preserve the site. Today the home is furnished as it was during Jackson's lifetime with original family pieces. The focal point of the entry hall is an airy elliptical staircase. Jackson's bedroom, with its portrait of Rachel over the mantel, is much as it was when he died.

The **Andrew Jackson Visitors' Center** features a museum with artifacts that include a miniature of Rachel and the family's Brewster carriage. The **tomb** in the garden is an architectural landmark in itself: a classical stone structure with fluted columns and a copper-covered dome. Other Jackson family members are buried nearby.

Just down the road is **Tulip Grove Mansion,** a Greek Revival home built in 1836 by Andrew Jackson Donelson, Rachel's nephew and the President's White House secretary. It contains family and period furnishings. Also on the property is the **Old Hermitage Church.** Jackson donated the three-acre site for the church's construction in 1823, and Rachel was one of the charter members. It has been restored to its appearance in 1837–1845.

LOCATION: Old Hickory Boulevard, 12 miles east of downtown Nashville. HOURS: 9–5 Daily. FEE: Yes. TELEPHONE: 615–889–2941.

Southwest of the Hermitage, off Lebanon Pike, stands **Two Rivers Mansion** (3130 McGavock Pike, 615–885–1112), so named because of its proximity to the Cumberland and Stones rivers. David McGavock built this Italianate mansion in 1859 on the eve of the Civil War. The economic difficulties of the time delayed the completion of the interior until the 1870s; the house is presently being restored to that period. Also on the grounds is a Federal-style house, built in 1802, where the McGavocks lived while the mansion was under construction.

Twenty miles west of Nashville is the **Narrows of Harpeth State Historic Area** (off Route 70, 615–797–9051). At a point west of Pegram, the Harpeth River doubles back on itself, forming two channels that are separated by only a narrow rocky ridge. In 1818 a pioneer industrialist, Montgomery Bell, had his slaves chisel a tunnel through the solid rock, allowing the river to flow beneath the ridge. By taking advantage of this abrupt change in the water's elevation, Bell generated power for a forge. Though the forge is gone, the approximately 290-foot-long tunnel may still be seen.

ROCK CASTLE

Rock Castle was built by Daniel Smith, the first settler in the area of present-day Hendersonville. He was a Virginia surveyor who brought his family to Middle Tennessee and began construction of the limestone house around 1785. Initially it consisted of only two rooms, but additions were made, and by 1796 the seven-room structure that stands today was complete. Smith continued to acquire land until his plantation consisted of over 3,000 acres. He also became active in politics and in 1798 was appointed to fill a seat in the U.S. Senate vacated by Andrew Jackson; in 1805 he was elected in his own right. During his frequent absences his wife, Sarah, oversaw the plantation. In 1793 she wrote to him, "I still find myself under the disagreeable necessity of conversing with you on paper or not at all." The house remains remarkably unchanged; its black walnut woodwork, original glass, and solid (thirteen-to-eighteen-inch) walls are intact. Furnished to reflect the period from 1790 to 1820, the house contains a number of Smith family pieces. A visitor center features exhibits on Smith and his times. The family cemetery stands nearby.

LOCATION: 139 Rock Castle Lane, off Route 31, Hendersonville. HOURS: February through December: 10–5 Wednesday–Saturday, 1–5 Sunday. FEE: Yes. TELEPHONE: 615–824–0502.

GOODLETTSVILLE

Prior to the arrival of whites, the two salt licks in this area were a gathering place for game. Buffalo trails wound their way through the forest, and one is still visible along Mansker's Creek in **Moss Wright Park** (Caldwell Road, off Route 65, 615–859–0362). This path served as the first road between Nashville and Gallatin. Also in the park is **Mansker's Station** (615–859–3678), reconstructed in 1986. The original fort, of which nothing remains, was built in 1779 and 1780 by Kasper Mansker, one of Middle Tennessee's earliest settlers. During the station's first year eight people lost their lives. Costumed interpreters demonstrate a variety of pioneer activities. Also in the park is the **Bowen-Campbell House** (615–851–2253), which may be the oldest brick house in Middle Tennessee. Captain William Bowen constructed the house in 1787, less than a decade after Mansker's arrival. Located near the fort for safety, the Federal-style home features a Flemish-bond brick pattern and illustrates the rapid improvement of living conditions in the area. It is believed that William Bowen Campbell, a grandson of the builder who went on to become Tennessee's sixteenth governor, was born in the house.

GALLATIN

Named in honor of Albert Gallatin, U.S. secretary of the treasury during the administrations of Thomas Jefferson and James Madison, the town was laid out on a forty-acre site in 1802. The Gallatin–Bethpage Pike, now known as Route 31, runs through the heart of the town. Two blocks west of the public square stands **Trousdale Place** (183 West Main Street), a two-story brick house built in 1813 by John H. Bowen, a Gallatin attorney and eldest son of William Bowen. In 1836 the house was purchased by William Trousdale, known as the "War Horse of Tennessee" because he served in four wars: the Creek War, the War of 1812, the Seminole War, and the Mexican War. By the end of his military career he had risen to the rank of brigadier general, and in 1849 he was elected governor of Tennessee. The home contains a number of family pieces, including Trousdale's hats and the suit he wore at his inauguration. Directly behind the home is the **Sumner County Museum** (615–451–3738), which displays a large collection of antique guns and farm implements and a number of early automobiles.

CASTALIAN SPRINGS

The mineral spring that gave this area its name was a gathering place for game and an early site of Indian habitation. Several mounds are still visible. The spring was originally known as Bledsoe's Lick after an early explorer, Isaac Bledsoe, arrived in the area in the latter part of the 1770s. In 1783 Isaac and his brother Anthony constructed Bledsoe's Fort on a hill overlooking the spring. Both brothers were killed by the Indians near the fort, and a **monument,** located just off Route 25, marks their graves.

Cragfont

General James Winchester, who completed his home, Cragfont, in 1802, had been a Revolutionary War soldier and was present at the British surrender of Yorktown. When Tennessee was admitted to the Union in 1796, he served as the first speaker of the state senate. A brigadier general during the War of 1812, Winchester, along with Andrew Jackson and John Overton, founded the city of Memphis. Winchester's son, Marcus Brutus, became the city's first mayor.

A marked contrast from the standard log home, Cragfont was constructed of Tennessee limestone by Maryland stonemasons. The T-shaped home was strengthened with iron rods attached to star-shaped anchor plates. The second-floor ballroom, believed to be the first in Tennessee, entertained such notables as Andrew Jackson, Sam Houston, and the marquis de Lafayette. During the Civil War the Winchesters were staunch Confederates, and when a portion of Union General Buell's army camped at the plantation, an officer appeared at the door asking for the gentleman of the house. A son who was too young to fight recalled that, "in answer to his inquiry . . . I simply replied that he was absent. I wish now that I had pertly responded Where he ought to be Sir! In the service of the Confederate States." The house was left unscathed. The home passed

out of the Winchester family around 1865 and had a procession of owners before being purchased by the state in the 1950s. Although the house was used as a barn at one point, much of the original interior has survived, including the stencilling on the parlor walls. Among the Winchester pieces returned to the home are the hat and epaulets the general wore during the War of 1812. The family cemetery is at the rear of the house.

LOCATION: Just off Route 25. HOURS: Mid-April through October: 10–5 Tuesday–Saturday, 1–5 Sunday. FEE: Yes. TELEPHONE: 615–452–7070.

Wynnewood

An impressive two-story log structure made of oak, walnut, and ash, Wynnewood was built in 1828 by A. R. Wynne and several business associates to serve as a stagecoach stop on the road between

Wynnewood was built in 1828 by A. R. Wynne as a stagecoach stop between Knoxville and Nashville. OPPOSITE: *Cragfont was built by General James Winchester in 1802. Constructed of Tennessee limestone by Maryland stonemasons, the house was strengthened with iron rods anchored by star-shaped plates.*

Knoxville and Nashville. When a new southern route through Lebanon became favored, Wynne moved into the building, and it remained the family home until 1973. Between 1830 and 1940 the Wynnes operated a summer resort centered around the nearby mineral springs. The upstairs has been furnished as a men's sleeping room typical of early stagecoach stops.

LOCATION: Just off Route 25. HOURS: 10–4 Monday–Saturday, 1–5 Sunday. FEE: Yes. TELEPHONE: 615-452-5463.

CLARKSVILLE

Located at the confluence of the Cumberland and Red rivers, the town was founded in 1784–1785 by Colonel John Montgomery and Colonel Martin Armstrong. Montgomery, who had fought with General George Rogers Clark during the Revolutionary War, named the town in honor of the general. Clarksville was laid out on several high bluffs that overlooked the rivers, and ferries were a necessity in the early days. Tradition says that boats were propelled across the river by a team of mules hitched to a wheel, and that blind mules were favored because it was thought they were less likely to become dizzy while treading an endless circle.

The city was a prominent tobacco port during the nineteenth century, and the area's preoccupation with the crop was reflected in the name of the town's newspaper, the *Leaf Chronicle*, which was founded in 1808. In the 1870s a fire destroyed a large portion of the business district, but the **Poston Block** (Public Square and Main Street), which dates to 1841, survived. Original nineteenth-century advertising, painted on the north side of the building, is thought to be some of the oldest extant in the nation. Fifteen downtown acres have been designated a historic district; the majority of the buildings date from the latter part of the nineteenth century.

The **Clarksville–Montgomery County Historical Museum** (200 South 2d Street, 615-648-5780) is housed in the Old Federal Building, which was constructed in 1898. The building combines Italianate ornamentation and Romanesque arches with Flemish and Gothic elements. Exhibits highlight the Civil War era, Victorian fashions, nineteenth-century firefighting equipment, and one of the most complete collections of horse-drawn vehicles in the state. The

OPPOSITE: *The roof and cupola of the Old Federal Building, built in 1898, are trimmed with copper plating. A copper eagle adorns each corner of the building, which now houses the Clarksville-Montgomery County Historical Museum.*

Smith-Trahern Mansion (Spring and McClure streets, 615–648–9998) was built in 1858 by a wealthy tobacco grower, Christopher Smith. The house, which overlooks the Cumberland River, combines Greek Revival and Italianate styles and has grand hallways, a winding staircase, "jib" windows, and a widow's walk. The original slave quarters remain on the property. Adjacent to the house is the **Riverview Cemetery,** where pioneer leader Valentine Sevier, who died in 1800, is buried. The site became a public cemetery in 1805.

Sevier Station (Walker Street), which has recently undergone restoration, was built in 1792 by Valentine Sevier, whose brother, John Sevier, was Tennessee's first governor. The stone blockhouse was repeatedly attacked by Indians, and over the years Sevier lost four sons, two daughters, two sons-in-law, and several grandchildren during such raids. One of Sevier's daughters, Rebecca, was scalped but survived. As Sevier wrote after one attack, "The news from this place is desperate with me . . . such a scene no man ever witnessed before. Nothing but screams and the roaring of guns, and no man to assist me for some time."

North of Clarksville on the Fort Campbell Military Reservation is the **Don F. Pratt Museum** (502–798–4986), dedicated to the history of the 101st Airborne Division, or "Screaming Eagles," who fought in Europe during World War II. Numerous weapons and aircraft are on display. North of the small town of **Adams** was the home of the legendary Bell Witch. Tradition says that in the early nineteenth century John Bell purchased a piece of property from a neighbor, Kate Batts, who soon regretted the bargain. On her deathbed she vowed to haunt Bell to his grave. Visitors reported that furniture was flung about, and that they heard screams, cries, and curses. After spending one night in the house, Andrew Jackson reputedly said that he would "rather fight the British again than have any further dealings with that torment." The mysterious activities ceased after John Bell's death, and though the home has been demolished, the Bell Witch has become a permanent part of Tennessee folklore.

FORT DONELSON
NATIONAL BATTLEFIELD

The capture of Fort Donelson on February 16, 1862, marked the first major Union victory of the Civil War and brought to prominence a relatively obscure officer, General Ulysses S. Grant. The general's insistence upon Confederate surrender without conditions gained him the nickname "Unconditional Surrender" Grant.

Fort Donelson and neighboring Fort Henry were critical links in the western line of the Confederate defense that stretched from the Mississippi to the Appalachians. Earlier Union attempts to penetrate this defense had failed, but Grant's tactics, including a successful encirclement of the fort, forced the Confederates to surrender. A number of southern troops, including Colonel Nathan Bedford Forrest's, eluded capture and continued to harass Federal forces in the West and South, but the fort's capture led to a general withdrawal of Confederate forces from southern Kentucky and much of Middle and West Tennessee.

The park preserves many of the original earthworks, and exhibits at the visitor center detail the battle and its consequences. **Fort Donelson National Cemetery** is on the grounds, and in the

The Union force under General Ulysses S. Grant, on horseback at center, fires on the fortifications around Fort Donelson on February 15, 1862, in this painting by Paul Philippoteaux (detail).

nearby town of **Dover,** the restored **Dover Hotel** (Petty Street, 615–232–5359) marks the site of the formal surrender of General Simon B. Buckner to Ulysses S. Grant.

> LOCATION: Route 79, west of Dover. HOURS: *Visitor center:* 8–4:30 Daily. *Dover Hotel:* June through August: 11–4 Daily; September through May: 1–4 Daily. FEE: None. TELEPHONE: 615–232–5706.

North of Dover, the **Land between the Lakes** (off Route 79, 502–924–5602) is a 170,000-acre national recreation area administered by the Tennessee Valley Authority and located between two man-made lakes formed from the Cumberland and Tennessee rivers. **The Homeplace–1850** (off Route 79, 615–232–6457) is a living-history farm that interprets life "between the rivers" during the mid-nineteenth century. Sixteen historic structures from throughout the region have been relocated to the sixty-acre site, where costumed interpreters portray everyday farm life on a typical two-generation homestead. Cooking, cleaning, farming, and hand-crafting implements are all done in traditional fashion. The interpretive center offers exhibits on seasonal farm activities.

Just south of The Homeplace stands the remains of the **Great Western Iron Furnace,** built in 1854, a reminder of an industry that once thrived in Stewart County. The furnace marks the site of a former "iron plantation," a self-sufficient community that included doctors and teachers as well as laborers. Once such furnaces were fired, they operated continuously for eight to ten months. The county's first furnace was opened in 1820, and in 1927 the last remaining furnace ceased production.

W E S T   T E N N E S S E E

West Tennessee is clearly delineated by two rivers: the Tennessee on the east and the Mississippi on the west. Still decidedly rural, the region's eastern portion is rolling, flattening to the west. Not until an 1818 treaty was signed with the Chickasaw did white settlers move into this part of Tennessee. Money made from the cultivation and sale of West Tennessee cotton helped build the city of Memphis, and it remains one of the world's largest cotton markets.

NATHAN BEDFORD
FORREST STATE PARK

Named in honor of the Confederate cavalry commander known for his daring raids, the park lies in a curve of the Tennessee River. Forrest harassed Union shipping along the Tennessee and destroyed the Federal arsenal at nearby Johnsonville on November 4, 1864. At the heart of the park stands Pilot Knob, the highest point along the river and a navigational landmark for generations of rivermen. The **Tennessee River Folklife Museum,** perched on top of the knob, offers a panoramic view of a stretch of the river that was dammed by the Tennessee Valley Authority in 1944 and is now known as Kentucky Lake. The museum provides a look at life along the river, including displays on such traditional activities as log rafting, musseling, commercial fishing, and the pearl industry.

> LOCATION: Route 191, 8 miles north of Camden. HOURS: *Park:* 8–4:30 Daily. *Museum:* April through November: 10–5 Wednesday–Sunday; December through February: 10–5 Saturday–Sunday. FEE: None. TELEPHONE: 901–584–6356.

JACKSON

The area around Jackson was first settled in 1819; soldiers who had fought under General Andrew Jackson during the War of 1812 named the town after their former commander. Jackson was incorporated in 1823 but grew slowly until the arrival of the railroad, which transformed the town into a commercial center. During the Civil War Jackson served as headquarters for Confederate general P. G. T. Beauregard, then later became a Union supply depot.

Casey Jones Home and Railroad Museum

In 1893 John Luther Jones, an engineer for the Illinois Central Railroad, purchased a one-story frame house near the Jackson railroad station. He lived there with his wife and three children until his death seven years later in a train wreck near Vaughan, Mississippi. Jones, nicknamed Casey for his hometown of Cayce, Kentucky, chose to stay with his engine and lessen its speed when a collision became unavoidable. His courageous act, which resulted in his death but prevented further fatalities, was soon immortalized in a song, now considered an American classic. The original verses are attributed to Wallace Saunders, a black engine wiper who had known Casey.

The museum was opened in 1956 by the city of Jackson as a tribute not only to Jones but to turn-of-the-century railroading. In 1980–1981 the house museum was moved from its original location at 211 West Chester Street to the present site. Items on display include the watch Casey was wearing at his death, its hands stopped at the moment of the crash, and other railroad memorabilia. On the grounds is an engine of the kind Casey operated.

LOCATION: Off Route I-40, on Route 45 Bypass. HOURS: June through October: 8–8 Daily; November through December: 9–5 Daily; January through February: 10–4 Daily; March through May: 9–5 Daily. FEE: Yes. TELEPHONE: 901–668–1223.

PINSON MOUNDS
STATE ARCHAEOLOGICAL AREA

This site, which dates primarily from A.D. 1–300, contains the largest extant Middle Woodland mound group in the United States. Unlike many mounds of this period, which were used for burials, most of the large mounds at Pinson are flat topped and were used for ceremonial purposes. The flat-topped mounds here are the earliest known in the United States. Archaeologists believe that groups from as far away as Georgia and Louisiana sometimes gathered here.

The mounds were rediscovered in 1820 by a surveyor, Joel Pinson, and in 1916 an archaeologist from the Smithsonian Institution, William E. Myer, mapped the site. Today twelve mounds and a large circular earthen enclosure survive. Sauls Mound, at seventy-two feet high, is the second-tallest earthwork in the United States. Trails marked for self-guided tours connect the various features of the site. A museum, built to resemble a mound, houses exhibits on prehistoric Indian cultures and displays numerous archaeological artifacts including fine stone pendants, stone projectile points, and engraved human skull rattles.

LOCATION: 460 Ozier Road, 10 miles south of Jackson, off Route 45. HOURS: April through September: 8:30–5 Monday–Saturday, 1–5 Sunday; October through March: 8–4:30 Monday–Friday. FEE: None. TELEPHONE: 901–988–5614.

SHILOH NATIONAL MILITARY PARK

The battle that occurred around Shiloh church on April 6 and 7, 1862, was one of the bloodiest of the Civil War. After victories at Forts Henry and Donelson, General Ulysses S. Grant camped at Pittsburg Landing on the Tennessee River to await the arrival of additional Federal forces under General Don Carlos Buell. The Confederate commander, General Albert S. Johnston, decided to launch a surprise attack before the two Union armies could join forces, and when one of his officers counseled caution, Johnston replied, "I would fight them if they were a million."

On the morning of April 6, thousands of Confederate soldiers poured from the woods around the church and advanced rapidly, driving Grant's army before them. Retreating to a sunken wagon road that afforded some protection, the Federal troops regrouped, defending the site with such tenacity that the southerners dubbed it the "Hornet's Nest." During fighting that day, General Johnston was killed when a bullet severed an artery in his leg. General P. G. T.

The Confederate Monument at Shiloh National Military Park, site of one of the bloodiest battles of the Civil War.

Beauregard assumed command and slowly pushed the Union forces back to hastily prepared fortifications along the river. The two exhausted armies got little sleep as torrents of rain fell and Union gunboats continuously lobbed shells into the Confederate lines. During the night General Buell's army arrived, as did a division led by General Lew Wallace (who survived the war and wrote the novel *Ben Hur*). When fighting resumed on the next morning, the tired Confederates faced fresh troops. They were attacked and forced to retreat over ground they had fought to secure the previous day. Late that afternoon, when Beauregard ordered a general retreat, the Federal forces offered only a token pursuit. Of the 110,000 troops engaged in the battle, more than 20,000 (divided equally between the two armies) were killed or wounded. Many of the casualties had been left unattended on the battlefield during the two days of fighting. "Their groans and cries were heart-rending," wrote one Union soldier. General William Tecumseh Sherman, who had been in the thick of the fighting, wrote, "The scenes on this field would have cured anybody of war."

Exhibits at the park's **visitor center** describe the events surrounding the battle. Uniforms, firearms, and numerous artifacts recovered from the field are also on display. A self-guided tour includes such sites as the **Hornet's Nest,** the **National Cemetery,** and **Bloody Pond,** whose water was stained red by the wounded and dying.

LOCATION: On Route 22 east of Route 45. HOURS: June through August: 8–6 Daily; September through May: 8–5 Daily. FEE: Yes. TELEPHONE: 901–689–5275.

BOLIVAR

Settlement in the area around Bolivar began one mile north at a trading post frequented by the Chickasaw. Hatchie Town, as it was then known, offered merchants a river connection from the Hatchie River to the Tennessee, then down the Mississippi to New Orleans. In 1825 the name was changed to Bolivar, in honor of the Venezuelan patriot Simón Bolívar.

During the Civil War much of the downtown area was burned by Union General Samuel D. Sturgis, but a few antebellum structures survived. **The Pillars** (Bills and Washington streets, 901–658–6554) was constructed some time before 1826 and became the home of

Major John Houston Bills in 1831. Bills, a surveyor, was one of the earliest settlers in West Tennessee. Believed to be the first brick home in Bolivar, the house has Greek Revival elements and period furnishings, many of which are original. Bills's diary is being used to restore the home to its appearance during his lifetime. The **Little Courthouse Museum** (116 East Market Street, 901–658–6554), built in 1824, was the first courthouse in Hardeman County and is one of the earliest surviving courthouses in the western part of the state. The central portion of the building consists of a two-story log structure, though additions were subsequently made and clapboards added. The upper floor also served as the jail. Period furnishings, including a rosewood piano shipped up the Hatchie River from New Orleans, are on display. **Magnolia Manor** (418 North Main Street, private) was built by Judge Austin Miller in 1849. It served as General Grant's headquarters for a time, though Mrs. Miller, a lady of some spirit, informed the general that she was giving up only half of her home for his use.

In the **Polk Cemetery,** on the south side of town, lies the grave of Colonel Ezekiel Polk, grandfather of President James K. Polk. The self-composed, anticlerical epitaph of the elder Polk so offended certain sensibilities that portions of it were used against his grandson during the presidential campaign. The colonel, who denounced "holy cheats," among other things, predicted dire consequences for the country if religion and politics were combined, and groused: "Methodists with their camp bawling/Will be the cause of this down falling."

MEMPHIS

Commerce has been the lifeblood of Memphis from its earliest days. The area was once Chickasaw country, claimed by France, Spain, Britain, and, finally, the United States. Shortly after the American Revolution, settlers from Middle Tennessee began to erect trading posts to counteract the Spanish influence among the Indians. The town of Memphis was laid out on a bluff overlooking the Mississippi River in 1818 by business partners Andrew Jackson, James Winchester, and John Overton. Large plantations based on slave labor sprang up, and soon cotton was king. Cotton brokers and bankers, known as factors, were among the town's wealthiest citizens. By 1850 Memphis was one of the busiest ports in the country. The

The drawing room of the Mallory-Neely House. OPPOSITE: *The house was built in the Italianate style in the 1850s by Isaac Kirtland; later renovations were made in the 1890s by James Columbus Neely.*

town was staunchly Confederate during the Civil War, and most of the population watched in dismay as Union gunboats sank most of the Confederate fleet during the Battle of Memphis on June 6, 1862. The town was under Union control for the remainder of the war.

The economic havoc wrought by the war was closely followed by a series of yellow fever epidemics; the worst occurred in 1878 and much of the population fled. Of the 6,000 whites that remained, over 4,000 died; the proportion of deaths among black residents was lower. At the height of the crisis, the city was quarantined from surrounding areas, and armed men turned back trains carrying those who sought to escape. Madam Annie, the proprietor of a noted brothel, turned her lavish establishment into an infirmary and nursed the victims until succumbing to the disease herself. A heavy frost halted the fever's spread, but the town's political structure had totally collapsed and the state revoked the city's charter. Not until 1893 was Memphis recognized as a municipality once again.

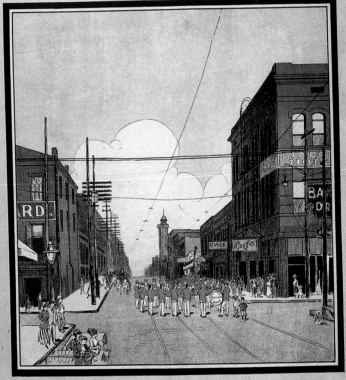

During the early part of this century a new style of music, the blues, developed in the honky-tonks that lined Beale Street. It was there that black composer W. C. Handy introduced such classics as "Memphis Blues" and "St. Louis Blues." In later years a fusion of black rhythm and country music, known as rockabilly, was popularized by the city's most famous resident, Elvis Presley.

The oldest surviving residence in the city is the **Magevney House** (198 Adams Avenue, 901–526–4464). This white frame house was built around 1836 by Eugene Magevney, an Irish immigrant who served as the city's first schoolmaster. Magevney taught in a log cabin on Court Square from 1833 to 1840 and was instrumental in establishing the city's public school system. The house was the site of the city's first Catholic mass (1839), Catholic wedding, and christening. Furnished as it would have been in the 1850s, the house contains numerous items originally owned by the Magevney family, including the trunk that Mrs. Magevney brought from Ireland, Mr. Magevney's secretary, and the mahogany bureau used as an altar for the celebration of mass. Next door to the Magevney house is **Saint Peter's Catholic Church,** built in 1851, the oldest Catholic church in West Tennessee. Magevney was one of its founders.

The **Victorian Village District,** on Adams and Jefferson avenues, preserves a number of imposing mansions built by the city's leading businessmen in styles ranging from Neoclassical to Late Victorian. The Italianate **Mallory-Neely House** (652 Adams Avenue, 901–523–1484) was constructed in the 1850s by Isaac Kirtland; a later owner, James Columbus Neely, undertook extensive renovations during the 1890s. Neely, a partner in one of the most successful cotton factor firms in Memphis, added a full third floor to the mansion and decorated the interior in lavish Victorian fashion. Barton Mallory, who was also in the cotton business, married Neely's daughter, Daisy. Because of continuous ownership by the Mallory-Neely family until 1969, the home remains remarkably unchanged. A stained-glass window purchased in 1893 at the Chicago Columbian Exposition graces the front door, the double parlor contains original stencilling on walls and ceilings, and the wall-to-wall carpeting of 1890 is still in place.

OPPOSITE: *The original cover of W. C. Handy's Beale Street Blues sheet music, which helped establish Memphis as the "Home of the Blues."*

The **Woodruff-Fontaine House** (680 Adams Avenue, 901–526–1469) was built in 1870 by Amos Woodruff for $40,000. In 1883 the mansion was purchased by Noland Fontaine, a successful cotton factor with eight children, whose family maintained it for the next forty-six years. Although few original furnishings remain, the home has been restored and decorated with antiques of the Victorian period, and the original cypress woodwork and elaborate ceiling medallions are intact. At the top of the third-floor staircase, forty-three feet above the first floor, is a hammered-tin ceiling. Portions of an extensive 2,000-piece collection of Victorian clothing and accessories are periodically on display.

Other houses in the district include the **James Lee House** (690 Adams Avenue, private), which dates from 1848, with later additions made in 1865 and 1871. The **Mollie Fontaine Taylor House** (679 Adams Avenue, private) is a brick Queen Anne, constructed around 1890 as a wedding present for one of Noland Fontaine's daughters. The oldest home in the district is the **Massey House** (664 Adams, private). The one-story frame house was constructed in the 1840s and is Greek Revival in style.

Mud Island

At one time this Mississippi River island was considered such an eyesore that city officials tried to dynamite it. Today Mud Island has been transformed into a downtown park, accessible by pedestrian walkway and a monorail over the Mississippi. At the heart of the park is the **Mississippi River Museum,** which offers a walk through time from prehistoric Indian villages to the present. A three-story reproduction of the prow of an 1870s steamboat includes a pilothouse as well as cargo on the lower deck. Other exhibits portray the Civil War along the river, river disasters, and the development of the blues, jazz, spirituals, rock-and-roll, and ragtime.

The **River Walk** runs the length of the park and is a scale model of the Mississippi River from Cairo, Illinois, to New Orleans. Constructed of concrete, the "river" is topographically accurate and details each bend, bridge, and major city along its course. The *Memphis Belle,* a B-17 bomber that was the first aircraft to complete twenty-five missions successfully during World War II, is housed in a special pavilion with accompanying displays.

LOCATION: 125 North Front Street. HOURS: *Park:* April: 10–7 Daily; May through August: 10–10 Daily; September through October: 10–7 Daily; November: 10–5 Daily; *Museum:* April: 10–5:30 Daily; May through August: 10–7 Daily; September through October: 10–5:30 Daily; November: 10–3:30 Daily. FEE: Yes. TELEPHONE: 901–576–7241.

Memphis Pink Palace Museum and Planetarium

One of the largest museums in the southeast, the Pink Palace is dedicated to the cultural and natural history of Memphis and the mid-South, which encompasses an area within a 150-mile radius of the city. Life in the Memphis area is illuminated by the exhibit "Memphis: 1800–1900," which features displays on pioneer life, the Civil War, and the city's devastating yellow fever epidemics. "From Saddlebags to Science" looks at health care in the city from 1830 to 1930, and another major exhibit is devoted entirely to the city's black citizens.

Constructed as a private residence in the early 1920s by a grocery entrepreneur, Clarence Saunders, the palace got its name from the color of its exterior walls, made of pink Georgia marble. In 1916 Saunders founded the Piggly-Wiggly grocery chain, the nation's first self-service food stores, but he lost his fortune before he could reside in the house. Today the mansion houses the museum's educational center, while a new building contains the exhibit areas.

LOCATION: 3050 Central Avenue. HOURS: 9:30–4 Tuesday–Saturday, 9:30–8:30 Thursday, 1–5 Sunday. FEE: Yes. TELEPHONE: 901–454–5600.

C. H. Nash Museum—Chucalissa

Chucalissa offers visitors a glimpse of Indian life along the Mississippi from A.D. 1000 to 1500. The site was used and abandoned several times during this period, thus the name *Chucalissa,* a Choctaw word meaning "abandoned houses." Following extensive archaeological work during the 1950s and 1960s, portions of the village, including several thatched-roof homes, were reconstructed as they may have stood around a central square. The museum has interpretive exhibits.

LOCATION: 1987 Indian Village Drive, off Route 61. HOURS: 9–5 Tuesday–Saturday, 1–5 Sunday. FEE: Yes. TELEPHONE: 901–785–3160.

ALEX HALEY STATE HISTORIC SITE

Alex Haley, internationally known for his Pulitzer Prize–winning novel *Roots,* spent much of his boyhood at his maternal grandparents' home in the tiny town of Henning. Here the youngster first heard the stories that eventually led him to search for his family's African origins. Says Haley, "The front porch of this home is, in fact, the birthplace of *Roots.*" The ten-room bungalow was constructed from 1918 to 1921 by Haley's grandfather, Will E. Palmer, who owned a successful lumber business in Henning. The home has been restored to its appearance in 1919 and is furnished with replica furniture and some original family pieces, including numerous family photographs and the Carleton upright piano Alex's mother played to entertain the townsfolk. An interpreter, Fred Montgomery, one of Haley's boyhood friends, recalls in vivid detail life in the home during the early part of this century.

LOCATION: 200 South Church Street, Henning. HOURS: 10–5 Tuesday–Saturday, 1–5 Sunday. FEE: Yes. TELEPHONE: 901–738–2240.

FORT PILLOW STATE HISTORIC AREA

One of the most controversial battles of the Civil War took place along the Mississippi River at Fort Pillow on April 12, 1864. Northerners called it a massacre while Confederates defended their actions as consistent with accepted conventions of war. Constructed by the Confederates in 1861–1862 to protect shipping along the Mississippi, Fort Pillow passed into Union hands without a fight in June 1862 after the southerners abandoned the position during a general withdrawal of the Confederate army from the west. For two years Federal forces occupied the site, effectively controlling the flow of traffic along this stretch of the river. On April 3, 1864, the fort's commander, Major Lionel F. Booth, wrote to his superiors: "I do not think any apprehensions need be felt or fears entertained in reference to this place being attacked, or even threatened."

Nine days later 1,500 Confederate cavalry under the command of General Nathan Bedford Forrest subjected the fort's defenders to withering artillery and rifle fire. Early in the battle Major Booth was killed by a Confederate sharpshooter. When Forrest offered the new commander, Major William F. Bradford, the opportunity to surrender, he refused, perhaps in the belief that reinforcements from a nearby Federal gunboat could be landed safely. The Confederates quickly drove the gunboat away and overran the parapet. In the ensuing rout, 231 Union soldiers, a large portion of them black, were killed. Some eyewitnesses maintained that they were systematically massacred. Within days of the incident, the U.S. Congress launched an investigation; the final committee report concluded that a massacre had indeed occurred and that blacks were treated with particular viciousness. Although Confederates labeled the findings propaganda, the truth of this massacre is now well established and generally accepted.

The park preserves the remains of the extensive earthen breastworks. The interpretive center features exhibits detailing the battle and displays artifacts recovered from the site.

LOCATION: Route 207, off Route 87, 18 miles west of Henning. HOURS: *Park:* 8–10 Daily. *Interpretive center:* 8–4:30 Daily. FEE: None. TELEPHONE: 901–738–5581.

THE DAVY CROCKETT CABIN

Now located on Route 45W in the town of Rutherford, the home of the legendary frontiersman originally stood four-and-a-half miles east, along the Rutherford fork of the Obion River. Crockett moved from Middle Tennessee to this sparsely settled area in the early 1820s, and when asked for directions to his home by a northerner, Crockett replied, "Why, sir, run down the Mississippi till you come to the Obion River, run a small streak up that, jump ashore anywhere, and inquire for me." The cabin was about to be demolished in the 1920s when it was purchased for the sum of twenty-five dollars. Many of the original handhewn logs were used in the reconstruction. The cabin displays nineteenth-century pioneer artifacts. The grave of Crockett's mother, Rebecca Hawkins Crockett, is nearby.

LOCATION: Route 45W, Rutherford. HOURS: June through August: 9–5 Monday–Saturday, 1–5 Sunday. FEE: Yes. TELEPHONE: 901–665–7166.

KENTUCKY

OPPOSITE: *The gently rolling hills of Kentucky's Bluegrass Country are dotted with horse farms. A subterranean layer of Ordovician limestone, deposited when the region was covered with a prehistoric ocean, gives its distinctive grass a high phosphorus and calcium content—excellent nourishment for thoroughbred horses.*

Kentucky—the Bluegrass State—is known for its coal mines, burley tobacco, bourbon whiskey, and thoroughbred horses. Kentucky has the world's oldest mountains, the Appalachians, forests that cover nearly one-half of the land in the state, natural bridges created by water and wind, one of the world's most elaborate underground cave systems, and more miles of running water (provided by nature or the U.S. Army Corps of Engineers) than any other state except Alaska. The state has been home to prehistoric people, explorers, presidents, and distinguished prize winners.

The abundant evidence of the prehistoric population in Kentucky includes signs of human occupation in cave shelters and burial remains in the east and the Middle Mississippian mounds at Wickliffe in the west. Explored initially as a potential westward extension of Virginia, the region's Allegheny Mountains presented a natural barrier that limited exploration from the east. The French seem to have laid first claim to the area when Marquette and Joliet in the 1670s and LaSalle in the 1680s explored the Mississippi and claimed the river and all its tributaries for France. French exploration motivated the English, who sent James Needham and Gabriel Arthur west across the Alleghenies around 1673. Though Needham did not return alive, he and Arthur probably were the first English explorers of Kentucky. English land companies began to back the exploration of this territory in 1750, when the Loyal Land Company of Virginia sponsored the expedition of Dr. Thomas Walker. In March 1750 Walker and his group left from Charlottesville and traveled through an Appalachian gap to a site near present-day Barbourville, where they explored until June of that year. In the next year the Ohio Land Company sent Christopher Gist into the region. He traveled down the Ohio River toward the site of present-day Louisville and returned through the mountains of North Carolina. English settlers were discouraged from moving west by the French and Indians; peace with the former was declared in 1763 in the Treaty of Paris. It allocated the land east of the Mississippi to the English, but in the same year, George III forbade settlers from moving beyond the Appalachians.

OPPOSITE: *The Cherokee chief Cunne Shote, one of three chiefs presented to George III as leaders of the Cherokee nation, painted in London in the 1730s by the court painter Frances Parsons. Cunne Shote wears a decoration given to him by the king.*
PAGES 352-353: *Ann Rice O'Hanlon's mural in the University of Kentucky's Memorial Hall depicts the growth of the Commonwealth of Kentucky (detail).*

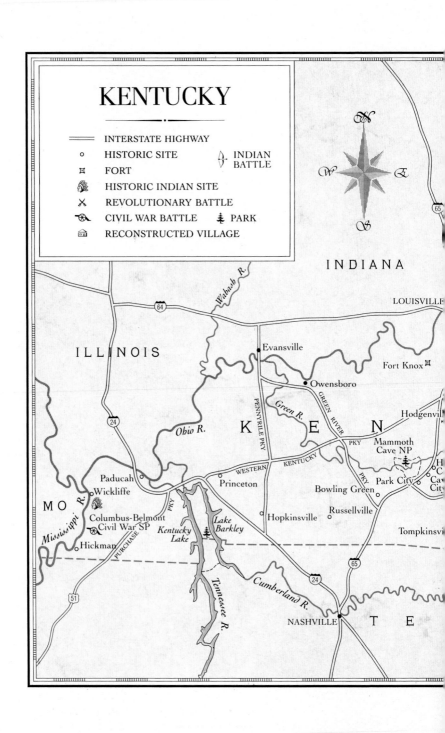

KENTUCKY

- ═══ INTERSTATE HIGHWAY
- ○ HISTORIC SITE
- ⚐ INDIAN BATTLE
- ⌂ FORT
- HISTORIC INDIAN SITE
- ✕ REVOLUTIONARY BATTLE
- CIVIL WAR BATTLE
- 🌲 PARK
- 🏠 RECONSTRUCTED VILLAGE

INDIANA

ILLINOIS

LOUISVILLE

Evansville

Fort Knox ⌂

Owensboro

Wabash R.

Hodgenvil

K E N

Green R.

GREEN RIVER

PENNYRILE PKY

Ohio R.

PKY

Mammoth Cave NP

WESTERN

KENTUCKY

Park City

H C Ca Cit

Paducah

Wickliffe

Princeton

Bowling Green

PKY

MO

Mississippi R.

Columbus-Belmont Civil War SP

Kentucky Lake

Lake Barkley

Hopkinsville

Russellville

Tompkinsvi

Hickman

PURCHASE

PKY

Tennessee R.

Cumberland R.

65

24

NASHVILLE

T E

51

64

24

65

OHIO

75 71

CINCINNATI
Covington
Big Bone Lick SP
8
Augusta Maysville
Washington
Cynthia
Blue Licks
Battlefield
SP
68
Paris
LEXINGTON
Shaker Village
of Pleasant Hill
Richmond
Harrodsburg
Danville
Perryville
Battlefield
Berea
William
Whitley
House
SHS
Daniel Boone NF
DANIEL BOONE PKY
CUMBERLAND PKY
Somerset
Levi Jackson Wilderness
Road SP
Barboursville
Monticello
Stearns
Middlesboro
Cumberland Gap NHP

KENTUCKY

NKFORT
54
Versailles
stown
gfield
ncoln
mestead
xto
U   K   Y

BLUE GRASS

Fort Boonesborough SP
BERT T. COMBS MTN PKY
Prestonburg
Hindman
23
80
PLATEAU

Portsmouth
10
Ashland
64

WEST
VIRGINIA

Big Sandy R.

Tug Fork

MOUNTAINS

VIRGINIA

Dutts Knob

Harlan

CUMBERLAND

APPALACHIAN

E   S   S   E   E

75 KNOXVILLE

NORTH
CAROLINA

Kentucky R.

71

Cumberland R.

0   60 Mi.

Scouts, explorers, and eventually land surveyors chose to ignore the king's proclamation, and such men as John Finley, Daniel Boone, Squire Boone (Daniel's brother), James Harrod, and Thomas Bullitt became well acquainted with the region between 1763 and 1775. Harrod led a party of surveyors to start the town now known as Harrodsburg; settled early in 1775 for Virginia, it is Kentucky's oldest Anglo-American settlement. Richard Henderson's Transylvania Land Company, organized in 1773, contracted with Daniel Boone to start a settlement, and Boone led thirty men through the Cumberland Gap toward the Kentucky River, where Boonesborough was begun in May 1775. In December 1776 Kentucky County was formed as a part of Virginia.

George Rogers Clark proposed to drive the Indians beyond the Ohio River and asked the governor of Virginia, Patrick Henry, to support a campaign against the English and the Indians. Between 1778 and 1779, Clark and his volunteer troops captured Indian villages and British forts, opening the western frontier as far as the Mississippi River. In 1782 the Indians and British, led by Captain William Caldwell and Simon Girty, began an offensive with an attack on Bryan Station, about six miles outside Lexington. The settlers, with reinforcements from Lexington and Boonesborough, held off their attackers for two days. Knowing more reinforcements were likely to arrive soon, Caldwell led a retreat toward the Ohio. Kentuckians pursued Caldwell and his men to the edge of the Licking River, where an inexperienced, hot-tempered officer, Major Hugh McGary, against the advice of Daniel Boone and others, refused to wait for reinforcements and led the Americans to defeat at the Battle of Blue Licks. It was the last significant battle with Indians in Kentucky.

Kentuckians met in Danville in December 1784, the first of ten conventions, to discuss separation from Virginia. By April 1792 they had agreed on a constitution, and in June of that year, Kentucky was admitted to the Union as the fifteenth state, the first one on the western frontier. Kentucky's boundaries were extended in 1818, when the westernmost area, from the Tennessee River to the Mississippi, was "purchased" from the Chickasaw Indians. Because Andrew Jackson was instrumental in these negotiations, the area is known as the Jackson Purchase, or simply the Purchase.

During the Civil War, Kentucky, like many border states, was sharply divided in its loyalties. (President Abraham Lincoln and President Jefferson Davis of the Confederacy, were born within one year and one hundred miles of each other in Kentucky.) Kentucky was a slave state, but after much maneuvering, it remained with the Union. The Confederate stronghold in Bowling Green set itself apart from the rest of the state, elected George W. Johnson its governor, and added a thirteenth star to the Confederate flag.

All significant action in Kentucky during the Civil War took place in 1861 and 1862. There were primarily three campaigns. The first, in western Kentucky, used Kentucky as a bridge from Illinois to Tennessee with General Ulysses S. Grant occupying Paducah, Kentucky in September 1861 in preparation for the campaign. In January 1862 Grant and Flag Officer Andrew H. Foote went down the Cumberland and Tennessee rivers to take Fort Henry and Fort Donelson in Tennessee. In November 1861 a second campaign was begun when General William Tecumseh Sherman was ordered to lead his Federal troops from east central Kentucky to eastern Tennessee to support the Unionist contingent there. He failed to execute these orders and so was transferred to Missouri. General Don Carlos Buell replaced him and ordered General George Thomas's army across the Cumberland Mountains. On January 19, 1862 Confederate forces under General George Crittendon attacked Thomas's forces at Loan's Cross Roads near Mill Springs and were routed by the Federals. Though Thomas won the battle and East Tennessee was left open to a Union occupation, he could not advance due to the hard winter rains and deep mud. When spring came and Thomas's army could move again, he was ordered to central and western Tennessee because of Union advances there.

The third campaign and the only one waged to capture Kentucky itself occurred in the summer and fall of 1862. Confederate generals Braxton Bragg and Edmund Kirby Smith had orders to invade Ohio by way of Kentucky. They hoped to increase their strength with men and arms from pro-Confederate sections of the state. After taking Corinth, Mississippi, Confederate generals Van Dorn and Price were ordered to take and occupy western Tennessee and then join Bragg in Ohio once he had made his invasion. Kirby Smith left Knoxville in August, took Richmond, Kentucky on August 30 in a surprise attack, and then occupied Lexington. Bragg moved from Chattanooga and captured a Union garrison at Munfordville on September 17, then went on to meet Kirby Smith.

Buell, meanwhile, moved from Mississippi in June after much prodding by Washington and slowly made his way to Kentucky via Alabama and Tennessee. The Confederate cavalry under generals Nathan Bedford Forrest and John Hunt Morgan harassed Buell's army with guerrilla raids all along the way, keeping the Federal movement as slow as possible. Buell finally caught up with Bragg at Perryville, Kentucky on October 8 before Bragg had the opportunity to join up with Kirby Smith. The Federals prevailed in this battle with General Philip H. Sheridan driving the Confederates through the streets. Bragg retreated to Knoxville and Chattanooga, convinced now that Kentuckians were not willing to provide the support he had expected and disheartened by the news that the Federals had retaken Corinth, depriving him of badly needed reinforcements. When Buell wasted more time and failed to trail Bragg into eastern Tennessee, Lincoln replaced him. Though Morgan's cavalry continued to harass Union forces and guerrilla warfare was constant, no other significant campaigns occurred in Kentucky.

Coal mining, which started on a large scale in the 1870s, was well established in the early twentieth century. When the boom brought about by the First World War subsided after the war ended, labor troubles developed and intensified, especially in Harlan County, which has been called the coal capital of Kentucky. In the 1930s bitter battles over unionization of the mine workers resulted in deaths of miners. A U. S. Senate subcommittee in 1937 investigated the violent situation and allegation of civil rights violations by the coal industry management in Harlan County. In 1939 the United Mine Workers of America was recognized as a valid union for most miners in Kentucky. Kentucky's original 9 counties have undergone reorganization and additions until they now number 120, in four main regions: eastern Kentucky, or the Appalachian region; north-central Kentucky, or the Bluegrass area; south-central and west-central region, or the Pennyroyal (sometimes referred to as the Mississippian Plateau region); and western Kentucky, or the Purchase.

This tour of Kentucky begins in the Appalachian region at Ashland, proceeds through Hindman and Middlesboro, then from Covington in the Bluegrass Region loops through Augusta and Maysville. It then moves back to Frankfort and Lexington before moving from Richmond to Louisville. From Somerset it proceeds through the Pennyroyal west to Bowling Green and finally through the Purchase to Paducah and Hinckman.

THE APPALACHIAN REGION

The eastern region of Kentucky includes almost one-third of the state, with rugged terrain, of which less than 10 percent is suitable for farming, and a relatively sparse population. The greatest number of settlers found their way to the Appalachian highlands around the turn of the century after the construction of railroads and the development of the coal-mining industry. A number of towns were established by mining companies from 1910 to 1940, and most of the homes and other structures in this area date from this time.

The mining industry affected the people in Appalachian foothills less than in the mountains, but the area remains the least densely populated in Kentucky, as much of the land is part of the **Daniel Boone National Forest** (100 Vaught Road, Winchester, 606-745-3100), which stretches across almost the entire length of the eastern region of the state. Territory Daniel Boone once explored—over 672,000 acres in twenty-one counties—has been designated as national forest land. The forest includes one lake at each end: the 8,400-acre Cave Run Lake in the north and the 5,600-acre Laurel River Lake near Corbin in the south. The 254-mile Sheltowee Trace National Recreational Trail extends from one end of the forest to the other, connecting the developed recreation areas with such impressive natural attractions as the Red River Gorge Geological Area. This area, approximately 50 miles southeast of Lexington, holds more than fifty major natural arches created by wind and water. Two of the most notable are the Natural Bridge, which stands more than seventy-eight feet tall with an opening sixty-five feet wide, and the tremendous arch under the ninety-foot stone span of Sky Bridge.

ASHLAND

Strategically located on the Ohio River, near the border of three states—Kentucky, West Virginia, and Ohio—Ashland had a prosperous beginning in the late 1700s as a major shipping and industrial center. Historic mansions along Bath and Montgomery avenues reflect that prosperity. The city's forty-seven-acre **Central Park** has Indian burial mounds dating back more than a thousand years.

Mayo Manor and Kentucky Highlands Museum

Built in 1917 and located in the heart of Ashland's historic district, the Beaux-Arts Mayo Manor was built by Alice Mayo Fetter, the widow of a wealthy eastern Kentucky coal operator. The three-story mansion has three stained-glass skylights: one in a Pompeiian entryway, one at the top of a cantilevered spiral staircase, and another in a third-floor ballroom, which is also lighted by two stained-glass lunettes and a two-story stone-columned conservatory. Once used for offices and apartments, Mayo Manor became the Highlands Museum in 1984. Its exhibits focus on the cultural and industrial history of eastern Kentucky, with memorabilia of the Kentucky writer Jesse Stuart, who lived in W-Hollow in nearby Greenup County, the Appalachian Collection of period clothing and household linens dating back to 1830, and exhibits about the influence of the steel, oil, power, railroad, and shipping industries on the area.

LOCATION: 1516 Bath Avenue. HOURS: 10–4 Tuesday–Saturday, 1–4 Sunday. FEE: Yes. TELEPHONE: 606–329–8888.

About three miles from **Prestonsburg,** the Civil War Battle of Middle Creek was fought in January 1862. Union Colonel James A. Garfield, who later became president, planned and led a campaign that forced the retreat of Confederate forces under General Humphrey Marshall from the Big Sandy Valley into Virginia. An early Union victory, the Battle of Middle Creek helped prevent the Confederates from using the Ohio River to enter Cincinnati.

The eastern area of **Pike County,** along the Kentucky–West Virginia border, is the site of the Hatfield-McCoy feud, which began on an election day in the late 1800s. A number of legends offer accounts of the origin of this conflict. One story maintains that the son of "Devil Anse" Hatfield of Tug Fork, West Virginia, eloped with the daughter of Randall McCoy of Kentucky. The feud began, according to this account, when the unwed McCoy mother returned home with a child. Motivated by hatred and the desire for revenge, the feud resulted in a number of deaths on each side. For years afterward, disputes over such matters as the ownership of a hog would renew the fighting. Coal-mine operators, who came to the

OPPOSITE: *The Daniel Boone National Forest preserves 672,000 acres in eastern Kentucky.*

The Hatfield-McCoy feud, which ranged along the Kentucky–West Virginia border, cost some forty to fifty lives. This portrait of the Hatfield faction shows "Devil Anse" Hatfield, the family leader, surrounded by his armed relations.

state and found the dispute hindering commercial development, pressured local authorities to intervene, but law enforcement officials of each state, often relatives of the feuding families, were reluctant to cross state boundaries to intercede. The fighting continued for fourteen years despite industrial development.

Off the Pikeville Bypass (which may be reached from Route 119E/23N), across from the north end of town in Pikeville is a peak called **Duty's Knob,** a reputed hideout of the Confederate raiders led by John Hunt Morgan.

Hindman, the seat of Knott County, is located at the forks of Troublesome Creek. The **Hindman Settlement School** (Route 160, 606–785–5475) was founded in 1902 at the urging of 82-year-old "Uncle Saul" Everidge to educate local students and promote the traditional arts of the area. **Uncle Saul's Cabin,** built in the 1840s, is now restored and furnished with period pieces.

LEVI JACKSON
WILDERNESS ROAD STATE PARK

Most of the land for this 896-acre park was originally given to John Freeman as payment for his service in the American Revolution. Named for Levi Jackson, the first judge of Laurel County (and John Freeman's son-in-law), the park includes parts of three of Daniel Boone's most famous routes, which survive as paved highways: the Sheltowee Trace, the longest, runs west to Laurel River Lake and south into Tennessee; the Daniel Boone Trace, most of which runs through the park, is also an automobile route that runs up Route 25; the Boone Trace branches off the third, the Wilderness Road, which is now Route 229. Boone and his group of thirty-six men marked the Wilderness Road in 1775, when they came west through the Cumberland Gap to the Kentucky River. Many historic markers along the Boone Trace show the route that an estimated 200,000 pioneers followed across the mountains to Kentucky and other areas of the western frontier from 1775 to 1796. Between 1777 and 1779, the Boone Trace was frequently closed by Indian attacks. The park has four marked trails, including the Boone Trace Trail (over two miles, beginning at the McHargue Mill) and the Wilderness Road Trail (over one mile), beginning at the Feltner 4-H Camp entrance). To the right of this entrance, the trail leads to two family cemeteries, those of Levi Jackson and John Freeman. This trail has the only marked burial grounds along the Wilderness Road. **Mountain Life Museum,** a restored pioneer village in the park, includes a log manor house, smokehouse, barn, and other buildings, as well as exhibits of pioneer firearms and domestic tools.

LOCATION: 2 miles south of London off Route 25. HOURS: *Museum:* April through mid-October: 9–5 Daily. FEE: Yes. TELEPHONE: 606–878–8000.

The **Dr. Thomas Walker State Shrine** (Route 459, off Route 25E, Barbourville, 606–546–4400) commemorates the explorations by Dr. Walker, who was sent to explore Kentucky by a Loyal Land Company of Virginia. He and his companions made the first documented trek through the Cumberland Gap in 1750. He reportedly built a cabin near Barbourville; the cabin here is a reproduction and is not located on the original site.

MIDDLESBORO

The town was created and settled by a British land company between 1886 and 1889, when the Scottish engineer Alexander A. Arthur arranged for English funds to begin the development of iron and coal industries. He chose the name Middlesboro, after the iron city in the English Midlands. **The Coal House** (North 20th Street, 606–248–1075), built in 1926 of forty tons of bituminous coal, now houses the Middlesboro chamber of commerce.

Cumberland Gap National Historical Park

Established in 1955, this park includes over 20,200 acres of the Cumberland Mountains shared by Kentucky, Virginia, and Tennessee. The area's historical importance arises from its use as a natural passage for migratory animals, Indians, frontier pioneers, and Civil War soldiers. Two miles from the Gap is the Great Saltpetre Cave, an important source of salt for early pioneers. The Cumberland Gap, first explored by Dr. Thomas Walker's expedition in 1750, was further explored by Daniel Boone, who blazed a way through the gap in 1775. With the resulting westward immigration, Kentucky's population increased to over 100,000 by 1792, the year the state was admitted to the Union.

A strategic location during the Civil War, the Cumberland Gap was first occupied by Confederates, under Brigadier General William Churchwell and General Felix Zollicoffer, in the summer of 1861, when they directed the construction of seven earthen forts facing north, and held the gap until abandoning their position. On June 17, 1862, the Union general George W. Morgan took control of the area and directed his troops to build nine earthen forts facing south. Confederate Lieutenant General Edmund Kirby Smith led his troops past the gap and cut off Morgan's supplies from Kentucky, thus forcing him to abandon his position, which the Confederates reassumed. In September 1863 Union troops under Major General Ambrose E. Burnside destroyed supplies stored at the Iron Furnace, prompting the Confederates to surrender their stronghold. After the surrender the Confederates found that they outnumbered their enemy. Though the gap changed hands four times before the end of the Civil War, no major battles took place there.

Within the Cumberland Gap National Historical Park is the **Hensley Settlement,** on Brush Mountain, along the Ridge Trail, an

George Caleb Bingham's painting Daniel Boone Escorting Settlers Through the Cumberland Gap, *honors the man who opened Kentucky territory for settlement when he blazed the Wilderness Road through the Appalachian Mountains (detail).*

isolated group of twelve self-sufficient Appalachian farmsteads that were worked from 1903, when Burton Hensley, Sr., first purchased 500 acres of land, until 1951, when Sherman Hensley, the last inhabitant, left. Without roads, electricity, or other modern conveniences, the Hensleys and Gibbonses began a settlement that grew to a population of between 60 and 100 people, who made their living from farming and the forests. About seventy acres of the original Hensley Settlement have been returned to farm and pasture land.

LOCATION: Cumberland Gap Parkway (Route 25E). HOURS: Memorial Day through Labor Day: 8–6 Daily; September through May: 8–5 Daily. FEE: None. TELEPHONE: 606–248–2817.

THE   BLUEGRASS   REGION

This fertile area west of the Appalachian Mountains, south of the Ohio River, and north of the Pennyroyal, was the destination of many of Kentucky's first settlers. Because the first communities grew up here—Harrodsburg (1774), Danville (1775), Bardstown (1778)—the area contains most of the surviving buildings from the eighteenth century. The productive farmlands later made possible Kentucky's greatest concentration of antebellum mansions. The tiny blue blossoms of bluegrass, which give the pastured countryside its distinctive dark blue-gray shade, appear only in May.

Within the Bluegrass are three areas: the inner Bluegrass, the Eden shale belt, and the outer Bluegrass, of which the inner Bluegrass is the most productive. The Eden shale belt, surrounding the inner Bluegrass, has poor soil with less phosphorus, more shale and silica. It is more suited for forests or pastures than crops, partly because it erodes so easily. The outer Bluegrass forms a wider belt that surrounds the Eden shale, and like the inner Bluegrass, is productive for farming.

COVINGTON

Charted in 1815 and named for a hero of the War of 1812, General Leonard Covington, the city of Covington is an Ohio River trade center that has always been more closely associated with Cincinnati than with Kentucky. The construction of Covington's renowned **Suspension Bridge** across the Ohio (at the northern end of Court Avenue) was approved by the Kentucky state legislature in 1846, interrupted by the Civil War, and then completed in 1867. Designed by John A. Roebling, this 1,057-foot-long bridge with towers 100 feet high predated the completion of Roebling's Brooklyn Bridge by about sixteen years. The **Riverside National Historic District,** located at the junction of the Ohio and Licking rivers, extends along Garrard Street between Riverside Drive and East 8th Street. The area includes the **Mimosa Historic Home** (412 East 2d Street, 606–261–9000), featuring original Edison electric lights, gaslights, a fine John Henry Belter parlor, and a player grand piano.

MainStrasse Old World Village (616 Main Street, off Route I-75, 606–491–0458) covers roughly thirty blocks in Covington and reflects the city's German heritage. The area's centerpiece is **Carroll**

Chimes Bell Tower in Goebel Park (near 5th Street on Philadelphia Street), next to the visitor center. It contains one of the world's two American-made animated clocks. On the hour the forty-three-bell carillon plays a concert with twenty-one figures depicting the story of the Pied Piper of Hamelin. **Mother of God Church** (119 West 6th Street) is a good example of Renaissance Revival architecture. Completed in 1871, the chapel contains five large murals, the artwork of Johann Schmitt, completed ca. 1890.

The interior of **Saint Mary's Cathedral, Basilica of the Assumption** (1140 Madison Avenue), was designed by Leon Coquard, begun in 1895 and completed by 1901. The facade, designed by David Davis in 1908 and added in 1910, is roughly derived from the Cathedral of Notre Dame in Paris; two projected towers, similar to Notre Dame's, have not yet been built. The facade rises 128 feet. On its north wall, the cathedral features one of the largest (twenty-four by sixty-seven feet) handmade stained-glass windows in the world. The stained and leaded glass portrays the Coronation of the Virgin, the Council of Ephesus, and the Fathers of the Church. The church also has three impressive paintings by Frank Duveneck, the important American artist who came from Covington. The exhibits in the **Behringer-Crawford Museum** (in Devon Park, 1600 Montague Avenue, 606–491–4003) focus on the cultural and natural history of the area, including paleontological and archaeological artifacts.

BIG BONE LICK STATE PARK

Approximately twenty-two miles southwest of Covington near Union is the site of an ancient salt lick and sulfur spring where the bones of prehistoric animals have been discovered in great numbers. In 1729 Indians guided a French-Canadian explorer, Charles Le Moyne, baron de Longueuil, to the site, which was littered with the bones of mammoths and mastodons. Many of these bones have since been removed, but the park museum has many artifacts on display, and the salt springs are still visible.

LOCATION: Route 338, 3380 Beaver Road. HOURS: *Museum:* April through October: 10–6 Daily; November through December: 10–6 Saturday–Sunday; February through March: 10–6 Saturday–Sunday. FEE: Yes. TELEPHONE: 606–384–3522.

AUGUSTA

On a high bank along the Ohio River is Augusta, site of a Civil War battle on September 27, 1862 between Union home guard, led by Colonel Joshua Taylor Bradford, and a detachment of General John Hunt Morgan's Confederate cavalry, led by his brother-in-law General Basil W. Duke. The Federals garrisoned themselves in brick houses in Augusta, firing from rooftops, but Duke, outnumbering his opponents by more than two to one, forced them to surrender. Two Union gunboats that had been at Augusta to help protect the town steamed away to avoid capture once the Confederates turned their guns on them. Despite Duke's victory, however, his casualties were so heavy that he aborted his plan to lead the cavalry across the Ohio and advance toward Cincinnati.

MAYSVILLE

This pioneer river town on the Ohio River was settled in 1784. The tobacco trade has always been important, and the town is the site of the world's second-largest burley tobacco market. The downtown historic district includes the **Olde Mechanics Row,** built about 1850 by John Armstrong with iron grillwork that shows the influence of early river trade with New Orleans. The **Mason County Courthouse,** built in 1844 as the city hall, became the courthouse in 1848, when Maysville was named the seat of Mason County. A cannon used in the 1811 Battle of Tippecanoe is on display at the courthouse. Pioneer records of such renowned citizens as Daniel Boone and Simon Kenton are held in the Clerk's Office (1860). The **Mason County Museum** (215 Sutton Street, 606–564–5865), built in 1876 and now restored, holds documents for historical and genealogical research as well as river dioramas and regional-history exhibits.

WASHINGTON

Incorporated in 1786, Washington claims to be the first town of many in the United States to be named for George Washington. Most of its residences date from 1785 to 1812, as the settlement was an outpost for pioneers traveling the Buffalo Trace, one of the oldest trails in the North American interior.

OPPOSITE: *Maysville, an important Ohio River port founded in the 1780s, retains many buildings from its mid-nineteenth-century period of prosperity.*

The Washington Historic District

Old Washington includes many sites of historical significance. Costumed guides offer tours of house museums as well as local churches and cemeteries, beginning at the visitor center located in the Cane Brake, one of the oldest surviving log structures in town. Sites open to the public include the home of Confederate general Albert Sidney Johnston, built around 1797; the log cabin of Simon Kenton, restored to resemble the store he owned in town; the Paxton Inn, built in 1819; the Pillsbury Boys School, dating to 1820; and the Mefford's Flatboat Fort, a cabin constructed in part from a 1787 flatboat.

> LOCATION: Junction of Routes 62 and 68. HOURS: Mid-March through December: 10–4:30 Daily, and by appointment.. FEE: Yes. TELEPHONE: 606–759–7411.

BLUE LICKS BATTLEFIELD STATE PARK

The park of roughly 150 acres near the Licking River in northern Kentucky is the site of the August 19, 1782, battle that ended the American Revolution in the West. A granite monument in the park honors the sixty pioneers, including Israel Boone, the son of Daniel Boone, and American leaders Major John Todd and Stephen Trigg, who died in this bloody battle with the Indians, who were led by British captain William Caldwell. Against the advice of more experienced fellow officers, American major Hugh McGary did not want to wait for reinforcements and convinced the youngest of the troops to follow him across the Ohio River in pursuit of Caldwell's force of several hundred Indians and about fifty British soldiers. Greatly outnumbered, the Kentuckians were ambushed, and the battle that resulted is said to have lasted only fifteen minutes. The park museum exhibits pioneer relics and a collection of prehistoric artifacts discovered here. During the nineteenth century, the site was well known for its mineral waters, and a health spa once operated here.

> LOCATION: Route 68, near Mount Olivet. HOURS: April through October: 9–4:30 Daily. FEE: None. TELEPHONE: 606–289–5507.

CYNTHIANA

Established in the 1790s and incorporated in 1806, Cynthiana was named for first settler Robert Harrison's two daughters, Cynthia and Anna. The Greek Revival **Harrison County Courthouse,** built in 1851, has an octagonal clock tower. In July 1862 Colonel John J. Landrum was not successful in defending the town against Confederate raiders led by General John Hunt Morgan. In 1864 Morgan's second raid into Kentucky ended here in defeat, when he decided to fight a larger Union force, despite a lack of ammunition. The Federal troops, led by General Stephen G. Burbridge, routed Morgan's men on June 12, 1864. Cynthiana suffered much damage, and there were heavy casualties on both sides.

PARIS

In the early days, Doyles Spring on 2d Street and fine bluegrass pastureland made the seat of Bourbon County a favorite rest stop for people and horses between Maysville and Lexington. Known as Hopewell when it was established in 1789, local appreciation for French assistance during the Revolutionary War prompted citizens to rename the town Paris. In 1790 Jacob Spears and others set up one of the first distilleries in Kentucky. Their distilled product was called *bourbon,* for the county in which it was produced. Later bourbon came to mean any deep-amber-colored distilled corn liquor.

Courthouse records reveal that Daniel Boone was once a resident of Maysville, and several suits for debts were filed against him. Boone is known to have frequented **Duncan Tavern Historic Shrine** (363 High Street, 606–987–1788), built in 1822 and now open as a historical and genealogical library, furnished with pre-1820 items. The collection includes the original manuscript of *The Little Shepherd of Kingdom Come,* by John Fox, Jr., the first in a series of books about life in the Appalachian region of Kentucky and the first American novel to sell 1 million copies. Fox was born near Paris. The ca. 1801 **Anne Duncan House,** adjoining the Duncan Tavern, is also constructed of native limestone and fully restored.

Approximately seven miles east of Paris on Route 460 onto Route 537 is the **Cane Ridge Meeting House,** built in 1791 by North Carolina Presbyterians. It is the parent church of the Disciples of

Christ, the Christian denomination formed following the religious revivals that swept Kentucky in the early nineteenth century. The oldest log church in the area and thought to be the largest one-room log church in the United States, the Cane Ridge Meeting House is constructed of ash logs on a stone foundation.

WARD HALL

Kentucky's finest Greek Revival house and one of the most distinguished in the nation, Ward Hall is in remarkably complete condition with fittings and period furnishings. The property on which this Greek Revival mansion rests was purchased in the 1770s by Colonel Robert Johnson from Patrick Henry. Johnson served as a member of the first constitutional convention for Kentucky statehood; in 1826 three of his sons (John Telemachus, William, and Richard Mentor)

Ward Hall's massive Corinthian columns are made of stone with cast-iron bases and capitals.

were serving in the U.S. Congress. William had been a major in the War of 1812. Richard was a congressman for twenty-nine years and was also vice president under Martin Van Buren.

Just west of the present site, William Johnson built the original house on the property in 1817. After William's death, his grandson Junius Ward bought the estate and began construction of Ward Hall during the late 1830s. In the drawing room, he used the 1817 door lintel, and throughout the house are other materials from the original structure. The house was not complete until 1853. At one time, it was under consideration for use as the Kentucky state capitol.

LOCATION: Route 460, 2 miles west of Route I-75. HOURS: May through October: 9:30–5 Monday–Saturday, 1–5 Sunday. FEE: Yes. TELEPHONE: 502–863–1619.

FRANKFORT

Frankfort, the capital city of Kentucky, lies in a valley alongside an S-shaped bend in the Kentucky River. A settlement in Frankfort was established by James Wilkinson, a general in the Revolutionary War, and a friend of Aaron Burr, who trusted him, and of the Spanish government, which paid him as a secret agent. In 1786 Wilkinson bought the property, which is now the downtown district, for about $400. Also in 1786, he asked the Virginia legislature to recognize 100 acres of the land as the town of Frankfort. The town is named after Stephen Frank, a pioneer who had been killed by Indians and whose name had already been given to his campsite beside the river: Frank's Ford became Frankfort. In exchange for a trade monopoly in New Orleans, Wilkinson agreed in secret to use his influence to move Kentucky toward becoming a colony of Spain, rather than a part of the federal union. Such a background of political intrigue, combined with his association with Aaron Burr, who was later also allegedly involved in a conspiracy with Spain, caused Wilkinson to be implicated in the treason charges Burr faced in 1805–1806. He testified against Burr and was later acquitted of all charges. Wilkinson platted the town, naming the streets Wilkinson Street; Washington Street; Ann Street, for his wife; and Miró Street, for his employer, the Spanish governor of Louisiana. The capitol burned twice, in 1813 and 1824, and each time the cities of Lexington and Louisville questioned the decision to rebuild in Frankfort. The capitol has remained here, however.

Frankfort has the only building in Kentucky designed by Frank Lloyd Wright. The **Reverend Jesse R. Zeigler House,** or **Frank Lloyd Wright House** (509 Shelby Street, private), is the result of a chance shipboard meeting between Wright and the Reverend Zeigler in 1910. The **Vest-Lindsey House** (401 Wapping Street, 502–564–6980), the early-nineteenth-century home of George Graham Vest, a Confederate lawmaker and a U.S. senator from Missouri, was later the home of Union general Daniel Lindsey. It is now a museum of period furnishings. Vest was best known for his "Tribute to a Dog" speech, in which he declared that "a dog is a man's best friend."

Ancient Age Distillery (Leestown Pike, Route 421, 502–223–7641) has been making Kentucky bourbon since 1869. It marks the site where a group led by Captain Hancock Lee established Leestown in 1773. A neighborhood known as the **Corner of Celebrities,** the oldest in Frankfort, has been home to two Supreme Court justices, two cabinet officers, nine U.S. senators, governors of Kentucky or Missouri, four U.S. congressmen, and five ambassadors. The area includes Liberty Hall, the home of John Brown, and the home of his son, Orlando Brown. John Brown was a friend of the first five presidents, and many of them visited his home. Dignitaries who were guests in this neighborhood included Thomas Jefferson, James Madison, James Monroe, Andrew Jackson, Theodore Roosevelt, the marquis de Lafayette, Louis-Philippe, Aaron Burr, Henry Clay, and Daniel Webster.

Kentucky State Capitol

At the south end of Capitol Avenue stands the impressive Kentucky State Capitol, begun in 1905 and completed in 1909. Because the plans by architect Frank Mills Andrews were for a structure too large to fit on the site of the old capitol, the new site was chosen. Andrews's structure incorporated elements of Greek and Roman architecture: paired Ionic columns, seventy in all, and pediment sculpture designed by Charles H. Niehaus and carved by Peter Rossack featuring "Lady Kentucky" attended by "Progress," "History," "Plenty," "Law," "Art," and "Labor." The three-story building's exterior is of Bedford limestone on a Vermont granite base, and its most impressive feature is the central dome on an Ionic peristyle base crowned by a lantern.

OPPOSITE: *The central corridor of the Kentucky State Capitol in Frankfort contains thirty-six columns, each made of a single piece of Vermont granite.*

The Kentucky Governor's Mansion, built of native limestone, was modeled after the Petit Trianon, Marie Antoinette's villa at Versailles.

The interior includes a vestibule inside the north, or main, entrance, which leads to the central corridor. The 403-foot nave holds thirty-six granite columns, each weighing ten tons. The floors are marble from Tennessee and Italy; wainscots and pilasters are Georgia marble. At either end of the nave are murals painted by T. Gilbert White of Michigan, one depicting Daniel Boone's role in Kentucky history, the second showing negotiations with the Indians for the purchase of land. The rotunda was modeled after Napoléon's tomb in the Hôtel des Invalides in Paris. A grouping of statuary located under the central dome centers upon a bronze statue of Abraham Lincoln by A. A. Weinmann. Located on the second floor of the capitol, the **State Reception Room** overlooks the north capitol grounds. Designed in the style of Louis XIV, the room resembles the Throne Room of the Charlottenburg Palace near Berlin. The walls are embellished with faux marble pilasters and hand-painted murals that resemble tapestries. The fireplaces are exact copies of those in the salon of Diane in Versailles, completed in 1670.

Thirty-four acres of landscaped grounds surround the State Capitol. The **Floral Clock** on the grounds is a working clock face thirty-four feet in diameter with approximately twenty thousand flowering plants planted in a base weighing 100 tons.

LOCATION: Capitol Avenue. HOURS: 8–4:30 Monday–Friday, 9–4 Saturday, 1–4:30 Sunday. FEE: None. TELEPHONE: 502–564–7318.

Kentucky Governor's Mansion

Constructed in 1914, the Beaux-Arts Governor's Mansion was built adjacent to the State Capitol on a bluff overlooking the Kentucky River. It resembles the Petit Trianon in Versailles. Designed by C. C. and E. A. Weber, the mansion features a portico with eight Ionic columns, a stone balustrade, and a terrace. Remodeled in the 1980s, the first-floor rooms include a formal reception room, a salon, and a formal ballroom. The semicircular state dining room has tall windows overlooking the grounds. Double stairways wind to the second and third floors, the private living space of the governor and his family.

LOCATION: Capitol Avenue. HOURS: 9–11 Tuesday, Thursday, 1:30–3:30 Wednesday. FEE: None. TELEPHONE: 502–564–3449.

Kentucky Military History Museum

The castellated Gothic Revival building that houses the museum was designed by Frankfort native Nathaniel C. Cook and constructed as the Kentucky State Arsenal in 1850. For reasons of safety it was sited outside the town. During the Civil War cartridges for the Union army were manufactured here, and the building was fired on by Confederate forces under General John Hunt Morgan. Through World War I the arsenal served as a matériel distribution point for the Kentucky National Guard.

In 1936 fire burned the interior of the building, leaving only the exterior walls intact. It was rebuilt by the National Guard, working without benefit of the original blueprints. Today the two-story brick building resembles a fortified castle, with three-story towers flanking the front entrance. Iron grillwork, befitting a symbolic stronghold, covers lower-level openings. In 1973 the arsenal became the home of the military collection that had been housed in the Old State Capitol. Exhibits interpret Kentucky's role in American military his-

tory from frontier days to the Vietnam conflict. The collection includes several Kentucky long rifles; original uniforms from the War of 1812 to the present; forty-eight Civil War flags; memorabilia from such famous Kentuckians as John C. Breckinridge, Vice President Richard M. Johnson, and Henry Clay; one of the four remaining Confederate Williams rapid-fire guns; and many captured enemy weapons from World Wars I and II, Korea, and Vietnam. The museum also has an extensive collection of automatic weapons.

LOCATION: East Main Street (Route 60) at Capitol Avenue. HOURS: 8–4 Monday–Saturday, 1–5 Sunday. FEE: None. TELEPHONE: 502–564–3265.

Liberty Hall

Named for the Virginia school that the Kentucky lawyer and legislator John Brown had attended and that his father had founded (now

ABOVE and OPPOSITE: *The Georgian Liberty Hall, built by John Brown in the 1790s, resembles the houses he left behind in his native Virginia. It is furnished with many Brown family pieces.*

Washington and Lee University), Liberty Hall was begun in 1796 when Brown bought four acres along a bend of the Kentucky River. John Brown served in Congress from 1787 to 1792 as a member of the Virginia delegation. He actively supported the movement to separate Kentucky from Virginia, and when Kentucky became the fifteenth state in 1792, Brown became one of the state's first two U.S. senators. He later served two six-year terms in the Senate.

The Browns moved into Liberty Hall in 1801. The bricks for their home were made and fired on the property. Nails were forged by the local blacksmith, and the wood was cut and dried in sheds for two years before its use—black walnut and poplar for the interior woodwork, white and blue ash for the floors, cherry for the stair banister and wall rail, cypress for the roof shingles and cellar windowsills. Glass windows and brass locks and fixtures were shipped from the east. The L-shaped house is a fine example of Georgian architecture. The entrance is recessed, with a fanlight below a second story featuring a Palladian window. The house is furnished with period pieces belonging to the Browns, including portraits and an extensive library. Thomas Jefferson corresponded with Brown and sent house plans that went unused because construction was already well under way when Jefferson's letter arrived.

Liberty Hall was visited by President James Monroe, Andrew Jackson, Zachary Taylor, and the marquis de Lafayette. An interesting "guest" who reportedly still appears is the ghost of Margaretta Brown's aunt, Mrs. Varick, called the Gray Lady. The story goes that soon after John and Margaretta's 8-year-old daughter died of an overdose of calomel, Mrs. Varick came to visit and died herself soon afterward. Since that time, the Gray Lady has supposedly appeared periodically at the head of the stairs. When John Brown died in 1837, his eldest son, Mason, inherited the property, and it was passed to Mason Brown's descendants until 1956, when it became a museum house of the National Society of the Colonial Dames of America in the Commonwealth of Kentucky. The formal garden was recently restored and is filled with old roses, azaleas, and boxwood.

LOCATION: 218 Wilkinson Street. HOURS: March through December: 10–4 Tuesday–Saturday, 2–4 Sunday. FEE: Yes. TELEPHONE: 502–227–2560.

Orlando Brown House

Orlando Brown, John Brown's younger son, inherited the southern half of his father's property and enough money to build a mansion next door to Liberty Hall, which had been the inheritance of his older brother. Designed by Gideon Shryock, the architect of the Old State Capitol, Orlando Brown's house was built between 1835 and 1836 on roughly the same floor plan as Liberty Hall, except reversed and with slightly smaller rooms. Though trained in medicine and law, Orlando Brown eventually turned to journalism, became editor of *The Frankfort Commonwealth* in 1833, and made his avocation his vocation. His home passed to generations of his family after his death in 1868, and it has been maintained as a museum since 1955. Most of the furnishings, the silver, and china are original to the Brown family, including chandeliers that originally burned whale oil.

LOCATION: 202 Wilkinson Street. HOURS: March through December: 10–4 Tuesday–Saturday, 2–4 Sunday. FEE: Yes. TELEPHONE: 502–875–4952.

The **Old Governor's Mansion** (420 High Street, 502–564–5500) was constructed of brick laid in Flemish bond between 1797 and 1798. The two-and-a-half-story Georgian home with its front door inside a semicircular keystoned archway is framed by engaged Doric columns beneath full entablature. Home to Kentucky governors from 1798 to 1914, it is now the residence of the Kentucky lieutenant governor.

Old State Capitol

Designed by Gideon Shryock, and built between 1827 and 1830, this Greek Revival building served as the state capitol until 1910. It was the first major work of Shryock, who pioneered Greek temple architecture in the West. The exterior has a gabled roof, a domed cupola with windows, and an Ionic portico with six columns. The most impressive interior feature is the self-supporting circular staircase. The old House chamber contains four original desks from about 1850, including the Speaker's desk, and larger-than-life-size portraits of Daniel Boone, George Washington, and the marquis de Lafayette.

LOCATION: Broadway and Lewis streets, at Saint Clair Mall. HOURS: 9–4 Monday–Saturday, 1–5 Sunday. FEE: None. TELEPHONE: 502–564–3016.

Across the river from the Capitol, located on a high bluff overlooking the river and the city, is the **Frankfort Cemetery** (215 West Main Street), incorporated in 1844, though some of the markers date to the eighteenth century. The most visited graves in the cemetery are those of Daniel and Rebecca Boone, who were moved here from Defiance, Missouri, near Saint Louis, where they were originally buried. Their large marker features marble relief carvings of Daniel Boone engaged in such activities as fighting an Indian and looking at a deer he has slain. Rebecca Boone is depicted milking a cow. Other important Kentuckians buried here include Governor William Goebel, who was assassinated near the Old State Capitol, as well as fifteen other Kentucky governors. In the center of the cemetery is the Kentucky Veterans War Memorial, a sixty-five-foot-tall monument originally dedicated in 1850. Hundreds of soldiers from all U.S. wars are buried here, including Marine lieutenant Presley O'Banion, the first person to plant the American flag on foreign soil.

VERSAILLES

The seat of Woodford County, Versailles is located between Lexington and Frankfort. The town was established in 1792 and named after Versailles, France. The **Jack Jouett House** (Craig's Creek Road, Route 33, 616–873–7902), home of Revolutionary War hero Captain Jack Jouett, was built around 1797 and fully restored in 1978. Jouett is known as the "Paul Revere of the South" because of his forty-mile gallop to warn Thomas Jefferson that the British were coming to arrest him at Monticello. His son Matthew Jouett was one of the foremost portrait painters west of the Appalachians. Briefly a student of Gilbert Stuart, Matthew Jouett was mainly self-taught.

The **Woodford County Historical Society Museum** (121 Rose Hill, 606–873–6786) is housed in an 1819 building that once served as Big Spring Church. In addition to an extensive genealogical library, the museum features rotating exhibits from its collection of local memorabilia about equine history and prominent citizens of the Woodford County area.

LEXINGTON

Though Lexington, the seat of Fayette County, is the second-largest city in the state, the countryside—particularly along the Iron Works Pike, Old Frankfort Pike, and the Paris Pike—reveals Lexington's

A peaceful street in Lexington, filled with early-twentieth-century houses.

past, with large thoroughbred horse farms, pastures, miles of white wooden fences, and fields of burley tobacco. Open since 1875, the **Red Mile Track** (847 South Broadway) is the oldest harness track in Kentucky. The **Keeneland Race Course** (4201 Versailles Road), site of the pre-Derby Bluegrass Stakes, was incorporated in 1935 on Keene family property that had been purchased from Patrick Henry, who received the acreage as part of a land grant in 1783.

Lexington was named in 1775 by frontiersmen in honor of Lexington, Massachusetts, site of the first battle of the American Revolution. Robert Patterson, one of the early settlers, constructed a cabin, which now stands on the Transylvania University campus. The town was officially organized in 1781. **Transylvania University** (North Broadway and 3d Street), the oldest institution of higher learning west of the Allegheny Mountains, made Lexington the leading academic center in the area. Its graduates have included at least 50 U.S. senators, 101 members of the House of Representatives, three House Speakers, 36 governors, 34 ambassadors, the president of the

Confederacy—Jefferson Davis—and 2 U.S. vice presidents—Richard M. Johnson and John C. Breckinridge. The **University of Kentucky** (South Limestone Street and Euclid Avenue) was also established during the nineteenth century. Its fine libraries and its **Museum of Anthropology** (606–257–7112) are important sources of information about Kentucky history and prehistory. The city has a number of historic districts. **Western Suburb Historic District,** along West Short Street, includes Mary Todd Lincoln's childhood home, built in about 1810 as an inn. One-half block east is the **Lexington Opera House,** built in 1887, at the corner of North Broadway.

A centrally located neighborhood of Lexington's leading citizens, **Gratz Park** (North Mill Street) is named for Benjamin Gratz, an early city leader, whose home stands in the area. Among the historic churches in the vicinity is the **First Presbyterian Church** (174 North Mill Street), designed by Cincinnatus Shryock, brother of the Greek Revivalist architect Gideon Shryock; the 1872 church is a restrained Gothic Revival structure. **Christ Church** (Church and Market streets), also a Gothic Revival building, houses one of the oldest Episcopalian congregations west of the Alleghenies. It was built between 1845 and 1848, but the site has been occupied by Episcopal churches since 1796.

Hunt-Morgan House

Hopemont, the Federal-style Hunt-Morgan House, built ca. 1814, was the home of John Wesley Hunt, who made a fortune outfitting pioneers for their westward trek. Hunt's descendants achieved fame in Kentucky and the world. His son Charlton Hunt was Lexington's first mayor, and another son, Francis Key Hunt, built **Loudoun** (209 Castlewood Drive, 606–254–7024) in 1850, a fine Gothic Revival villa designed by Alexander Jackson Davis of New York.

Hopemont was the home of John Wesley Hunt's grandson, John Hunt Morgan, a Confederate general, called the "Thunderbolt of the Confederacy" by southerners and a "horse thief" by northerners. Hunt's nephew, Dr. Thomas Hunt Morgan, winner of the Nobel Prize for genetics research in 1933, was born here. The house was occupied for nearly a century by the family and few changes were made. The front central entrance has an impressive fanlighted doorway with a Palladian window spanning nearly nine feet. Unusual features include a cantilevered staircase in its own separate room and elaborate woodwork with much reed-ing, fluting, and bull's-eye designs. Family furnishings include a piano with a fourth pedal to give drum and fife accompaniment. The house also holds many original family portraits and porcelains.

LOCATION: 201 North Mill Street. HOURS: March through December: 10–4 Tuesday–Saturday, 2–5 Sunday. FEE: Yes. TELE-PHONE: 606–253–0362.

Mary Todd Lincoln House

In 1832 Mary Todd's father, Robert, bought the 14-room structure, built between 1803 and 1806, to house his large family. The lower half had been turned into a tavern soon after the house was built. Mary Todd lived here from about the age of 13 until she was 21. Her grandfather, Levi Todd, was one of the city's first settlers. During the Civil War, most of the members of her family were Confederate sympathizers, while her half sister, a brother, and three sisters supported the Union. The brick L-shaped structure with Georgian elements has a gabled roof with paired brackets. The front center entrance with a classical frame is slightly recessed. After the Todd family moved in 1852, the house was occupied by a variety of tenants before the state bought the property in 1969. Except for the dining room and family parlor, the house retains its original Kentucky ash floors as well as its original staircase with a sunburst design. An inventory list aided in the restoration of furnishings, and the house contains many portraits and personal items belonging to the Todd family.

LOCATION: 578 West Main Street. HOURS: April through mid-December: 10–4 Tuesday–Saturday. FEE: Yes. TELEPHONE: 606–233–9999.

The first rural cemetery in Lexington, **Lexington Cemetery** (833 West Main Street) was laid out in 1849. Its landscaped acres of flowering trees and other plants resemble Mount Auburn Cemetery outside Boston. Buried here are women's suffragist Laura Clay (1849–1941), daughter of Cassius M. Clay, in 1920 the first woman to have her name placed in nomination for U.S. president; John Breckinridge (1760–1806), framer of the Kentucky constitution; Confederate general John Hunt Morgan (1825–1864), whose raids are said to have cost the Union $10 million in property damages; and Henry Clay (1777–1852), whose monument is a landmark.

ABOVE *and* OPPOSITE: *Ashland, built in 1857 on the foundations of Henry Clay's earlier house by his son, James, contains many family portraits and furnishings.*

Eight miles south of downtown Lexington, **Waveland** (225 Higbee Road, off Route 27 South, 606–272–3611) was built in 1847 by Joseph Bryan, a grandnephew of Daniel Boone. Waveland is an outstanding example of the Greek Revival house in Kentucky. The grounds boast an impressive array of nineteenth-century dependencies, including brick slave quarters, an icehouse, and a smokehouse. The house is furnished with period pieces, and the slave quarters contain special exhibits highlighting the craftsmanship and household activities of the time.

Ashland

Originally built by the statesman Henry Clay, who lived there from at least 1812 to 1851, the present house was reconstructed on the site in 1857 by Clay's son, James, who used the same foundations and the original floor plan, though he added many Italianate elements. Benjamin Henry Latrobe, one of the architects of the U.S. Capitol, designed the wings added to the original house. As revised,

the exterior of the house has stone quoins and elaborate cast-iron hood molds. The two-story central part of this brick mansion is flanked on either side by one-story wings. The main entrance projects from the house in the form of a bay. The front doorway has a half-circle fanlight with a plain-molded architrave and cornice, as well as a Palladian window above. Roughly 95 percent of the furnishings are original to the house. Interior features include Sheffield silver doorknobs and silver hardware, a collection of campaign gifts given to Clay (who ran unsuccessfully for president three times), dining room china from Paris which includes an ice-cream service, twelve carved Italian-marble mantels, and an octagonal-shaped walnut-paneled library with an eighteen-foot-high domed ceiling. The property, which once comprised 600 acres, now includes twenty wooded and landscaped with gardens. Henry Clay imported thoroughbred horses and pedigreed livestock to Kentucky and built a private racetrack. A number of original outbuildings including two icehouses, a smokehouse, a dairy cellar, and a coach house, remain on the estate.

Clay was a U.S. senator when he was 29. He also served as Speaker of the House of Representatives. He pushed for the War of 1812 and then helped to negotiate the peace in 1814. He also negotiated the Missouri Compromise of 1820, which maintained a balance between free and slave states by admitting Maine and Missouri to the Union at the same time. When Clay ran for the presidency for the first time in 1824, he was one of four candidates, along with John Quincy Adams, Andrew Jackson, and William H. Crawford. Clay came up fourth in electoral votes and threw his support to Adams, who was elected and soon after appointed Clay as his secretary of state. Clay's expertise as a leader and legislator soon earned for him the nickname of "the Great Compromiser" or "the Great Pacificator," for his role in the Missouri Compromise and the Compromise of 1850.

LOCATION: 120 Sycamore Road. HOURS: 10–4 Monday–Saturday, 1–4 Sunday. FEE: Yes. TELEPHONE: 606–266–8581.

The **Henry Clay Law Office** (178 North Mill Street, private) was built specifically for Henry Clay in 1803 and used by him until 1810. The Flemish bond one-story building is one of the two remaining buildings originally built as professional offices in Lexington.

RICHMOND

Named for Richmond, Virginia, the seat of Madison County was settled by Colonel John Miller in 1784. Its first county courthouse was Colonel Miller's barn, where the present courthouse, built in 1849, now stands. The **Madison County Courthouse** (Main Street) has a clock tower with two octagonal stages set back from a pedimented Doric portico. An ornamental iron fence added in the 1850s was used to imprison Union soldiers captured in the Battle of Richmond. Remaining portions of that fence now enclose the Richmond Cemetery. Parts of the courthouse were used as a Civil War hospital. Federal troops took control of the Richmond area in 1861. Then on August 30, 1862, a battle began between the Union forces of General William Nelson and Confederates led by General Edmund Kirby Smith. The first clash was about six miles south of Richmond, and the struggle continued through Richmond toward Lexington, as the Confederates gained their first victory in Kentucky. Richmond was the home of Kit Carson and Cassius Marcellus Clay; today it is the site of Fort Boonesborough State Park.

Fort Boonesborough State Park

Sponsored by Colonel Richard Henderson, Daniel Boone established Fort Boonesborough near a salt lick beside the Kentucky River at the site where the replica fort now stands. Boone and his company of thirty men blazed a trail through the wilderness, reaching the river in April 1775. They began work on the fort that was first called Henderson and then Transylvania before becoming Boonesborough. Henderson himself arrived later that same month and called a meeting of people from the surrounding stations—Saint Asaph (or Fort Logan, now Stanford), Harrodsburg, Boiling Springs, and Boonesborough—to discuss local government. The fort was completed in July 1776 with four blockhouses and a palisade. On July 14, 1776, Daniel Boone's daughter and two daughters of Colonel Calloway were captured by Indians just outside the fort, though Boone's party was able to rescue the young women unharmed. Early in 1778, Boone and a party of men were captured by Shawnee and held captive for months before Boone escaped to warn Boonesborough of the impending Indian attack. He led the pioneers, who had given Boone up for dead, in preparing for the ten-day attack which began in September 1778. Boonesborough and Harrodsburg

were the only Kentucky settlements that survived the Indian campaign of that year. Afterward, when Boone was tried for conspiracy
and treason, his eloquent self-defense at the court martial proceed-
ings won for him not only an acquittal but also a promotion to major.
For a time after George Rogers Clark's success in the Northwest
Territory, Boonesborough thrived, but thereafter the settlement
declined and then disappeared. Today craftspeople demonstrate
pioneer skills in a reproduction of the fort, using authentic tools
from the eighteenth century. A museum in the park offers interpretive exhibits about Daniel Boone and the settlement of the area.

LOCATION: Exit 95 from Route I-75, 4375 Boonesboro Road (about
12 miles north of Richmond). FEE: Yes. TELEPHONE: 606–527–3131.

White Hall

White Hall was the home of Cassius Marcellus Clay—publisher of an
abolitionist newspaper, ambassador to Russia under Abraham
Lincoln and Andrew Johnson, founder of Kentucky's Republican
party, influential negotiator in the purchase of Alaska, and founder
of racially-integrated Berea College before the Civil War.

The original house was built in 1798 and called Clermont. It was
here that Clay was born in 1810. It was remodeled in the Italianate
mode from 1864 to 1868, producing its irregular shape. The three-
story house has seven stair levels plus an attic and many differing
ceiling heights in its forty-four rooms. The tripartite facade has a
projecting entrance pavilion and a balcony and porch with tracery;
pilasters run the height of the house between the bays. The back of
the house includes late-eighteenth- and early-nineteenth-century
sections. White Hall was the first home in the area to have central
heating and indoor plumbing. Heat ducts run to each fireplace
from a basement furnace. Clay installed a water storage tank on the
third floor and pipes to drain water from the roof. The sewage system allowed the operation of a toilet and bathtub.

Clay's outspoken ways and unpopular ideas resulted in an active
life. He participated in more than 200 documented fights and duels.
He always carried a bowie knife, sometimes supplemented by a pistol.
He married twice: first to Mary Jane Warfield, who mothered ten

OPPOSITE: *White Hall, originally called Clermont, was extensively remodeled in the popular Italianate style in the 1860s.*

children but divorced Clay (in 1878) after a woman brought a 4-year-old boy to White Hall and presented him saying, "Mr. Clay, I've brought you your son." Clay adopted the child. At the age of 83, he married Dora Richardson, the 15-year-old daughter of a sharecropper. The marriage lasted two years before they were divorced. After Clay's death in 1903 at the age of 93 in the White Hall library, the contents of the house were auctioned. The parlor contains original woodwork, and the house contains some of its original pieces, subsequently recovered—silver, china, law books, and furniture. Before the restoration of the house began, tenant farmers used the front rooms as a barn, parking their tractors in the reception hall and allowing chickens to roost on the only piece of furniture that remained after the auction, the 1859 Steinway grand piano. All obvious traces of abuse have been removed.

> LOCATION: Exit 95 from Route I-75, 7 miles north of Richmond on Clay Lane, off Route 25/421. HOURS: April through August: 9–5:30 Daily; September through October: 9–5:30 Wednesday–Sunday; November though March: By Appointment. FEE: Yes. TELEPHONE: 606–623–9179.

Over five generations of the Cornelison family have owned and operated **Bybee Pottery** (Route 52, nine miles east of Richmond, 606–369–5350), one of the oldest existing potteries west of the Alleghenies. Sales records go back to 1845, although tradition has it that the business traces to 1809. The central log building with its solid walnut beams has a floor several inches higher than its original level due to the buildup of clay dust. Clay is mined from an open pit located about three miles away, where pioneer settlers from Fort Boonesborough also mined.

BEREA

Located in the foothills of the southern highlands, where the bluegrass meets the Appalachian Mountains, Berea is the site of **Berea College,** founded in 1855 by John G. Fee, John A. R. Rogers, and Cassius Marcellus Clay. The **Berea College Appalachian Museum** (Jackson Street, 606–986–9341, ext. 6078) features a permanent exhibit of textiles—coverlets, quilts, and other woven items. The Appalachian area was industrialized later than other parts of the country, and craftsmanship here remains several generations closer to the values of a preindustrial society. There are at least four temporary exhibits per year featuring the work of contemporary Appalachian photographers, folk artists, or craftspeople. **Churchill Weavers** (Route 1061 off Route 25N, 606–986–3126) was opened in 1922 by Carroll and Eleanor Churchill, former missionaries to India, and grew into a nationally recognized hand-weaving studio. Inspection stations and weaving rooms where weavers work at hand-looms are open for viewing.

WILLIAM WHITLEY HOUSE STATE HISTORICAL SITE

Two miles west of Crab Orchard, near Stanford, stands the first brick house built by Anglo-Americans west of the Alleghenies. It was planned and constructed by the scout and state legislator William Whitley, who began the building in 1785 and completed it in 1792. Whitley located his home on acreage he received as land grants from the American government for his service in fighting Indians. He designed a number of features to make his home a refuge: high placement of first-floor windows, twenty-three-inch-thick walls, a windowless, centrally located kitchen that can be entirely shut off from all other rooms, and a hidden interior stairway, so steep that hand grips were cut into the center of each stair, leading from this kitchen to the third story, where the ballroom floor has a secret hiding place for children. On his property, called Sportsman's Hill, Whitley built the first circular track for horse racing in Kentucky in 1788. An Irishman, Whitley reversed the English practice of racing in a clockwise direction; the races on his track were run counterclockwise, as they still are today in Kentucky and throughout the United States.

LOCATION: Off Route 150, between Stanford and Crab Orchard. HOURS: July through August: 9–5 Daily; September through June: 9–5 Tuesday–Sunday. FEE: Yes. TELEPHONE: 606–355–2881.

DANVILLE

Located near the old Wilderness Road and called "the birthplace of the Bluegrass," Danville was founded in 1775 and named the official seat of government west of the Alleghenies by Virginia in 1785. The town was the site of ten conventions held between 1784 and 1792, before Kentucky was recognized as a state separate from Virginia. The **Boyle County Courthouse** (West Main Street), built from 1860 to 1862 after the 1844 courthouse burned, was designed by James R. Carrigan and, soon after its completion, was occupied by Federal troops as a hospital following the Battle of Perryville. The **Kentucky School for the Deaf** (South 2d Street, 606–236–5132), founded in Danville in 1823, was the first state-supported school in the nation for the education of deaf children. The campus administration building, **Jacobs Hall,** built in 1857, once housed female students and staff. The building is a remarkable structure designed especially for the deaf, with a central open stairwell measuring over seventy feet from the ceiling to the floor.

Ephraim McDowell House

Ephraim McDowell made medical history in this house on December 25, 1809, when he removed a twenty-two pound ovarian tumor, a procedure that had never before been tried, from 46-year-old Jane Todd Crawford. During the twenty-five-minute operation,

Danville's Ephraim McDowell House, where the Scottish-trained doctor made medical history on Christmas Day, 1809, by removing an ovarian tumor.

performed without anesthesia, the patient sang hymns and quoted scripture. The house, built around 1800 and restored in 1938, contains family portraits by P. H. Davenport and Chester Harding in addition to some McDowell family furnishings, period pieces, and several items, including surgical tools, that belonged to Dr. McDowell. The Apothecary Shop is impressively stocked with a collection of period apothecary glassware, scales from Vienna, and other medical instruments. The trap door in the apothecary leads to the autopsy room downstairs.

LOCATION: 125 South 2d Street, facing Constitution Square. HOURS: March through October: 10–12, 1–4 Monday–Saturday, 2–4 Sunday; November through February: 10–12, 1–4 Tuesday–Saturday, 2–4 Sunday. FEE: Yes. TELEPHONE: 606–236–2804.

Old Centre (West Walnut Street, 606–236–5211), the administration building of **Centre College,** established in 1819, was erected in 1820 by Robert Russel, Jr., at a cost of $10,000. It was used as a

Ephraim McDowell's Apothecary Shop, which adjoined his Danville house, is stocked with nineteenth-century medical items.

Confederate hospital in 1862, after the Battle of Perryville, and as a Union hospital after the Confederate soldiers left the area.

Constitution Square State Shrine

This complex of buildings includes reproductions and original structures important to the history of the state and the local region. The replica buildings include the log courthouse, originally built in 1785 to house the constitutional conventions that preceded Kentucky's statehood. Replicas of the courthouse building, log meetinghouse, and log jail were constructed in 1942. Original structures include the first post office in Kentucky, built prior to 1792, which was moved from its original location on Walnut Street, two blocks away, to the square; the 1817 Flemish bond two-story two-unit row house; and Grayson's Tavern, built in 1785 by Benjamin Grayson, a meeting place for Kentucky constitution delegates.

LOCATION: 105 East Walnut Street. HOURS: 9–5 Daily. FEE: None. TELEPHONE: 606–236–5089.

HARRODSBURG

Harrodsburg, named for its founder, James Harrod, is the oldest permanent settlement in Kentucky. Harrod and thirty-one frontiersmen explored the area in May 1774, and, after participating in the Battle of Point Pleasant, West Virginia, Harrod returned to the site in 1775 to establish the fortified settlement. Also in 1775, Kentucky's first political meeting was held at the fort: George Rogers Clark and James Gabriel Jones were chosen to represent the settlers in the Virginia assembly. When the area was still part of Virginia, Harrodsburg was the site of Kentucky's first law courts, the first religious service, and the first school. The **Dutch Reformed Church,** or **Old Mud Meeting House** (three miles southwest of Harrodsburg on Dry Branch Road), built in 1800, is the first church of that denomination constructed west of the Alleghenies. The **Beaumont Inn** (Routes 127 and 68, 606–734–3381), built at the site of the 1806 Greenville Springs Spa, was constructed in 1845 as a school for women. It has been open as a country inn since 1917. **Morgan Row** (South Chiles Street), built in 1807, is the oldest standing brick rowhouse in Kentucky. The four-unit rowhouse is of Flemish bond construction, with a separate entrance for each unit and with interior fire walls dividing them.

Old Fort Harrod State Park

The fort is an accurate replica, built in 1927, of the Fort Harrod built in 1774. Three corners of the fort are occupied by two-story blockhouses: the Ann McGinty Block House, featuring an unusual log and mortar chimney; the George Rogers Clark headquarters, where Clark planned his Indian campaigns that opened western territories to white settlers; and the James Harrod Block House, home of the fort's founder and leader. A palisade in the fourth corner shelters a spring. Other buildings on the site include approximate replicas of the first school in Kentucky, taught by Jane Coomes, and cabins housing pioneer beds, tools, and other artifacts. Costumed craftspeople demonstrate spinning, weaving, woodworking, and other pioneer activities.

Outside the fort, the park grounds also include the **Pioneer Cemetery.** To the right of the park entrance is the **Lincoln Marriage Temple.** A brick building with stained-glass windows houses the cabin where Abraham Lincoln's parents, Thomas Lincoln and

The reconstructed Old Fort Harrod, originally built to protect the early Kentucky settlers from Indian attacks.

Nancy Hanks, were married on June 12, 1806. The small cabin was moved from its original site near Springfield, Kentucky.

LOCATION: Route 68. HOURS: Mid-March through November: 8:30–5 Daily; December through mid-March: 8–4:30 Tuesday–Sunday. FEE: Yes. TELEPHONE: 606–734–3314.

Mansion Museum

The core of this house, built in 1813 by Felix Matheny, was two stories with a one-story kitchen. Major James Taylor, a representative to the Kentucky constitutional convention in 1792, bought the house in 1830 and completed the construction of the Greek Revival front ell addition in 1836. The museum contains the house's original flooring and woodwork throughout.

In recognition of the divided sympathies in Kentucky during the Civil War, the museum displays portraits and memorabilia of the Kentucky native Abraham Lincoln, the Union president, in the front room on the north side of the house. The Lincoln Room contains a life-size portrait by the Kentucky artist Clifton J. Long, a replica of the Lincoln life mask of his face and hand, and other Lincoln artifacts, including an itemized account of his funeral expenses. On the south side of the house, the exhibit focuses on another native Kentuckian, Jefferson Davis, president of the Confederacy. The room contains portraits of Confederate general Robert E. Lee and Kentuckian John Breckinridge, vice president under James Buchanan, as well as a collection of Civil War weapons and other memorabilia. The museum's collection also includes original furnishings, Indian relics, antique musical instruments, documents and paintings of James Harrod, Daniel Boone, and George Rogers Clark, and the McIntosh Gun Collection.

LOCATION: Lexington Street and Route 127. HOURS: Mid-March through November: 9–5:30 Daily. FEE: Yes. TELEPHONE: 606–734–2927.

SHAKER VILLAGE OF PLEASANT HILL

This Shaker village, the most complete of the extant Shaker communities, is a living-history museum comprising twenty-eight restored buildings on their original sites and nearly 2,500 Shaker items, from tools to furnishings. Now designated a National Historic Landmark, it covers over 2,700 acres. Eighty guest rooms in fifteen buildings are furnished simply with reproductions of Shaker pieces, wooden pegs on the walls instead of closets, handwoven rugs, and curtains. The term "Shaking Quaker" or "Shaker" was originally a derogatory name given to the members of this religious sect because of their frenetic whirling, twirling, shaking movements performed during worship services. The sect eventually accepted the name and used it themselves. The name took on more favorable connotations as these people earned a reputation for their industry, quality craftsmanship, and ingenuity. Well known for their furniture making and successful farming, the Shakers developed a number of practical items, including the wooden clothespin, the flat broom, the circular saw, and packaged garden seeds.

The Shaker Village of Pleasant Hill had its beginnings in 1805 when three missionaries from the parent village in New Lebanon,

The attic of the Centre Family Dwelling, built between 1824 and 1834 in the Shaker Village of Pleasant Hill, contains wooden drawers and pegs for storage.

New York, converted three Mercer County farmers, who accepted the four central tenets of the religion: celibacy, separation from the world, public confession of sins, and the common ownership of property. Notable buildings here include the **Meeting House** (1820) with an elaborate internal truss system; the 1839 **Trustees Office,** with its impressive twin spiral staircases; and the **East Family Dwelling** (1817) and the **West Family Dwelling** (1821), where the celibate men and women lived as brothers and sisters, instead of husbands and wives. The **Centre Family Dwelling** is now a museum illustrating the crafts that sustained the Shakers' daily life. Pleasant Hill grew to a membership of 491 by 1823, its holdings to about 4,500 acres. Orchards were planted, along with crops of wheat, rye, oats, flax, hemp, and broom corn. The Shakers were also successful in the breeding of seeds and livestock. Angus/Hereford crossbreeds and Border Leicester sheep still graze on the grounds of this living-history museum and working farm.

The society declined with the shift from an agrarian society to an industrial one between 1837 and 1857. Both sides in the Civil War depleted the supplies of the pacifist community. In 1910 the remaining twelve Pleasant Hill Shakers deeded their property to a Harrodsburg merchant under the condition that he would take care of them for the remainder of their lives. The last Shaker in the community, Sister Mary Settles, died in 1923.

LOCATION: Route 68, 7 miles northeast of Harrodsburg. HOURS: 9:30–5 Daily. FEE: Yes. TELEPHONE: 606–734–5411.

PERRYVILLE BATTLEFIELD STATE SHRINE

The final Confederate attempt to gain control of Kentucky took place on the afternoon of October 8, 1862, only a few miles from the town of Perryville. This ninety-acre park is located at the northern end of the battleline, where 16,000 Confederates led by General Braxton Bragg charged 22,000 Union soldiers. There were heavy casualties on both sides. At nightfall Federal troops held the field, and General Don Carlos Buell expected the fighting to resume in the morning. Bragg, realizing his troops were outnumbered, began a midnight retreat to Harrodsburg. The Federal forces spent four days treating their wounded, burying their dead, and reorganizing.

Buell's failure to pursue the retreating Confederates cost him his command. The Confederates eluded capture, moving into Tennessee through the Cumberland Gap. A number of monuments and markers stand in the park in memorial to the nearly 3,400 Confederates and over 4,200 Union soldiers who lost their lives in this, the bloodiest battle fought in Kentucky. The **Perryville Battlefield Museum** exhibits battle artifacts.

LOCATION: Off Route 68 and 150, approximately 3 miles west of Perryville. HOURS: *Park:* 9–9 Daily; *Museum:* April through October: 9–5 Daily; November through March: By appointment. FEE: For Museum. TELEPHONE: 606–332–8631.

LOUISVILLE

Located on a curve of the Ohio River across from New Albany and Jeffersonville, Indiana, the original settlement of Louisville was called Falls of the Ohio, named for the natural landmark that interrupted river traffic and thus determined the location of the city. Captain Thomas Bullitt surveyed the land in 1773. George Rogers Clark, the city's founder, was responsible for bringing settlers and constructing a fort between 1778 and 1779. By May 1, 1780, the city's official charter had been signed by Thomas Jefferson and the governor of Virginia. The city was named Louisville for the French king Louis XVI to acknowledge French assistance to America during the Revolution. Between 1781 and 1782, Fort Nelson, named in honor of the governor, was constructed and became the headquarters of General Clark, who led military campaigns against the British and their Indian allies during the Revolutionary War. **Nelson Park** (7th and Main streets) is the site where Fort Nelson once stood.

The city grew into a river port that profited immeasurably by the invention of the steamboat in the early nineteenth century. The **Belle of Louisville** (4th Street and River Road, 502–625–2355), a 1914 steam-powered stern-wheeler with its original engines, is one of the few remaining traditional Mississippi River steamboats still in operation. The Portland Canal, completed in 1830, opened Ohio River traffic from Pittsburgh to the Mississippi. In the late 1850s, the completion of the Louisville & Nashville Railroad also contributed to Louisville's success as a commercial center. Its key location made it a valuable site for the Union army, which maintained military head-

quarters and a supply depot there throughout the Civil War. After the war, Louisville had to struggle to reestablish trade with the South. Louisville survived the disastrous fire of 1840, tornado of 1890, and flood of 1937. It is the largest city in Kentucky, with five historic districts of houses and commercial buildings. Notable buildings downtown include the **Jefferson County Courthouse** (West Jefferson Street, between South 5th and 6th streets), the work of Gideon Shryock, architect of the Old State Capitol in Frankfort. The **Seelbach Hotel** (500 Fourth Avenue, 502–585–3200) has in its marble lobby a number of historical murals of pioneer life featuring an Indian, a farmer, a slave, and a whiskey distiller, as well as important people in the history of Kentucky—Colonel Henderson, Daniel Boone, and George Rogers Clark—painted by Arthur Thomas in 1904; the hotel's Rathskeller restaurant is tiled completely in Rookwood pottery. The **Bank of Louisville** building (320 West Main Street), now occupied by the Actor's Theatre of Louisville, was long attributed to Shryock. A splendid, small Greek Revival structure, it was designed in 1834 by James Dakin and completed in 1837.

Completed in 1852, the **Cathedral of the Assumption** (443 South 5th Street, 502–587–1354) was constructed of brick trimmed with limestone in the Gothic Revival style to designs by William Kelly. The 287-foot spire holds a cross twenty-four feet in height. The cathedral has leaded stained-glass windows and a 4,500-pound bell given to the church by the archbishop of Mexico.

Brennan House

This preserved 1868 Victorian townhouse in the Italianate style has original furnishings of the Brennan family, who lived here from 1884 to 1969. The house is owned and operated by the Filson Club. Thomas Brennan, an Irish immigrant machinist, created and presided over Brennan and Co., manufacturers of seed-drilling equipment. Notable furnishings include the ornately carved solid walnut Centennial bedroom suite, which won first prize in the 1876 Centennial exhibition in Philadelphia. The Brennans' collection of antiques, art, and curios reflect the changing tastes of a family during their eighty years of travel and occupation of the same house. There are family portraits throughout the house, a

OPPOSITE: *A bronze statue of Thomas Jefferson by Moses Ezekiel stands in front of Louisville's Jefferson County Courthouse.*

hand-carved Bedford limestone mantel in the dining room, and a
Bohemian glass chandelier.

LOCATION: 631 South 5th Street. HOURS: 10–3:30 Monday,
Wednesday, and Friday; 1–3:30 Saturday. FEE: Yes. TELEPHONE:
502–584–7425.

J. B. Speed Art Museum

Kentucky's largest and oldest art museum was designed by Arthur
Loomis and completed in 1927. The building is a memorial to James
Breckinridge Speed of Louisville. The Preston Pope Satterwhite addition features an oak-paneled Elizabethan Renaissance hall with suits
of armor and other artifacts from The Grange in Devon, England.

Oakland House and Race Course (detail), as painted in 1840 by Robert Brammer
and Augustus A. Von Smith. Patrons of the Louisville race course stayed in Oakland
House.

The museum also houses the works of Rembrandt, Rubens, Tiepolo, Monet, Picasso, and other artists.

LOCATION: 2035 South 3d Street. HOURS: 10–4 Tuesday–Saturday, 1–5 Sunday. FEE: Yes. TELEPHONE: 502–636–2893.

Churchill Downs (700 Central Avenue, 502–636–3541) was the site of the first Kentucky Derby in May 1875. The race is held here annually on the first Saturday in May. Churchill Downs covers over 150 acres on a site three miles south of downtown. The grandstand's Edwardian spires date from 1895. Adjacent to Churchill Downs, the **Kentucky Derby Museum** (704 Central Avenue, 502–637–1111) is a showcase for memorabilia and trophies concerning thoroughbred horse racing. A central attraction of the museum is the 360-degree multi-image show of a Derby race, with the viewer in the center of the oval screen.

The Filson Club

The Filson Club, a historical society, was named for Kentucky's first historian and established in 1884. John Filson began his biography of frontiersman Daniel Boone, published in 1784, stating "Curiosity is natural to the soul of man, and objects have a power-ful influence on our affections," and established the credo of the society that would later bear his name. The first club, of nine Louisville gentlemen, established the traditions of reading a paper on Kentucky history at each meeting, drinking crab-apple cider, and smoking Filson cigars. The name Filson for a time took on the connotations of high quality, like the Ritz, and it appeared as part of a number of product names. The Filson Club is now located in the Beaux-Arts Ferguson Mansion (1905). The club maintains a large collection of manuscripts concerning Kentucky history, over 1 million documents, with its greatest strength in the area of pio-neer and Civil War history. The Filson Collection includes the Shaker manuscripts, letters, account books, and other materials necessary to establish the authenticity of the museum/farm at Pleasant Hill, Kentucky. There is also a 50,000-item collection of photographs and prints. **The Filson Club Museum** is housed in a former carriage house. A rare piece on display is a Rocky Mountain ram horn brought back from the expedition of Lewis

and Clark. The museum also displays part of its large collection of Rogers Clark Ballard Thruston's early (ca. 1884) photographs of Appalachia; the tree trunk inscribed by Daniel Boone with "D. Boone kill a bar 1803"; Chester Harding's famous portrait of Daniel Boone; one of the oldest copper stills in existence; a textile collection from the 1880s–1920s; and a collection of nineteenth-century jewelry. Because of a lack of display space, much of the Filson Club's holdings are in storage, and the exhibits are changed several times a year.

LOCATION: 1310 South 3d Street. HOURS: 10–4 Monday–Friday, 9–12 Saturday. FEE: None. TELEPHONE: 502–635–5083.

Locust Grove

The retirement home of General George Rogers Clark, western military leader of the American Revolution and founder of Louisville, has been authentically restored to its ca. 1790 appearance. Clark lived here the last nine years of his life with his sister, Lucy, and her husband, Major William Croghan, from 1809 to 1818. The brick residence has two-and-a-half stories, a reconstructed full-length porch with slender Doric columns, and pilasters framing the door. The interior woodwork is mostly solid walnut. Locust Grove had many famous visitors, including Aaron Burr, John James Audubon, Cassius Marcellus Clay, and three U.S. presidents: James Monroe, Andrew Jackson, and Zachary Taylor. William Clark, General Clark's youngest brother, returned to Locust Grove from his expedition to the Pacific with his partner Meriwether Lewis.

LOCATION: 561 Blankenbaker Lane. HOURS: 10–4:30 Monday –Saturday, 1:30–4:30 Sunday. FEE: Yes. TELEPHONE: 502–897–9845.

Farmington

Built in 1810 as the home of John and Lucy Fry Speed, this house is Jeffersonian in its design, especially in its symmetry, two octagonal rooms, and the narrow, steep, hidden interior staircase, only eighteen inches wide and enclosed to conserve heat and space. The fourteen-room house has three fanlighted windows over its doors, original blue ash floors, and original woodwork of yellow poplar. The 1840 inventory was used to furnish the house. Abraham

OPPOSITE: *Churchill Downs, where the mile-and-a-quarter Kentucky Derby takes place each May. The first Derby took place on the track's opening day, May 17, 1875.*

Lincoln visited the house for about three weeks in August 1841, as a guest of the second-eldest son, Joshua. On exhibit is a copy of Lincoln's four-page letter thanking the family.

LOCATION: 3033 Bardstown Road, just off the intersection of Bardstown Road and Watterson Expressway (Route I-264). HOURS: 10–4:30 Monday–Saturday, 1:30–4:30 Sunday. FEE: Yes. TELEPHONE: 502-452-9920.

Located within the **Zachary Taylor National Cemetery** (4701 Brownsboro Road, 502–893–3852) are the graves of fifty members of the Taylor family. Zachary Taylor and his wife, Margaret Smith Taylor, are interred in a limestone mausoleum of classical Roman design. Some thirty feet from the mausoleum stands a fifty-foot granite shaft surmounted by a statue of President Taylor, erected in 1883 by the state of Kentucky. The twelfth U.S. president, Taylor was born on November 24, 1784 in Virginia, shortly before his parents moved to Kentucky. He fought in the War of 1812, the Black Hawk War, and the Florida Wars with the Seminole, and was an outstanding general in the Mexican War. With more military than political experience, he was elected to the presidency in 1848, defeating former president Martin Van Buren. He died of typhus on July 9, 1850, after serving only sixteen months in office.

Theodore Scowden designed and built the city of Louisville's first water system, which began operation in 1860. The engine house and boiler room were housed in a brick, two-story main block building with one-story wings. The center pavilion resembles a temple, with a Corinthian portico. In front of the waterworks building stands the 169-foot **Louisville Water Tower** (3005 Upper River Road at Zorn Avenue, 502–896–2146) enclosing a water standpipe, surrounded by a Corinthian colonnade in the manner of a Roman triumphal column. The complex was rebuilt after a tornado struck it in 1890. The building now houses the offices and exhibits of the Louisville Water Tower Art Association.

FORT KNOX

South of Louisville on Route 31W/60, the U.S. military reservation Fort Knox covers over 100,000 acres. Active since 1918, Fort Knox

OPPOSITE: *The Louisville Water Tower, part of River Pumping Station Number One, was first constructed in 1860 and completely rebuilt after a tornado destoyed it in 1890.*

was named for Henry Knox, a Revolutionary War general and first secretary of war. It is the site of the U.S. Army Armor Center as well as the **U.S. Gold Depository** (Gold Vault Road). In 1936 the Treasury Department built the Gold Bullion Depository building. Surrounded by a high iron fence, a great part of the U.S. gold reserve, in standard mint bars of mined gold or melted gold coin, is stored here in vaults, where a number of high-security measures are in constant operation. No tours of the interior are allowed, but the two-story bullion depository, constructed of steel, concrete, and granite, may be viewed from outside. The **Patton Museum of Cavalry and Armor** (Keyes Park, off Route 31W, 502–624–3812) features many personal items of the controversial World War II general, George S. Patton, Jr., as well as historic tanks and other armored fighting vehicles. Uniforms, weapons, and other military equipment from the Revolutionary War to Vietnam are also on display.

Beside Freeman Lake, about two miles north of Elizabethtown off Route 31W, the **Lincoln Heritage House** (502–765–4941) is the site of two pioneer log cabins, built between 1789 and 1805. Thomas Lincoln, Abraham Lincoln's father, who lived in Hardin County, did the joinery work on the larger of the two.

HODGENVILLE

The seat of Larue County is the site of a farm, mill, and tavern that were owned and operated by Robert Hodgen in the 1790s. His tavern guests in 1797 included French botanist André Michaux and Louis-Philippe. After Hodgen died in 1810, the settlement that had grown up around his property was named for him.

Abraham Lincoln Birthplace National Historic Site

On February 12, 1809, Abraham Lincoln was born in a one-room log cabin on this site. The restored cabin, thought to be part of the original, is enclosed in a granite and marble Memorial Building, designed by John Russell Pope and completed in 1911. A broad stone stairway leads to the entrance, marked by six Doric granite columns and the words "With Malice Toward None and Charity for All" engraved above. Sinking Spring, located on the site and still producing water, was used by the Lincoln family when they lived here between 1808 and 1811. When Abraham was 2 years old, the

The log cabin thought to be Abraham Lincoln's birthplace is now encased in a memorial designed by John Russell Pope. It was constructed with funds raised by the Lincoln Farm Association, a group that included Mark Twain, William Jennings Bryan, and Samuel Gompers as members.

family relocated to **Knob Creek Farm** (Route 31E, eight miles east of Hodgenville, 502–549–3741), where they lived until moving to Indiana when Abraham Lincoln was about seven.

> LOCATION: 3 miles south of Hodgenville on Route 31E. HOURS: June through August: 8–6 Daily; September through June: 8–4:45 Daily. FEE: None. TELEPHONE: 502–358–3874.

The **Maker's Mark Distillery** (Route 52E, Loretto, 502–865–2881) began operation in 1889, built on the foundation of a water-powered gristmill on the site. A visitor center is housed in the restored 1840s home of the former resident distiller. The restored Quart House is where local residents brought empty quart jars to be filled with whiskey. Tours of the distillery trace the process of whiskey making.

In 1812, about six miles from the present site of the **Loretto Motherhouse** (Route 152, north of Loretto, 502–865–5811), Sister Mary Rhodes and two other women formed one of the first religious orders of American women, the first west of the Allegheny Mountains and north of the French and Spanish settlements. In

1824 the convent had added so many members that it needed a new home, so the move was made to Saint Stephen's farm, former home of the co-founder of Roman Catholicism in Kentucky. In 1860 a brick convent was constructed to replace the one destroyed by fire.

Located on land originally settled by Thomas Lincoln's family, the **Lincoln Homestead State Park** (off Route 528 north of Springfield, 606–336–7461) has the original cabin where Lincoln's mother, Nancy Hanks, lived during her courtship with Thomas Lincoln. There is also a reproduction of the 1782 cabin where Thomas Lincoln grew up, built on its original site, and replicas of blacksmith and woodworking shops.

BARDSTOWN

Incorporated in 1778, Bardstown is one of Kentucky's oldest cities, and was the home of John Fitch, one of the inventors of the steamboat, who died here in 1798. A monument to him and his work stands on the Courthouse Square. The **Saint Joseph Proto-Cathedral**

The container room in the Oscar Getz Museum of Whiskey History displays a variety of bottles, barrels, and jugs, along with a barrel scale and a model of a warehouse interior.

A Kentucky whiskey distillery, ca. 1900.

(310 West Stephen Foster Avenue), the first Catholic cathedral west of the Alleghenies in the United States, was begun in 1816, dedicated in 1819, and completed in 1825. Designed by John Rogers of Baltimore, it was built from local materials: poplar trees, covered with plaster, form the columns of the pedimented Ionic portico. The bricks were made of native clay and baked on the site. Nearby limestone cliffs supplied the foundation stone and the altar. Hardware was forged by local blacksmiths. When the seat of the Roman Catholic see was relocated from Bardstown to Louisville, the church became known as the "proto" (or first) cathedral. Completed ca. 1826–1839, **Spalding Hall** (114 North 5th Street, 502–348–2999) was originally part of Saint Joseph College. Still owned by the Catholic church, the building now houses two museums: The **Bardstown Historical Museum,** which opened in 1973, exhibits items relating to local history, Civil War weapons, gifts of French kings Louis-Philippe and Charles X, Jesse James's hat, and Indian relics. The **Oscar Getz Museum of Whiskey History,** which opened in 1984, contains a

large collection of artifacts relating to American whiskey distillation. Said to be the oldest inn in continuous operation west of the Alleghenies and north of the Gulf Coast, the **Old Talbott Tavern** (107 West Stephen Foster Avenue, 502–348–3494) was built around 1800 as a stagecoach stop. General George Rogers Clark stored provisions in the cellar during the Revolution. Guests included Daniel Boone, Jesse James, Abraham Lincoln and his family, John J. Audubon, and Stephen Foster. A favorite story of the innkeepers is that Louis-Philippe, later king of France, stayed here during his exile. Wall murals on the second floor may have been painted by one of Louis-Philippe's brothers during their stay. **The Mansion** (1003 North Street, 502–348–2586) is a ten-room Greek Revival mansion just outside of Bardstown. According to local legend, the Confederate raider John Hunt Morgan hid here after escaping from prison in Ohio. It is also said to be the site where the first Confederate flag was raised in Kentucky. The house is privately owned but open by appointment.

My Old Kentucky Home

The home that inspired Stephen Foster's song is a stately late Federal mansion, completed around 1818 by Judge John Rowan. Rowan devised a number of ways to make symbolic use of the number of original American states—thirteen—in his home. He built ceilings thirteen feet high and Flemish bond brick walls thirteen inches thick. There are thirteen windows on the front of the structure, thirteen steps in each flight, and thirteen railings at each stair landing. Stephen Foster visited his cousins here in 1852 and soon afterward wrote the famous ballad. The house, part of a 255-acre state park, contains many original family furnishings, including such unusual items as a large square crib made for family twins and the 1835 piano made of rosewood with mother-of-pearl keys. Outside buildings include a carriage house and a smokehouse as well as a kitchen.

LOCATION: Route 150, 2 miles off the Blue Grass Parkway. HOURS: January through February: 9–5 Tuesday–Sunday; March through May: 9–5 Daily; June through September: 8–7:30 Daily; October through December: 9–5 Daily. FEE: Yes. TELEPHONE: 502–348–3502.

OPPOSITE: *Bardstown plantation house Federal Hill was the inspiration for Stephen Foster's ballad "My Old Kentucky Home." Foster visited his cousins here in 1852.*

T H E   P E N N Y R O Y A L

Named for the herb, a variety of mint, this region of Kentucky called
the Pennyroyal, or Pennyrile, includes the watersheds of the Green,
Cumberland, and Lower Ohio rivers. Its rather vague boundaries
extend west from the southern Appalachian Mountain region of the
state, south and west of the Bluegrass, to the Ohio River on the
north, roughly to the Land Between the Lakes in southwest
Kentucky, to the state boundary between Kentucky and Tennessee.
The landscape of this plateau region reflects its Mississippian period
history,.when shallow seas covered the surface and left behind varied limestone formations and caves. Kentucky has roughly 3,000
caves, including the longest explored system in the world,
Mammoth Cave. (Its closest rivals are the second-longest cave,
Optimisticeskaja, in the USSR, and the third-longest, Holloch H–hle
in Switzerland.) In October 1981 the United Nations Educational,
Scientific, and Cultural Organization (UNESCO) agreed to name
Mammoth Cave National Park to its list of World Heritage Sites, sites
identified as cultural and natural monuments important to the heritage of all peoples of the world.

SOMERSET

This town, just west of the Cumberland Mountains, was established
as the Pulaski County seat in 1801. West of Somerset, off Route 80,
are **Zollicoffer Park** and **Logan's Cross Roads National Cemetery,**
near the site where Confederate general Felix K. Zollicoffer, who led
the attack, was killed at the Battle of Logan's Cross Roads on
January 19–20, 1862. Zollicoffer's death started a panic among the
southern troops and began the retreat that turned into a rout at the
hands of the Union forces commanded by General George H.
Thomas at this battle (also known as the Battle of Mill Springs).

STEARNS

This turn-of-the-century coal company town has been preserved
with little change. The **Stearns Museum** (1 Henderson Street,
606–376–5730) has exhibits on the railroad, coal mines, sawmills,
and local history. From Stearns the **Big South Fork Scenic Railway**
(Route 92, 606–376–5330) offers a two-hour eleven-mile round-trip
train ride, May through October, descending 600 feet into the

rugged gorge cut by the Big South Fork of the Cumberland River. The train travels through a tunnel 265 feet long, completed in 1902, and past mining camps established in the early 1900s.

Mill Springs Park (Route 1275, off Route 90), ten miles northeast of Monticello, features an 1877 mill with a forty-foot overshot water-wheel, which is still in operation. Built in 1804 and used as a church until 1885, the **Old Mulkey Meeting House** (two miles south of Tompkinsville on Route 1446, 502–487–8481) is the oldest log meet-inghouse in the state. The building has a gabled roof, large interior cross beams, and peg-leg benches. Heat was provided by bags containing heated stones. The cemetery includes the grave of Daniel Boone's sister Hannah.

MAMMOTH CAVE

Humans discovered Mammoth Cave at least 4,000 years ago and left evidence of activities from 2500 B.C. to the year of Christ's birth. Low humidity, sulfate salts, and the cave's constant temperature of 54

Mammoth Cave, an underground system that extends for more than 300 miles, has been used for weddings, Shakespearean performances, concerts, and was also the site of an experimental tuberculosis hospital. OVERLEAF: *Winter at Lake Cumberland, formed by a widening of the Cumberland River, in southern Kentucky.*

degrees Fahrenheit preserved many artifacts, such as clothing and tools. Human bones, broken and bearing marks like those made on animal bones, suggest the possibility that these people practiced cannibalism. Soot from their torches marks the walls from the natural entrances of Mammoth Cave and Salts Cave to narrow passageways that lead two-and-a-half miles into the caves. After the caves were abandoned around the time of Christ's birth, they remained apparently undisturbed until around 1800.

The date of the rediscovery of Mammoth Cave is in dispute. A hunter named Houchin may have found the entrance about 1797 when chasing a bear. A Warren County survey book provides the first written reference to Mammoth Cave in an entry dated August 18, 1798. During the War of 1812, the owners of Mammoth Cave, Hyman Gratz and Charles Wilkins, made their living from the sale of saltpeter, used for curing meat and for the manufacture of gunpowder. In 1838 Mammoth Cave was developed further as a tourist attraction when Franklin Gorin brought Stephen Bishop, a 17-year-old black slave, to the cave to explore it and serve as a tour guide. Two other slaves, Matt and Nick Bransford, succeeded Bishop after his death in 1859 and began a tradition, which continues today, of passing down knowledge in a direct line to each succeeding generation of tour guides. The cave, part of a 52,000-acre national park, contains approximately 300 miles of explored territory on five levels. Experts speculate that there may be as many as 500 miles of passageways still unexplored. It is the longest cave system known in the world. The Historic Cave Tour, one of ten tours of varying length, winds down 138 stairs and through passages past prehistoric artifacts left by ancient peoples; tools, ashes, wooden vats, and other remains of the 1812 saltpeter mining operation; and a demonstration of torch throwing to illustrate how visitors before the installation of electric lights would have viewed the darkest recesses of large chambers.

LOCATION: Off Route I-65 between Louisville and Nashville. HOURS: *Visitor Center:* June through August: 7:30–7 Daily; September through May: 8–5:30 Daily. *Tours:* July through August: 8:30–5, September through June: 9–4 Daily. FEE: Yes. TELEPHONE: 502-758-2251.

Cave City, Horse Cave, and Park City form a triangle south of Mammoth Cave. The area's main attractions are privately owned caves. In **Cave City,** the **Crystal Onyx Cave** (Route 90, 502–773–2359) contains beautiful onyx formations and a working archaeological site, where human remains from around 680 B.C. have been discovered. **Mammoth Onyx Cave** and **Kentucky Buffalo Park** (Route 218, off Route I-65, Horse Cave, 502–786–2634) contains many high-ceilinged chambers featuring onyx of many hues and formations resembling flowers, trees, and human features. The park also features a large herd of American buffalo in a natural setting.

Southeast of the approach to Mammoth Cave in **Park City** is **Kentucky Diamond Caverns** (one mile north on Route 255, off Route I-65, 502–749–2891), one of the most beautiful in the area. The **Jesse James Cave** (one mile west of Route 31W, off Route I-65, 502–749–4101) was reputedly a hideout for Jesse James and his gang. In 1963 a 6,000-year-old Indian burial ground was also discovered in the cave.

BOWLING GREEN

Incorporated in 1798, the city's name purportedly comes from the sport of its earliest settlers, George and Robert Moore, who enjoyed a form of lawn bowling, rolling hand-carved wooden balls across the green meadows. During the Civil War, both Union and Confederate troops occupied Bowling Green, because of its strategic location on the Barren River and along highways and railway lines. The city served as the Confederate capital of Kentucky. Bowling Green has five historic areas. The Downtown Commercial Historic District features commercial, religious, and government structures dating from 1818 to 1940. The Saint Joseph Historic District, a residential area from the late nineteenth and early twentieth centuries, is named for **Saint Joseph's Catholic Church** (434 Church Street), at its center. Constructed between 1870 and 1884 in the German Romanesque style, it has recently been restored. Finally, the **Brinton B. Davis Thematic Resource,** on the Western Kentucky University campus, includes eleven structures designed by Davis, a Louisville architect, between 1910 and 1937.

Riverview–The Hobson House

Riverview, the home of Colonel Atwood Gaines and Juliet Van Meter Hobson, was begun in 1857, interrupted by the Civil War, and then completed in 1872. Only the raised stone basement was completed

The Italianate Riverview was built by Colonel and Mrs. Atwood Games Hobson between 1857 and 1872, when the style was very popular in Bowling Green. OVER-LEAF: *The ceiling of Riverview's parlor was frescoed by a French painter, who lived in the house with the Hobson family for a year while the work was completed.*

when the war began, and Hobson, a Union sympathizer, offered the structure for use as a Confederate munitions depot rather than see it destroyed. The Italianate mansion's furnishings are principally Victorian, appropriate to the period from 1860 to 1890. The double parlors downstairs have frescoed ceilings, restored in 1973 to their original design, and pocket doors with tall glass panels. A staircase leads to the second-floor landing, where an unusual circular opening reveals a view of the interior of the cupola. A circular staircase leads to a landing inside the cupola from which there is an impressive view of the countryside and the Barren River.

LOCATION: 1100 West Main Street in Hobson Grove Park. HOURS: 10–12, 1–5 Tuesday–Saturday, 1–5 Sunday. FEE: Yes. TELEPHONE: 502–843–5565.

SHAKERTOWN

Shakertown was the last Shaker village in Kentucky. The South Union group was founded in 1807 by Issachar Bates to encourage the westward spread of Shaker beliefs. The Shaker village at South Union eventually included 6,000 acres of land and over 150 buildings. Membership peaked at about 350 between 1840 and 1860. Important commercial industries were the sale of packaged garden seeds and "sweetmeats," or fruit preserves. South Union Shakers were also known for their handmade silk, not for sale to outsiders but used within the community and given as gifts to Shakers in other villages. The society was the last western Shaker colony to disband, in 1922, when only nine members remained.

The hall in Shakertown's Centre House has two doorways leading to a meeting room beyond, one for each of the sexes. OPPOSITE: *The 1824 Centre Family Dwelling House now houses the Shaker Museum.*

A nonprofit organization currently owns four of the six remaining buildings. **The Shaker Tavern** (Route 73, 502–542–6801), built in 1869, provides a sharp contrast to the simplicity of other Shaker buildings with its columned facade and ornate interior staircase. Two privately owned structures may be viewed from the road: **The Ministry's Shop,** currently a private residence, was built in 1847 as a workshop space and living quarters. **The Sister's Shop,** owned by Saint Mark's Monastery, was built in 1854 for use by the Shaker women of the community.

The Centre Family Dwelling House, a forty-room, two-and-a-half-story brick building completed in 1824, houses the **Shaker Museum** (Route 68/80, 502–542–4167). Its double room doors and staircases illustrate the Shaker practice of separating the sexes. Along the walls are strips of wooden pegs (for hanging anything from clothes and tools to chairs not in use) and built-in cabinets. The museum houses a collection of distinctively western Shaker furniture, which differs from that made elsewhere in that it is a little more ornate. Exhibits demonstrate Shaker skills in weaving, broom making, and production of herbal and patent medicines. Original artifacts include Shaker tools, oval boxes, baskets, silk, and linen, as well as many furnishings.

Russellville was the home of the parents of the outlaw Jesse James, and the site of a bank robbery by the James gang. Markers at the **Southern Deposit Bank** (ca. 1810) on the corner of 6th and Main streets tell of the $9,000 holdup on March 20, 1868. Nimrod Long, the only bank officer present during the holdup, suffered a gunshot wound. Ironically, Long had helped the outlaw's father, Robert James, through college. The elder James was a Baptist minister.

JEFFERSON DAVIS
MONUMENT STATE SHRINE

The Jefferson Davis monument, an obelisk constructed in 1924 at a cost of $200,000 (paid for by the United Daughters of the Confederacy) commemorates the birth of Jefferson Davis, president of the Confederacy, in Fairview (then known as Davisburg) on June 3, 1808. It is 351 feet in height; an elevator inside the monument carries visitors approximately 300 feet up for a panoramic view of the area. At the base of the monument is a twenty-foot-square room featuring Frederick Hibbard's life-size bas-relief sculpture of Jefferson Davis. Davis's original birthplace was torn down in the spring of 1886 to clear the site for the Bethel Baptist Church. Davis donated the property for the church and dedicated the building to his mother, Jane Cook Davis. The birthplace materials were shipped to Nashville and reassembled in Centennial Park for the Tennessee Centennial Exposition of 1897. The materials were lost after being shipped to Richmond, Virginia.

LOCATION: Route 68/80, 10 miles east of Hopkinsville. HOURS: May through October: 9–5 Monday–Sunday. FEE: Yes. TELEPHONE: 502–886–1765.

HOPKINSVILLE

Housed in the 1914 post office building, the **Pennyroyal Area Museum** (217 East 9th Street) exhibits early pioneer artifacts such as clothing, tools, and furniture. Also on display are items connected with tobacco, the railroad, the Civil War, Jefferson Davis, the Hopkinsville-born clairvoyant Edgar Cayce, and the Cherokee Trail of Tears. Between 1838 and 1839, thousands of Cherokee Indians camped near Hopkinsville during their forced removal from their eastern homelands to the Indian Territory in Oklahoma. Chiefs Whitepath and Fly Smith died in Hopkinsville and are buried at the edge of the local campground within the city limits.

The **Adsmore Museum** (304 North Jefferson Street, Princeton, 502–365–3114) is a restored house built in 1857 with a Corinthian portico added in the early 1900s. The house has been restored to the late-Victorian era, with furnishings and personal items.

THE JACKSON PURCHASE

The westernmost portion of Kentucky, bounded by the Land Between the Lakes, the Ohio and Mississippi rivers, and the Tennessee state line, called "the Purchase," was bought from the Chickasaw Indians on October 19, 1818, in a settlement negotiated by General Andrew Jackson and Kentucky governor Isaac Shelby. The Indians then left this land, which had been given originally to George Rogers Clark in 1795 as a land grant for military service. The Purchase became the property of William Clark, George's brother, of the famed Lewis and Clark expedition, in 1827.

The people of this relatively flat area with fertile farmlands traditionally relied on river transportation and commerce as well as on the Illinois Central Railroad. This area was the final portion of Kentucky to be opened for settlement, so few buildings here were constructed before the 1820s and 1830s. The Tennessee Valley Authority's Land Between the Lakes Recreation Area has significantly displaced the population of this region, and according to the Kentucky Heritage Council, "no area of Kentucky has lost more of its early heritage to Federal projects than this area."

Whitehaven, originally a simple farmhouse built in the 1860s, was extensively remodeled between 1903 and 1908 by the Paducah architect A. L. Lassiter, who added the portico and Corinthian columns.

PADUCAH

In 1827, for the sum of five dollars, General William Clark purchased 37,000 acres of western Kentucky that had been part of the Revolutionary War land grant to his brother George. William Clark laid out the town in 1827 and named the site Paducah for his Chickasaw friend Chief Paduke. By 1856 Paducah had become a city, with proximity to four navigable rivers. Its location also made it a strategic port during the Civil War. Union general Ulysses S. Grant began military occupation of Paducah in September 1861, and throughout the war the city was an important Union supply depot.William Clark platted South 2d Street as a market area when he laid out the town. Part of the present Market House, built in 1905 at a cost of $25,000, is occupied by the **Market House Museum** (South 2d Street and Broadway, 502–443–7759). Its chief exhibit is the complete interior of the 1877 L. S. DuBois drugstore. Other exhibits include memorabilia of Paducah residents Alben W. Barkley and the writer Irvin S. Cobb; the city's first motorized fire engine, a 1913 LaFrance; and a life-size wooden carving of Henry Clay, done in the 1850s by a Paducah teenager.

Whitehaven (exit 7 off Route I-24, 502–554-2077), a two-story mansion constructed in the 1860s, houses a welcome center for tourists. The house maintains a collection of furnishings from 1903–1910, as well as two rooms of former vice president Alben W. Barkley memorabilia, including his collections of walking canes and senatorial shaving mugs, the teakwood desk and hand-carved chair presented to him by the president of the Philippines, his congressional rolltop desk, 1948 inaugural Bible and tuxedo, and a magnifying device that allowed him to read his speeches without the aid of glasses. Barkley's Greek Revival home in Paducah, where he lived from 1937 to 1956, was built in 1859 by Colonel Quintus Quincy Quigley. The house is privately owned but visible from the road, about one-and-a-half miles from Whitehaven on Route 62 (540 Alben Barkley Drive). Housed in the 1852 Greek Revival and Italianate home of Paducah mayor David A. Yeiser, the **Alben W. Barkley Museum** (Madison and 6th streets, 502–444-9356) preserves furnishings, books, and memorabilia of Alben W. Barkley, the state legislator, U.S. senator, and thirty-fifth U.S. vice president, as well as a collection of period furnishings, toys, a Belgium ceramic-tile cook stove, and photographs of leaders and businessmen from Paducah and McCracken County. The museum is owned by the schoolchildren of Paducah as a project of their Junior Historian groups.

WICKLIFFE MOUNDS

Located on the steep river bluffs overlooking the Mississippi River floodplain, Wickliffe Mounds is the site of a Middle Mississippian prehistoric community that occupied the area from A.D. 1000–1350. The first researcher to publish a description of the site (1888) was Robert Loughridge. In 1932 Colonel Fain White King, an amateur archaeologist and entrepreneur, purchased the site and opened it to the public as a curiosity while continuing excavations. None of King's field records survive. By 1945, when he donated the site to Western Baptist Hospital, King had done enough relic collecting to frustrate and distress generations of archaeologists. In 1984 professional archaeological study was resumed by the Wickliffe Mounds Research Center. Buildings cover three open excavation sites. The Lifeways Building has artifacts including pottery and stone tools. The Architecture Building reveals the posthole patterns of original structures built on the site.

LOCATION: North of junction of Route 51/60/62. HOURS: March through November: 9–4:30 Daily. FEE: Yes. TELEPHONE: 502–335–3681.

COLUMBUS-BELMONT CIVIL WAR STATE PARK

The park is the site of the northernmost Confederate fortification on the Mississippi, Fort de Russey, established at Columbus by General Leonidas Polk in September 1861. Occupied by 12,000 to 19,000 soldiers from September 1861 through the winter of 1862, the area was protected by earthwork forts, trenches, and 140 pieces of heavy artillery, mostly thirty-two- and sixty-four-pound guns, arranged at different levels from slightly above the water to the top of the 200-foot bluff. General Ulysses S. Grant landed his Union forces on the Missouri side of the Mississippi on November 7, 1861, and burned the Confederate camp at Belmont, but Polk's army forced Grant to retreat. Grant then moved south by way of the Tennessee and the Cumberland rivers.most unusual of the defenses was a two-ton deep-sea anchor and chain stretched across the river. The chain could be allowed to sink when Confederate supplies were arriving and pulled taut to prevent Union gunboats were advancing southward down the Mississippi. Stretched from the bluff at Columbus to two sycamore trees on the Missouri side of the river, the chain had links weighing about twenty pounds each. Eventually, however, the weight of the mile-long chain combined with the river current caused the chain to break near the Kentucky shore. This broken portion of the chain and the anchor are displayed in the park.in the park is an 1840s two-story farmhouse used first by the Confederates as a hospital from September 1861 to March 1862 and then by the Union army until 1865. Since 1935 when the federal government remodeled the interior, it has been used as the Park Museum, which houses items discovered in the trenches, firearms, cannonballs, and a Civil War diorama of the Battle of Belmont.

LOCATION: Approximately 10 miles southwest of Bardwell on Route 123S/80W. HOURS: April through October: *Park:* 7 AM–9 PM Daily; *Museum:* 9–5 Daily; November through March: 9–5 Saturday –Sunday. FEE: Yes. TELEPHONE: 502–677–2327.

HICKMAN

Samuel Clemens, in his *Life on the Mississippi,* called this town one of the most beautiful towns along the Mississippi River. The seat of Fulton County, Hickman is built on different levels with the business district closest to the water. On the bluff above, allowing a fine view of the river, are the residential areas, including some homes dating to 1850s; the **Fulton County Courthouse** (Moulton and Wellington streets), built 1906; schools and churches, the oldest of which is the **Episcopal Church** (Buchanan Street), built in the 1840s.

The town of **Murray** claims as one of its most famous citizens Nathan B. Stubblefield who, in 1892, three years before Marconi, demonstrated radio principles. Murray is also home to **Murray State University,** and its **Wraather–West Kentucky Museum** (502–762–4771), a regional history museum with exhibits illustrating the cultural, social, and economic development of the area.

WEST VIRGINIA

OPPOSITE: *The West Virginia Governor's Mansion in Charleston, designed in the Colonial Revival style by Walter F. Martens and completed in 1925.*

The history of West Virginia has been shaped by its mountains. Prior to the white man's arrival in the early eighteenth century, several Indian tribes (Shawnee, Delaware, Iroquois) shared the land as hunting grounds but found these uplands not as inviting for year-round habitation as the more fertile and benign valleys around them. Only a few footpaths, used by the Indians for trading, hunting, and waging war, wound through the otherwise unbroken forest. The first white explorers who journeyed into the region were searching for an outlet to the "South Sea" but found instead peaks of endless green. Said Robert Fallam in 1671, "It was a pleasing tho' dreadful sight to see mountains and Hills as if piled one upon another." The first permanent settler in what is now West Virginia was Morgan Morgan, a Welshman who lived in Delaware before moving west. In 1728 he settled on a thousand-acre tract along Mill Creek near present-day Bunker Hill. As increasing numbers of settlers trickled across the mountains, clashes with the Indians were inevitable. Almost every European community began as a cluster of homes near a stockade, and few areas escaped bloodshed during the frontier years of the eighteenth century. At times the settlers were victims of their own ignorance, as in 1753, when Robert Files built his cabin on the Seneca War Trail, a mistake that cost him his life.

Both sides committed their share of atrocities. In 1774 James Logan, a Mingo leader friendly to whites, returned home to find his entire family massacred. "I had . . . thought to live with you," Logan said bitterly. "Then, last spring, in cold blood and unprovoked [were] cut off all the relatives of Logan, not sparing even my women and children. There runs not a drop of my blood in the veins of any creature. . . . Who is there to mourn for Logan? Not one." The murder sparked a general Indian uprising known as Lord Dunmore's War (after Virginia's royal governor), along the western frontier. A militia under General Andrew Lewis won the deciding battle of the war at Point Pleasant, beside the Ohio River, on October 10, 1774. The Indians sued for peace, and the subsequent treaty enabled the frontiersmen of West Virginia to turn their attention eastward during the early days of the American

OPPOSITE: *The abolitionist John Brown, whose raid on Harpers Ferry in 1859 was a bloody preamble to the Civil War.*

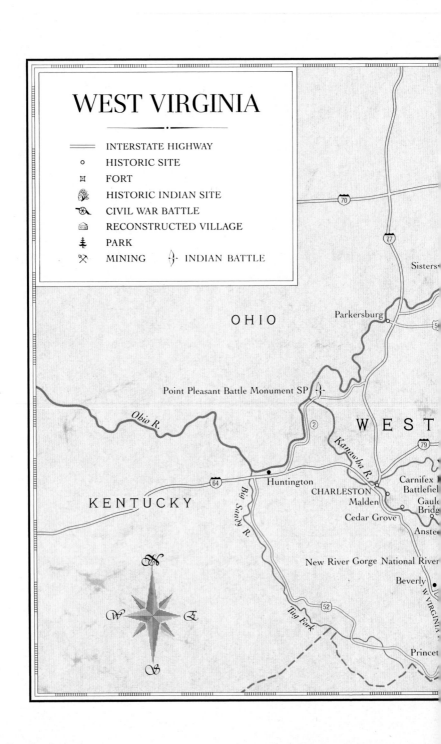

WEST VIRGINIA

═══ INTERSTATE HIGHWAY
○ HISTORIC SITE
⛉ FORT
HISTORIC INDIAN SITE
CIVIL WAR BATTLE
RECONSTRUCTED VILLAGE
PARK
MINING INDIAN BATTLE

OHIO

Parkersburg

Sisters

Point Pleasant Battle Monument SP

Obio R.

WEST

KENTUCKY

Huntington

CHARLESTON
Malden
Cedar Grove

Carnifex
Battlefiel
Gaule
Bridg
Anstee

New River Gorge National River

Beverly

Princet

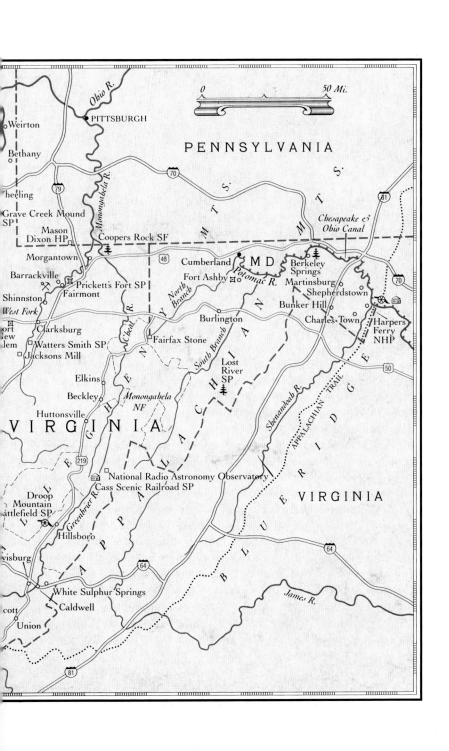

Revolution. A large contingent joined General Washington at
Boston in 1775, having covered 600 miles in only twenty-four days,
an accomplishment known as the "Bee Line March."

After American independence was assured, the settlers once
again turned their attention to taming their wilderness home. By
1795 Daniel Boone, who lived near the site of present-day
Charleston, found the land too crowded, the game too scarce, and
he loaded his family on a flatboat and headed west. Others shared
Boone's desire for elbowroom. One frontiersman wrote that,
before the Revolution, "There was no law, no courts and no sheriffs and [everyone] agreed pretty well . . . then came the lawyers
and next the preachers, and from that time they never had any
peace anymore. . . . I would rather take my chances and live
among the savages than live among justices and sheriffs and
lawyers who, with all their civility, have no natural feeling in them."

Sure signs of civilization were the region's small but growing
industries, such as milling, powder making, and boat building. The
first iron furnace west of the Alleghenies roared to life near present-day Weirton in 1794, and salt was being commercially produced along the Kanawha River by 1797. In 1784 the Potomac
Company was incorporated with the goal of building a canal-river
route linking the Potomac with the Ohio, while the James River
Company hoped to reach the Ohio by connecting the James, New,
and Kanawha rivers. George Washington, who had invested heavily
in western lands, was president of both companies. Neither project
proved successful, but in 1800 the James River Company completed
the James River–Kanawha Turnpike to the Ohio, which traversed
much the same route as present-day Route 60. Other roads soon
followed: the National Road (Route 40) in 1818, the Northwestern
Turnpike (Route 50) in 1838, and the Staunton–Parkersburg
Turnpike (Route 250/33) in 1847. Rail lines were slow to appear in
the mountainous state. The Baltimore & Ohio Railroad had penetrated the Eastern Panhandle at Harpers Ferry by 1836, but it took
another seventeen years for the line to make its way to Wheeling.
Large sections of the state were without rail connections until the
industrial boom of the 1870s and 1880s.

Despite improvements in road and rail, the jumbled valleys and
ridges of the Alleghenies were an effective barrier between the
inhabitants of the eastern and western portions of Virginia. Even
before the Civil War erupted in 1861, Virginians in the western part

of the state flirted with the idea of breaking away from the mother state. Westerners felt the government in Richmond catered to Tidewater concerns and apportioned taxes unfairly. The eastern part of the state had a slave-based economy, while slavery never really took hold in the mountainous west. In the years after John Brown's dramatic raid on Harpers Ferry, the differences between the two portions of the state became more and more pronounced. When war broke out and Virginia seceded from the Union, a convention held in Wheeling proclaimed the western section of the state loyal to the federal government, an act that led, in 1863, to West Virginia's admission to the Union as the thirty-fifth state.

Although most West Virginians were pro-Union, a sizable minority joined the rebellion. Stonewall Jackson, a native of the region, became one of the South's most able commanders. Federal troops slowly pushed the Confederate army southward in fighting at Rich Mountain, Carnifex Ferry, and Droop Mountain. Despite the Union advance, pockets of guerrilla resistance remained, and bands of southern sympathizers, such as McNeill's Rangers, conducted raids throughout much of the state. Even in the midst of war, the beauty of the mountains was continually remarked upon. Colonel Rutherford B. Hayes, a Union officer (and future president) wrote to his wife: "You will think me insane, writing so often and always with the same story: Delighted with the scenery." On the opposing side, Robert E. Lee took time out from preparing his troops to defend Cheat Mountain to write, "The views are magnificent, the valleys so beautiful, the scenery so peaceful. What a glorious world Almighty God has given us . . . and how we labor to mar his gifts."

After the war, towns along the rail lines experienced a burst of growth while those less favorably situated languished. Fortunes were made in coal and timber, and company towns sprang up almost overnight. Conditions were often primitive, the hours long, the work dangerous, and by the turn of the century, labor unrest was common. A prominent figure in the mining strikes that shook the state in 1912 was Mary Harris "Mother" Jones, a grandmotherly figure who helped publicize mine conditions. Frequently jailed at the insistence of coal operators and government officials, Jones remarked tartly that she could "raise just as much hell in jail as anywhere." For much of this century, West Virginia's economy has been tied to the coal industry, but a renewed awareness of the state's scenic beauty has led to the development of an outstanding park system, where recreational opportunities abound.

This chapter covers the state beginning with the Eastern Panhandle, from Harpers Ferry to Berkeley Springs; it then moves to the north-central region, winding southwest from Fort Ashby to Davis, west to Grafton, and then north to Morgantown and south to Droop Mountain. The southwest part of the state is toured next; and the chapter closes with the northern portion of the state from Parkersburg up through the Northern Panhandle.

THE EASTERN PANHANDLE

The first area of the state to be settled, the Eastern Panhandle still retains a hint of the aristocratic lifestyles of Tidewater Virginia, typified by a number of fine estates, many connected with the Washington family. The peaceful countryside, still decidedly rural, is known for its fine orchards. Martinsburg is the major industrial city in the region, a position held by Harpers Ferry until the middle of the nineteenth century. As a gateway to the west, the area was of great strategic importance during the Civil War, and both armies had devastating effects on the region's economy. Entire villages in the panhandle remain relatively untouched by the twentieth century; large numbers of historic structures, representing a broad range of architectural styles, have survived. The Appalachian Trail hugs the region's eastern boundary, while the Chesapeake & Ohio Canal, out of business since 1924, runs across the panhandle's northern border. To the west is the 6,000-acre Cacapon State Park, with panoramic views from the summit of Cacapon Mountain. The tour of the Eastern Panhandle begins at Harpers Ferry, meanders westward, and ends in the old resort of Berkeley Springs.

HARPERS FERRY
NATIONAL HISTORICAL PARK

The convergence of the Potomac and Shenandoah rivers at Harpers Ferry has elicited superlatives from visitors for centuries. Thomas Jefferson declared the view "one of the most stupendous scenes in nature." From its earliest days, the town was a transportation center,

Located at the confluence of the Potomac and Shenandoah rivers, Harpers Ferry retains many nineteenth-century buildings.

having grown up around a ferry operated by Robert Harper in the middle of the eighteenth century. During the nineteenth century, both the Baltimore & Ohio Railroad and Chesapeake & Ohio Canal passed through the town. The construction of a federal armory in 1796 brought a surge of growth to the area; over the years the weapons facility developed into a twenty-building complex along the Potomac River. Firearms crafted on the site were carried by Lewis and Clark on their expedition westward in 1804.

John Brown, a Kansas abolitionist who sometimes quoted the biblical passage "Without shedding of blood there is no remission of sin," slipped into town on the evening of October 16, 1859, with the objective of capturing the armory and distributing weapons to the slaves he felt sure would rise in rebellion. Brown's band of eighteen men easily overpowered the lone night watchman and took control of the armory, but the alarm was soon raised, and the raiders found

themselves trapped and hopelessly outnumbered. Refusing to surrender, Brown and the remainder of his men barricaded themselves
in the armory's fire-engine house along with several hostages,
including Lewis Washington, a great-grandnephew of George
Washington. Some thirty-six hours after the raid began, a contingent of U.S. Marines, under the command of Colonel Robert E. Lee
and Lieutenant J. E. B. Stuart, stormed the building, taking Brown
prisoner. The only slaves actually freed by Brown's action were those
belonging to Fontaine Beckham (the town's mayor and one of the
raid's sixteen casualties). Beckham's will stipulated the manumission
of his five slaves upon his death. Almost immediately many in the
North hailed Brown as a martyr, while others denounced him as a
madman. During his hasty trial and subsequent execution, the abolitionist maintained a dignified demeanor. "I am worth inconceivably
more to hang than for any other purpose," Brown told his brother.
Brown's suicidal mission helped precipitate the Civil War; two years
later, thousands of Union soldiers marched off to war to the tune of
"John Brown's Body."

Much of the town was destroyed during the war. Federal troops
burned the armory early in 1861 to prevent its capture by the
Confederates, and the complex was never rebuilt. In the late nineteenth century, a series of floods devastated the town, ending hopes
that the area could reclaim its pre-war industrial vitality. Today many
of the town's buildings are part of the National Historical Park. The
park's **visitor center** is housed in a restored stagecoach stop built
from 1826 to 1834. A brick fire-engine house, crowned with a wood-
en cupola, was used by the raiders and is now known as **John
Brown's Fort.** The only building left standing when the armory was
destroyed, it was dismantled in the early 1890s and shipped to the
World's Columbian Exposition in Chicago. It now stands near its
original site. The **Master Armorer's House** (1858), which was the
home of the armory's principal gunsmith, now houses a museum
devoted to gun making. Both the **Civil War Museum** and the
Pharmacy contain exhibits depicting the town's war experiences, as
well as the postwar years, and such artifacts as artillery pieces.

Stone steps, cut into the natural rock around 1810, lead to the
heights above the town. The two-and-one-half-story stone **Harper
House** was built between 1775 and 1782 and is the oldest structure
in the park. Its furnishings reflect a typical household during the
1850s. **Saint Peter's Catholic Church,** near the top of the steps, was

constructed of granite in High Victorian Gothic style during the 1830s. It survived the war by flying both the Union and Confederate flags. A footpath leads from the church to **Jefferson Rock,** which offers a panoramic view that Jefferson considered "worth a voyage across the Atlantic." **Harper Cemetery** contains the grave of the town's founder, Robert Harper, who died in 1782. The former campus of **Storer College** (Filmore Street) is now part of the park. Founded in 1869 as an institution of higher learning for blacks, it was one of the first integrated colleges in the United States and continued to operate until 1955. The early Federal-style, two-story buildings, constructed in the 1840s and 1850s, once housed armory officials. Self-guided walking tours are available of early industrial works on nearby Virginius Island as well as the remains of area Civil War fortifications.

LOCATION: Off Route 340. HOURS: 8–5 Daily. FEE: Yes. TELEPHONE: 304–535–6371.

CHARLES TOWN

Charles Town was laid out in 1786 on an eighty-acre site owned by Charles Washington, a younger brother of George Washington. Several of the early streets (Samuel, George, Lawrence, Mildred) were named in honor of members of the Washington family. By the end of the eighteenth century, Charles Town was an educational center for western Virginia, with academies for both boys and girls.

The **Jefferson County Courthouse** (North George and East Washington streets, 304–725–9761), a Greek Revival structure built in 1836, was the site of John Brown's trial in 1859. Cannon were ranged around the courthouse, and the prisoner was escorted from the jail to the courtroom between long files of militiamen. In 1922 a number of coal miners were tried here on charges of treason following large-scale protests against mine conditions (one miner was convicted and received a ten-year sentence). The **Jefferson County Museum** (200 East Washington Street, 304–725–8628) displays Civil War artifacts, including John Brown's gun, stove, cot, and the wagon that carried him, perched on his own coffin, to his execution. The site of the **John Brown Gallows,** identified by a historic marker, is on South Samuel Street. Fifteen hundred troops were stationed around the scaffold, and as he rode into their midst Brown reputedly

remarked, "This is a beautiful country. . . . I never had the pleasure of seeing it before." One of the militiamen who witnessed the execution was John Wilkes Booth, the future assassin of President Abraham Lincoln. The **Old Opera House Theatre Company** (Liberty and George streets, 304–725–4420), with a simple, red-brick facade, built in 1910 and undergoing restoration, was the cultural center of the city and continues to be used. The 1836 Colonial-style **Carriage Inn** (417 East Washington Street, 304–728–8003) was the site of an 1864 strategy session between generals Ulysses S. Grant and Philip Sheridan. The **Tate-Fairfax-Muse House** (201 East Washington, private) is an early-nineteenth-century brick home built over a spring-fed pool.

Three miles west of Charles Town on Route 51 is **Harewood** (private), built around 1770, probably to designs by John Ariss, for Colonel Samuel Washington, brother of the future president. In 1794 the home was the site of James Madison's marriage to Dolley Payne Todd. (Dolley's sister, Lucy Payne Washington, was mistress of the estate at that time.) The home is still the residence of the Washington family.

BUNKER HILL

Morgan Morgan, the first European settler in what became the state of West Virginia, arrived in this rich valley around 1728. Morgan was a Welshman who lived in Delaware before settling on a thousand-acre tract along Mill Creek. The simple log **Morgan Cabin,** located off Route 11, was completed in 1734 and restored in 1976. Nearby is **Morgan's Chapel,** constructed in 1851. The Greek Revival church, containing Civil War graffiti, is the third building on the site. The graves of Morgan Morgan and other early settlers are in the adjacent cemetery. The **Bunker Hill Flour Mill** (Route 26, one mile east of Route 11, 304–229–8707) stands on one of the state's oldest mill sites. The first mill was constructed in 1738; the present stone building dates to 1800 and contains nineteenth- and twentieth-century milling equipment.

OPPOSITE: *Harewood, built ca. 1770 by George Washington's brother Samuel. His descendants still live in the house.*

MARTINSBURG

Martinsburg was chartered by the Virginia assembly in 1778. Laid out by General Adam Stephen, the town was named in honor of Colonel T. B. Martin, the nephew of Lord Fairfax, from whom General Stephen purchased the tract. Stephen was a Scottish physician who had practiced in Fredericksburg before accepting a military commission and moving to the Virginia frontier in 1754. He settled in Martinsburg around 1770. Martinsburg began to grow rapidly after the Baltimore & Ohio Railroad arrived in town in 1837. During the Civil War, the railroad became a strategic prize in the fighting, and the town suffered a great deal of damage from both sides. In 1861 Confederate cavalry burned railroad bridges and tore up miles of track. The Rebels later regretted these acts of destruction when they controlled the town. To salvage some of the stranded engines, they were forced to put broad wheels on them and haul them over country roads to Winchester, Virginia. It is said that thirty-two horses were needed to move each engine. The town witnessed a major railroad strike in 1877 when workers for the B & O line halted all freight passing through Martinsburg. Attempts to break the strike proved futile, and the company appealed to President Rutherford B. Hayes, who sent in federal troops. Through this intervention, the strikers were forced to return to their jobs at reduced wages.

The downtown area has been declared a historic district, and a number of antebellum residences, predominantly Federal and Greek Revival in style, have survived along John, Race, and North streets. The **Boarman Art Center** (208 South Queen Street, 304–263–0224) has been restored and offers visitor information as well as an arts center. The Federal-style structure was built around 1802 and is one of the oldest brick homes in Martinsburg. Boarman was a rear admiral in the U.S. Navy who helped open trade with South America and supervised the outfitting of the Perry expedition to Japan in 1853. The **Apollo Civic Theater** (128 East Martin Street, 304–263–6766) was built in 1913 and is still in use. The lavishly decorated Baroque structure is one of the state's first motion-picture theaters. The **General Adam Stephen House** (309 East John Street, 304–267–4434) was constructed of limestone between 1774 and 1789 by the town's founder. Stephen served in the French and Indian War and fought during the Revolutionary War at Trenton,

Princeton, Chadds Ford, Brandywine, and Germantown. The house contains period furnishings. On the grounds are several dependencies as well as the **Triple Brick Museum,** devoted to local history. This 1876 building, which was built in three sections, housed railroad crews awaiting engine maintenance in the town. **Boydville, The Inn at Martinsburg** (601 South Queen Street, 304–263–1448), built around 1812 by General Elisha Boyd, is one of the area's finer estates. The two-story stone structure has a hipped roof and one-story flanking wings. The house has retained its original wallpaper and brass chandeliers.

Just east of Martinsburg on East Burke Street is the **Van Metre Ford Bridge.** A three-arched stone structure built in 1832, it was heavily used during the Civil War, as both armies frequently passed through the area.

York Imperials are among the varieties of apples being picked and put in barrels in this 1910 photograph of an orchard in Berkeley County, West Virginia.

SHEPHERDSTOWN

The oldest continually settled town in the state, Shepherdstown was settled around 1730 by a band of German immigrants who crossed the Potomac River at Pack Horse Ford and called the new community Mecklenburg. Chartered in 1762, the town was renamed in 1798 in honor of Thomas Shepherd, an early settler. During the Revolutionary War, Shepherdstown supposedly furnished a proportionally greater number of soldiers than any other town in the state of Virginia. In 1775 a company of riflemen gathered at Morgan's Spring and set off, under the command of Captain Hugh Stephenson, to join General George Washington in Boston. Their remarkable 600-mile, twenty-four-day trek is remembered as the "Bee Line March."

On December 3, 1787, the first successful public demonstration of a steamboat took place at Shepherdstown on the Potomac. The small craft, built by James Rumsey, cruised back and forth at four miles per hour. The amazed spectators included the Revolutionary War general Horatio Gates, who reportedly exclaimed, "By God! She moves!" as the boat pulled away from the bank. Rumsey's early steam experiments were never developed commercially; it was nearly twenty years before Robert Fulton successfully demonstrated steam's feasibility for water transport. The **James Rumsey Monument** (north end of Mill Street), a seventy-five-foot granite column, overlooks the Potomac and commemorates Rumsey's accomplishment. The **Shepherd Grist Mill** (High Street, private) was built around 1738 by the town's founder. The mill's forty-foot overshot waterwheel is one of the largest in the world. The **Entler Hotel** (German and Princess streets, 304–876–2435), the heart of which is a log building constructed around 1786, now houses a museum devoted to the town's history. The collection includes a Sheetz rifle and a Joseph Kraft tall clock. During the Civil War, the hotel housed troops from both sides. The **Public Library** (King and German streets), part brick, part frame, was constructed in 1800 at the town center to serve as a market house. The second floor was added in 1845 by the Odd Fellows Lodge. It was here that the town whipping post once stood. The **Sheetz Rifle Works** (corner of German and King streets, private) was originally a tavern built sometime prior to 1810. In the days before the Civil War, William Sheetz made gun stocks here and sold them to the federal armory at Harpers Ferry. After the armory's destruction, legend says that Sheetz took his worthless supply of stocks and used them to build a "picket" fence.

BERKELEY SPRINGS

Before the town was settled, the warm springs here were considered neutral territory by the Indians. Even tribes that were bitter enemies met peacefully here to enjoy the water's refreshing (and, many believe, curative) powers. George Washington first visited the springs in 1748 as a young surveyor working for Lord Fairfax, an English nobleman whose grandfather had been royal governor of Virginia. Eventually Fairfax, probably at Washington's urging, granted the area to the colony of Virginia "to be free to the publick for the welfare of suffering humanity." By the end of the Revolution, the site had become a popular resort, but its ebullience was not to everyone's taste. The renowned Methodist circuit rider Francis Asbury wrote in his journal, "My spirit is grieved at so much vanity as is seen here. . . . The living is expensive, four dollars per week." During the first half of the nineteenth century, the popularity of the Berkeley springs waxed and waned. After the Civil War, the town went into a slump, but the springs are still frequented by bathers at **Berkeley Springs State Park** (Washington Street, 304–258–2711). **Berkeley Castle** (Route 9W, 304–258–3274), built in the English Norman style, stands on a hill overlooking the town. It was conructed in 1885 by Colonel Samuel Taylor Suit and furnished in Victorian style.

T H E   M O U N T A I N S

Two mountainous regions, the North-Central region and the Potomac Highlands, are crisscrossed by rivers—the Cheat, Tygart, Greenbrier, Blackwater—and dotted with state parks and recreation areas. In the north-central region, the discovery of coal, oil, and gas led to extensive industrialization and the development of such towns as Clarksburg, Fairmont, and Morgantown as industrial centers. By contrast, the Potomac Highlands has few towns of any size and comprises the state's highest peaks and most rugged terrain. Timbering, which had spread throughout the region by the turn of the century, remains a major industry. The traveler through these highlands will understand the mountaineer who said, "It's right spread out, and it's might rough; but it's a damned good state for the shape it's in." This tour follows Route 50 (with frequent side trips) from Fort Ashby across a corner of the Potomac Highlands and into the north-central portion of the state to Clarksburg. This road was once part of the Northwestern Turnpike, which was cut from Winchester, Virginia, to the Ohio River in the first half of the nineteenth century, and it is still the region's major east–west thoroughfare. Upon reaching Clarksburg, the route heads north to explore sites in the Morgantown area, then south to the town of Jackson's Mill, near Weston. From there the road turns eastward to Elkins, and south into the heart of the Potomac Highlands.

FORT ASHBY

This small town, originally settled in the 1730s, takes its name from a small fort built here in 1755. During that decade a chain of forts, ranging from simple blockhouses to elaborate stockades, marked the intrusion of the Anglo-Americans in lands previously occupied by the Indian tribes. Of these early fortifications, only **Fort Ashby** (intersection of Routes 28 and 46, 304–298–3319) has survived. Built by Lieutenant John Bacon and garrisoned with twenty-one men, it survived an attack in August 1756 by a combined force of Indians and French. After the French and Indian War, the site served as a private residence and schoolhouse. Although the stockade has disappeared, the log barracks building, with its large center chimney, remains. Much of the interior woodwork is original.

Twelve miles south of Route 50 at Burlington, on the Patterson Creek Road at Williamsport, stands **Lyon's Mill,** a restored and fully operable 1882 structure with a twenty-four-foot overshot waterwheel. It was named for David Lyon, who purchased the mill in 1907 from its original owner, Acey Alt.

An interesting, though lengthy, side trip is to the **Lost River State Park** (304–897–5372), near Mathias. Some of the acreage encompassed by the park was part of a land grant given to General "Light-Horse Harry" Lee for his service as a cavalry commander during the Revolutionary War. In 1800 the general constructed a cabin here, which became his summer retreat. One of Harry's sons, Charles Carter Lee, erected a hotel on the property that became a popular resort known as Lee's White Sulphur Springs. Another son, Robert E. Lee, chose a military rather than a business career. The sulfur spring and the **Light-Horse Harry Lee Cabin,** with furnishings of the period, are all that remain.

Near the town of **Thomas,** a small park surrounds the **Fairfax Stone,** which marks the boundary of 5 million acres of land granted to four Cavaliers by King Charles II in 1669 and later acquired by

Baron Thomas Fairfax. The original marker was a sandstone pyramid with the carved letters *F X*. The present stone, which dates from 1910, is the fourth of five placed near this site since 1746; only the last two remain. The stone now marks the boundary between West Virginia and Maryland as determined by the U.S. Supreme Court in 1912. The Court's decision put an end to a 200-year-old boundary dispute. The **Old Stone House** (Route 50, two miles east of Aurora, private), once known as the Red Horse Tavern, was a favorite mid-nineteenth-century stopping point for travelers on the Northwestern Turnpike. The building was constructed by Henry Grimes between 1825 and 1827. At nearby **Cathedral State Park** (Route 50, one mile east, 304–735–3771) is a stand of virgin forest composed of hemlocks and hardwoods, a remnant of the great forests that once covered much of the eastern United States.

FAIRMONT

First settled in the 1790s, Fairmont was primarily a convenient halfway point between Clarksburg and Morgantown until an 1850s mining boom brought new life to the area. The first coal mine was opened by Francis H. Pierpont, sometimes referred to as the "father of West Virginia." A Union supply depot during the Civil War, the city saw little military activity, with the exception of a sudden strike on April 29, 1863, by General William Ezra Jones's Confederate cavalry division. The raiders raced through town, destroyed the railroad bridge over the Monongahela River, and ransacked the home of the Unionist governor Pierpont. Through the years, Fairmont's fortunes have ebbed and flowed with those of the coal industry. The imposing **Marion County Courthouse** (Adams and Jefferson streets) is a fine example of Beaux-Arts Classicism and reflects the region's prosperity at the turn of the century. In 1910 James Edwin Watson, a wealthy coal operator, constructed his palatial home, **High Gate** (801 Fairmont Avenue, private), an outstanding example of Jacobean Revival architecture. On the campus of Fairmont State College stands the **Snodgrass One-Room Schoolhouse Museum** (304–367–4231). Built in 1871, the structure was moved to its present location and now displays learning materials and furniture typical of a late-nineteenth-century classroom.

Northwest of Fairmont, just off Route 250 at Barrackville, is the **Barrackville Covered Bridge.** Built by Lemuel and Eli Chenoweth in 1853, the 145-foot-long span is the second-oldest covered bridge in

the state. Ten miles northwest of Fairmont on Route 250 stands the
East Run Church, one of the oldest in the area.

PRICKETTS FORT STATE PARK

To protect his fur-trading operations and a few intrepid settlers,
Virginia's royal governor Lord Dunmore ordered a series of forts
constructed throughout the region; Pricketts Fort, named for Jacob
Prickett, who was operating a trading post in the area as early as
1759, was completed in 1774. The original fort was dismantled in
1799; the present structure was built in the mid-1970s and is an
effective reproduction of a frontier refuge fort, where a variety of
frontier activities, including blacksmithing, spinning and weaving,
and gunsmithing, are under way. Also on the grounds is a visitor
center and the **Job Prickett House,** a brick structure built about
1860 by Jacob Prickett's great-grandson. Several architectural
details, such as the dentil work along the cornice line and the carefully cut stone foundation, are of particularly high quality.

LOCATION: North of Fairmont, off Route I-79 (exit 139). HOURS:
Mid–April through October: 10–5 Monday–Saturday, 12–5 Sunday;
Park: Dawn–Dusk Daily. FEE: Yes. 304–363–3030.

MORGANTOWN

Fort Morgan, on the site of present-day downtown Morgantown, was
constructed in 1772. Just a few years later, in 1785, the Virginia
assembly established Morgans-Town, named for its founder, Zacquill
Morgan. When the Baltimore & Ohio Railroad proposed to lay track
through town, residents objected that the "soulless corporation with
their screeching locomotives would affect wagon traffic, reduce the
price of horse feed, set our haystacks on fire, and frighten to death
our hogs and wives." Protesters succeeded in diverting the rail line
to neighboring Fairmont, which prospered as a result. **The Old
Stone House** (313–315 Chestnut Street, 304–296–7825), built of
native sandstone around 1795, is the oldest surviving house in
Monongalia County. The house's first owner was Jacob Nuze, who
had previously spent three years in Indian captivity. Over the years
this simple structure has housed a pottery, tannery, tavern, and

OPPOSITE: *The reconstructed Pricketts Fort compound contains sixteen cabins, a meeting hall, and a storehouse.*

church; it is now a craft shop. The **Monongahela County Courthouse** (243 High Street) is the third courthouse to stand on this site. The first was built in 1802, the second in 1848, and the present structure, which is Romanesque Revival in style and features both a five-story tower and a round turret, was completed in 1891. A wooden statue of Patrick Henry, which stood atop the 1848 building, is on display inside. The West Virginia University Medical Center houses the **Cook-Hayman Pharmacy Museum** (304–293–5101), a replica of a nineteenth-century pharmacy.

Northwest of Morgantown, along the West Virginia–Pennsylvania state line, is the **Mason Dixon Historical Park** (304–879–5526), which is still under development. On Brown's Hill, near the center of the park, is a small monument marking the western end of the Mason-Dixon survey, which was undertaken to settle a long-term boundary dispute between William Penn's heirs and those of Lord Calvert of Maryland. Completed in 1767, the survey took two years and a crew ranging from 40 to 100 men. As the terrain was traversed, a swath twenty-four feet wide was cut to mark the line. Charles Mason and Jeremiah Dixon, from the Royal Academy in England, made their calculations on clear nights using a sextant and distant stars as points of reference. When the line was resurveyed by the National Geodetic Society, it was found to be astonishingly accurate—no more than one-and-one-half inches off. The park is located along Route 39 between Core, West Virginia, and Mount Morris, Pennsylvania.

East of Morgantown, the remains of the **Henry Clay Iron Furnace** (304–594–1561) may be viewed in **Coopers Rock State Forest.** Built between 1834 and 1836 by Leonard Lamb to produce nails, the furnace is a relic of the flourishing iron trade that existed here prior to the Civil War. The operation was named after Clay in a vain attempt to enlist his aid for the area's slowly declining iron industry.

CLARKSBURG

Clarksburg's **Downtown Historic District,** which retains nearly all of its original structures from the late nineteenth and early twentieth centuries, is one of the most historically intact business districts in the state. A variety of architectural styles, from Neoclassical to Gothic Revival, are represented. A bronze **plaque** at 326–328 West Main Street marks the site of the birthplace of the Civil War general

Thomas "Stonewall" Jackson. After he was orphaned at the age of 2, Jackson left Clarksburg to live with his uncle at nearby Jackson's Mill. The **Nathan Goff, Jr., House** (463 West Main Street, private) is a two-and-one-half-story brick house built around 1880 in a modified Second Empire style. Several blocks away is the **Stealey-Goff-Vance House** (123 West Main Street, 304–842–3073), the town's oldest brick house. It was built in 1807 by Jacob Stealey. The Harrison County Historical Society maintains a small museum inside.

In the town of **Shinnston,** just north of Clarksburg, stands the **Levi Shinn House** (Route 19, private), a two-and-one-half-story log cabin built in 1778 by the town's founder. Shinn came from New Jersey and claimed the land by tomahawk rights, marking trees that bounded his property, a common practice on the frontier. The cabin may be the oldest house in Harrison County.

West of Clarksburg, costumed interpreters at **Fort New Salem** (off Route 50, 304–782–5245) portray the Appalachian frontier period from 1790 to 1830 through crafts such as weaving, woodworking, candle making, and gardening. Comprising twenty pioneer structures that have been relocated to the site, the fort operates as a museum during summer months and a year-round educational center for Salem College. Watters Smith, originally from New Jersey, served in the army of the newly formed federal government during the Whiskey Rebellion, before moving to western Virginia in 1796 from Pennsylvania. South of Clarksburg, in **Watters Smith State Park** (304–745–3081), the Smith family's pioneer homestead has been preserved. Smith's descendants donated their homestead on Duck Creek to the state in 1949. Log farm buildings, some from the late eighteenth century, dot the site, and the family's 1876 frame farmhouse is now a museum, full of original furnishings. A second museum displays farm implements of the late nineteenth century.

JACKSONS MILL

This gristmill beside the West Fork River was the site of the boyhood home of General Thomas "Stonewall" Jackson, who was raised by his uncle, Cummins Jackson. In addition to a gristmill, the Jackson homestead had a sawmill, carpenter and blacksmith shops, and a store. The first gristmill on the site was built by Edward Jackson, Stonewall's grandfather, in 1801. In 1842 Thomas Jackson left home to attend West Point; later he served in the Mexican War and held a professorship at the Virginia Military Institute. When the Civil War broke out, he joined the Confederate army. Jackson's strategy was to "always mystify, mislead, and surprise the enemy." He played key roles in the first Battle of Bull Run (where he earned the nickname "Stonewall") and at the battles of Antietam and Fredericksburg. At Chancellorsville in 1863, he was mistakenly shot by a Confederate sentry and died eight days later. Most of the original buildings, including the Jackson family house, have disappeared; only the 1841 gristmill, built by Cummins Jackson, has survived. It is unusual because it was powered by two horizontal waterwheels located beneath the floor of the building. Today the mill contains numerous nineteenth-century artifacts. Also on the grounds are the **Henry McWhorter Cabin** (1703) and **Blaker's Mill** (ca. 1796), which were moved to the site.

LOCATION: 2 miles north of Weston on Route 19. HOURS: June through August: 1–5 Daily. FEE: None. TELEPHONE: 304–269–5100.

ELKINS

Situated beside the Tygart Valley River, Elkins, originally known as Leadsville, was a tiny farming community until 1889, when the main line of the Western Maryland Railroad was laid through town. In 1890 the town changed its name in honor of Stephen Benton Elkins, a U.S. senator with an active interest in the railroad industry. Elkins served as secretary of war during the presidency of Benjamin Harrison. Originally an adversary of Theodore Roosevelt, Elkins came to support the president's "trust-busting" policies, explaining that when the "political horse is running away," it is wisest to be "on the seat with the driver, ready to grab the reins." Senator Elkins's palatial home, **Halliehurst** (100 Sycamore Street, 304–636–1900), stands on the crest of a ridge above the town and was built in 1890 at a cost of $300,000. The mansion was named for his wife, Hallie Davis, the daughter of Henry Gassaway Davis. The Elkinses' son, Davis Elkins, became West Virginia's senator in 1911.

South of Elkins on Route 219 is the town of **Beverly,** home to the **Randolph County Historical Society Museum** (Main Street, 304–636–4120), which is housed in one of the first brick commercial buildings erected west of the Allegheny Mountains. The two-and-one-half-story building, known as the Blackman-Bosworth store, was constructed in 1828 by slaves. The **Tygarts Valley Presbyterian Church,** in the small town of **Huttonsville** (approximately eighteen miles south of Elkins), is one of the best examples of High Victorian Gothic architecture in the state. Designed by Isaac Purcell, a Philadelphia architect, and built by Lemuel Chenoweth, who built many covered bridges throughout the state, the church was dedicated in 1883.

CASS SCENIC RAILROAD STATE PARK

Cass, a remarkably well preserved company town, now a state park, was built around the turn of the century to support the logging industry that flourished in these mountains. By 1911, West Virginia had over 3,000 miles of railroad line devoted to the logging industry; today, only Cass's 11 miles of logging track remain. The state park has an excellent collection of Shay engines, including the last one ever built. The Shay engine, with its direct gearing to each wheel, became the workhorse of the timber industry, because regular rod-driven locomotives were unable to climb the steep grades leading to the logging sites. A train still travels to Bald Knob, the second-highest point in West Virginia. In town, the managers lived in large frame homes, which still stand on "Big Bug Hill," while working men resided in much smaller houses at the foot of the hill. Many of the workers' cottages have been restored. The **Cass History Museum** documents the logging industry through photographs and artifacts.

LOCATION: Off Route 28/92 between Dunmore and Green Bank. HOURS: May through October: Phone for current excursion schedule. FEE: Yes. TELEPHONE: 304–456–4300.

Just north of Cass, at the **National Radio Astronomy Observatory** (Route 92, 304–456–2011), is the Reber Radio Telescope, the first radio astronomy telescope. Astronomer Grote Reber used it in 1939 to study radio waves coming from the Milky Way. It was reerected here in 1957.

PEARL S. BUCK BIRTHPLACE MUSEUM

Pearl Buck, author of *The Good Earth* and the only American woman to win both the Pulitzer and Nobel prizes for literature, was born in this spacious farmhouse in 1892. The home was constructed in 1858 by Pearl's maternal grandfather, Hermanus

An 1857 organ and other family memorabilia, in the Hillsboro house where the author Pearl S. Buck was born on June 26, 1892.

Stulting, an immigrant from Holland who crafted the walnut woodwork found throughout the house. Family furnishings fill the rooms, and the parlor contains Oriental souvenirs collected by Pearl's missionary parents. Though the author spent most of her childhood years in China, memories of her grandparents' home remained vivid. She wrote: "From that house there has come so much life that it ought never to die or fall into ruin. . . . For me that house was a gateway to America."

LOCATION: Route 219, Hillsboro. HOURS: May through October: 9–5 Monday–Saturday, 1–5 Sunday. FEE: Yes. TELEPHONE: 304–653–4430.

DROOP MOUNTAIN
BATTLEFIELD STATE PARK

Here, on top of Droop Mountain with a view thirty miles up the Greenbrier Valley, the last major Civil War battle on West Virginia soil was fought on November 6, 1863. During the preceding months, the Confederate forces in West Virginia had been pushed slowly southward into a narrow corridor in the southeastern corner of the state. The main road (now Route 219) running south to Lewisburg crossed Droop Mountain; the Confederates, led by General John Echols, built breastworks on the brow of the mountain, and General William W. Averell's Union troops, advancing from the north, had to seize this fortified position if they hoped to proceed any farther. The six-hour battle, which involved 7,000 soldiers and left 400 dead, was fought primarily by West Virginia troops. Many had friends or relatives fighting on the opposing side; in at least two cases, the battle was literally brother against brother. Averell massed most of his troops at the base of the mountain, then sent more than 1,000 on a looping nine-mile march in an attempt to circle behind the Confederate lines. From daylight until early afternoon, the two sides exchanged artillery fire with little change in position, until the Union flanking party, which had gone undetected, arrived and opened fire. The southerners, sensing they would soon be trapped, retreated in disarray. The defeat ended Confederate hopes of maintaining more than a token military presence in West Virginia.

The 288-acre park is the oldest in the state system and has a small museum, battle markers, and a lookout tower that offers a breathtaking view of the valley below.

LOCATION: Just off Route 219 near Droop. HOURS: *Park:* 6–10 Daily. *Museum:* 8–5 Daily. FEE: None. TELEPHONE: 304–653–4254.

THE SOUTHWEST CORNER

Despite its name, the New River may be the oldest river in North America. The river cuts its way northward through a deep gorge that remained almost totally isolated until the latter part of the nineteenth century, when rich coal deposits lured miners and rail lines into the rugged terrain. Northeast of the New River is the rich Greenbrier Valley, where some of the earliest settlements in the southern portion of the state took root. A small-scale plantation economy, similar to that found in the Eastern Panhandle, developed here prior to the Civil War, and a string of mineral spring resorts became known throughout the antebellum South as fashionable places to summer. Many old historic structures still stand along the **James River–Kanawha Turnpike** (Route 60), which cuts across the region from one side of the state to the other. It was completed in 1800 by a private company whose first president was George Washington. This tour begins on Route 60 at White Sulphur Springs, moving west to Lewisburg and making a detour southward before looping northwest again, back to Route 60 and following it along the Kanawha River to Charleston, Huntington, and the Ohio River.

WHITE SULPHUR SPRINGS

The sulfur spring on this site has drawn health seekers since the eighteenth century; the water, remarked one visitor, was believed to cure every ailment known to man "except chewing, smoking, spitting and swearing." The first recorded "cure" was in 1778 when a woman, crippled with rheumatism, was walking normally a few weeks after bathing in the spring water. In 1808 James Calwell built a tavern on the site and later added a dining room, ballroom, and row of cottages. By the 1830s the resort was a favorite gathering place for southern society. The ever-expanding rows of cottages were given names such as Paradise Row, Virginia Row, and Wolf Row. The latter was the bachelors' domain, and it was said that "unless you be young and foolish, fond of noise and nonsense, frolic and fun, wine and wassail, sleepless nights and days of headache, avoid Wolf Row."

The White Sulphur Springs Hotel, affectionately dubbed the Old White, was constructed in 1858 and served first as Confederate, then Union headquarters during the Civil War. After the Battle of White Sulphur Springs, August 26 to 27, 1863, the hotel's elegant dining room was lined with the wounded and dying. The present imposing Georgian Revival building, the **Greenbrier Hotel,** was constructed in 1913 after the demolition of the Old White. The **President's Cottage** (304–536–1110) was built in 1835 and has housed five U.S. presidents: Van Buren, Tyler (who honeymooned here), Fillmore, Pierce, and Buchanan. Since 1932 it has served as a museum depicting the history of the resort.

The **Greenbrier River Inn** (Route 60, Caldwell, 304–647–5632) is an imposing two-and-one-half-story structure with Greek Revival elements. The inn was built in 1824 as a stagecoach stop near a toll bridge erected across the Greenbrier River. In 1837 the tavern hosted a reception for President Martin Van Buren. The bridge was burned in 1862 after Confederate troops retreated across the river in the Battle of Lewisburg. During the skirmishes that followed, the tavern was struck by several shells. A private home for many years, the building is again an inn.

LEWISBURG

Shawnee Indian attacks on settlers in 1763 abruptly halted efforts at settlement here. By 1774, however, there were enough settlers in the area for Andrew Lewis to raise a militia of over 1,000 men and mount a campaign against the Indians, which culminated in a victory in the Battle of Point Pleasant in the western part of the state. The town, named for Lewis, was chartered in 1782 and prospered as an important stop on the James River–Kanawha Turnpike, today Route 60. A remarkable number of eighteenth- and early-nineteenth-century structures have survived. The two-story **Old Stone Presbyterian Church** (200 Church Street, 304–645–2676), which still contains its original galleries and pews, is the oldest church building in continuous use west of the Alleghenies. It was built in 1796. The original congregation numbered only twenty, and legend says the women helped with the construction, carrying sand for the mortar on horseback from the Greenbrier River. The adjacent cemetery, established in 1797, contains the graves of many of the town's early residents.

The **John A. North House** (301 West Washington Street, 304–645–3398) was built in 1820 for North, who was the clerk of the Greenbrier District Court of Chancery. The house's limestone walls are faced with brick made nearby. In 1830 North sold the house to James Frazier, who converted it into the Star Tavern. Today the building houses a museum operated by the Greenbrier Historical Society, and the museum serves as the society's headquarters. The two-story brick **Greenbrier County Library** (301 Courtney Drive) was built in 1834 to house the law library of the Western Division of the Supreme Court of Appeals of Virginia. A section of plaster featuring graffiti carved by Civil War soldiers has been preserved. The **Greenbrier County Courthouse** (200 North Court Street) is a three-story brick building, constructed in 1837. Behind it is the **Lewis Spring,** which was the focal point of early settlement and is protected by a limestone structure built in 1785. Across the street from the spring stands **The Barracks** (200 North Jefferson Street), built ca. 1770 near the site of the original Fort Savannah. The log structure was built by the British before the American Revolution and housed American soldiers during the War of 1812. It now contains a museum of pioneer artifacts.

The **Jessie B. Bowlin House** (300 East Washington Street), a log building covered with weatherboarding, was constructed in 1784. During the Civil War, it served as a commissary and at various other times has been used as a drover's office and schoolhouse. The oldest portion of the rambling **General Lewis Inn** (301 East Washington Street, 304–645–2600) was built in 1834 as a private residence. The inn's walnut-and-pine front desk dates from 1760 and was formerly in the Sweet Chalybeate Springs Hotel, which is no longer standing. Guest rooms are furnished with antiques. Ninety-five unknown Confederate soldiers are buried in a cross-shaped common grave in the **Confederate Cemetery.** They were killed during the Battle of Lewisburg, May 23, 1862, an unsuccessful attempt to wrest control of the town from Colonel George Crook's Union forces.

UNION

Although Union is the seat of Monroe County, the town came into being only after the county was formed in 1799. James Alexander, the first settler in the area, donated the land for the original courthouse, which was constructed in 1800. The **Monroe County Historical Society Museum** (Route 219, 304–772–5317), located in a brick bank building built sometime prior to 1842, contains numerous historical items, including a Civil War collection with, among other memorabilia, a Confederate uniform and a folding Civil War hospital bed. The museum also displays Shoshone Indian artifacts.

Two miles east of Union just off Route 3 stands **Rehoboth Church,** constructed in 1786 and believed to be the oldest Protestant church building west of the Alleghenies. The one-story log building measures twenty-two by twenty-nine feet and has split-log pews and an interior gallery around three sides. The church was visited frequently by Bishop Francis Asbury, a circuit rider who helped spread Methodism into the frontier areas. He noted in his journal on March 19, 1792, that he "preached with satisfaction" despite "difficulties in getting to Rehoboth. It was very dark and we were bewildered in the woods." In 1980 a museum building was built on the property. It displays a wide variety of items, including the church's original communion table, eighteenth- and nineteenth-century kitchen utensils, and a number of military uniforms.

South of Union stands **Salt Sulphur Springs** (Route 219, private), once a popular resort, which opened in 1823 and hosted such prominent guests as Henry Clay, Martin Van Buren, and John C. Calhoun. The remaining hotel buildings, now used as private homes, make up one of the largest native-stone antebellum groupings in the state. During the Civil War, the hotel served as a hospital.

On the outskirts of **Talcott** stands a **statue** erected in 1972 to honor John Henry, the legendary steel driver who supposedly challenged and beat a steam-powered drill but died in the effort. The Big Bend Tunnel, where John Henry is said to have worked, is near Talcott. Opened in 1873, it is over 6,000 feet long and took three years to complete. A folk song commemorating Henry's deed includes the words, "The Big Bend Tunnel on the C. & O. road / Is gonna be the death of me, Lawd, Lawd."

NEW RIVER GORGE NATIONAL RIVER

For centuries the only way to cross the New River Gorge was to descend its steep slopes, ford the swift-moving river, and climb the opposite canyon wall. The arduous route was avoided whenever possible, and the earliest Indian trails and settler's roads stuck to the canyon rims on either side. Finally, in 1977, the canyon rims were connected at Fayetteville by the **New River Gorge Bridge,** the world's longest single-arch steel span (1,700 feet) and the second-highest bridge in the country (only Colorado's Royal Gorge Bridge is higher). The National Park Service administers a fifty-two-mile stretch from the bridge, upstream to Hinton. The river contains twenty-one major rapids along a single fifteen-mile stretch. The **Canyon Rim Visitor Center** (304–574–2115) is located at the north end of the bridge and features exhibits on the river's history.

In nearby **Babcock State Park,** located a few miles south of the old James River–Kanawha Turnpike (Route 60), the **Glade Creek Grist Mill** (Route 41) was constructed on this site in 1976 using parts salvaged from nonfunctioning mills around the state. Over 500 similar mills, most now gone, were in operation in West Virginia at the turn of the century. The Glade Creek reconstruction is fully operable. East of Babcock State Park along Route 60 is **Big Sewell Mountain.** Robert E. Lee's headquarters were here in the fall of 1861, and according to tradition, Major Thomas Broun and Captain Joseph Broun presented

The Glade Creek Grist Mill in Babcock State Park was constructed near the site of the earlier Cooper's Mill, using pieces salvaged from several other grist mills.

the general with a prize-winning four-year-old colt under a large sugar maple that stood near the summit (recognized by a historic marker). Lee named the horse Traveller and rode him throughout the war. Traveller survived his owner and was led, with empty saddle, behind the general's casket in 1870.

CARNIFEX FERRY BATTLEFIELD STATE PARK

The Civil War battle of Carnifex Ferry on September 10, 1861, was an important conflict in the struggle for control of Virginia's western lands. Union troops, led by General William S. Rosecrans, assaulted a Confederate force entrenched on the heights above the Gauley River Gorge. Though outnumbered by the Union forces, the Confederate troops, commanded by General John B. Floyd, took advantage of log and rail breastworks to halt several Union attacks. As Union reinforcements continued to arrive, the eventual capture of his army appeared certain, and Floyd ordered his men to retreat across the

Gauley River under cover of darkness. Floyd then destroyed the ferry so Rosecrans was unable to pursue him. The Confederate withdrawal left the majority of western Virginia free to become an independent state, a goal that was achieved in 1863. The park preserves the **Patteson House,** which was caught in cross fire during the day-long battle. The simple frame farmhouse now serves as a small visitor center and museum. A number of trails traverse the park, including the route Floyd's men used during their nighttime retreat.

LOCATION: Route 129, 5 miles off Route 19. HOURS: June through August: 9–5 Daily; September through May: 9–5 Saturday–Sunday. FEE: Yes. TELEPHONE: 304–872–3773.

ANSTED

Ansted was originally named New Haven by a group of New England Spiritualists who settled there in 1830. The following year the name was changed to honor Professor David T. Ansted, a British scientist whose positive reports about coal in the area encouraged a number of English businessmen to invest in the fledgling industry. Despite this early interest, no large mines were opened near the town until the 1870s. The Fayette County Historical Society is headquartered in a one-story frame house known as **Contentment** (Route 60, 304–465–5032), which was built along the James River–Kanawha Turnpike in 1830. In 1872 it became the home of Colonel George Imboden, a prominent businessman who had served on Robert E. Lee's staff during the Civil War. Today it is furnished with period pieces and houses a museum. A restored one-room schoolhouse is also on the grounds. Just off Route 60 is **Westlake Cemetery,** where General Stonewall Jackson's mother, Julia Neale Jackson, is buried. Jackson, then a major, visited the cemetery in 1855 and noted that the grave was unmarked. After the general was accidently killed in 1863 by picket fire from his own men, one of his subordinates, Captain Thomas D. Ranson, had a marble monument erected over Mrs. Jackson's grave.

Hawk's Nest State Park (Route 60, north of Ansted, 304–658–5196), one of the state's scenic wonders, is named for the massive cliff that stands at the northern end of the New River Gorge. Ambrose Bierce, a Union soldier turned writer, set one of his stories at Hawk's Nest, having served here under General Jacob Cox in 1861. In the 1930s the Hawk's Nest Tunnel was blasted through Gauley Mountain, diverting the New River and generating large quantities of hydroelectric power. The park offers breathtaking vistas and a museum displaying pioneer artifacts.

GAULEY BRIDGE

As the name implies, there has long been a bridge spanning the Gauley River near the town site. The first bridge, constructed in 1822, was the subject of heated debate, as it put out of business the ferrymen who had previously plied their trade along the river. When the bridge burned in 1826, the ferrymen were blamed. A second bridge was completed in 1828 and stood until November 1861, when General John B. Floyd's retreating Confederate forces burned it in the face of pursuit by General William S. Rosecrans. The stone piers of this bridge are still visible.

CEDAR GROVE

The oldest settlement in the Kanawha Valley, Cedar Grove was first inhabited by a North Carolinian named Walter Kelly who arrived in 1773. When word reached him that hostile Indians were in the area, Kelly sent his wife and children to Fort Savannah in Lewisburg but insisted on staying behind to plant his crops. Only a few hours after the family's safe departure, the Indians scalped Kelly and his slave. In its early days, the town marked the terminus of the developed roadway, and from here travelers transferred their goods to flatboats and poled them down the river to reach points farther west. For a few years, boat building flourished, and the village became known as Boat Yards, but with the completion of the turnpike to the Ohio River in 1800, the once thriving industry withered away.

The **Tompkins House** (just off Route 60, private), in the heart of Cedar Grove, was built in 1844 and is still owned by the Tompkins family. The house's first owner, William Tompkins, developed a process that used natural gas to extract salt from brine, one of the first known industrial uses for the gas. During the Civil War, Federal cavalry spared the house when Mrs. Tompkins produced a letter from her uncle, General Ulysses S. Grant. **Virginia's Chapel** (private), also on Route 60, was built in 1853 by William Tompkins at the request of his daughter, Virginia. The one-story brick building features Gothic Revival elements and was constructed as a nondenominational chapel. It served both sides during the Civil War.

MALDEN

Malden was once the center of Kanawha County's prosperous salt industry. During the first half of the nineteenth century, salt was considered as desirable a commodity as money, and local newspapers advertised property for sale for either "salt or money." In 1815 there were thirty salt furnaces in the vicinity, but the industry slowly declined; by 1876 only one remained in operation. Booker T. Washington, the educator, spent his boyhood in Malden, where he worked in the salt furnaces. The **Malden Historic District** contains such landmarks as the **African Zion Church,** constructed in 1872, where Washington was a member of the congregation from age 9. Also of interest are the **Richard Putney House** and the **Kanawha Saline Presbyterian Church.**

CHARLESTON

In 1788 Colonel George Clendenin supposedly paid less than one dollar for forty acres on the bank of the Kanawha River. Here he built a fort, which he named for Governor Henry "Light-Horse Harry" Lee of Virginia, just east of present-day Brooks Street. One of the earliest settlers in the vicinity was Daniel Boone, who built a cabin in what is now the eastern part of the city. In 1789 Boone was elected to the Virginia assembly; one of his reports on frontier defense reads in part: "Two spyes or Scutes will be nesery at the pint to sarch the Banks of the River at Crosing places." Boone lived here until 1795, when he returned to Kentucky. One of Boone's contemporaries was Anne Bailey, an Englishwoman who became an Indian scout after her husband was killed by the Indians at the Battle of Point Pleasant. Nicknamed "Mad Anne," she completed (according to legend) a 200-mile trip to Fort Savannah (Lewisburg) for gunpowder in only three days when Fort Lee was besieged by Indians in 1791. Charleston was officially chartered in 1794 and named for Clendenin's father. The salt industry, centered at nearby Malden, spurred the economy of the town in its early years. During the Civil War, the city was spared the destruction visited on many other West Virginia towns. After West Virginia was admitted to the Union as the thirty-fifth state, both Charleston and Wheeling aspired to be the state's capital, and for years the capital shuttled back and forth, a compromise that pleased no one. In 1877 a special election was

called to decide the issue. Charleston's representatives cleverly stumped for votes during the performances of a traveling circus, a technique that resulted in Charleston's victory by a landslide. The city became the state's permanent capital in 1885.

The **State Capitol** (1900 Washington Street East, 304–348–3809) was designed by Cass Gilbert, whose other achievements include the U.S. Supreme Court Building in Washington, DC. The building was completed in 1932 after fire destroyed the previous capitol building several blocks to the west. The building's massive gold dome is four-and-one-half feet taller than that of the U.S. Capitol. The chandelier that hangs from the center of the dome is of hand-cut Czechoslovakian crystal, weighs two tons, is eight feet in diameter, and is lit during the gubernatorial inauguration every four years and for other special occasions. The exterior of the building is Indiana limestone, while two-thirds of the interior consists of marble. On the capitol grounds are a statue of Abraham Lincoln and a bust of Booker T. Washington.

The **West Virginia State Museum** (304–348–0230), adjacent to the capitol, offers numerous exhibits depicting the history of West Virginia, including a re-creation of a settler's cabin and an old-fashioned country store. The wooden-columned Governor's Mansion (1716 Kanawha Boulevard East, 304–348–3588), completed in 1925 in Georgian Revival style, has thirty-three rooms and is open twice a week for tours. Hollygrove (1710 Kanawha Boulevard East, private) is one of the oldest homes in Charleston. Constructed in 1815 as a Federal-style plantation home, the house became an inn and hosted such notables as Henry Clay, Sam Houston, John Audubon, and Andrew Jackson. A front portico and other Classical elements were added in 1902. The **Craik-Patton House** (2809 Kanawha Boulevard East, 304–925–5341) is a Greek Revival structure built in 1834 by James Craik, a son of George Washington's personal secretary and the grandson of Dr. James Craik, Washington's close friend and physician. The younger Craik moved to the Charleston area to practice law but later became an Episcopalian minister. The house, which was moved to its present site in 1973, is furnished to reflect the year it was built. One of the more unusual items on display is a remarkably well preserved ingrain carpet, a woven carpet that is reversible. In contrast to

OPPOSITE: *Dwarfed by the dimensions of the West Virginia State Capitol dome is a massive chandelier made of 10,080 pieces of cut Czechoslovakian crystal.*

The Greek Revival Craik-Patton House, home to the grandson of George Washington's physician and to the grandfather of World War II general George S. Patton.

the rest of the house, the Patton room is furnished to reflect the period around 1865 in honor of Colonel George S. Patton, a Confederate officer who bought the house in 1858. (Patton's grandson and namesake was the distinguished World War II general.) Colonel Patton was killed at the Battle of Winchester in 1864.

The **Sunrise Museum** (746 Myrtle Road, 304–344–8035), located across the river from the central city, was originally the home of William A. MacCorkle, the ninth governor of West Virginia. The thirty-six-room stone mansion, named after MacCorkle's family home in Virginia, was constructed in 1905 and was the culmination of years of hard work by a man who had arrived in Charleston practically penniless. "I slept on a bare table for one whole winter,"

The bedroom of the Craik-Patton House, furnished as it might have been in 1834, the year it was constructed.

MacCorkle recalled. "What was the use of telling people about it? I knew I would sooner or later have a bed!" Sunrise and an adjacent mansion, **Torquilstone** (built for MacCorkle's son in 1928), now house an art museum, children's museum, and planetarium.

The **Criel Mound** (304–744–0051), located in South Charleston, is a thirty-three-foot-high prehistoric burial mound attributed to the Adena people, an ancient Indian civilization (1000 B.C. to the first century A.D.). The second-largest Adena mound in the state, it was constructed near the beginning of the Christian era and was excavated in the 1880s by the Smithsonian Institution. One skeleton found within the mound reportedly wore a copper headdress. No artifacts are on display.

The portion of the state south of Charleston is still largely rural, and such names as Coalwood, Coal City, and Coal Mountain attest to the importance of its mining industry. Coal was first discovered near Racine in 1742 by a German explorer named John Peter Salley, but only small-scale mining was feasible until the latter part of the nineteenth century, when rail lines were laid in the region. In 1921 the Battle of Blair Mountain pitted 3,000 angry miners against a combined force of Logan County lawmen and federal troops. County officials even borrowed a plane and dropped a homemade bomb on the battlefield. Following the three-day struggle, 600 miners were indicted, 54 of them for murder and treason. Most were acquitted, and the resulting publicity heightened public awareness of deplorable mine conditions.

The infamous feud between the Hatfield and McCoy families occurred along the Kentucky–West Virginia border. Trouble first erupted around 1881 over two separate issues: the ownership of a razorback hog and the birth of an illegitimate child to Johnson Hatfield and Rose Anne McCoy. The feud continued for years with fatalities on both sides. The worst violence occurred between 1882 and 1888, but the last recorded incident was in 1896. The **Hatfield Family Cemetery** (Route 44 near the small town of Sarah Ann) contains a life-size statue of the clan's patriarch, "Devil" Anse.

POINT PLEASANT
BATTLE MONUMENT STATE PARK

This small park, which lies at the confluence of the Ohio and Kanawha rivers, marks the site of the fierce day-long struggle on October 10, 1774, between 1,100 frontier militiamen under the command of Andrew Lewis and 1,000 Shawnee, Miami, and Wyandot warriors, led by Shawnee Chief Cornstalk. The Indians had risen up five months earlier to drive the settlers from their lands and to retaliate for atrocities committed against them by whites. Lewis's army was attacked in the early morning hours of October 10. He sent out two divisions, one led by his brother, Charles. After a day of fierce hand-to-hand combat in which heavy casualties were suffered by both sides, the discouraged Indians retreated across the Ohio River, their power broken. Charles Lewis was one of the casualties. Point Pleasant was probably named by George Washington, who camped here in the 1770s. A series of log forts stood near this site; the first was built shortly after the 1774 battle. The oldest structure on the battlefield is the **Mansion House,** a two-story log cabin built in 1796. Restored by the D.A.R. in 1901, the cabin houses a potpourri of eighteenth- and nineteenth-century artifacts, including a massive rosewood piano, reputed to be one of the first brought over the Alleghenies. The focal point of the two-acre park is an eighty-four-foot granite shaft commemorating the battle. A reconstruction of **Fort Randolph,** originally built in 1776 by Captain Matthew Arbuckle, stands in nearby Krodel Park.

> LOCATION: Just off Route 2, Point Pleasant. HOURS: April through November: 8–4:30 Monday–Saturday, 1–5 Sunday. FEE: None. TELE-PHONE: 304–675–3330.

T   H   E   N   O   R   T   H

The Ohio River, which forms a natural boundary between West Virginia and Ohio, has shaped this region's development from earliest times. Long before white settlers arrived, the river valley was a favored place for human habitation. Elaborate ceremonial complexes, burial mounds, and petroglyphs attest to the presence of a prehistoric Indian tribe known as the Adena people well before the birth of Christ. The river served as a highway to western lands during the eighteenth century, and the availability of river transport spurred the region's impressive industrial growth a century later. The discovery of oil in the 1890s brought a burst of life to many once-sleepy river towns; competition was fierce as hundreds of oil companies set up operations, and some homeowners, hungry for instant wealth, allowed oil wells to be dug on their front lawns.

   William Penn's charter gave him a southern boundary "extending from the Delaware River five degrees west." The Pennsylvania boundary thus stopped short of Ohio by about sixteen miles, creating the Northern Panhandle. Small iron furnaces were in operation in the panhandle by the 1790s; by the late nineteenth century, the area contained some of the nation's largest iron and steel mills. The industrial entrepreneurs who flocked to Wheeling were followed by craftspeople (woodworkers, stained-glass makers, tin workers) eager to market their skills; together they produced some of the nation's finest Victorian homes.

PARKERSBURG

In 1770 George Washington camped near the site of present-day Parkersburg while attempting to identify lands awarded to him for his service in the Virginia militia. Settlers began to trickle into the area during the 1780s, many traveling down the Ohio River by flatboat. The town of Parkersburg was chartered in 1820, but the lack of adequate roads leading to the site slowed the city's growth until 1838, when the Northwestern Turnpike, which connected the town with Winchester, Virginia, was completed. In 1847 the Staunton–Parkersburg road, cutting across the midsection of the state, was completed as well. A decade later the Northwestern Virginia Railroad was completed, and in 1859 the rush to the nearby oil fields began. Soon Parkersburg was one of the most important towns on the Ohio River and became home to many of the leaders in the movement that led to the founding of the state of West Virginia in 1863. The **Blennerhassett Hotel** (4th and Market streets, 304–422–3131), an eclectic brick structure, was built in 1889 by W. N. Chancellor while the town was a major oil-refining center, and it was fully restored in 1986. The public areas are furnished with antiques gathered from every corner of the United States; the ballroom wall sconces originally hung in New York's Chase Manhattan Bank, the entryway chandelier came from an office building in Chicago, and the heart-pine wood in the library came from a barn near Savannah. The **Henry Cooper Log House,** constructed around 1804, is one of the few reminders of Parkersburg's nineteenth-century beginnings. The cabin was moved to its City Park location in 1910 and is said to be one of the earliest two-story log homes built in the area.

Blennerhassett Island Historical Park

Located on 500-acre Blennerhassett Island in the Ohio River, this historical park features a reconstruction of a two-story mansion with covered walkways connecting to flanking buildings. It was built about 1800 by a wealthy Irishman, Harmann Blennerhassett, whose visitors were effusive in their praise: "Until I go to my grave

OPPOSITE: *An enormous hollow sycamore tree on Blennerhassett Island, 1912.*

he large
camore tree
Blennerhasset
land
1912

The reconstructed Palladian mansion of the Irish aristocrat Harmann Blennerhassett, which was originally constructed on an island in the Ohio River around 1800 and burned to the ground in 1811.

I must bear remembrance of the beautiful Blennerhassett . . . this Paradise," wrote John Bernard, an English actor, in the early nineteenth century. Archaeologists uncovered the mansion's original foundations in the mid-1970s, and after careful research the house was reconstructed. Blennerhassett was undoubtedly the most controversial figure in Parkersburg's history. In 1805 he met Aaron Burr, who had fled south to escape indictment for killing Alexander Hamilton the previous year in a duel, and was drawn into Burr's scheme to seize territory in the Southwest held by Spain and create a new republic, thereby perhaps inciting Spain to war with the United States. Alerted to the plot, the Virginia militia raided the island on December 11, 1806, but Blennerhassett had already fled. After the two conspirators were arrested for treason, Burr was acquitted, and Blennerhassett was never brought to trial. Afterward Blennerhassett's creditors seized the estate; the mansion was destroyed by fire in 1811. The **Blennerhassett Museum** (Second and Juliana streets) in downtown Parkersburg contains exhibits ranging from Ice Age tools that were found on the island to original furnishings owned by the Blennerhassett family.

Excursions to the island begin at Point Park, just a few blocks from the museum, where visitors board riverboats for the brief journey downriver. The reconstructed mansion is open for tours, craftspeople demonstrate traditional skills, and horse-drawn wagons tour the island.

LOCATION: Blennerhassett Island. HOURS: 11–6 Tuesday–Sunday. FEE: Yes. TELEPHONE: 304–428–3000.

SISTERSVILLE

First settled by Charles Wells sometime between 1802 and 1810, Sistersville was named in honor of Charles's seventeenth and eigh-

A late Adena mound known as the Grave Creek Mound, built in successive stages over a period of more than one hundred years. OPPOSITE: *A hollow sycamore tree of enormous proportions on Blennerhassett Island in 1912.*

teenth children, Sarah and Delilah, upon whose property it was laid out. Charles, rather prayerfully one assumes, called his twenty-first child Plenty; he was destined to have one more, twenty-two in all. In the 1890s the discovery of oil in the area transformed the village; almost overnight the town's population rose from 300 to 15,000. While only a few oil companies maintain offices in Sistersville today, 192 had operations here in 1902. Many of the structures in the downtown historic district were built during this period, including the **City Hall** (Main Street), a building with Georgian Revival elements that is set on a diamond-shaped plot.

GRAVE CREEK MOUND STATE PARK

The town of Moundsville, which surrounds the park, takes its name from this large conical mound built by the Adena people who lived along the Ohio River some 2,000 years ago. The largest such mound in the state of West Virginia and one of the largest in the United States, it is sixty-nine feet high and was completed around 150 B.C. It was the focal point of a large ceremonial complex consisting of earthworks and smaller mounds that covered much of the present Moundsville town site. The area around the mound was first settled in 1770 by the Tomlinson family, who, unlike many early whites, respected and protected the mounds. A museum was constructed adjacent to the mound in 1978 and contains exhibits on the Adena culture and the controversy surrounding the Grave Creek Tablet, allegedly recovered from the mound, which supposedly indicates contact with Mediterranean cultures long before the earliest documented voyages.

LOCATION: 801 Jefferson Avenue, Moundsville. HOURS: 10–4:30 Monday–Saturday, 1–5 Sunday. FEE: Yes, for museum. TELEPHONE: 304–843–1410.

WHEELING

Like so many frontier towns, Wheeling grew from violent beginnings. According to John Brittle, a captive of the Delaware Indians in the late eighteenth century, the town got its name from the Delaware Indian word *Weeling*, or "Place of the Skull." The Indians told Brittle that the first white settlers in the area had been decapitated and their heads placed on poles as a warning to others who

The 1849 Wheeling Suspension Bridge, designed by Charles Ellet, Jr., was the first bridge to span the Ohio River and may be the oldest surviving cable suspension bridge in the United States.

encroached on Delaware territory. The first successful settlement occurred in 1769, but Indian uprisings were a constant danger, and around 1774 a fort was constructed along Wheeling Creek. Originally called Fort Fincastle, the name was changed to Fort Henry in honor of the fiery orator Patrick Henry. In September 1782 the fort withstood an attack by a combined force of British and Indians in what has been called the final confrontation of the American Revolution.

In 1861 Wheeling was the site of two conventions called to explore the possibility of carving a new state out of Virginia's western lands. When the idea became a reality, Wheeling was chosen as the first capital. A Unionist stronghold, the town escaped damage during the Civil War, then experienced a burst of industrial growth. During these boom years, Wheeling became famous for its glass, china, nails, and other manufactured goods. One of its most prominent landmarks is the **Wheeling Suspension Bridge** (10th Street).

When constructed in 1849, it was the longest suspension bridge in the world and the first over the Ohio River. Henry Clay called the impressive span "Wheeling's Rainbow."

The original site of Fort Henry is not known. The area where it is believed to have stood, marked by a plaque, is on Main Street, between 11th and 12th streets. Every resident of the city knows the story of Betty Zane, who, when the garrison was under Indian attack in 1782, bravely volunteered to venture out and retrieve additional gunpowder, thereby saving the fort. Because of its numerous examples of outstanding Victorian architecture, the city has been officially declared "Victorian Wheeling," and several areas of the city are National Register Historic Districts. **Centre Market Square,** on Market between 20th and 24th streets, contains two market buildings, a one-story structure with a gabled roof, built in 1853, and an open-air building with wide overhanging eaves, built in 1890. **Chapline Street Row** (2300 block of Chapline Street) contains townhouses that reflect the city's wealth during the second half of the nineteenth century. The rowhouses in the **Monroe Street East** district (12th and 13th streets on Eoff and Jacob streets) were constructed during the period 1850 to 1890, as were the buildings in the **Downtown Central District** (between 10th and 16th streets on Market, Main, and Chapline streets). Four restored Victorian structures may be toured by contacting **Yesterday's Ltd.** (823 Main Street, 304–233–2003). The interiors of the homes feature tin ceilings, stained glass, and walls decorated with Lincrusta, a technique that simulates the look of Moroccan leather.

West Virginia Independence Hall

A Renaissance Revival structure, Independence Hall was constructed between 1857 and 1859 to house Wheeling's custom house, post office, and federal court. It has been carefully restored to its 1861 appearance, when it was the scene of the Second Wheeling Convention, which denounced Virginia's secession from the Union, leading to the drafting of West Virginia's Declaration of Independence. The third-floor courtroom, where the convention was held, displays its original Corinthian columns. The iron columns

OPPOSITE: *The third-floor courtroom in the West Virginia Independence Hall, an 1859 building designed by Ammi B. Young, where the second Wheeling Convention denounced Virginia's secession from the Union.*

were not only decorative but functional; some conducted hot air to the upper floors, while others served as cold-air returns. Other notable elements are functioning gas fixtures and ironwork.

LOCATION: 1528 Market Street HOURS: 10–4 Monday–Sunday. FEE: None. TELEPHONE: 304–233–1333.

OGLEBAY INSTITUTE MANSION MUSEUM

This imposing white mansion with its Greek Revival portico began as a simple red-brick farmhouse, constructed in 1846. In 1900 the house was purchased by industrialist Earl W. Oglebay, who transformed the house and acquired the surrounding 750 acres. At his death he left the entire estate to the city of Wheeling, and today it serves as a park and museum. Eight period rooms, ranging from the 1750s to the 1870s, portray the history of the Upper Ohio Valley. The museum's extensive glass collection features many pieces manufactured in the Wheeling area, including the Sweeney Punch Bowl, believed to be the largest piece of cut glass ever produced. The massive vessel holds sixteen gallons of liquid and stands four feet high. A smaller version was presented to Henry Clay and was reputedly used by the family as a baptismal font.

LOCATION: Route 88, off Route I-70. HOURS: 9:30–5 Monday–Saturday, 1–5 Sunday. FEE: Yes. TELEPHONE: 304–242–7272.

Four miles from Oglebay is the **Stifel Fine Art Center** (1330 National Road, 304–242–7700), housed in the turn-of-the-century home of Edward Stifel, a businessman whose family fortune was based on the production of calico. At Stifel's insistence, the home was built entirely of concrete, steel, and brick to make it fireproof; however, hardwood panelling, plaster, and marble were used to soften the interior. The house retains much of its architectural integrity, and the estate's formal gardens have been preserved.

BETHANY

This small town retains much of the quiet charm of a nineteenth-century village, with the buildings of **Bethany College** (304–829–7285) sitting high on a hill overlooking the main street.

Founded in 1840, the college is the oldest degree-granting institution in the state. When the original college building was destroyed by fire in 1857, the school's founder, Alexander Campbell, replaced it with **Old Main,** a Gothic Revival structure loosely based on the buildings he had known as a student at the University of Glasgow. Down the street stands the **Old Meeting House** of the Bethany Church of Christ, which served the village from 1852 to 1915. It retains potbellied stoves, straight-backed pews, and oil chandeliers.

The Alexander Campbell Mansion

For fifty-five years, this white frame structure was home to Alexander Campbell, one of the nineteenth century's foremost religious figures. A Scotch-Irish immigrant, Campbell became the leading spokesman for a revival that spawned several sects, including the Disciples of Christ, the Churches of Christ, and the Christian Churches. The house was begun by Campbell's father-in-law in 1793, and Campbell made frequent additions over the years, including a guest wing that townsfolk dubbed "Stranger's Hall." Guests to the home included Henry Clay, Daniel Webster, and John C. Calhoun. Many original furnishings remain, such as an early recliner, Campbell's well-worn writing chair, and the rosewood piano reputed to be the first in the area. One of the mansion's most interesting features is its original handcrafted French silk wallpaper, which portrays incidents from the *Odyssey*. The family cemetery, known as God's Acre, lies across the road.

LOCATION: Route 67. HOURS: April through October: 10–12 and 1–5 Tuesday–Saturday, 1–5 Sunday. FEE: Yes. TELEPHONE: 304–829–7285.

As far back as the eighteenth century, the area around **Weirton** has been known for its industry. Sometime between 1790 and 1794, Peter Tarr constructed an iron furnace along King's Creek, probably the first furnace built west of the Alleghenies and a forerunner of the steel industry that flourished along the Ohio in later years. Cannonballs cast here were used during the War of 1812 by Commodore Oliver Hazard Perry. The simple stone remains of the furnace stand alongside King's Creek Road, two miles off Route 2, north of town.

Notes on Architecture

EARLY COLONIAL

CUPOLA HOUSE, NC

In the eastern colonies, Europeans first built houses using a medieval, vertical asymmetry, which in the eighteenth century evolved toward classical symmetry. Roofs were gabled and hipped, often with prominent exterior chimneys. Small casement windows became larger and more evenly spaced and balanced on each facade.

GEORGIAN

DRAYTON HALL, SC

Beginning in Boston as early as 1686, and only much later elsewhere, the design of houses became balanced around a central axis, with only careful, stripped detail. Sash windows with rectilinear panes replaced casements. Hipped roofs accentuated the balanced and strict proportions inherited from Italy and Holland via England and Scotland.

FEDERAL

FEDERAL HILL, KY

The post-Revolutionary style sometimes called "Federal" was more flexible and delicate than the formal Georgian. It was rooted in archaeological discoveries at Pompeii and Herculaneum in Italy in the 1750s, as well as in contemporary French interior planning principles. As it evolved toward the Regency, rooms became shaped as polygons, ovals, and circles and acquired ornamentation in the forms of urns, garlands, and swags. Lacking the strong color of English and Scottish prototypes, this style was sweetly elegant: a fan shaped window over the door is its most characteristic detail.

GREEK REVIVAL

MILFORD PLANTATION, SC

The Greek Revival manifested itself in severe, stripped, rectilinear proportions, occasionally a set of columns or pilasters, and even in a few instances Greek-temple form. It combined Greek and Roman forms—low pitched pediments, simple moldings, rounded arches, and shallow domes, and was used in public buildings and many private houses.

GOTHIC REVIVAL

RUGBY PRESBYTERIAN CHURCH, SC

The Gothic Revival brought darker colors, asymmetry, broken skylines, verticality, and the pointed arch to American buildings. New machinery produced carved and pierced trim along the eaves. Roofs became steep and gabled; "porches" or "piazzas" became more spacious. Oriel and bay windows became common and there was a greater use of stained glass.

ITALIANATE

WHITE HALL, KY

The Italianate style began to appear in the 1840s, both in a formal, balanced "palazzo" style and in a picturesque "villa" style. Both versions of the style had round-headed windows and arcaded porches. Commercial structures were frequently made of cast iron, with a ground floor of large arcaded windows and smaller windows on each successive rising story.

QUEEN ANNE

EXECUTIVE MANSION, NC

The Queen Anne style emphasized contrasts of form, texture, and color. Large encircling verandahs, tall chimneys, turrets, towers, and a multitude of textures are typical of the style. The ground floor might be of stone or brick, the upper floors of stucco, shingle, or clapboard. Specially shaped bricks and plaques were used for decoration. Panels of stained glass outlined or filled the windows. The steep roofs were gabled or hipped, and other elements, such as pediments, Venetian windows, and front and corner bay windows, were typical.

RENAISSANCE REVIVAL OR BEAUX ARTS

STATE HOUSE, SC

In the 1880s and 1890s, American architects who had studied at the Ecole des Beaux Arts in Paris brought a new Renaissance Revival to the United States. Sometimes used in urban mansions, but generally reserved for public and academic buildings, it borrowed from three centuries of Renaissance detail—much of it French—and put together picturesque combinations from widely differing periods. The Beaux Arts style gave rise to the "City Beautiful" movement, whose most complete expression was found in the late nineteenth– and early–twentieth century world's fairs in Chicago and San Francisco.

I N D E X

PHOTO CREDITS

The editors gratefully acknowlege the assistance of Ann J. Campbell, Rita Campon, Virginia Dooley, Moira Duggan, Fonda Duvanel, Julia Ehrhardt, Ann ffolliott, Carol McKeown Healy, Lydia Howarth, Brigid A. Mast, Margaret Stanek, Catherine Shea Tangney, Linda Venator, and Rebecca Williams.

Composed in Basilia Haas and ITC New Baskerville by Graphic Arts Composition, Inc., Philadelphia, Pennsylvania. Printed and bound by Toppan Printing Company, Ltd., Tokyo, Japan.